German Footprints
in America

ALSO BY SUDIE DOGGETT WIKE

Women in the American Revolution
(McFarland, 2018)

German Footprints in America
Four Centuries of Immigration and Cultural Influence

SUDIE DOGGETT WIKE

McFarland & Company, Inc., Publishers
Jefferson, North Carolina

All maps courtesy of Glenn McCroskey

ISBN (print) 978-1-4766-8575-5
ISBN (ebook) 978-1-4766-4518-6

LIBRARY OF CONGRESS AND BRITISH LIBRARY
CATALOGUING DATA ARE AVAILABLE

Library of Congress Control Number 2021062283

© 2022 Sudie Doggett Wike. All rights reserved

No part of this book may be reproduced or transmitted in any form or by any means, electronic or mechanical, including photocopying or recording, or by any information storage and retrieval system, without permission in writing from the publisher.

Front cover: Three generations of German immigrants at an Ellis Island inspection station in the early 1900s (National Park Service)

Printed in the United States of America

*McFarland & Company, Inc., Publishers
Box 611, Jefferson, North Carolina 28640
www.mcfarlandpub.com*

For Americans,
especially those 46 million with German heritage,
including my husband,
Sidney Wike,
our children,
Martha Wike and Sid Wike, Jr.,
and our grandchildren—
Sid's children, Abi and Miles Wike,
and Martha's children, Christopher and Katie Lyne

Table of Contents

Acknowledgments   ix
Introduction   1

1. England Sends German Metallurgist to America   15
2. German Immigrants to Jamestown   20
3. German Immigrants to Massachusetts Bay Colony   25
4. New Netherland, New Sweden and New Jersey   29
5. Protestant Reformation and the Thirty Years' War   41
6. Germans Flee Rhineland for America   50
7. Jamestown Welcomes a German Explorer   56
8. Quakers Migrate to Penn's Colony and Delaware Valley   65
9. German Protestants Migrate to Colonial America   83
10. France vs. England Conflict: Phase I Glorious Revolution   91
11. Phase II: War of Spanish Succession: Queen Anne's War   99
12. The Great Exodus of the Palatines and Conrad Weiser   105
13. Phase III: War of Austrian Succession: King George's War   116
14. Phase IV: French and Indian War and Bouquet's Royal Corps   123
15. Pontiac's War, Bouquet's Regiment and the Delaware Indians   137
16. Germans and Scots-Irish Migrate to Virginia: Hite vs. Fairfax   150
17. Germans in Colonial Maryland, the Carolinas and Georgia   155

Table of Contents

18	The Great Wagon Road and the Carolina Road	169
19	Quaker and German Longhunters and the Wilderness Road	177
20	American Revolutionary War Soldiers of German Descent	184
21	Germans Begin Migrating to Kentucky, Ohio and the Old Northwest	191
22	The Revolution of the 1848-ers	199
23	German Influx: Indiana, Illinois, Michigan, Wisconsin and Minnesota	205
24	Go West, Young Man: Louisiana, Oregon, California and Texas	219
25	Americans of German Heritage During World War I	225
26	World War II German Rocket Scientists Immigrate to USA: 127 Exceptional Men—BY JAMES EVANS LYNE	232
27	Interview with a Contemporary German Immigrant	243

Appendix: Chronology: The Germans in America	247
Chapter Notes	251
Bibliography	265
Index	273

Acknowledgments

Special thanks go to my husband, eye surgeon Sidney Wike, MD, for repeatedly reading the manuscript of *German Footprints in America*. Appreciation also is expressed to our son, Attorney at Law Sid Wike, Jr.; daughter Martha Wike, PhD, East Regional Psychologist for Children's Services, State of Tennessee; and her son, our grandson, Christopher Lyne (who is working on his PhD in aerospace engineering at Urbana, Illinois), for carefully reading and critiquing parts of this book. In fact, the encouragement of our whole family is greatly appreciated. A warm thank-you goes to Christopher's father, university professor Evans Lyne, who has an MD degree as well as a PhD in aerospace engineering. Not only did Dr. Lyne write this book's chapter on World War II involving 127 exceptional German scientists and Operation Paperclip, but he also critiqued the entire manuscript. I am indeed grateful for the enthusiasm of family friend Myra Orr who, when this manuscript was in its early stages, kindly scrutinized the entire first draft while wielding her schoolteacher's red pencil which she, as promised, did not hesitate to use. Another thank-you is for the late Dr. John Gaines, professor emeritus of King College, for sharing his knowledge of European history and for offering the use of books from his personal library. Kudos also to Glenn McCroskey, who drew the maps for this book. Another special thank-you is extended to Dylan Lightfoot, an editor at McFarland. This nonfictional history, *German Footprints in America*, simply would not have materialized without his encouragement and guidance.

Introduction

Prior to 500 CE migrating Germanic tribes, always searching for land and food, moved south from Scandinavia and then spread throughout Europe, creating independent German states. A thousand years later, in the 1400s the emerging middle class of Western Europe—bankers and merchants hoping to increase their wealth—financed explorers and invested in trading posts that made possible the Age of Discovery. Portugal, Spain, France, the Netherlands, Sweden and England all sent voyages of discovery to the Americas, and German merchants contributed substantial loans to Spaniards and Portuguese for their New World enterprises. German financiers and their Spanish colonists zealously believed in the existence of El Dorado, a city of fabulous riches in the interior of South America, and native stories supported their obsession. Searching for gold, they opened vast swathes of the New World. El Dorado was not found by European explorers in South America, but a new El Dorado indeed was discovered centuries later on a German-American entrepreneur's settlement in present-day Sacramento, California, and the gold rush was on!

Although specific reasons for monarchs sending out explorers varied from nation to nation, the motivation generally involved a desire to increase national wealth, gain territory and spread religion. However, individual explorers, according to tradition, were motivated by three Gs: the desire to please God, find gold and win glory. In May 1493, six months after Columbus landed in America, Pope Alexander VI, a Spaniard by birth, issued his famous bull—a papal charter bearing his seal (bulla)—which protected Spain's title to territory discovered by Christopher Columbus. Dividing the world in half between the two Iberian powers, the papal bull of 1493 drew an imaginary line through the Atlantic about 300 miles west of the Azores and Cape Verde islands. Portugal received all the newly discovered land (including Africa) to

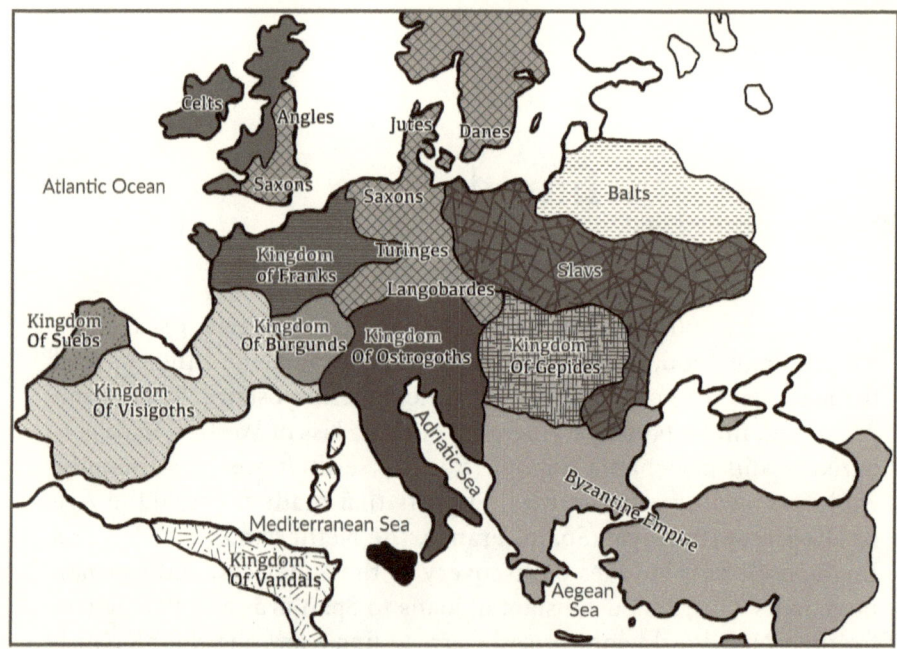

German Tribes, 500 CE.

the east of the line, and Spain got all the land to its west. This gave the yet-to-be-discovered continent of South America as well as the West Indies to Spain. Backed by his mighty fleet, however, Portuguese King John II persuaded Spain to adjust the line. The agreement of June 7, 1494, known as the Treaty of Tordesillas, moved the boundary westward, from 38° to about 46°30' longitude. This gave Portugal a claim to part of the continent of South America and so secured much of present-day Brazil to the Portuguese Crown.

When the Pope divided the American Continent between Portugal and Spain, the excluded nations of the world did not passively accept the new arrangement. Mariners from England, Sweden, the Netherlands and even His Most Catholic Majesty of France set their sails westward to flout the Pope and frantically stake out claims in North America and the West Indies. Starting with Spain, and soon followed by France and England, these three European powers engaged in fierce competition to claim, explore and colonize the New World. The race was soon joined by the Netherlands, Sweden, and Russia.

The discoveries of Columbus and Magellan, plus the conquests of Cortés and Pizarro, added the gold and silver of what is now Latin

America to the spices of the East, all of which began to pour into their sponsoring country—Spain. Tobacco, potatoes, and sugarcane soon followed. The New World offered places for Europeans to live and opened doors to the interchange of goods and services. Merchants, traders and bankers welcomed the age of opportunity. "The future lay not in the Mediterranean, but on the shores of the Atlantic, where the new powers, England, France and Holland had ports and harbours which gave easy access to the oceans."[1]

The contest for the ownership of that portion of North America which became the United States began in the 1600s and remained undecided for a century and a half. Until then Spain had concentrated most of its efforts in New Spain (Mexico), Central and South America. In the 1600s, however, the exploratory expeditions of Ponce de Leon, Hernando de Soto and Coronado supported Spain's claim to a large strip of southern North America which it called La Florida. For more than a century Spain defended its entitlement against both France and Britain.

This book, *German Footprints in America*, begins by describing a conflict between the Protestant Queen Elizabeth I of England and the Catholic Habsburg King Philip II of Spain. It tells how Queen Elizabeth I of England sent two of her favorite knights, Sir Walter Raleigh and Sir Francis Drake, to establish an English colony on what is now the North Carolina coastline. They persuaded a well-known German scientist, Joachim Gans from Prague, Bohemia, the metallurgy capital of the Western world, to sail to America in 1585 and work with them in an attempt to find precious metals in their new colony. Joachim Gans is thought to be the first German as well as the first Jew to set foot in British America.

Elizabeth, in order to finance her venture, commissioned pirates to intercept the flow of wealth to Spain by seizing the treasure-filled galleons of Philip II returning from the Spanish colonies. The queen hoped to increase her country's wealth and forestall any plans Spain might have to subjugate rival maritime nations—the Netherlands and England.

The Royal House of Habsburg to which Philip belonged was a German family-based Catholic dynasty which was continuously occupied by the Habsburgs for many centuries. The Habsburg King Philip II led Spain into its golden age, holding territories in a global network of nations and establishing an empire where "the sun never sets." In 1588, in an attempt to further expand his horizon, Philip organized the Spanish Armada to invade England and overthrow Elizabeth I. In the main battle, which occurred in the English Channel, the English outsailed and outgunned the Spanish. England's naval victory over Spain's Armada elevated Elizabeth's England to a first-class power and placed England in a position to found a North American empire of her own. North America was named *Virginia* in honor of Elizabeth I, the Virgin Queen. Thereafter, English monarchs claimed all the land on America's Atlantic seaboard north of Spanish Florida.

The second chapter describes the founding of Jamestown, Virginia, by the Virginia Company under the auspices of Elizabeth's successor King James I. Early in the endeavor the company recruited a few skilled German and Polish workers to manufacture glass. In 1620 four millwrights from Hamburg were sent to Jamestown to erect sawmills. These craftsmen contributed greatly to increase the industry and commerce of Virginia. The mass migration of Germans to America began early in the next century.

Subsequent chapters focus on the Palatines (a synonym for Germans) who inhabited the Black Forest area of Southern Germany near the junction of the German-French-Swiss borders. Palatines were an agricultural people producing grains for livestock and grape vineyards for red and white wines. These Palatine farmers were living on land that was overpopulated and overworked. Although they were industrious, they were also poor, politically oppressed and torn by religious chaos between Catholics, German Lutherans and Swiss Zwinglians (Protestants).

Many Germans who migrated to the English colonies around 1683 sent word back to their homeland that land in the British colonies of America was plentiful and also offered religious freedom and political stability. By 1717 three groups of Palatine emigrants had gone to America, and some 3,000 were there by 1730. Most of the German immigrants were young people, both married and single, who felt able to survive the rough journey. Usually the elderly were too attached to their beloved Deutschland or too infirm to leave. Moving to a new land, these young immigrants packed up farm equipment, home furnishings and all they thought they would need and set out for Rotterdam. (Rotter means muddy river.) The city's port, lying in the Rhine delta 20 miles upstream from the North Sea, was then—and still is—a vital trading center that connects the industrial heartland of Europe with the rest of the world.[2]

"They loaded their belongings on river freighters when the Rhine River was free of ice in the spring. Journeying down the river they would have to pay customs from local custom houses, costing much money and long delays. The freighters would dock at Rotterdam,

Holland where the Rhine meets the English channel, and the transfer was made to ocean sailing vessels. This was another long and expensive process. From Rotterdam, the vessels would sail to the southern coast of England, Portsmouth or Plymouth, but most often to the Port of Cowes on the Isle of Wight. There goods from the continent would be exchanged for merchandise going to the colonies, more taxes levied, more delay encountered, often in waiting for a favorable wind. With the most favorable conditions, the ocean voyage alone was at least seven weeks long. The total move usually took from May to October in a vessel wretched due to crowded, unsanitary conditions."[3]

Most entered the port of Philadelphia because the colony of Pennsylvania offered religious freedom. Beginning in 1727, each ship's captain entering Philadelphia was required to keep a list of those continental Europeans on board, chiefly German, Dutch, Swiss and French.[4] Each immigrant was examined by port and health officials and required to swear and sign an oath of allegiance to the King of England. "Deutschlanders" would then fan out in a 100-mile radius from Philadelphia to settle mainly in Lancaster and Berks counties. Their descendants are still called Pennsylvania Dutch because the German word "*Deutsch*" was mistaken for "Dutch."

Several chapters discuss why many other Germans chose to leave their European homeland. There are stories of the tribulations and triumphs of these immigrants as they disembarked in colonial America and spread throughout the 13 colonies and into Ohio Country (the Old Northwest Territory north of the Ohio River), the New Northwest Territory (west of the Mississippi River) and eventually to Texas and throughout America. This history chronicles the determination of German immigrants to acculturate but at the same time blend their inherent, straightforward, blunt but kind behavior and indefatigable work ethic into American traditions.

German culture and language were never confined to the boundaries of a German national state. Even into the 20th century "a state called Germany included only parts of the regions of central Europe where people speak German and are part of the German culture." One source identifies German-Americans as "those whose ancestors came from the German-speaking regions of Central Europe, whether or not they were citizens of a German national state as a political entity." It includes Swiss Germans, Austrians, and people from regions bordering Czechoslovakia, Poland and Alsace.[5] Another source points out that, like the immigrants themselves, we should consider as "German any of those people from a conglomerate of central European countries who spoke different but mutually intelligible German dialects and, if literate, read High German. At various times they have included people from not only modern Germany but also Luxembourg, the Alsace, parts of Switzerland and Poland, Austria, the rimland [peripheral area] of Bohemia, local regions in Hungary, Yugoslavia, and other southeastern European countries, as well as the Black Sea and central Volga regions in European Russia."[6]

Germanic peoples of Europe shared much in common, even though their boundaries changed continually, and for many centuries, there was no German national state. German regions existed as autonomous feudal states without a central government. German peoples traditionally have identified with their regional roots and with specific local leaders rather than with governments. It was not until several years after the German Habsburg Emperor of the Holy Roman Empire (which had lasted 1,000 years) abdicated in 1806 that the German Confederation was organized. The Confederation was "an organization of 39 German states, established by the Congress of Vienna in 1815 to replace the destroyed Holy Roman Empire. It was a loose political association, formed for mutual defense, with no central executive or judiciary. Delegates met in a federal assembly dominated by Austria."[7] Germany became a unified nation for the first time in 1871. But even to this day Germans "identify with their regional roots much more intensely than with the national state."[8] Moreover, Germanic peoples are markedly diverse spiritually and include Catholics, a wide array of Protestant groups (Lutheran, Reformed, Pietists, Quakers, Mennonites, Amish, Anabaptists, etc.) and Jews.

In the first half of the 1600s (when English colonists first settled Jamestown, Virginia, and the Bay Colony of Massachusetts) there were an estimated 700,000 Native Americans scattered along the Atlantic coast and throughout the foothills of the Appalachians. By the early 1700s, the Native American population of these coastal and Piedmont areas had dwindled drastically. The natives were supplanted by 250,000 British colonists and other immigrants, with African slaves making up 11 percent of the population.[9] Some Americans make the distinction that British settlers are called colonists since they simply moved from one part of the British Empire to another, whereas non–English settlers of colonial America are referred to as immigrants.

During the first three-quarters of the 1700s, before the American Revolution, hundreds of thousands of non–English-speaking European immigrants and captured African slaves began putting their stamp on

America where the great majority of the white inhabitants had once been of English descent. German-speaking immigrants were the largest group of Europeans who came to British North America in the century between 1683 and 1775. By 1776—the time of the American Revolution—large numbers of Germans, Scots, Irish and immigrants of other nationalities inhabited the colonies along with hundreds of thousands of people of African descent. Thus, "the ethnic English population had become a minority."[10]

The most important cause of German emigration in the 17th century was religious persecution by state and church in Germany.

> The religious persecution that drove settlers from Europe to the British North American colonies sprang from the conviction, held by Protestants and Catholics alike, that uniformity of religion must exist in any given society. This conviction rested on the belief that there was one true religion and that it was the duty of the civil authorities to impose it, forcibly if necessary, in the interest of saving the souls of all citizens. Nonconformists could expect no mercy and might be executed as heretics.[11]

The Protestant Reformation, a 16th-century religious movement, created a schism in the Catholic Church. The Reformation was led by a Catholic priest, Martin Luther, who not only posted a lists of protests—95 theses, or Disputations, on the Power of Indulgences—on the door of Wittenberg's Castle Church (also known as All Saint's Church) in 1517, but he also gave the German people a Bible which he had translated from Latin, the language of scholars and the clergy, into German, the dialect of the people. Both Martin Luther and another Catholic priest, John Calvin, protested corruption, especially the sale of indulgences (spiritual privileges, remission of sin in the afterlife) by the Catholic clergy.

Yet the Protestant Reformation fell far short of satisfying the discontent of the persecuted sects, mainly among the lower classes, who wanted to abolish not only the priesthood but also nobles and kings. The persecuted Protestant sects suffered death by fire and sword, imprisonment and harassment by the authorities and forcible conversions. Compounding these intolerable conditions came the Thirty Years' War (1618–1648), when Germany became a desolate wilderness, and many of the oppressed and starving people resorted to robbery, murder and the eating of human flesh. Spiritual consolation was all that was left, and so the Germans looked to heaven for solace. But they looked beyond the conventional Lutheran, Reformed and Catholic churches. The Rhine country from which most of the emigrants came was the home of Mysticism and Pietism which sprang up following the Protestant Reformation.[12] Eighty percent of these displaced German people went to Pennsylvania and arrived in three distinct phases: the first phase spanned 26 years, 1683 to 1709; the second phase lasted five years, 1709–1714; and the third stretched out over 58 years, from 1717 to 1775.[13]

Throughout the 1700s "The settling of the British colonies by small German-speaking religious groups continued. The groups included Swiss Mennonites, Baptist Dunkers, Schwenkfelders, Moravians, Amish, and Waldensians. But most German immigrants belonged to the main Lutheran and Reformed churches. The central colonies, especially Pennsylvania, received the greatest part of this immigration. As many as half of these immigrants came as redemptioners [indentured servants], that is, they agreed to work in America for four to seven years in exchange for free passage across the Atlantic."[14]

The first phase (1683–1709) of German immigrants to America came mainly from the Rhine country. Their emigration was spurred by religious intolerance against Mennonites, Quakers and many other small, well-organized Pietist groups. Pietism was a reform movement, a protest, originating in 1675 within German Lutheran Christianity in reaction to the religious formality and orthodoxy observed by the Lutheran Church. Pietists embraced primarily the betterment of mankind. Pietists stressed practicing a personal faith rather than conforming to the traditional Lutheran doctrine and theology. They focused on devotional experience and Bible study. They favored a warm, heartfelt, personal relationship with Christ that avoided preaching and teaching. They were also greatly concerned with social and educational matters. Continual, devastating warfare in southwest Germany (the Rhenish Palatinate, Swabia, Württemberg, Silesia and the many small principalities between Bavaria and Austria) and Switzerland also drove Pietists from their homeland.

Typical of the Pietist groups were 300 Mennonites and Quakers led by Franz Daniel Pastorius, Johannes Kelpius and Daniel Falkner to Penn's Colony. The Quaker William Penn and other Friends and Mennonites along with Pietists and Mystics persuaded all persecuted German-speaking groups to escape and embark on a long, weary, overland journey and then cross perilous seas in overcrowded, sick and starving conditions to reach an alien, English-speaking land.[15]

The second phase of German immigration (1709–1714) was driven by agricultural disaster. In addition, the rulers of small principalities exacted heavy taxes to pay for their attempt to emulate the lavish court of Louis XIV. Not only that, but the game in Louis's hunting parks was allowed to run amok across the planted fields of the farmers. Also significant was the reality that the government of the Palatinate was Roman Catholic while the population was predominately Protestant, although not all the emigrants were Protestant. These conditions caused thousands of Germans and Swiss to migrate to England to accept the generous aid of Queen Anne during the War of Spanish Succession, called Queen Anne's War in America.

The third phase (1717 to 1775) saw hundreds of thousands of Germans ousted by overpopulation and its resultant land scarcity in Europe. These refugees were lured to America by the active recruitment of laborers to settle in the American colonies. Some of the recruiters were unscrupulous. German-Americans went on to fight on British America's side in the French and Indian War and later as American Patriots or Loyalists during the American Revolution.

And then there were the political refugees known as the 1848-ers. These thousands of German middle- and working-class people from across many nations of Europe had staged widespread rebellions against monarchal rule. The Forty-Eighters advocated for new leadership in which the common man, like the aristocracy, would have a voice in government. After the failed German Revolution of 1848, these defeated rebels fled their homeland. However, for a few short months during the European Revolutions of 1848 throughout Western Europe, liberalism had been on the march against autocracy. "National unification, individual freedom, greater economic opportunities, and popular self-government were the watchwords of a long-overdue revolt against the censorship, espionage, repression, militarism, and special privilege which marked" the previous age.[16] Many Forty-Eighters held onto their dreams and immigrated to America's Old Northwest.

And so it happened that economic refugees of earlier times were soon balanced by political refugees of the 1830s and 1840s seeking freedom in America. Otto Von Bismarck's intolerance of socialists in the 1870s and 1880s sent to America a small but influential number of educated Germans with a variety of liberal, freethinking and religious views.

It was during the 1800s and early 1900s (specifically between the years 1815 and the beginning of the First World War in 1914) that 38 million immigrants from Europe and Asia arrived in America. These newcomers played a vital part in the continuous reshaping of this multiethnic country. However, during World War I, a significant number of Americans developed Germanophobia: spitting at Germans in the street; barring the teaching of the German language in schools; burning German books; kicking dachshunds; renaming German shepherds "Alsatians"; dubbing sauerkraut "liberty cabbage"; and forcing Germans in America to purchase war bonds as proof of patriotism. World War II saw less anti–German sentiment, and yet 10,000 German-Americans were imprisoned as enemy aliens. "President Franklin Roosevelt conspicuously appointed military commanders with names like Eisenhower and Nimitz to fight the Axis powers. But the Holocaust gave German-Americans yet another reason to hide their origins."[17]

Today German-Americans are quietly successful. Note German beer barons such as Jacob Best, Joseph Schlitz, Frederick Pabst and Frederick Miller of Milwaukee who have dominated the brewing trade. The German-American "median household income, at $61,500, is 18% above the national norm. They are more likely to have college degrees than other Americans, and less likely to be unemployed. A whopping 97% of them speak only English at home.... Germans have assimilated and prospered without any political help specially tailored for their ethnic group."[18]

Although Americans encouraged German immigration, Colonial America did not welcome every immigrant or colonist who tried to enter. In 1639, the Pilgrims of Massachusetts attempted to expel foreign paupers and set fines for shipmasters who brought criminals and paupers to its shores. Virginia and other colonies did the same. The General Assembly of Maryland passed a law in 1676 that required shipmasters to declare whether convicts were on board, and if so, they were prohibited from landing.

However, the English government frequently shipped its "idle poor" to its North American colonies and in 1717 began exporting felons. From 1717 until the American Revolution, 50,000 criminals were sent to America from the British Isles, "20,000 of them to Maryland between 1750 and 1770."[19] The colonies protested the landing of criminals and some indentured servants. But as long as the colonies were subject to British rule and had no voice in Parliament, they were unable to change the mother country's immigration policy. Pennsylvania passed a law in 1722 to impose a duty upon persons convicted of heinous crimes and imported into the province. Shipowners were held accountable for the conduct of their passengers.

Ever since colonial times, the foremost ethnic groups in America have considered each subsequent influx of newcomers as an enemy to be feared and subdued. Even Theodore Roosevelt, in 1915, before the United States entered the First World War in 1917, declared "that no good American could possibly be a 'hyphenated American'—say a German-American or an Italian-American." Later, "In 1919, Woodrow Wilson would put the matter more starkly, likening the hyphen in a hyphenated American to a 'dagger' plunged into the 'vitals of this Republic.'"[20] Frequently these very same newcomers, once they assimilated and prospered, treated new immigrants exactly as they, themselves, had been treated. Thus the achievements and opportunity of each alien group were diminished and deemed inferior by the people who had preceded them.[21]

Today, if Hispanics are classified in separate groups such as Mexican-Americans, Cuban-Americans, etc., those of Germanic ancestry are the largest single ethnic group in America: According to the U.S. Census Bureau, for the year 2000, 15 percent of the United States population (42.8 million Americans) claimed to be of German descent. In comparison, those of Irish and English descent number approximately 33 million and 25 million respectively. However, these numbers regarding German heritage may be significantly higher because German-Americans often acculturate so completely that they are frequently unaware of their German ancestry.

Popular media covering World War II, military films and later television repeatedly portrayed Germans negatively. That's part of the reason why knowledge of one's German heritage has often been suppressed, and numerous Americans may be uninformed about, or reluctant to claim, their culture. Many may not be aware of the positive: Colonial Germans' contributions to America included improved farming methods, the rapid establishment of schools, the first paper mill and the first glassmaking factory. Jacob Leisler convened the first intercolonial congress in North America.

Jacob Leisler (1640–1691) was born in Frankfort, a large city in western Germany on the river Main, a few miles upstream from its confluence with the Rhine River. At age 20 he immigrated to the Dutch colony of New Netherland. He had become a wealthy merchant and a militia captain of the West India Company (WIC) by the time the British overtook New Netherland and renamed it New York in honor of the Duke of York, who soon became King James II. When James was overthrown in 1689 by co-monarchs William III and Mary II, Leisler led a revolt of small farmers and city workers against the new Crown-appointed governor of New York. One theory for why Leisler revolted explains that he was a committed Calvinist who objected to Anglican government because he feared that Anglicans would eventually revert to Catholicism. Seizing control of government, Leisler became commander in chief of the New York revolutionary government and was elected by revolutionaries as lieutenant governor of the province of New York. He then summoned the first intercolonial congress in North America to plan a united action against the French and Indians. English co-regents William and Mary commissioned a British governor for the New York province and hanged both Leisler and his brother-in-law for treason. Parliament subsequently reversed the sentence and restored the confiscated estates to the heirs of the executed men.

There is some controversy about whether it's fact or fiction that in 1735 Anna Zenger of New York became the first woman newspaper publisher in the new nation. "Christopher Saur, a German printer in Philadelphia, printed the first Bible in America" in 1742.[22]

"In whole swathes of the northern United States, German-Americans outnumber any other group.... Some 41% of the people in Wisconsin are of Teutonic stock. Yet despite their numbers, they are barely visible.... [Few] ... notice that John Boehner, the Speaker of the House of Representatives, and Rand Paul, a senator from Kentucky ... are of German origin. Companies founded by German-Americans tend to play down their roots, too: think of Pfizer, Boeing, Steinway, Levi Strauss or Heinz."[23]

Multiple catastrophes of German history in the 20th century have almost swept away public awareness of the "great reputations of those who, like Helmholtz, had raised German science to the heights."[24] Albeit he was not an immigrant, Prussian-born Hermann von Helmholtz (1821–1894) was a renowned scientist whose discoveries and inventions contributed much to American and world science. He was one of the first to describe the conservation of energy, the concept that energy can be neither created nor destroyed. As an army surgeon who aspired to be a physicist, Helmholtz invented the ophthalmoscope, which shines a light into a patient's eyes and allows the medical practitioner to diagnose and treat eye diseases and abnormalities. His work on electromagnetism led to breakthrough radio and wireless transmissions.

The tremendously influential Helmholtz served as an idol for the work of Albert Einstein and Nobel Prize winner Max Planck. Einstein (b. 1879 Württemberg, Germany; d.1955 Princeton, New Jersey) was a German immigrant to America who revolutionized our understanding of gravity, space and time. Although not an immigrant to America,

Introduction

German-born Planck, a theoretical physicist who studied in Munich and Berlin universities, originated the quantum theory which revolutionized our understanding of atomic and subatomic particles and processes.

Another vastly important event was the immigration of German rocket scientists to the U.S. at the end of the Second World War. Hundreds of scientists and engineers fled toward the U.S. forces to avoid being taken by the Soviets. The program to bring them to the U.S. was known as Operation Paperclip, and those 127 exceptional men formed much of the core group that developed the American space program.

Germans have brought to America and shared their auspicious heritage, not only in science and theater but also in music. The incredible list of German classical composers includes musical maestros like Beethoven, Bach, Brahms, Handel, Strauss, Schumann, Wagner, Mozart, Mendelssohn and many, many more who are applauded throughout the Western world.

Despite the relative obscurity of German immigrants and their role in the development and prosperity of America, peoples of Germanic descent have made and continue to make significant and widespread contributions to American culture and technology.

1

England Sends German Metallurgist to America

The Habsburg dynasty was a royal German family whose members became the hereditary rulers of the Holy Roman Empire. The Hapsburgs ruled middle Europe for 500 years, from the 15th to the 20th century. In 1556 the first Habsburg King of Spain, Charles I, who was also the Emperor of the Holy Roman Empire, abdicated and split his duties, which had become too heavy for one person to handle. He gave the title Holy Roman Emperor to his brother, Ferdinand. The more significant title at that time, however, King of Spain, went to his son, Philip II.

As the second Habsburg king of Spain, Philip II reigned for 42 years, and during his sovereignty the Spanish Empire attained its greatest power. The Venetian ambassador described Philip as "slight of stature and round-faced, with pale blue eyes, somewhat prominent lip, and pink skin, but his overall appearance is very attractive…. He dresses very tastefully, and everything that he does is courteous and gracious."[1] Philip II was an avid Catholic Christian. He exterminated Protestantism in Spain and suppressed Lutheran heretics everywhere without mercy.

Philip combined the two great rivals of the Age of Discovery, Spain and Portugal, when he acquired the Portuguese throne. Spain then entered its golden age, holding territories in a global network of nations and establishing an empire where "the sun never sets." Philip's colonial empire stretched from South America to his namesake, the Philippines, and the Spice Islands and to Florida.

Sir Winston Churchill noted that by the late 1500s the rivalry between England and Spain was pushing the two countries toward war. Streams of silver and gold from the mines of Mexico and Peru flowed across the ocean on galleons, greatly enhancing the wealth of the Spanish Empire. Together, Spain's King Philip II and England's Queen

Elizabeth I dominated the Western world in the second half of the 16th century.

England's Queen Elizabeth I commissioned privateers—licensed pirates—to intercept the flow of wealth to Spain by seizing Philip's galleons returning from the Spanish colonies. She hoped to increase her country's wealth and forestall any plans Spain might have to subjugate rival maritime nations—the Netherlands and England. She ordered the strengthening of the Royal Navy so it could "fight and sink anything the Spaniards might send against them." Sir Francis Drake, one of Elizabeth's privateers, was confident that England could win a war against Spain. Vowing to start a war with Spain, Drake earned the epithet "Master thief of the unknown world." His incessant raids on Spanish harbors and his plundering of Spanish ships became a seafaring legend.[2]

The pirate Drake executed a secret mission for Queen Elizabeth in 1577. He embarked on a several years voyage to "annoy the King of Spain in his Indies." After rounding the tip of South America and entering New Spain's previously uncontested Pacific waters, Drake sailed northward and swooped down upon the unsuspecting Spanish outposts. He sacked Spanish towns in the New World and captured ship after ship, stuffing his ship, the *Golden Hind*, almost to the sinking point with treasure.

Sir Francis Drake worked with his friend Sir Walter Raleigh in attempting to establish a colony on what is now the North Carolina coast. Therefore, the first temporary settlement in North Carolina was an English outpost founded in the 16th century by Elizabeth's favorite knight, Sir Walter Raleigh, at Roanoke Island on the Outer Banks. This was more than 20 years before the permanent colony at Jamestown, Virginia, was established.

Joachim Gans, born in Prague, Bohemia (now the Czech Republic), was both the first German and the first Jew as well as one of the first scientists known to have immigrated to British colonial America. Gans's birthplace, 16th-century Prague, was the most advanced European center of innovation for mining and metallurgy. Arriving in England in 1581, Gans introduced his new invention, an improved method for smelting copper. He was subsequently employed at the Mines Royal in the Lake District of northwestern England. There, working with a German-speaking shareholder in the mines, Gans shortened the time required to refine copper and reduced the cost of production.

When Sir Walter Raleigh first attempted to colonize Roanoke Island, he needed a metallurgist with enough scientific expertise to discover and identify valuable metals in the New World. Raleigh wanted to prevent voyages from returning to England with another shipload of fool's gold. At the time, war between England and Spain was imminent. England, a relatively poor and backward European country, needed copper, tin and cannon to arm her ships. No Englishman was available to do the job of locating and analyzing metals. That's why the German metallurgist Gans was employed by the Ralph Lane Colony on Roanoke Island. Sir Ralph Lane, first governor of the first English colony in America, was invited by Sir Walter Raleigh to command an expedition to America. He sailed on April 9, 1585, under Sir Richard Grenville, with whom he soon began to quarrel. Towards the end of June, they arrived on the North Carolina Outer Banks and established a colony with Lane as governor.

After Grenville departed for England in August, the colony moved to Roanoke Island, North Carolina, where it remained for the next eight months. Among the colonists of this expedition were John White, an artist, and a mathematician, who took meticulous notes and made remarkably accurate drawings of the wildlife, fauna, and Natives of the New World. Gans, a German-Jew, was one of the 100 would-be settlers who hoped to enable England to compete with Spain in acquiring wealth for their king and country. The catch was that Jews, like Muslims and other non–Christians, were forbidden to live in or even visit England. Raleigh therefore obtained a visa for the scientist Gans, who built a laboratory on the island to conduct experiments. "The small band of Europeans in the American wilderness was far from home, but Joachim had come farther than any. Moreover, he was a foreigner among the English and a Jew among the Christians.... Therefore, the burden of adjustment may have been greater for Gans than for his companions, yet he adapted himself well and made his technological contributions."[3]

Thomas Harriot, another scientist on the expedition, reported that Gans, the "mineral man," discovered both iron and copper in America.

When food supplies dwindled, however, and the Indian threat heightened, Joachim Gans, along with the other 100 settlers, gladly evacuated Roanoke Island a year later when Sir Francis Drake rescued them from a hurricane, took them aboard ship and in 1586 returned to England.[4] In 1589 Gans was arrested in Bristol, England, as an infidel. When he admitted that he was a circumcised Jew who did not believe in the Christian religion, he was taken to London for trial. It was probably because he was known by such important persons as Sir Walter Raleigh that no trial seems to have taken place. In England Gans gave

Hebrew lessons to English gentlemen who wanted to read the Bible in its original tongue. It was also in 1589 that a bishop visited Gans who proclaimed himself a Jew. Bishop Curteys asked Gans, "Do you deny Jesus Christ to be the Son of God?" Gans replied, "What needeth the almighty God to have a son? Is he not almighty?"[5]

What's more, since there is no record of his burial in the Jewish cemetery of Prague, it is unlikely that he returned there. "The register of St. Andrew's Church, Plymouth, under date of 13 Oct. 1589 notes the marriage of one John Geynes and Alce, whose surname is not recorded; whether Geynes is a form of Gans is, of course, not known."[6]

In the 1990s, archaeologists excavating the former Roanoke settlement discovered the remnants of Gans's equipment and workshop; "the material is the only undisputed physical evidence we have of the Roanoke settlement."[7]

Raleigh's next attempt to settle the Outer Banks would become known as the Lost Colony. It was established and then abandoned virtually without a trace. That's partly because Philip II sent his Spanish Armada to attack England. Therefore, the English could not return to America to check on and aid Raleigh's newest colony.

By 1588 King Philip II of Spain had spent two years organizing the Spanish Armada's attack on England. He wanted Protestant England to return to the Catholic faith. He also intended to halt England's hostility to his effort to reconquer the Netherlands. Most emphatically he needed to stop the maritime raids of Queen Elizabeth's pirates on Spanish trade. To this end, his giant fleet of 130 ships carrying 8,000 seamen and 19,000 well-trained soldiers prepared to invade England.

The Spanish planned to win control of the English Channel before invading England. Throughout England volunteers and militiamen mobilized to identify and reinforce possible landing sites. The English knew that if Philip's strong Spanish Army invaded England, the weak English army would be powerless against them. Any hope of English success depended on her sea power.

The war between Queen Elizabeth's English navy and the Spanish Armada of King Philip II occurred offshore. This is just what the queen wanted. Britain's long-range cannons boomed victory for the queen in a series of naval battles. One leader of the English fleet was Sir Francis Drake. Artillery was key to the battle. The English guns were more effective than those of the Spanish. The English outsailed and outgunned their Spanish opponents.[8]

During the battle, a dreadful storm with harsh wind and rain

1. England Sends German Metallurgist to America

contributed heavily to the Spanish losses. "The armada," wrote Winston Churchill, "had indeed been bruised in battle, but it was demoralized and set on the run by the weather."[9] Protestant England celebrated. A commemorative medal was struck bearing the inscription, "God blew and they were scattered." The jubilant queen and her people believed the storm to be the work of a Protestant God. Elizabethan England's naval defeat of Philip's Spanish Armada elevated England to a first-class power and placed the English nation in a position to found a North American empire of her own.

Throughout the 16th and most of the 17th centuries, however, Spain was Europe's first modern great world power. In the Americas alone, the Spanish Empire eventually included claims to most of South America, Central America, present-day Mexico and much of the American West from Cape Horn to the Great Plains and beyond.

2

German Immigrants to Jamestown

Today, Historic Jamestowne is the actual site of the colony at Jamestown, Virginia. On the other hand, Jamestown Settlement is a living history museum.

1608—Several Germans were among the settlers at Jamestowne.[1]

By right of Cabot's discovery of the North American mainland, probably Newfoundland or Labrador, the English monarchs claimed all the land on America's Atlantic seaboard north of Spanish Florida. They called this land *Virginia* in honor of Elizabeth I of England, the Virgin Queen.

James I (r. 1603–1625), the King of England and Scotland, who was Queen Elizabeth's successor, established a global network of charter colonies. Each province (colony) received a written contract authorizing a private trading company—joint stock company—to establish the colony. The charter granted the stockholders the right to self-govern. Joint stock companies, an outgrowth of medieval guilds, were made up of groups of entrepreneurs, mainly merchants and bankers as well as many gentlemen and noblemen.[2] Some companies, however, had non-entrepreneurial motives, such as providing sanctuary and economic opportunities for religious dissenters.[3] By granting royal charters, the king hoped to "gain import duties and taxes, and the commercial venture—for the ultimate benefit of the country—would be managed and expanded by knowledgeable people at no expense or risk to the crown. The advantage to the company, of course, was that all business flowed through its hands."[4] James encouraged charter colonies to harvest natural resources, develop new industries and create markets for English-made goods. The stockholders received shares in the

2. German Immigrants to Jamestown

company as well as a percentage of the profit. In the case of America, they also received grants of land. Between 1575–1630 more than 6,300 English men and women owned stock in joint stock companies.

In 1606 England's King James I chartered two English companies of entrepreneurs, the Virginia Company of London and the Virginia Company of Plymouth, to colonize Virginia (British America). Colonization is a "form of conquest in which a nation takes over a distant territory, thrusts in its own people, and controls or eliminates the native inhabitants."[5] At the king's request, the companies sought not only to found colonies but also to discover gold, find a northwest water route (passage) to the silks and spices of the Orient, and to convert American Indians to the Anglican religion.

After choosing English privateer Christopher Newport as captain of its first expedition, England's Virginia Company of London handed him a sealed envelope with instructions not to open it until his ships arrived at their destination. Commanded by Newport, three ships—*Susan Constant, Godspeed*, and the smaller vessel, *Discovery*—set sail on December 20, 1606. At that time Spain still dominated the Atlantic Ocean. That is why Newport carefully avoided Spanish waters south of Virginia.[6]

More than 100 male passengers were on board. Among them were carpenters, a blacksmith, a mason, a tailor, a barber, two surgeons, and cartographer John Smith. An auburn-haired and bearded soldier-sailor, Smith had earned the rank of captain while fighting the Turks in Europe. When 26-year-old Captain Smith challenged Captain Newport's command, Newport threw the troublemaker into the ship's prison and planned to execute him.

Newport and the first Jamestown colonists sailed into the Chesapeake Bay on April 26, 1607. Upon landing at Cape Henry, present-day Virginia Beach, Captain Newport opened the sealed envelope and read the names of 13 Englishmen designated by the London Company to serve as councilmen. When Newport saw that one of the 13 was John Smith, he released him from prison. The letter instructed the councilmen to elect a president from among their numbers.

Newport's fleet entered the mouth of a river which they named "James" and continued to sail upstream where they founded a settlement now called Jamestown, Virginia. Jamestown was the first permanent English settlement in British America. Most of the Jamestown settlers were colonists, not immigrants, because they were born in England under the rule of an English monarch and moved from one part of the English empire to another. At the time of colonization, the Tidewater–Chesapeake Bay area was inhabited by indigenous peoples, the Powhatan Confederacy, a league of some 30 Algonquian-speaking North American Indian tribes named for their powerful leader, Chief Powhatan.

The Jamestown colonists built James Fort on territory claimed by the Paspahegh tribe, one of several tribes of the Powhatan Confederacy. In less than a fortnight, hostilities between the settlers and Native American tribes accounted for the killing of 200 Indians and several colonists. Even so, over the ensuing years these Indians occasionally supplied the settlers with food.

The reason male English colonists went to Jamestown in the early 1600s was because poverty in England had intensified. The struggle with Spain and defeating the Spanish Armada had absorbed the vivacity and treasure of Englishmen. Wage earners faced hardships; beggary and vagabondage were everywhere. The cost of living was steadily rising. Inflation was a problem, said 20th-century British Prime Minister Winston Churchill, "prices rose sixfold, and wages only twofold."[7] King "James's craven eagerness for peace," said Princeton University Professor (later American President) Woodrow Wilson, "had put an end to the wars with which Elizabeth's day had resounded, and London was full of idle soldiers, mustered out of service. Younger sons and decayed and ruined gentlemen seemed to abound more than ever. It was men out of work or unfit for it who chose to go to America."[8] It was thought that the creation of colonies might help to lift the hope and provide livelihood for the English peasantry.

Although Jamestown, Virginia, the cradle of Anglo-Saxon America, was primarily an English colony, the Virginia Company recruited skilled German and Polish immigrants to promote trade and craft in the colony. In 1608, one year after the first English settlers reached Jamestown, some German mechanics came there by special invitation to carry on their trade.

Back in the fall of 1607 John Smith began scouting the countryside, bargaining with the Indians for food and furs in exchange for copper, beads, axes, knives, hatchets, guns, swords, iron pots and cloth. All the time he was canoeing the rivers and mapping the new colony. Searching for a navigable river leading northwestward to the South Sea (Pacific Ocean), Smith and his crew, aboard a small, open boat rigged with sails, charted the course of the James River and the Chesapeake Bay area.[9]

Half of the original Jamestown settlers died of disease and starvation within six months of their arrival. Soon additional colonists arrived in the new colony. Newport returned with supplies and more Englishmen. He also brought two women and five men from Poland. The Polish immigrants were pitch, tar and soap makers. On April 20, 1608, the ship *Phoenix* docked with 40 more and carried cedarwood back to London.[10]

In September 1608, the second council president of Jamestown was killed by Pamunky Indians as he attempted to bargain for supplies and food. Immediately Captain John Smith was chosen president of the council. Shortly thereafter, the first German settlers arrived at Jamestown.

Southeastern Virginia Historical Highway Marker WT 2 located on Jamestown Road (Rt. 31) in James City County describes the first German immigrants at Jamestown:

> The first Germans to land in Jamestowne, the first permanent English settlement in Virginia, arrived aboard the vessel *Mary and Margaret* about 1 October 1608. These Germans were glassmakers and carpenters. In 1620, German mineral specialists and saw-millwrights followed, to work and settle in the Virginia Colony. These pioneers and skilled craftsmen were the forerunners of the many millions of Germans who settled in America and became the single largest national group to populate the United States.

When the Virginia Company sent German (*Deutsch*) contract laborers (glassblowers and carpenters) to Jamestown, Captain John Smith characterized his array of workman of that time as "labourers … that never did know what a days work was except the Dutch-men, Poles, and some dozen others." Holland was the main embarking point for people living along the Rhine in areas of Germany contiguous with Holland. Hence, not only Hollanders but also Germans embarking from a Dutch port were classified as Dutch. Smith praised the German (*Deutsch*) and Polish craftsmen for their quality workmanship which generated profits for the Virginia Company. The Germans and Polish were brought over to manufacture glass. In 1620 four millwrights from Hamburg were sent to Jamestown to erect sawmills.[11] Captain John Smith recorded several German names (e.g., Unger and Keffer) in his list of original settlers. One of the "Dutch" that Smith mentioned was referred to as a "Switzar," a person from Switzerland. The skilled German craftsmen contributed greatly to increase the industry and commerce of Virginia. "There still stands on the east side of Timber Neck, on the north side of the York River, a stone chimney, with a mighty fireplace, nearly eight feet wide, built by these Germans."[12]

In retrospect, the notion that North America would supply raw materials proved to be futile. For surprisingly it was not so much raw materials but a novel crop, tobacco, that turned out to be immensely profitable in the new colony of Virginia. Therefore, in the mid–1600s it was the tobacco industry that attracted Germans to Virginia. Among these immigrants were Dr. Georg Nicolaus Hacke, a native of Cologne who was perhaps the most highly educated citizen of Northampton County; Thomas Harmanson from Brandenburg, who founded a prominent eastern shore family; and Johann Sigismund Cluerius, also of German birth, who owned a large estate in York County.

3

German Immigrants to Massachusetts Bay Colony

Although the first permanent English settlement in America was made at Jamestown, Virginia, in 1607, the first English Great Migration to America occurred 23 years later, in 1630. This was the Puritan migration to the Bay Colony when John Winthrop led a large group of colonists, including some Germans, to settle the Massachusetts Bay Colony. This greater Bay Colony migration happened ten years after the small group of *Mayflower* Pilgrims had anchored and thrived at Plymouth Rock, Massachusetts.

Because the strict anti–Puritan policy of King Charles I cost English Puritan Lawyer John Winthrop his government position, he joined the Massachusetts Bay Company. Winthrop pledged to sell his estate and take his family to Massachusetts if a charter could be obtained. The other Bay Colony company members elected him governor.

In 1629 Winthrop and a number of his fellow Puritan noblemen and gentry from East Anglia received a royal charter from King Charles I naming their organization "Governor and Company of the Massachusetts Bay in New England."[1] The charter granted them permission to trade between the Charles and Merrimack rivers. Having long dreamed of escaping intolerable living conditions in England, they now sold their possessions and set sail. Their Bay Colony charter to Massachusetts made Winthrop's new government virtually free of rule by the king. They would be 3,000 miles away and across the ocean, far from the threat of religious persecution of Puritans.

The Bay Colony Puritan migration was a religious movement of Christians, the most successful English effort to colonize the North American mainland during the first half of the 17th century. It was an exodus which "for size and wealth and organization was without precedent in English colonization of North America." The myriad ships carried livestock, passengers, and supplies—bread, butter, oatmeal, beef, beer and food to be cooked on deck on a common hearth as weather permitted. Leading the Great Migration was the eagle figurehead of the 28-gun flagship *Arbella*, carrying highly skilled, middle-class passengers—yeomen and artisans, pious and literate; "very few came from the bottom of English Society." Traveling in a cabin was the ship's namesake, Lady Arbella Fiennes. Also on board were her rich landowner husband, high stewards and Suffolk lawyer, John Winthrop, who would become governor.[2] The first passenger ashore at Boston was a nine-year-old girl who remembered "a land very uneven, abounding in small hollows and swamps and covered with blueberry and other bushes."[3] They dug burrows into the riverbank for temporary shelter and ate fish and dried peas. Many died of scurvy, whose etiology would not be discovered until two centuries later, or "burning fever" of unknown cause.

Over a six-month period in 1630, the colony welcomed 17 ships carrying 1,000 women, children, men, livestock and supplies.[4] Over the next ten years, nearly 200 ships, each carrying 100 emigrants, sailed into Boston. Bringing their unique folkways, patterns of speech, town meetings, and Puritan churches, they became the backbone of New England Society. Speaking with a high-pitched "Norfolk whine" which evolved into "Yankee twang," their austere society associated "plain cooking with piety." They dressed in dull colors—sad green, liver and russet. To them, "marriage was not a religious ceremony but a civil contract"[5] performed by a civil magistrate, not a minister. These staunch New Englanders did not kneel to pray but stood, open-eyed, looking toward heaven, talking directly to God. Sitting erect and unmoving—pinned by the all-seeing eye of God carved on the pulpit—they listened for hours to hellfire and brimstone preaching.

The Bay Colonists were committed to establishing a "city upon a hill," "a new Canaan—an experiment in Christian living ... with all eyes upon them ... (proving) that it was possible to lead a New Testament life, yet make a living."[6] On a special day of prayer, July 8, 1630, Governor Winthrop presented this creed to his colonists:

> Wee must be knitt together in this worke as one man, wee must entertaine each other in brotherly Affeccion ... wee must delight in eache other, make others Condicions our owne rejoyce together, mourne together, labour, and suffer together, allwayes haveing before our eyes our Commission and Community in the worke.[7]

In the early to mid–1600s more than 60,000 Englishmen sought refuge and opportunity in the New World.[8] Most were Puritans who came to America from East Anglia where more than half the people were sheep farmers and cloth traders engaged in the cottage wool-weaving industry.

Some Germans accompanied Winthrop's Puritan fleet, according to a tract published after Winthrop set sail for America. The pamphlet specifically mentioned Germans by saying: "It is not improbable that partly for respect to some Germans that are gone over with them and more that intend to follow after."[9] But the main history of German immigration would not begin in earnest until more than a half-century later, 1683, with the settlement of Germantown, Pennsylvania, by Quakers and kindred spirits such as Mennonites. Quakers and Mennonites were usually called "harmless sects" in contrast to the aggressive, sword-wielding Bay Colony Puritans who praised the Almighty for political or religious victory on ground soaked in human blood.[10] Especially bloody was King Philip's War. Fought by Puritans in 1675 against the Wampanoag Indian Nation, King Philip's War has been called the "toughest battle, not excepting Bunker Hill, ever fought on New England soil."[11] In the same year Bay Colonists followed King Philip's War by a preemptive strike against the Narragansett tribe.

Although a few Germans were admitted, Quakers were discriminated against in the Bay Colony because Puritans were obsessed with order. "Everything was put in its proper place and held there by force if necessary."[12] Quakers failed to conform to that order and were automatically accused of witchcraft and heresy and then were prosecuted and punished, sometimes severely. Two Quaker women, 22-year-old Mary Fish and Ann Austin, a mother of five, arrived in Boston Harbor on the ship *Swallow* in 1656. They were confined to the ship while Massachusetts authorities searched their belongings, which a hangman then publically burned in the marketplace. The women were strip searched for signs and items pertaining to witchcraft. After five weeks they were allowed to sail to a Quaker colony in Barbados. Nevertheless, Quakerism still spread throughout the colonies from Maine to South Carolina.[13]

The Rev. John Norton, who succeeded Matthew Cotton as minster of the First Church of Boston, agreed with other Puritans in their belief that Quakers had no place in the "Lord's Kingdom." Norton said: "I would carry fire in one hand and faggots in the other, to burn all the Quakers in the world."[14] Another time, Norton made a joke of the flogging nearly to death of a Quaker missionary. "He endeavored to beat the gospel ordinances black and blue," said the Reverend Norton, "and it was but just to beat him black and blue." In 1660 the usual punishment for any Quaker who dared set foot in Massachusetts was death by hanging. Next to hanging, the most violent common punishments for Quakers were slitting the nostrils, amputation of ears, and the very deep branding of an "H" for blasphemous heretic on the face with a red hot iron. Four Quaker women were stripped to the waist, tied to a cart and wheeled from constable to constable through 12 New England towns to be whipped and flogged so that blood ran down their naked backs and breasts until "the horrified townsmen of Salisbury [MA] rose against the constables and rescued them."[15]

In 1662, English King Charles II, a Catholic sympathizer and no friend of Puritans who had executed his father, responded to a plea for help. The king sent a letter to Massachusetts ordering Quaker persecution to stop. The accused were to be sent unharmed to England for trial. But the persecution of Quakers in Massachusetts lessened only gradually.

4

New Netherland, New Sweden and New Jersey

While the New England Puritan, the Pennsylvania Quaker and the Maryland Catholic colonists came to America seeking religious freedom to worship as they saw fit, "The Dutch—who invented many aspects of modern capitalism and became immensely rich in the process—came to Manhattan to make money.... They were so busy trading beaver pelts they didn't even get around to building a church for 17 years."—*Wall Street Journal*[1]

1626—Peter Minuit, a German, came to New Amsterdam to serve as the governor of the Dutch colony, New Netherlands. Later he governed the Swedish colony in Delaware.

Between 1607 and 1611, while Jamestown settlers were searching for gold and a river route to the South Seas, English navigator Henry Hudson skippered four voyages seeking a northern route to the Orient—an ice-free passage from Europe to Asia via the Arctic Ocean. On his first voyage, financed by a Russian (Muscovy) company in which members of his family probably were stockholders, Hudson piloted the ship *Hopewell*, plying due north of Norway for a passage across the North Pole to China and Japan. He abandoned his search. On his second voyage, still sailing under the Russian flag through the hazardous, ice-gorged waters of the Arctic north of Russia, he soothed his restless crew but again failed to find the Northeast Passage and returned to England.

In 1609, on his 3rd voyage, Hudson's ship *Half Moon* was put to sea under an orange, white, and blue Dutch flag bearing the VOC (Verenigde Oostindische Compagnie) logo of the prosperous Dutch East India (Trading) Company. The East India Company was chartered in 1602 by the Republic of the United Netherlands which had formed when several Dutch coastal cities on the North Sea joined together for mutual benefit. The united Dutch then grew strong enough to revolt against Spain and gain their independence. The East India Company supported the Dutch War of Independence and protected the Netherlands' interest in the Indian Ocean trade. Dutch shipwrights built stout vessels and became the ocean carriers for Europe. On the high seas their great fleets made conquests to the far corners of the earth.[2]

The East Indian Archipelago provided the East India Company with spices: salt, pepper, nutmeg, cloves and cinnamon. The company obtained silk and cotton, including chintz, from India. It traded Bengal opium, which was smoked as a recreational drug on Java and in Europe. Silk, porcelain and tea were traded in China. The Dutch East India Company even traded elephants in Asia.[3]

The great maritime nation of Dutchmen financed their exploring and colonizing by founding the modern stock exchange. The Dutch East India Company (also called the East India Company or the VOC) was a prosperous, joint stock company with many investors. The East India Company was the first multinational corporation in the world and the first company to issue stock. "Among the early shareholders of the [East India Company], immigrants played an important role. Among the 1,143 tenderers were 39 Germans and no fewer than 301 Zuid-Nederlanders (roughly present-day Belgium and Luxemburg, then under Habsburg rule).... The [Company's] total capitalization was ten times that of its British rival."[4] The majority of the stock of the Dutch East India Company, however, was owned by the Jesuit Order, the Roman Catholic Society of Jesus. Jesuits were priests and brothers who took the religious vows of obedience, chastity and poverty. One of the East India Company's chief moneymaking ventures was smuggling involving the opium trade. Thus, in addition to being the first international stock corporation, the Jesuit-controlled East India Company formed the first international drug cartel. Not only that but, in 1600, Protestant England chartered the omnipotent East India Company as a mercantile and mercenary pirate enterprise. England contracted the VOC mercenary pirates to carry on commercial trade ventures.[5]

On Hudson's third voyage, when his *Half Moon* crew spotted icebergs and threatened mutiny, he bore west. Navigating along the east coast of North America, Hudson discovered the territory which he named New Netherland. It stretched from Delaware in the south to Albany, New York, in the north and encompassed parts of the

4. New Netherland, New Sweden and New Jersey

present-day states of Delaware, Connecticut, Maryland, Pennsylvania, New Jersey, and New York.

After rounding Cape Cod, Hudson found what his master mate, Robert Juet, called a "very good harbor for all windes," and there Hudson steered the *Half Moon* into the mouth of a large river which now bears his name. Juet, the sailing mate, recorded in his journal of the voyage that the Dutch ship *Half Moon* set "sayle" from Amsterdam on March 20, 1609, and began exploring the Hudson River on September 12 of the same year.[6] (This was the same majestic river noted but not navigated by Verrazano exploring for the French in 1524.) Juet duly logged his "compasse" readings as well as the daily weather. He described the visit of the *Half Moon* far up the river to the mouth of the Mohawk near the present site of Albany, New York.

Hudson anchored the *Half Moon* at the crossroads of two American Indian trails, one running north-south paralleling the Hudson River, the other traveling east-west from Massachusetts to Niagara. "The people of the Countrie came flocking aboard," he wrote, "and many brought us Bevers skinnes, and Otters skinnes."

The Dutch based their extensive claim to New Netherland on Hudson's third voyage. As logged by the master mate aboard the *Half Moon*, Hudson navigated the Hudson River, identified the Delaware River and pointed the way for Dutch traders to explore the Connecticut River.

When Hudson returned to England, he was arrested for sailing under a foreign flag. Despite his arrest, he found English backers for an ill-fated fourth voyage in 1610. Piloting the ship *Discovery*, he actually discovered and established the British claim to a huge body of water—now called the Hudson Bay—in northern Canada. Trapped in the frigid waters of Hudson Bay, starving mutineers set their captain, Hudson, and a few others adrift on a small boat and took their ship the *Discovery* back to England. Master Mate Juet, who was one of the mutineers, died of hunger. The marooned Hudson and his valiant crew vanished and were never heard from again. His body has never been found. So, the question of whether Henry Hudson was murdered or succumbed to the harsh environment of northern Canada has never been answered. And—although speculations including a multitude of legends, books, articles and hypotheses abound—the history of his final days remains a mystery.

Soon after Henry Hudson spotted his namesake river, Captain Hendrick Christiansen, a ship captain-trader, explored the Hudson River. Christiansen, a German navigator employed by the Dutch, built the first houses on Manhattan. Christiansen was born in Kleve, Germany, a town on the lower (northern) part of the Rhine Province near the Dutch border with Germany. At that time Holland was still a part of Germany and remained so until 1648.[7] In 1614 (six years before the Mayflower Pilgrims settled Plymouth Colony, Massachusetts) Christiansen, the founder of Albany, New York, built Fort Nassau at the future site of Albany. Fort Nassau served as a busy trading post for four years and for sporadic trading thereafter. Thus the foundation for an amicable trading relationship between settlers and the Mohawk Indian Nations was laid.

Five years after Hudson charted the course for three rivers, Adriaen Block, a privateer and fur trader from Amsterdam, explored the Connecticut River. Block discovered local shells which the Native Pequots called *sewan* or *wampum*. Far to the northwest the Mohawks, who prized these shells for making jewelry, eagerly bartered them for beaver pelts. The Dutch set up a three-way trade, exchanging English cloth and cookware for the Pequot's shells and then swapping the shells to the Mohawks for beaver furs. This business was bustling long before the English had ever heard of the word *wampum*.

The Dutch East India Company failed to colonize the Hudson Valley. Therefore, the Parliament of the Republic of the United Provinces of the Netherlands chartered the Dutch West India Company (WIC) to populate the Hudson Valley. The WIC was modeled after the Dutch East India Company. However, in contrast to the Jesuit-owned Dutch East India Company, the West India Company was answerable to secular investors.

In March 1624 a WIC ship, *Nieu Nederlandt*, brought the first permanent settlers—not Dutch, but 30 Flemish and Walloon families—to the Dutch colony of New Netherland.[8] Walloons were a "mixture of Germans and French on a Celtic base" who spoke a French dialect and lived west of the Lys River[9] in Belgium and France. Over the next two years, six additional ships brought colonists, livestock and supplies. The expansive colony of New Netherland sprawled through parts of the present-day states of New York, New Jersey, Pennsylvania, Maryland, Connecticut and Delaware.

In 1624 the first permanent settlers—18 mostly Walloon families from Holland—built a second fort at the site of Albany and named it Fort Orange in honor of the ruling house of Holland.[10] Like the no-longer-thriving Fort Nassau, Fort Orange, the first Dutch settlement in America, was a forerunner of present-day Albany, New York. Fort

Orange began trading with Iroquois Indians who brought pelts from the Mohawk Valley. Many Germans were among the first Dutch settlers of both Fort Orange and New Amsterdam (now New York City).

In 1625 the WIC sent Peter Minuit (Minnewit), a Dutch broker and diamond cutter, to the province of New Netherland which included today's New York State. Minuit, who was born in Wesel, a town in Northwestern Germany, was to negotiate for trade goods and manage the trading post in what would become the city of New Amsterdam. Before he became a broker, Peter Minuit had studied theology and served as deacon of the Dutch Reformed Church. Minuit's parents were religious refugees from the Rhineland, specifically Wesel, Rhenish Prussia, the westernmost province of the Kingdom of Prussia where Peter was born in 1590. Minuit was probably of "French speaking, Belgian Walloon stock."[11] On his arrival Minuet found a town of 30 log cabins on Manhattan. Recognizing his first duty to be finding ways to protect the colonists from Indians and pirates, he bought the island from the Indians.[12] For his famous purchase of 22,000 acres on Manhattan Island ("the Manhatoes") Minuit paid Native Americans a few trinkets and 60 guilders (florins, $20).[13] Sixty guilders equates to almost $1,000 today. Here Minuit built Fort Amsterdam, which would become the village of New Amsterdam. The next year, in 1626, the WIC appointed Minuit director of the struggling colony of New Netherland. As the first governor-general of New Netherland, Minuit surrounded the stone Fort Amsterdam at the southern point of Manhattan Island with cedar palisades. Today's Wall Street takes its name from the palisade wall of that settlement. Outside the wall, a large second-floor room of the fur warehouse served as a church. Windmills were built but failed to work inside the fort because the walls of the fort blocked the wind.[14] The horses, therefore, continued circling round and round, powering the mill that ground the grain into flour for colonial consumption and for export. Soon, under Minuit's dynamic leadership, Fort Amsterdam blossomed into New Amsterdam, a village of wooden houses with thatched roofs. Its lumberyard was powered by windmills, their blades turning "in drowsy arcs across the blue sky." It was a community of "creaking carts ... snorting hogs ... tavern ... backwoods traders ... sailors and colonists babbling in Swedish, French, Danish, German, and Portuguese for the colony welcomed all."[15] Manhattan was curiously cosmopolitan; within 20 years of its founding, a French priest heard at least 18 languages spoken on the streets. Taking advantage of New Amsterdam's large natural harbor at the mouth of the Hudson, which afforded access to America's interior, Manhattan's merchants traded pelts, slaves, lumber, oysters and other goods not only within the colonies but around the world.[16]

Minuit developed amity with the Puritans of New England. Under his government, New Amsterdam prospered until the WIC chartered a patroon system against his advice. The ensuing friction led to Minuit's recall. A patroon was an aspiring proprietor who received a government land grant with manorial rights in return for colonizing his land with 50 settlers. The patroon then had authority over his colonists and could charge rent. He had a monopoly of grinding, hunting, fishing and mineral rights. Lords of the manor had rights to hold fairs and markets.

In 1630, land surrounding Fort Orange was purchased from the Indians and settled by Dutch, Norwegians, Danes, Germans and Scots. Sawmills, grist mills, homes and barns were built by the absentee patroon who supplied food and cattle. He also enforced laws regulating trade, hunting and fishing and, of course, collected rentals. Later, in 1652, Peter Stuyvesant, who was the West India Company's general director of New Netherland, developed the village of Beverwijck (Beverwyck) around Fort Orange.

New Netherland had several directors after Minuit left there in 1631. Sixteen years and three directors later, the WIC appointed Dutchman Peter Stuyvesant, the son of a Calvinist minister, as New Netherland's first director-general (governor). The peg-legged Stuyvesant became the New Netherland colony's most successful director-general. Having sustained injury and amputation of his right leg in a previous military expedition, Stuyvesant wore a wooden leg. Stumping into New Amsterdam in 1647, Stuyvesant curtailed smuggling, regulated taverns, and enforced laws. As the colony grew, Dutch settlements wedged a toehold and then a foothold on Native American lands and infringed on English settlements, especially in the Connecticut Valley. Stuyvesant purchased farmland on the southeastern bank of the Hudson from the Algonquian-speaking Indians in the Esopus Valley. But Stuyvesant's delay in making promised payments for the property precipitated the Battle of Wiltwyck, one of two wars between the Esopus Munsee Nation, a branch of the Delaware Indians known as the Lenapes, and the Dutch. Barely winning the skirmish, the Dutch employed the Iroquoian-speaking Mohawk Indians to give chase to the retreating Esopus warriors.[17] After befriending the Iroquois Confederacy in the Upper Hudson Valley and crushing the Esopus Indians in the Lower Valley, Stuyvesant built a palisaded fort. Its 40 houses, protected by a wall, sat perched on a bluff overlooking Esopus Creek. He called the village "Wiltwyck," which is present-day Kingston, New York.

Under Stuyvesant, the New Netherland colony produced immense wealth for the Dutch. The zealous Calvinist Director-General Stuyvesant, however, discriminated against Quakers and Jews even though, back in 1579, the United Provinces of the Netherlands had proclaimed: "No one shall be persecuted or investigated because of his religion." In this spirit, almost a half-century later, in 1625, when the Dutch West Indies Company set up a trading post at the southern tip of Manhattan, the director's mission was to welcome all and "establish trade, not save souls." When Peter Stuyvesant became director-general of New Amsterdam in the mid–1600s, however, he supported the Dutch Reformed Church and only grudgingly tolerated most other faiths, except for Quakers and Jews. Even though he was biased against both Quakers and Jews, he especially discriminated against Quakers, "who then had a reputation of obnoxious rabble rousers." Stuyvesant ordered one 23-year-old Quaker preacher to be publicly tortured. Stuyvesant then issued an ordinance punishable by fine and imprisonment against anyone harboring Quakers. The people of Flushing (Vlissingen), a neighborhood in what is now the New York City borough of Queens, immediately objected to the edict. Thirty ordinary Flushing citizens signed a document citing a Flushing town charter which promised liberty of conscience. This Flushing town charter was a precursor of the U.S. Constitution. The citizens courageously sent their document to Director-General Peter Stuyvesant.[18] The citizens of Flushing, though none were Quakers, stood up for the oppressed. They wrote the "Flushing Remonstrance," a plea for establishment of religious freedom. "You have been pleased to send unto us a certain prohibition that we should not receive or entertain any of these people called Quakers.... For our part we cannot condemn them.... Nor can we punish, banish, or persecute them, for out of Christ, God is a consuming fire, and it is a fearful thing to fall into the hands of a living God. We desire therefore, in this case, not to judge, neither to condemn lest we be condemned, but rather let every man stand and fall to his own.... We are bound by the law to do good unto all men."[19]

Stuyvesant arrested the author of the document plus the officials who presented it and jailed two magistrates who signed it. Quakers, nevertheless, continued to meet in Flushing at the home of farmer John Brown. Brown then was banished from the colony. But when he went to Amsterdam to plead for the Quakers, Brown won his case. Even though the WIC proclaimed Quakerism "an abominable religion," it ruled against Stuyvesant and ordered him to "allow every one to have his own belief." Religious toleration then became the law of the colony. Today, within a few blocks of the still-standing Brown house, a visitor can see a Quaker meeting house, a Dutch Reformed Church, an Episcopal Church, a synagogue, a Hindu temple and a mosque. "All coexist in the most diverse borough in the most diverse city on the planet."[20]

Stuyvesant's council also discriminated against Jews in the village of New Amsterdam in 1655, forbidding them from entering armed service and then imposing a "special" tax on them *because* of their exemption from military.[21] During the 40 years of Dutch control, villages, trading posts and forts flourished along the Hudson and became the towns of today. As the settlements expanded, they spilled into the Delaware and Connecticut River valleys.

New Sweden—a Swedish Colony on the Delaware River spanning parts of the present-day states of Delaware, New Jersey and Pennsylvania—was founded after the WIC (Dutch West India Company) dismissed Dutch colonizer Peter Minuit as director of the Dutch province of New Netherland. German-born Minuit was employed by a Swedish commercial trading company, sponsored by investors from Holland, Sweden and Germany. Minuit was hired to explore and establish colonies in North America. Since the plan for founding New Sweden had originated on German soil, the subsequent European management of the colony was in the hands of a German treasurer, a German bookkeeper and other officers, many of whom were Germans.[22] From 1623 to 1633 the Swedes distributed printed circulars in Germany to entice Germans to join them in their settlements on the Delaware. And indeed, many German names are among the first settlers of New Sweden.

The Swedish expedition to settle New Sweden sailed their flagship, the *Kalmar Nyckel*, into the Delaware Bay in 1638. The celebrated Protestant captain of the expedition was none other than German-born Peter Minuit who in 1626, as the leader of the Dutch province of New Netherland, had bought Manhattan from local Lenape Indians. And now on the Delaware River, Captain Minuit and his Lenape translator met with five Lenape chiefs and purchased 67 miles of riverfront where he built a fur-trading post on "the Rocks"—a site on the Christina River near present-day Wilmington in the Delaware Valley. Naming the post Fort Christina for the reigning Swedish monarch, Minuit designated the entire Delaware River area the colony of New Sweden. To help populate the land the Swedish settlers imported Finnish woodsmen. It was

4. New Netherland, New Sweden and New Jersey   37

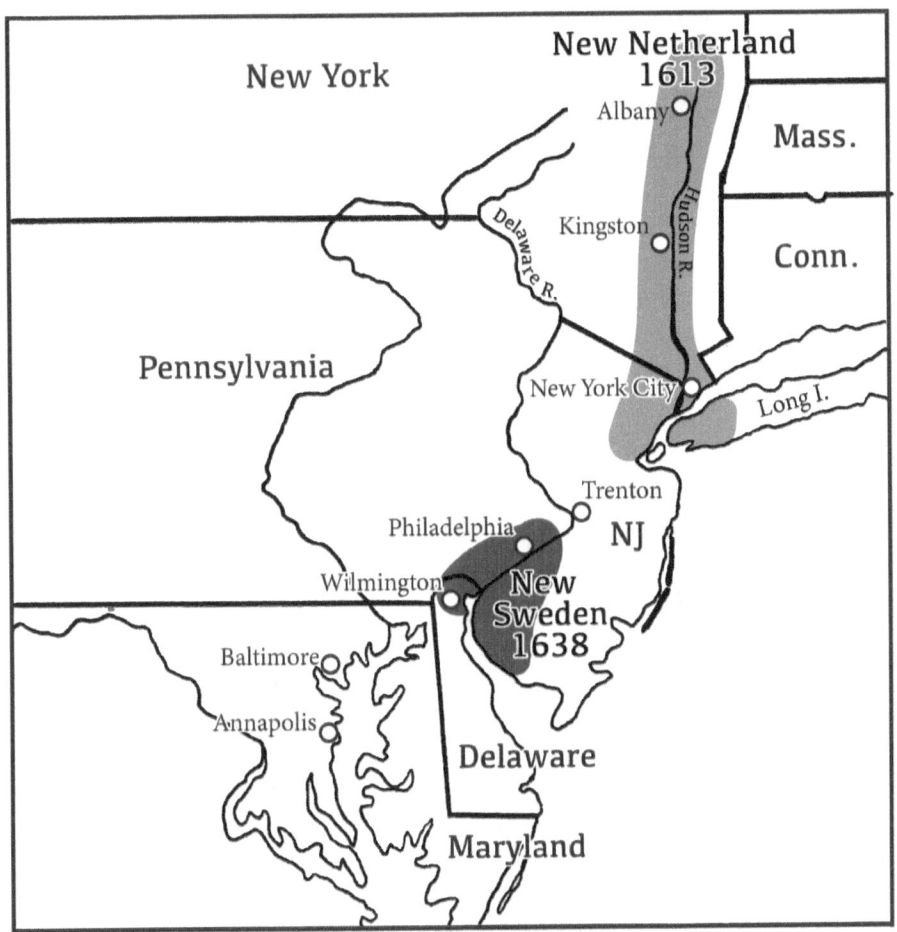

New Netherland and New Sweden.

difficult to attract settlers from the Netherlands since that country was prosperous and its citizens saw little need to emigrate. There were, however, many Germans among the first Dutch settlers of New Sweden. The Swedish colony expanded as far north as Trenton, New Jersey.

Later in the same year (1638) Minuit set sail with two vessels to open trade relations between New Sweden and the West Indies but was caught in a hurricane and drowned at sea.

Johann Printz Von Buschure, a German nobleman and Holstein native, succeeded Minuit as the governor of New Sweden. Governor Printz, a huge man weighing 400 pounds, was named "Big Guts" by the Lenni-Lenape (Delaware) Indians who sold land and pelts to his settlement. Printz and his settlers worked hard; the Finns cleared the land with fire; the Swedes raised log cabins with corner fireplaces. Stout hausfraus "stuffed straw into cloth bags for mattresses."[23] Although Big Guts was in the Swedish service, he brought 54 German families from Pomerania with him to New Sweden. Pomerania was a region between what is now Poland and Germany. Thus New Sweden developed a semi-German character.[24] "All these Germans, however, were in the minority in the respective settlements, and freely intermingling with the mass of the population, soon lost their identity."[25]

Although Printz ruled the colony quite successfully, New Sweden was attacked and annexed by New Netherland. The attack was led by Peter Stuyvesant, the director-general of New Netherland. "New Sweden vanished, but its Lutherans and log cabins [said to be the first log cabins built in America] remained to help shape the New World."[26]

Stuyvesant wanted to protect the original Dutch claim to New Sweden. For, despite the current Swedish and Finnish settlements, the Dutch still claimed the Delaware area as Dutch country because the ill-fated Dutch colony of Swaanendael (Zwaanendael) had been built there first. Therefore, the Dutch of New Netherland had no intentions of allowing an incursion into their territory. Consequently, New Sweden survived for only 17 years until 1655 when Peter Stuyvesant led a military expedition against the Swedish Fort Christina on the Delaware and brought the short-lived New Sweden to an end. Nevertheless, despite its physical boundaries being erased and engulfed by New Netherland, the social, cultural and religious tradition of the Swedish settlement of New Sweden lived on. Eventually, the colony that had once been New Sweden became parts of the states of Delaware, New Jersey, Pennsylvania, and Maryland.

In 1664 the Dutch lost the now-prosperous province of New Netherland, which at that time included New Sweden, to England. The British easily captured the city of New Amsterdam when a small English fleet sailed into Manhattan, surrounded the village and took possession of it. Stuyvesant—virtually defenseless—surrendered the entire province to Commander Richard Nicolls who served under the Duke of York and Albany, the future King James II of England.[27]

Though Stuyvesant surrendered to the English, he retained the Dutch West India Company's trading rights with the Mohawks.[28] New Amsterdam became New York, named for the Duke of York, but the Dutch stayed on, and so did their ways, richly preserved in the writings of Washington Irving, *Rip Van Winkle* and the *Legend of Sleepy Hollow*.

"And Irving tells us that thunder from the Catskills signals the return each 20 years of Henry Hudson and the *Half Moon* Crew, who play at ninepins and look down on the great river they explored long ago."[29]

The Dutch merchants adjusted readily to British rule. As the English colonies flourished, New York City emerged as one of North America's most prominent cities.

England's King Charles II granted his recently conquered New Netherland, which would become New York and New Jersey, to his brother the Duke of York. Not long after receiving his charter in 1664 and unbeknownst to Commander Nicolls, the Duke of York gave that part of his grant located between the lower Hudson and Delaware rivers to two of his Cavalier friends, Lord John Berkeley and Sir George Carteret.[30]

The province of New Jersey stretched from New York to present-day Cape May, New Jersey, where the Delaware Bay flows into the Atlantic Ocean. The duke gave the western part to Lord John Berkeley and the eastern part to Sir George Carteret, naming the entire land New Jersey in honor of Carteret, who had governed the Isle of Jersey and held it for the Crown during the English Civil War. Jersey Isle served as a refuge for the young royals until the restoration.

Carteret and John Berkeley developed the colony of New Jersey by selling the land to settlers and granting them political and religious freedom. New Jersey and New York shared a royal governor until 1738. New Jersey's first European immigrants settled East Jersey. Carteret conveyed his East Jersey estate to several persons, one of whom was Quaker William Penn, whose Anglican father was a friend of King Charles II.[31] Berkeley sold West Jersey, Delaware and eastern Pennsylvania to Quakers.[32]

The Delaware Colony, founded as New Sweden in 1638 by Peter Minuit, was one of the four Middle Colonies which included Pennsylvania, New York and New Jersey. The Duke of York, before he became King James II, leased Delaware to William Penn. Thus he subjected Delaware to British rule and insured that Penn's Colony would not be landlocked. However, in 1776 Delaware established a separate government, declaring itself free not only of British rule but of Pennsylvania.

There are diverse opinions about the chronology of the first German settlers of German Valley, New Jersey. One oral tradition has it that in 1705 a number of German Reformed residing between Wolfenbuttel and Halberstadt fled to Rhenish Prussia. From there they went to Holland. In 1707 these people embarked for New York, but adverse winds blew their ship into the Delaware Bay. Determined to live among the Dutch, they took the overland route toward New York, but upon reaching a particularly enchanting valley, they decided to settle in what is now known as German Valley of Morris County, New Jersey. This version, however, is not substantiated. Another historian speculated that the early Germans of New Jersey were the "poor Palatines" who came to New York in the massive emigration of 1710 and afterwards.[33]

Aside from oral tradition and speculation, the written record documents an act of service performed by the first German Lutheran pastor to preach in the colony of New Jersey. It was on August 1, 1714, "'at the house of Ari de Guinea' [Harry from Guinea, a Christian Negro and his wife Jora], on the Raritans [Raritan River] at our Christian Lutheran gathering"[34] at which time a child was baptized who had been born March 25, 1714. From this record it was decided that the year 1713 was the most probable date for the beginning of the history of German Valley, New Jersey.

After the early German immigrants came to New Netherland and New Sweden, a mass migration of Germans was triggered by the destruction wrought by Europe's Thirty Years' War, 1618 to 1648, and its aftermath, which will be covered in the next chapter following a discussion of the Protestant Reformation.

5

Protestant Reformation and the Thirty Years' War

Europe had been a patchwork of city states and small principalities for more than a century before religious differences split Western Christendom into two warring camps: the Protestant Reformation (1517–1648) led by Anglicans, Lutherans and Calvinists, and the Counter-Reformation (1534–1789) directed by the Jesuits, a Roman Catholic order of austerely religious men established in 1534 and renowned for their scholarship, the founding of schools and their charitable work.

This schism between Protestant reformers and Catholic counter-reformers divided the continent. Meanwhile the staunchly traditional Catholic Habsburgs, a royal German family, had begun to acquire new fiefs and increase their power. Mainly through marriage and inheritance, they assembled a multinational empire stretching from Gibraltar to Hungary and from Sicily to Amsterdam "exceeding anything which had been seen in Europe since the time of Charlemagne 700 years before"[1] when Charlemagne's Carolingian Empire, precursor of the Holy Roman Empire, controlled much of Western and Central Europe.

German-born Jan Hus, the harbinger of the Protestant Reformation, protested the sale of indulgences in 1451. Jan Hus was a Catholic priest from Prague, Bohemia, the capital city of what is now the Czech Republic. Because Hus protested the Pope's practice of granting indulgences (favors, mercy, forgiveness or remission of sin in the afterlife) in return for donations, he was burned at the stake for heresy. Jan Hus, who disbelieved in the ability of man to buy his way to heaven by contributing to the Pope, became a Protestant martyr more than a half-century before another German Catholic priest, Martin Luther, posted his 95 theses—his list of grievances or protests.

The Roman Catholic Church was a major political and military

Charlemagne's Empire.

power in Western Europe when Martin Luther, a German monk, Catholic priest and professor of theology at the University of Wittenberg, nailed a list of 95 theses to the door of Castle Church Cathedral in Wittenberg. Luther had vowed to become a monk after nearly being killed by a bolt of lightning. Nailing a list to the church door was the customary way to open public debate on controversial issues. Armed with his conviction that the sale of indulgences was wrong, Luther posted his complaints on October 31, 1517, the Eve of All Saints' Day, which marked the traditional beginning of the Protestant Reformation. Martin Luther's interpretation of the Bible encouraged him to attack the leadership of the Roman Catholic Church. "First, Luther insisted that religious

5. Protestant Reformation and the Thirty Years' War

authority lay not primarily in church traditions, nor in the hierarchy of bishops and popes, but in the Bible alone."[2] Protesting certain traditions of the Catholic Church, especially the Pope's practice of granting indulgences, Luther believed that faith alone was the source of salvation and that God could not be bought off. The Catholic Church's view was that salvation could be achieved by good works and donations.[3] Petitioning for reformation or restructuring of the Catholic Church, Luther's grievances questioned the dogma or beliefs of the Roman Catholic Church and initiated the Protestant Reformation movement. The Gutenberg Bible printed in the German language promoted the Protestant Revolution.

The publisher, German-born Johannes Gutenberg, grew up in the city of Mainz in the Rhineland-Palatinate where he worked as a blacksmith, goldsmith and jeweler. In 1439 Gutenberg invented a metal, movable type system that revolutionized the printing industry. Six years later, in 1455, he published his most famous work, the Gutenberg Bible. Thus, when Martin Luther insisted that all Christians be able to read the Bible in their own language, Gutenberg's printing press smoothed the progress of the Protestant Revolution by making Luther's translation of the New Testament from Latin into the German language, as well as his pamphlets, available to the general public. His conversion of biblical Scripture into everyday German language could be understood by mothers, children and the common man. Luther did not want to split the Catholic Church. He merely intended to purge it, not only of indulgences but also of other abuses listed in his 95 theses.

The Roman Catholic view that one could achieve salvation by good works differed from the Lutheran view that one could achieve salvation by faith, which implied a direct, individual relationship with God. Both differed from the Calvinist view that God had predestined every individual to be either among the elect (the saved) or the damned and that mortals could do nothing to influence their predetermined destiny.

The founder of Calvinism, John Calvin, an admirer and successor of Martin Luther, was a key mover in the ongoing Protestant Reformation. The Protestant Reformation was challenged by the Catholic Counter-Reformation led by the Society of Jesus or Jesuits, founded by Spaniard Ignatius Loyola.

It was religious differences, a Protestant versus Catholic confrontation, that started the Thirty Years' War. The conflict began as a German Civil War, spread from Prague throughout the German states, and soon engulfed much of Europe.

Distribution of Roman Catholics and Lutherans, 1560 CE.

The Thirty Years' War (1618–1648) uprooted numerous Germans who relocated and found safe haven as well as employment in America. The first conflict of the Thirty Years' War which presaged the breaking up of Germany was precipitated by a religious dispute between Catholics and Protestants at the Palace of Prague in Bohemia in what is now the Czech Republic. The ruckus occurred in the same city where a monument now stands in memory of the martyred Catholic heretical Priest Jan (John) Hus, the cleric who first protested indulgences and, in essence, initiated the Protestant Reformation which was furthered 66 years later by Martin Luther. In the aftermath of the Protestant Reformation, which had greatly disrupted the German states, the 1618 free-for-all in Prague broke out when a quarrel arose between Jesuits and Calvinists. Each was accused of forcing their respective religions on the other. A union of Protestants formed for mutual protection. The Catholic League had triple protection: the Pope, the Spanish King and the Emperor of the Holy Roman Empire. The brawl occurred in the Prague palace ballroom, a huge hall almost 200 feet long, 52 feet wide and 40 feet tall, where knights competed in indoor horse races. Mounted on horseback, knights charged each other with lances in jousting tournaments. When the messy track was mucked, the horse manure was shoveled out the window into the courtyard two stories below. In the fracas, Protestants gathered in the freshly mucked ballroom, grabbed two of the emperor's Catholic councilors and a secretary and shoved them out the window. The toss is known as the "Defenestration at Prague." The Habsburg representatives dropped 50 feet and landed unhurt into the pile of dung which cushioned the fall, according to Protestants.[4] But Catholics believed that the Virgin Mary intervened, softened the fall and prevented injury.[5]

The news of the defenestration initiated religious wars among Catholics, Calvinists and other Protestants that spread throughout Europe. Most of the fighting occurred on German soil. Soon the cause of the war was forgotten. It was no longer only a religious war. It escalated throughout Europe into "a series of wars fought by various nations for various reasons, including religious, dynastic, territorial and commercial rivalries."[6] Catholics fought in Protestant armies and vice versa. Nations and provinces raised armies at great expense and used the war as a pretext for the conquest of neighboring countries. Ill-paid soldiers, mercenaries from faraway lands, rampaged through the countryside. Plundering, poverty and famine were rampant. As the prolonged, cruel and destructive war dragged on, the question of pay for the military became as important as the quest for food or munitions. The financial distress increased until the commanders of both sides were forced to loot towns and villages both for supplies and to augment their soldiers' pay. "The Thirty Years' War set up a tradition of looting as a legitimate operation in warfare and of outrage as a soldier's privilege that has tainted the good name of Germany right down to the First World War of 1914."[7]

In the first half of the 1600s an estimated two-thirds of the people of Germany perished from war, pestilence and famine. The war destroyed almost all trade and commerce. Even after the lapse of two centuries, the line of march of 1,000 soldiers sent by French King Louis XIV to destroy Huguenots (French Protestants) seeking refuge in the Palatinate could be traced up the Rhine Valley from Drachenfels (near Bonn) to Heidelberg. Crumbling walls, ruined battlements and blown-up towers still remained as reminders of French vandalism.[8]

The war broke apart the German states and adversely affected much of Europe for years to come. It led to the poverty, persecutions and religious intolerance that uprooted Germans from their Fatherland and sent massive numbers of immigrants, mainly through Dutch ports, to America.

"Nothing less than the material and political annihilation of Germany could explain as it does the voluntary expatriation of almost all at one time of whole communities ... moved by a common impulse such as ... a mighty hope or a widespread despair." In this case it was more despair than hope that propelled the flight from the Fatherland.[9]

Before the Thirty Years' War, Germany compared favorably with other European countries in material prosperity. Even the average peasant was comfortable, had some training in school and church, and stashed away at least a small savings in coin for a rainy day. But the devastation beginning with the religious conflict of the Thirty Years' War in Central Europe and extending through the territorial conquests of French King Louis XIV later in the 17th century totally erased all wealth and sense of well-being for most Germans.

Death and destruction resulting from the Thirty Years' War affected various territories of Germany differently. Some areas lost one-third to two-thirds of their population. Others were almost unscathed. Epidemics of typhoid, plague and syphilis were the greatest killers. Decreased agricultural production, plus destruction of buildings and livestock, wrecked the fragile economy. Some say that it took almost a century after 1648 for the German population to regain its pre–1618 levels.[10]

The war wrecked not only sections of Germany but also much of 17th-century Europe, leaving in its wake uninhabited wildernesses, burnt villages and miserable people, some of whom became murderers, robbers and cannibals. Many of the desolate, oppressed and persecuted Germans looked to heaven outside of the conventional tenets of the established churches.[11] They embraced Pietism, a movement originating in the Lutheran Church in Germany in the 1600s. Pietism was

5. Protestant Reformation and the Thirty Years' War 47

Holy Roman Empire during the Thirty Years' War and the maximum extent of the Holy Roman Empire (based on map from *The Economist*, Dec. 22, 2012).

based on spiritual equality, not political equality. Pietism stressed personal piety (devoutness and goodness) over religious formality and orthodoxy. Eschewing formalism and intellectualism, Pietists stressed Bible study and personal, devotional experiences and practices. "The name Pietist, like Puritan and Methodist, was given to these devotees by their critics as a term of ridicule; it was accepted by them, and became a badge of humble pride."[12]

The Thirty Years' War (1618–1648) began as a German civil war won by the Catholic Habsburgs and then became increasingly international. England was the only powerful European country not to join the Thirty

Years' War. The English were fighting their own revolution, the English Civil War (1642-1651). By 1630 the wider set of conflicts involved Sweden, France and Spain. The war evolved into despair with cynicism and brutality while morals and morale collapsed. Ideals of religion and patriotism vanished. After a generation of violence "Simple men now fought for food or drink or hate while their masters mobilized their passions in the competition for taxable lands and political power...'God send that there may be an end at last,' wrote a peasant in his daybook."[13]

The rulers and their diplomats sent out feelers for peace. But the bickering, delays, quarrels and unproductive negotiations went on while men died in the battlefield until, at long last, the Treaty of Westphalia was concluded.

The 1648 Treaty (Peace) of Westphalia ended the Thirty Years' War, redrew the map of Central Europe and left the German states broken into bits and pieces under separate rulers. The Holy Roman Empire began to dissolve, and the power of the Habsburgs was diminished. Austria and Prussia, the largest of the German states, vied for dominance. The smaller states, allying first with one and then with the other, struggled to retain their independence. The Thirty Years' War radically changed the balance of power in Europe: Switzerland and the United Provinces (Dutch Republic, the Netherlands) won recognition of their independence; the Upper (south) Palatinate went to Bavaria; the Lower (north) Palatinate was restored to the Holy Roman Empire; Brandenburg, which was the heart of the Kingdom of Prussia and the site of the kingdom's capitals, Berlin and Potsdam, gained territory which increased the power of the Hohenzollern dynasty, the ruling House of Brandenburg-Prussia, over that of the rivaling Habsburg dynasty, also known as the House of Austria. Sweden gained towns and territories, became mistress of the Baltic, and kept the title until Peter the Great captured marshland adjoining Sweden, dredged it out, built a seaport on the site and named it St. Petersburg.[14] The German princes were granted full sovereignty over their 360 now shattered and still un-unified German states.[15] Europe became a community of sovereign states similar to its structure of today.

By the time the German princes elected Habsburgian Leopold I as Holy Roman Emperor (r. 1658-1705), the title was merely honorary. Leopold, however, shared the Habsburg love of the arts and maintained his ancestral sense of duty. As a devoted champion of German rights, he directed all Germans, Catholic and Protestant, in opposing the ambitions of almighty France.[16] During the time when Emperor Leopold I ruled, the Holy Roman Empire—just as it was under the rule of Rudolf I—was neither Roman nor holy since the Pope no longer chose the emperor. Nor, after the Thirty Years' War, was it any longer an empire. The only real power that Leopold, as emperor, held was over Austria, Hungary and Bohemia: Whereas "In Germany the power was in the hands of numerous German Princes who ruled over Bavaria, Saxony and many other big and small states."[17]

After the Thirty Years' War, the Holy Roman Empire was made up of hundreds of loosely knit, weak sovereign states, each with a separate ruler. Although the German states—especially the Austrian city of Vienna and the Bohemian city of Prague—were at its heart, the Holy Roman Empire also included Hungary. However, not all the Hungarian nobility accepted Austrian rule. Some refused to pay imperial taxes and hated Austrian government. That's because Hungary had been torn apart by sorties of soldiers repeatedly crossing its borders due to religious contention between Christians and Turks.

The estates of the Holy Roman Empire were owned by nobles and clergy, plowed by serfs, and inherited by the primogeniture rule—that is, passed down to the oldest son. Younger sons were appointed to posts in the army, the Church, or to administrative positions in the court of the emperor. Administrators in the court of Emperor Leopold I numbered 40,000. There was no middle class.[18] Germany consisted of many non-united German states or electorates ruled by a body of princes (noblemen) called prince-electors. Only the prince-electors of seven of the strongest German states were permitted to vote for the Emperor of the Holy Roman Empire. The majority vote of electors always selected the emperors, almost all of whom, since 1438, were born into the Royal House of Habsburg (House of Austria). In contrast, Germany's arch rival, France, under King Louis XIV (r. 1643–1715) from the Royal House of Bourbon, was "geographically compact, united under one strong central government."[19]

6

Germans Flee Rhineland for America

The 1648 Peace Treaty of Westphalia, which ended the Thirty Years' War, granted territory in Spain and Germany to France. The Westphalia Treaty made France, under the wily Cardinal Richelieu, the biggest winner of the Thirty Years' War. Richelieu had been chief minister of Louis XIII. By the treaty, France's longtime goal was achieved: the power of the Habsburgs was broken, though not crushed, and the peril of a united Germany was prevented.[1] France exploited the devastated region and captured a few German fortresses near the Rhine for France.

Under the sickly, delicate Louis XIII, Cardinal Richelieu had become the chief minister and the real ruler of France. With the expert guidance of Richelieu, France had replaced Spain as the dominant European power. Spain had lost the Netherlands, which became an independent republic. The formidable and gifted, skilled and cunning Cardinal Richelieu had gradually reduced the powers of the nobility and assumed them for himself. Richelieu had diminished the might of surrounding countries and elevated the status of France: He had helped weaken the German states in the Thirty Years' War; he had decreased Habsburg power, reduced Spain to poverty, and diminished Italy.[2] As a result, France was in a dominant position when Louis XIV ascended the throne.

Louis XIV (r. 1643–1715) became King of France in 1643 when he was five years old and his tubercular, effeminate father from the House of Bourbon died. Louis XIV's mother, Anne of Austria, was a Spanish princess of the House of Habsburg. The queen mother took control of the government for her son and appointed the charming Italian-born Cardinal Jules Mazarin as her chief minister.[3] Mazarin had served for one year as chief minister under the sickly Louis XIII after the death of the powerful politician Cardinal Richelieu in 1642. "Anne and

6. Germans Flee Rhineland for America

Peace of Westphalia 1648 CE.

Mazarin were devoted to one another, and some historians have concluded that they were secretly married."[4]

Louis XIV is said to have little education in early life except for the counsel of the politically savvy Cardinal Mazarin. The child Louis XIV was decidedly not fond of the clever, persuasive and diplomatic Mazarin.

In 1651 13-year-old King Louis XIV ended the regency of his mother and discharged Mazarin because ordinary people as well as merchants, the nobility and the French Supreme Court (*Parlement*) protested Mazarin's fiscal policy. Mazarin upset peasants and merchants and stifled commerce by imposing heavy taxes to finance his wars. He offended the nobility by opposing feudalism. A Paris mob demonstrated against him and the Crown in a series of French civil wars called the Fronde. Rebels involved in the Fronde used slings (which the French called *frondes*) to shoot stones through windows of buildings associated with Mazarin and his friends.

Later, however, when Louis won the respect of the people and became strong enough, he reinstated Mazarin as French chief minister. Mazarin "deflected military appropriations into personal coffers, sold crown offices for his own benefit, and lent money to the King at a high rate of interest." France recognized him as the ablest of ministers but never forgave him his personal greed. When Mazarin died in 1661, Louis was free of his guardian. He took the government into his own hands and assumed all the power that Richelieu and later Mazarin had held. Louis played his role as king with dignity and ceremony to the end. He confiscated Mazarin's "hoard" and "became the richest monarch of his time."[5]

Louis XIV chose Apollo, the Greek sun god of peace and the arts, as his emblem. Dubbing himself the "Sun King," he emblazoned the sun crest on his magnificent Château de Versailles and furnished it with fancy carved and gilded wood furniture. He depended on grants from the Catholic Church to maintain his majestic quality of life.

Both Cardinals Richelieu and Mazarin had upheld the 1598 Edict of Nantes, which for almost a century had granted religious and civil liberties to French Protestants (Huguenots). The edict protected Huguenots, most of whom were Calvinists, from persecution by the state. Protestants depended on and needed the edict, which permitted "those of the Reformed Religion to dwell in all cities and places ... under our obedience without being inquired after, vexed, molested or compelled to do anything in Religion contrary to their conscience." It made Huguenots eligible to hold all public offices of the state.[6]

The Catholic Church hated the Edict of Nantes. Catholics had never approved the toleration granted to Protestants by the edict a half-century earlier. Thus in 1655 the Catholic clergy finally pressured King Louis XIV to close Huguenot (French-speaking Calvinist) colleges and hospitals. They condoned Catholic attacks on Protestant churches and homes. The clergy insisted on forcible repression of Protestants by the state. By degrees, Louis XIV, who craved money to wage war and support his elegant lifestyle, yielded to Catholic Church demands. In return he received Catholic grants for outlawing Protestant worship, closing their institutions, confiscating their property and demanding that Protestants convert to Catholicism. His dragonnades tortured Huguenots, "poured boiling water down their throats ... burned their arms and legs with candle flames ... pulled out the hair of their beards." Some Huguenots pretended conversion. Others fled.[7]

In 1660 the Holy Roman Empire and France had roughly equal populations, 20 million each. The empire had lost half its people during the Thirty Years' War, but regained it by 1660. However, the Holy Roman Empire, which included Germany, Austria, Bohemia and Hungary, was an empire in name only. Devastated by the Thirty Years' War, the Holy Roman Empire was divided into hundreds of "jealously sovereign," small, weak states, "each with its own ruler, army, currency and laws," while the French government was united under one strong monarch.[8]

In 1685 when Louis XIV finally revoked the Edict of Nantes, which had offered crucial protection to Protestants, Huguenot clergymen were given two weeks to leave the country. With few exceptions, the departure of other French Protestants was prohibited. Violators would be sentenced to hard labor, pulling the oars of a galley. A regular galley required 260 rowers or galley slaves. Louis XIV had 40 galleys. Galley slaves were branded with G-A-L and chained to live or die in their own filth on the galley ship. Eventually galleys would be replaced by convent prisons, while the galley ships would be modernized and converted to sailing ships. Meanwhile, the very real threat of the galleys facilitated the efforts of French soldiers to bring in thousands of converts to Catholicism.

All Huguenot children were to be baptized by priests and brought up in the Catholic faith. Louis forced 400,000 "Converts" to attend mass and receive the Eucharist. Those males who spat out the communion wafer were burned alive or imprisoned in cold, underground dungeons. Another 400,000 Huguenots escaped to the surrounding Protestant provinces: the city-state of Geneva (now in Switzerland), Brandenburg-Prussia (surrounding Berlin), Holland and even to England and her colonies.[9] Large numbers of Huguenots fled France and crossed into the Palatinate. Four years later, Louis XIV sent soldiers to destroy the Palatinate. The Palatinate probably lost more of its population than any other region. Almost all the emigration from German-speaking lands came from southwest Germany (the Palatinate) and Switzerland.[10]

The revocation of the Edict of Nantes by Louis XIV in 1685 ousted thousands of intelligent and capable Huguenots (French Protestants). Fleeing to England and Holland, many immigrated to America and settled in South Carolina, Virginia, Pennsylvania, New York, Rhode Island, and Massachusetts. Huguenots blended smoothly and contributed competent physicians, artisans, craftsmen, farmers, workers, ministers and military personnel to the professions and businesses of the colonies.[11]

Germans were the largest group of non–English-speaking Europeans to settle in colonial America. Because most German emigrants came through England from the Palatinate, as well as from many small principalities of the Rhine adjoining the Palatinate, the English began to speak of the whole emigration as from the Palatinate, and the term "German" became synonymous with the term "Palatine." In fact, many emigrants who called themselves Palatines were from the Upper Rhine and not from the Palatinate at all.[12]

The Great Palatine immigration began in 1683. The years between 1683 and 1776 brought 120,000 German-speaking immigrants to the colonies. Philadelphia was the chief port of entry for German immigrants. From there they spread west beyond the 441-mile course of the Susquehanna River and south into Maryland across the Potomac River and into the Great Appalachian Valley of Virginia.

The grateful refugees escaped from the Rhineland and settled in other countries, bringing with them crafts, skills in the silk industry, pottery throwing, furniture carving and painting plus their expertise in operating paper and textile mills. Protestant Europe then benefited economically from the victory of Catholicism in France as the ousted Huguenots (French Protestants) brought with them the industries learned in France. Pennsylvania or Kentucky rifles as well as the Conestoga wagon were among the best-known contributions of Germans in America.

Protestant soldiers and sailors who had fled France now enhanced the armies of France's enemies. The French Navy lost 9,000 sailors, the army 600 officers and 12,000 troops. But the Catholics of France praised Louis, for now there could be a unified France. The Calvinistic spirit had "distrusted adornment ... and levity ... and discouraged art, elegance and wit ... the French Renaissance, unimpeded by Protestantism, passed directly into the Enlightenment after the death of the King."[13]

At his best Louis XIV was a lavish patron of the arts and literature. Only two years after taking over the government he gave royal pensions to 45 French and 15 foreign authors, scholars and scientists. Like his father who took under his protection a group of actors who had been excommunicated by the Church, and like Richelieu who supported drama and like Mazarin who imported comedy from Italy, Louis XIV encouraged French theater, which had long been outlawed by the Church. Above all, he was the protector of philosopher-dramatist Molière who humorously "exposed the vices and hypocrisies of the age."[14]

Since Louis ruled absolutely without French courts of law ("parlements"), 20 percent to 30 percent of the national income was in the hands of the top 2 percent of the population. The nobility gladly accepted wealth in lieu of political power and therefore expressed no will to dethrone their king. During his long life, Louis raised the strongest army and largest fleet in the world. His huge military made a revolt of poor peasants impossible. The Catholic Church prospered under Louis's tax system as long as its church doctrine defended the divine rights of the king.[15]

Louis XIV reigned as King of France for 72 years, from 1643 until 1705. Louis ousted French Protestants (Huguenots) and devastated the Palatinate in an attempt to convert France into a completely Catholic country.

7

Jamestown Welcomes a German Explorer

Sir William Berkeley, Louis XIV's contemporary, was the longest-serving governor of the Virginia colony in America. Berkeley ruled from 1642 until 1652 and again from 1660 to 1677. Like King Louis, Governor Berkeley cleansed his realm of those religions that did not agree with his. Berkeley ousted Quakers as well as the Dutch/North German and the Swiss/South German groups called Mennonites. He eschewed all religious denominations who did not support his Anglican Church. Like Louis, who wanted France to be a country for Catholics only, Berkeley turned Virginia into an almost totally Anglican colony.

William Berkeley was born in 1606 to parents who were shareholders in the Virginia Company of London, a joint stock company of entrepreneurs established that very year by King James I of England. The Virginia Company was formed to finance the colonization of the land in the New World called *Virginia*, which included all the land on America's eastern seaboard north of Spanish Florida. The king also appointed a royal council, which was a board of directors in England, to manage the company. The king's charter granted the Virginia Company—a privately owned business—exclusive rights to explore, settle, and trade on the coast of North America from 34° of north latitude in the south to 45° in the north. There were two divisions of the Virginia Company. One, the London Company—based in London—was authorized to settle the Chesapeake Bay area, which covered all the land between the Carolinas and northern New Jersey. The other, the Plymouth Company—based in Plymouth, England—was granted the Northern Virginia area (now New England) from southern New Jersey to Maine. There was overlap in the middle between the two companies.[1] Jamestown, the first permanent English settlement in America, began as a charter colony established by the Virginia Company of London. The stockholders of the London Company chose the colony's governor, his council, and assembly.

William Berkeley graduated from the University of Oxford with baccalaureate and master's degrees. He became a gentleman of the king's privy chamber (the private council of the British sovereign), a commissioner of Canadian affairs, and a playwright for the London stage. Berkeley was knighted by King Charles I of England in 1639. Two years later, the king appointed him governor of the Virginia colony to succeed Sir Francis Wyatt. So, when Jamestown Colony was 35 years old, 35-year-old Sir William Berkeley—destined to control the tiller of that Tidewater colony—boarded an emigrant ship for America. Berkeley and Virginians would remain loyal supporters of the British Monarchy and the Anglican Church throughout the English Civil War and long afterwards.

Sir William Berkeley, a wig-wearing English nobleman whose long ringlets swung in the sea breeze, strode the ship's deck with the air of a soldier, sword at side.[2] Sailing into Jamestown in 1642, the aristocratic Berkeley with patrician face and scholarly speech took up official as well as private residence in the statehouse as the newly appointed governor of Virginia. Before long he became embroiled in the Third Anglo-Powhatan War, which began with an Indian massacre and ended two years later when he captured its perpetrator, Opechancanough, the brother of Chief Powhatan. This was the same Chief Opechancanough who had organized the Jamestown Massacre two decades earlier. Subduing the Powhatan Confederacy, Berkeley gained control of the Jamestown Colony and its satellite settlements: Kecoughtan (Elizabeth City), Henrico (Richmond) and Bermuda Hundred (Charles City) named for the shipwreck during the Bermuda tempest of 1609. Berkeley also controlled the surrounding Tidewater area—all of which together comprised the entire Virginia colony at that time. He governed successfully during the first decade of his governorship (1641–1652).[3] His term was interrupted by the English Civil War.

During the English Civil War (1642–1651), Berkeley launched a tidal wave of British migration when he enticed Anglicans and their indentured servants to emigrate from the South of England to Jamestown, Virginia, the nucleus of the British colonies in America. One of the governor's chief demands was for religious uniformity and loyalty to the Anglican Church. His intolerance toward other faiths became more and more apparent as the years went by.

Berkeley's Anglican Virginians, whose church was patterned after the Church of England, sympathized with Royalists (Cavaliers) and supported the king during the English Civil War (1642–1651).[4] In the strictest sense of the word, to be a Cavalier meant that regardless of birth or rank, whether plow-hand or duke, he supported royalty, the power of the king; in this case it was King Charles I. The majority of Virginians of the time were yeomen farmers, small farm owners—one class below the gentry. They were self-made men. Most of the few Oxford graduates and nobility who had founded the colony had returned to England or were killed in the first Jamestown Massacre.

Following the 1622 Jamestown Massacre, King James I had revoked the London Company's charter and converted Virginia from a charter colony to a royal colony. He appointed a royal governor and council but left other Virginia Company institutions intact. Under Crown rule, the House of Burgesses exercised more power than it had under the London Company. Both King Charles I and England's Lord Protector of the Commonwealth, Oliver Cromwell, had allowed the Virginia colony to self-govern. Parliament's enforcement of trade laws was lax. Thus, left alone under "salutary neglect," the colony developed in a natural way. Virginia prospered. Berkeley reported that despite the Anglo-Powhatan wars, Virginia's population grew from 1,100 in 1624 to 15,000 by 1648 and to over 40,000 in 1671, excluding Native American populations.

Although Cromwell's Roundhead insurgents gained power in England, only a sprinkling of refugee Cavaliers from the English aristocracy trickled into Virginia to escape the Roundheads. Not until the 1800s did Virginians concoct and perpetuate the myth that Virginia Cavaliers were highborn gentlemen of nobility.

Cavaliers (supporters of the king) were horrified and saddened when Calvinist Oliver Cromwell and the Roundheads (Puritan parliamentarians) overthrew the monarchy and beheaded King Charles I for treason in 1649. In the first year of his reign, Charles had offended his Protestant (Anglican, i.e., Church of England) subjects by marrying a Catholic French princess. Back in America, remaining loyal to the Crown, Berkeley was forced to give up his governorship of the Virginia colony for seven years. During this interim he experimented with agricultural diversification, timber, rice, silk, flax, fruit, potash, and a wide variety of commodities, looking for a way to wean Virginia farmers from their dependency on tobacco sales.[5]

Virginians cheered the fall of Cromwell's British government.

When the monarchy was restored in 1660 and King Charles II inherited the throne, the new king named Sir William Berkeley one of the eight Lords Proprietors of Carolina and reappointed him governor of Virginia. King Charles II rewarded Berkeley's Colony of Virginia for its loyalty during the war. He gave Virginia, along with Ireland, Scotland, and France, equal status as a "dominion"—a self-governing division of the British Empire that acknowledges the British monarch as chief of state—hence Virginia's nickname "Old Dominion."

Berkeley's second period as governor of colonial Virginia (1660—until his death in 1677) was a stormy time, weathering Indian raids, crop failure, economic depression, high taxes and Bacon's Rebellion, a belligerent uprising of colonists against his (Berkeley's) moderate Indian policy.

Stepping into a land of 8,000 colonists led by "rough, violent, hard drinking men," Berkeley had transformed Virginia. He created an elite governing class from "distressed cavaliers and indentured servants" by recruiting younger sons of great families from the southwestern region of England. In Virginia they reconstructed a cultural system comparable to the one in England, where they were essentially excluded because of the primogeniture laws of inheritance in which the eldest son was the principal heir. By encouraging a cavalier migration of the younger sons of England's great families—who by reason of their birth order were forced to leave the land and seek their fortunes elsewhere—Berkeley enhanced and expanded Virginia. In this Second Great Migration from England to America, the Virginia colony grew from 8,000 to 40,000 in 35 years. By advertising in pamphlets sent to England, Berkeley recruited royalist elite for Virginia. He provided them large estates and thus created a governing class. In a master stroke of social engineering, Berkeley determined the nature of immigrants to his Anglican colony in Tidewater (eastern) Virginia. But these royalist elite comprised only a small fraction of Tidewater's total population. Three-fourths of Virginians were indentured servants.[6]

While devastating wars in Europe destroyed the boundary lines of Germany, explorers crossing the Appalachian Mountain barrier marked a major milestone in early American history. "Long before men thought of conquering the mountains, the mountains had conquered men.... Every high mountain was idolized by people who lived in its shadow."[7] Asia had its Himalayas, Europe its Mont Blanc and the Matterhorn, and Japan its Fuji. The Greeks had Mt. Olympus, Moses his Mt. Sinai—and frontier America was challenged by the Appalachians. Beckoned by what he called the "endless mountains," Virginia's colonial Governor Berkeley sent expeditions from Jamestown to open a path through the Appalachians, establish trade with the Indians and seek a water route to the South Sea. The search for water routes to Cathay (China) had been going on ever since the destruction of the Silk Road.

German-born Dr. Johann (John) Lederer, a young physician from Hamburg, Germany, was the first European to stand on the highest peak of the Blue Ridge, look down into the Shenandoah Valley, gaze across it to the Allegheny Mountains and explore Piedmont Carolina. In 1669-1670 Virginia Governor William Berkeley commissioned Lederer to make three expeditions to cross the Blue Ridge, look for a water route to the Orient, and open up trade with Native Americans. Looking for a route to the Indian Ocean and traveling unmolested and alone, except for a guide, John Lederer made three hikes from settlements near the fall line in Virginia and from there westward through the lands of American Indians: first to the vicinity of Big Meadows (now on Skyline Drive in the Shenandoah National Park), second to the area called Carolina, but not as far southwest as the Smokies, and third into the Blue Ridge Mountains of what is now Rappahannock County[8] (whose current county seat is Washington, Virginia, about 120 miles northwest of Richmond, the state capitol).

At the confluence of the Shenandoah and Potomac rivers in the Blue Ridge Mountains, where West Virginia, Virginia, and Maryland converge, Lederer found the gap, now called "Harper's Ferry," named after another German immigrant. Lederer's work has been disparaged by some since many of his maps seemed to be inaccurate. But his work is significant in that it was instrumental in negotiating with the Indians and opening the great Indian Trading Path to Europeans. In addition, his perceptive observation of Indian settlements and his comments on the location, customs and beliefs of Native Americans established rapport and influenced a lucrative fur trade with Catawba and Cherokee nations for several decades.[9]

A big fish in a little pond, Sir William Berkeley was an ocean of vice and virtue, bullying those beneath him, fawning on those above him, and yet he was a man of candor, courage and fidelity to family. His seismic predilection for self-enrichment—openly embezzling public funds—set a sad example for Virginians for years to come. But his loyalty to a cause accomplished tsunamic achievements. Good mixed with bad, for better and for worse, for 35 years Berkeley kept his intelligence, energy and unwavering devotion fixed on guiding and transforming his

Anglican colony. He acted as its helmsman and lawgiver, shaped its pattern of immigration, and defined its culture.[10]

Governor Berkeley was an Anglican, faithful to the Church of England and totally intolerant of all other religious beliefs. Almost from the beginning the Anglican Church, the Church of England, was the official church in the Virginia colony. In the mid–1600s the House of Burgesses passed laws on a wide range of ecclesiastical matters which established "the church as an official, tax-supported institution of colonial life. From this point to near the end of the eighteenth century, church and state were inexorably linked in Virginia."[11]

In the 1640s almost all members of the First Families of Virginia—such as John Carter of unknown, or at least unproven, parentage—rose to fame and fortune from a middle-class origin. In 1670 John Carter directed construction of Christ Church, the first Anglican Church in Lancaster County, Virginia.

At that time a typical parish of the Anglican Church in Virginia was immense, scattered along the riverbank for as much as 50 miles and usually without a minister. Before 1693—when William and Mary College was founded for the training of Anglican clergy—Virginia had no colleges where Virginians could study and qualify for ministry in the Anglican Church. In 1672 "four out of five Virginia parishes were vacant; and of the remaining ones that were not vacant, two out of three had only lay readers instead of ordained ministers."[12] Governor Berkeley earlier had sent out a plea to English universities calling ordained ministers to come to the colony of Virginia. One minister responding to Berkeley's call was the Rev. Benjamin Doggett, whose ancestors were woolen merchants in Ipswich, England, and who was educated at St John's College, Cambridge. He and his family arrived in Berkeley's colony of 40,000 Virginians in 1670.

Governor Berkeley appointed Doggett as rector of Trinity Parish. Soon thereafter the parish was divided into two separate parishes, Christ Church and St. Mary's Whitechapel in what is now Lancaster County. Serving as rector of both parishes, Doggett gave pastoral care, baptized newborns, buried the dead and delivered sermons. The Ball family, including George Washington's grandfather, belonged to his St. Mary's Whitechapel congregation.[13] St. Mary's Whitechapel parish was the birthplace of Washington's mother, Mary Ball. The Anglican Church, then and now, was not only a place of worship but an important center of Virginia's social and political life.[14]

In the early 1700s John Carter's son Robert was Virginia's most powerful planter, owning 30,000 acres and 1,000 slaves. He became so immensely wealthy from tobacco that his sobriquet was "King Carter."[15] Church creation and construction were important parts of Virginia culture at the time. "King" Carter financed the rebuilding of Christ Church of Lancaster County and became the acting colonial governor of Virginia.

Initially, under the colony's first governors, a small number of Puritans had settled in Anglican Jamestown. One of the Puritans was Steven Hopkins, who most likely was the same Steven Hopkins who would sail with Pilgrims on the 1620 *Mayflower* to establish Plymouth Colony. Another Puritan was the Rev. Richard Buck, an Oxford graduate, who had performed the marriage ceremony of Pocahontas and John Rolfe. Buck had opened Virginia's first legislative assembly with prayer in 1619. Just 23 years later, however, in 1642 Anglican Governor Berkeley, a staunch supporter of the king, ordered "all nonconformists" including Puritans to "depart the colony" of Virginia "with all conveniency." Puritans fled to Maryland and New England. Berkeley's ideal colony would tolerate only Anglicans. In 1658 he fined Quakers for failing to attend Anglican services and then banished all Quakers from the Virginia colony. One defiant female barely escaped whipping, 20 strokes on her bare back, by promising to conform and confessing her error on bended knee. By 1661 Anglicans were punished for being "loving to Quakers."[16] Mennonites—a Dutch/North German group and a Swiss/South German group—were religious dissenters who had much in common with Quakers and, in fact, were often called "German Quakers." Mennonites, too, were absolute pacifists and, like Quakers, were frequently persecuted in Britain. Mennonites, however, believed in adult baptism and in the Lord's Supper, but as a memorial rather than a sacrament or Christian rite.

The Mennonite founder was Menno Simon, whose name lives on in the word Mennonite. Born in Frisia, a province of the Netherlands, Menno died at Wüstenfelde, a German province of Schleswig-Holstein, in 1561, 25 years after his withdrawal from the Catholic Church. Menno was a former Catholic priest who converted to the Anabaptist faith. After witnessing the martyrdom of an Anabaptist, Menno was so powerfully moved that he wrote protests against violence toward the Anabaptist sects. He then became an early leader of the Mennonite Church, which was a peaceful wing of Anabaptists.

The Anabaptist (from Greek *ana*, "again") was the spiritual ancestor of modern Baptists, as well as the historic "peace churches," Quakers and Mennonites. However, although Quakers sprang from the Anabaptist movement, Quakers rejected all church ceremony, including baptism. They rejected even baptism of the adult. Therefore, Quakers separated from the Anabaptist sects. The Anabaptists held that Christian faith is a conscious and voluntary commitment of the heart. Thus, they rejected the coercion of any state church and also rejected infant baptism in favor of the baptism of adult believers. In fact, "the movement's most distinctive tenet was adult baptism. In its first generation, converts submitted to a second baptism...[but] rejected the label Anabaptist, or Re-baptizer, for they repudiated their own baptism as infants as a blasphemous formality. They considered the public confession of sin and faith, sealed by adult baptism, to be the only proper baptism... [T]hey held that infants are not punishable for sin until they become aware of good and evil and can exercise their own free will, repent, and accept baptism."[17]

In mid–17th-century Virginia, where there was no separation of church and state, Quakers were the largest nonconformist sect. In general Quakerism was regarded as "inimical to the welfare of the community as a whole."[18] Quakers believed in a personal spiritual communication with their savior and God. They eschewed formal, religious ceremonies and listening to sermons delivered by preachers from a pulpit. The conformist citizens of the colony were suspicious of Quakers. "Their style of worship was an oddity by itself. They had no clergy, no pulpit, no ceremony, nor did they worship in a church. Quakers met in a simple meetinghouse with rows of benches and a partition to separate the men and women. No one spoke unless moved to speak by God; then if so moved, anyone was permitted to speak, man or woman."[19]

Each member of Berkeley's Virginia colony was required by law to pay tithes, parish taxes for support of the minister of the Anglican Church. If Quakers were allowed to be exempt from the levy because they needed to pay their own ministers, then the tax burden for supporting the established church would be unendurable for the rest of the community. In addition to pleading exemption from the levy for Anglican ministers, Quakers opposed war and therefore demanded freedom from military service. Thus they avoided bearing their fair share of protecting the community from the ever-present threat of Indian raids. Their refusal to bear arms threatened the safety of every man, woman and child in the settlement.

By the early 1700s, only a few dissenters remained in Virginia. Later in the century—when Berkeley was no longer governor—Presbyterians, Methodists and Baptists began to increase in the colony, but Anglican orthodoxy remained strong and grew stronger.[20] The dissenters, however, would be welcomed in Penn's Colony, which was known for its religious tolerance.

8

Quakers Migrate to Penn's Colony and Delaware Valley

William Penn, one of the best loved of all our colonial founders, established a cornerstone of American democracy—the principle of religious liberty—in Pennsylvania. Penn called his new colony Sylvania (woods), and Charles II, King of Great Britain and Ireland, added Penn in honor of Penn's father, Admiral William Penn. William Penn's beneficence, philanthropy and religious tolerance attracted the Migration of Friends from England and drew German refugees from the devastated Rhineland to the Delaware Valley. Historian S.E. Morison wrote: "No colony or state of the Union so well fits Emerson's dictum, 'An institution is the lengthened shadow of one man,' as Pennsylvania."[1]

William Penn (1644–1718) shocked fellow Londoners, as well as his father, when he scorned Anglicanism, the traditional religion of the mother church of Britain, and converted to the Society of Friends (Quakers), a sect "destined to have an influence on American life far greater than their numbers."[2] Founded in England by George Fox about 1650, the Quaker Friends dressed simply, rejected rituals and oaths, and opposed war. Penn, a student of divinity and law, traveled and preached with George Fox throughout England where they were often incarcerated for preaching without a license. When the jailers realized that Penn was highborn and wealthy, they offered to release him, but he refused. On their missions the two preachers found thousands of Quakers and other oppressed non–Anglican Protestants eager to immigrate to a land of religious tolerance. Penn resolved to find a home overseas and establish a Quaker colony for the persecuted followers of Fox.

George Fox and his fellow Quakers were unique in believing that wisdom begins in silence. Quakerism is differentiated by its distinctive form of silent worship. "Quakers believe that only when we have silenced our voices and our souls can we hear the 'still small voice' that dwells within each of us—the voice of God that speaks to us and that we express to others through our deeds." Fox, the son of a weaver, was a persuasive though unlettered young preacher, born in Leicestershire, England. Leaving his job as a shoemaker's apprentice, he began wandering through the countryside, searching his soul, developing radical ideas about religion, and seeking the inner light. One day when Fox was at a low point in his life, he had a mystical experience. Like the early prophets, he heard the voice of God speaking directly to him. Then he realized that everyone has the ability to communicate directly with God without clerical intervention. Fox believed that God appears to us through a divine inner voice, an inner light shared by all. Continuing revelation would occur if people joined together in silence and opened their hearts to the divine voice within. As Psalm 46 directs: "Be still, and know that I am God."[3]

Quakers believe that man and woman are equal in the eyes of God. In the earliest days of Quakerism, many women were among the Quaker's first itinerate preachers. One of the women was Mary Fisher, who survived brutal physical flogging in England and imprisonment in Massachusetts and then traveled to the Ottoman Empire with six other Quaker women. The English consul put them on a boat bound not for Turkey but for Venice. Not to be deterred, Mary was able to disembark and travel alone on foot over land and mountains, seeking an audience with the Turkish Emperor, Sultan Mehmen IV. She said that she had "something to declare to him from the great God." After sitting in his tent with Mary for a while in silence, the Sultan encouraged her to speak. He listened. Mary asked, through an interpreter, if the Sultan had understood her message. The Sultan answered, "Yea every word, and it is true."[4]

George Fox's wife, Margaret Fell Fox, pleaded for women's rights. She argued for women's ministry in her pamphlet, "Women's Speaking Justified." Led by Fox, Quakers advocated for the education of girls as well as boys. In his "Journal of George Fox, an Historical Account of his Life" volume I, Fox wrote that in the year 1667, "After I had visited Friends, and the men's monthly meetings were settled there, I had a great meeting at Baldock, of many sorts of people. Then returning toward London by Waltham, I advised the setting up of a school there for teaching boys, and also a girls' school at Shacklewell, for instruction them in whatsoever things were civil and useful in creation."

After traveling with Fox, and still eager to establish a Quaker colony, William Penn appealed to King Charles II of England for support.

Penn's father, British Admiral Sir William Penn, had advanced loans totaling 16,000 pounds to the government of Charles II. As repayment to his deceased father's estate, the admiral's son and heir, William, proposed that Charles grant him a tract of unsettled land in America. The tract would lie east of the Delaware and as far north of Maryland "as plantable." Penn's proposition was accepted, and a charter was granted.[5]

> In 1681 "CHARLES the Second, by the Grace of God, King of England, Scotland, France, and Ireland" granted to the "sonn and heire of Sir William Penn" a "tract of parte of land in America." It was "in memory ... of his late father for his divers services ... under our Dearest brother James Duke of York ... against the Dutch Fleet ... in the yeare One thousand six hundred and sixty-five."[6]

In return for the land grant, the king exacted an annual fealty of "Two Beaver skins, to be delivered at our castle of Windsor, on the first day of January, in every year; and also the fifth part of all gold, and silver oar, which shall, from time to time, happen to be found within the limits aforesaid."[7] The next year Penn sent three commissioners to compensate the Indians for the land described in his charter. A few Germans and Dutch already lived there.

The charter made young William Penn a Lord Proprietor and guaranteed him possession of the proprietary colony. A Lord Proprietor (principal landowner) was a person, rather than a company, to whom the king granted a charter authorizing him to establish a colony at his own expense and finance it by attracting settlers. The charter allowed the proprietor to create courts, make laws and appoint the governor and council members of his colony. The Lord Proprietor was also permitted to establish the churches for his region.[8] Privately owned proprietary colonies soon became the dominant method of settling America.

Eager to establish his colony, Penn sent out a modest pamphlet, understated and simple in comparison with similar recruitments of the day. It offered easy terms and complete religious freedom to the sort of people he wanted to settle his new province. The tract, titled "Some Account of the Province of Pennsylvania," was translated into German, French, and Dutch and widely circulated.

The British colonies, especially Pennsylvania and the other central colonies, were settled by small German-speaking religious groups, including Quakers,[9] Swiss Mennonites, Baptist Dunkers, Schwenkfelders, Moravian, Amish and Waldensians. Most German immigrants, however, belonged to the main Lutheran and Reformed churches.[10]

Penn began building his colony by attracting Quakers (Friends) from the North Midlands of England and Wales to the Delaware Valley. Although a few Quakers had migrated to the American colonies as early as the 1650s, the ship carrying the first large-scale migration of Quakers to America reached Salem in West Jersey in 1675, followed by other ships docking in Delaware Bay.

Before William Penn established Pennsylvania, Robert Wade was probably the first Quaker to settle in that future colony. Wade emigrated from England in 1675 and went to Chester, which is now the oldest city in Pennsylvania and is located on the western bank of the Delaware River between the cities of Philadelphia and Wilmington, Delaware. There, in Chester, he helped establish Pennsylvania's first Quaker meeting house. By 1681, 1,400 Quakers resided in West Jersey. The real influx of Friends began the next year when 23 ships carrying more than 2,000 Quakers sailed into Delaware Bay.[11]

The ship *Welcome* with William Penn and 120 Quakers on board docked at New Castle in the Delaware Bay. Penn then traveled overland and soon met with local Friends at Chester. Penn and his Quakers intended to establish the colony of Pennsylvania free of religious persecution. While conducting this "holy experiment," Penn was also committed to making peace with local Indians. Penn's entourage was pleased with the rich, fertile and abundant land as well as the pleasant air, fresh water and plentiful fish, fowl and deer. That's why William Penn soon published a plan for his city.

"Penn laid out Philadelphia in checker-board fashion, a reflection of the tidy Quaker mind that has been a permanent influence on American city planning."[12] He established the foundation for the Quaker province by 1684, guaranteeing liberty to all. Penn dreamed of a place where peoples of all races and religions could live together in peace, harmony and brotherly love. Therefore the population quickly became cosmopolitan. Penn described Delaware Valley settlers in 1685 as a "collection of divers nations in Europe: as, French, Dutch, Germans, Swedes, Danes, Finns, Scotch, French and English, and the last equal to all the rest."[13] In 1688 German Quakers were the first to protest against property laws applying to people—human slavery, the buying, selling or owning of other humans.

Over a 50-year period the Friends' migration transplanted thousands of Friends to the Delaware Valley. Quakers believed the Word of God emanated from the human soul. Their deity was a God of love and light. Protected by the radiant presence of Jesus Christ dwelling within their souls, the inner light was "divine goodness and virtue passed from

Jesus to every human soul."[14] "Quakers, also called Friends, believed that all individuals had a divine light within them, and therefore no one could ever be justified in participating in any kind of violence or murderous activity against a fellow human being. Wholehearted pacifists, they embraced a culture of widespread equality, defiance against institutional religious practices, and tolerance for the native inhabitants of Pennsylvania."[15]

Although Quakerism originated within the Anabaptist movement, Quakers were not Anabaptists since they rejected all sacraments, even baptism and the Lord's Supper. Quakers celebrated no Christmas or Easter holidays because they believed that every day is holy, although they might mark these days as secular festivals. They believed that rituals are unnecessary in order to communicate directly with God.

Early Friends gathered for worship at monthly meetings without ordained ministers, liturgy or any prearrangement except an agreed upon time and place.

Quakers had no pulpit and no ceremony. They did not worship in a church but in meeting houses with rows of benches separating men and women. There was no preaching and no speaking unless one felt moved to speak by the presence of God, and then anyone, whether man or woman, was permitted to talk. Their differences in dress, the belief that all were equal and men should remove their hats only in the presence of God, their way of worship and their refusal to bear arms made them targets of ridicule and persecution.

Quakers were willing to withstand vilification because they believed that if they gave themselves to Christ, and allowed Him into their souls, then He would control their lives. His presence would set them free and shine through, illuminating and uniting the world in brotherly love. Passivity was a way of proving their submission to and faith in Jesus, a way of expressing brotherly love toward their detractors.

Rejecting the social hierarchy and calling themselves "Friends" because all humans are equal, Quakers addressed all persons as "thee" and "thou" and refused to doff their hats.[16] Strictly adhering to the commandment "Thou shalt not kill," Quakers were pacifists. Some were imprisoned in Britain during the first two years of the reign of Charles II because they accepted the authority of the Bible over that of the Church. Yet the king tolerated Quakers more than he tolerated other non–Anglicans because Quakers took no part in the English Civil War in which Puritans beheaded his father, Charles I.

Practicing nonviolence and finding salvation, redemption and victory in hardship and defeat, Quaker ideas spread through the British Empire.

Quakerism permeated Holland and Germany and filtered even into Russia. Every American colony except Rhode Island and Pennsylvania restricted Quakers. In Boston Quakers were hanged. In New York they were whipped, imprisoned, and tortured. Peter Stuyvesant, the governor of New Netherland, imposed a fine on any Dutch farm owner of New Amsterdam who provided overnight lodging for a Quaker. Quakers gradually won some tolerance through passive resistance. Before Pennsylvania was established, Quaker communities were founded in North Carolina, Rhode Island, Nantucket Island, and the fringes of Plymouth Colony.[17] At monthly meetings in England, Quakers recorded oppressions against them in Books of Suffering. The "Anglican clergy, whose income was threatened by Quaker refusal to pay church taxes," were especially abusive. The Friends' migration was a "flight from persecution," and yet their main religious goal for leaving England was "to show Quakerism at work unhampered by restrictions."[18]

One of Penn's first gestures of brotherly love in America involved the Iroquoian-speaking Conestoga Indians. These aboriginals had greeted immigrants to Pennsylvania with "presents of venison, corn and skins; and entered into a Treaty of Friendship with William Penn." Benjamin Franklin noted that the covenant of peace with the tribe was to last "as long as the sun should shine, or the waters run in the rivers."[19] A century later, the dream of peace and brotherly love would be broken in Pennsylvania's Lancaster County when the 1763 Conestoga massacre made this peaceful Christian tribe extinct.

Protesting the Proclamation of 1763[20] which provided protection for American Indians, 57 Scots-Irish Paxton Boys of Pennsylvania invaded the peaceful Conestoga Manor which the government had assigned as living quarters for the 20 surviving members of the Conestoga tribe. Benjamin Franklin wrote that without provocation the mounted invaders surrounded huts and murdered the defenseless Indians. The Paxtons killed three men, two women and a boy. They then sought out others of the tribe who were vending their wares among the "neighboring White people, some to sell baskets, brooms and bowls they manufactured…. In cold blood" they chopped an old man to pieces, scalped families and burned their huts. The Quakers Lancaster magistrates sequestered the remaining 14 Indians and promised them protection, but to no avail. The Paxton Boys broke down the door and slaughtered the entire—now extinct—tribe.

8. Quakers Migrate to Penn's Colony and Delaware Valley

Franklin philosophized:

> If an *Indian* injures me, does it follow that I may revenge that Injury on all *Indians*? It is well known that *Indians* are of different Tribes, Nations and Languages, as well as the White People. In *Europe*, if the *French*, who are White People, should injure the *Dutch*, are they to revenge it on the *English*, because they too are White People? The only Crime of these poor Wretches seems to have been, that they had a reddish brown Skin, and black Hair; and some People of that Sort, it seems, had murdered some of our Relations. If it be right to kill Men for such a Reason, then, should any Man, with a freckled Face and red Hair, kill a Wife or Child of mine, it would be right for me to revenge it, by killing all the freckled red-haired Men, Women and Children, I could afterwards any where meet with.[21]

Back in 1683 William Penn proselytized among Rhine Valley dissenters and welcomed them to his colony. The settlement of Germantown, Pennsylvania, began when 13 non–English-speaking Mennonite and Quaker families left the lower Rhine Valley town of Krefeld, Germany, on their way to America. On July 6, 1683, this first German immigrant group embarked from Rotterdam on the *Concord*, a ship which to the descendants of the first German settlers is comparable to the 1620 *Mayflower* for Pilgrim descendants. On July 24, 1683, the *Concord* set sail from London, England, landing in Pennsylvania on October 6. Led by Francis D. Pastorius, the real estate agent in the New World for the Frankfort Land Company, they purchased 43,000 acres of Pennsylvania land from William Penn and in 1683 founded Germantown, six miles north of Philadelphia.[22]

Here, in Pennsylvania, they could freely worship God in their own way, unmolested and in their own meeting house. This Krefeld colony founded the first permanent Mennonite Settlement of the New World in what would become Germantown. They were Anabaptists, religious dissenters who believed in adult baptism. Mennonites were committed to nonviolence, nonresistance, and absolute pacifism. The leader, next to Pastorius, of the Krefeld community was Mennonite Bishop Wilhelm Ryttinghuysen, proprietor of a paper mill at Arnheim, Holland. Being oppressed on account of his religion, he immigrated to New York with his two sons, Claus and Gerhard, in 1674.[23] Leaving New York with his sons, Ryttinghuysen settled in Germantown where he and his sons built the first paper mill in the colonies. He was an ancestor of the well-known David Rittenhouse, a "self-taught genius surveyor, orrery maker, philosopher, astronomer and patriot."[24] The orrery was an instrument devised to represent the motions of the planets about the sun. Seven years after its founding, the Germantown district comprised a cluster of small communities consisting of 44 families. At that time, two-thirds of Germantown citizens were Quakers. The remaining third were of the Reformed Church (including Lutheran and Mennonites) and the Catholics who were greatly opposed to Quakerism.

In 1685 the Quakers of Krisheim (a town in Baden-Württemberg) Germany followed the immigrants from Krefeld (a city in North Rhine-Westphalia) who had arrived two years earlier. Among them were the Hendicks, the Cassells and the Shoemakers.

> Mennonites then followed in large numbers and settled in Germantown, and in the country west of it. Among them were many whose names are very familiar to us, but their names were by an order of the Lord Proprietary anglicized, when they were naturalized as English citizens; it was then that the name of Langeneicher was changed into the well-known Longnecker, Ferne into Forney, Neukomm into Newcomer, König into King, Baumann into Bowman, Steinemann into Stoneman, Zimmermann into Carpenter, Ried into Reed, Weber into Weaver, Burghalter into Burkholder and afterwards Burke, Herr into Hare. This was done so extensively, that the names of many of *our* old families are no criterion as to their origin. This anglicising of German names became for a time very common. The Jäger changed into Hunter, Knecht into Knight, Gottwalter into Cadwallader, Hinkel into Hinkley, Goebel into Gable, Huth into Hood, Schott into Scott, Wehn into Wayne, Schürmann into Shermann, Mohl into Moale, Schürholz into Sherwood."[25]

Carefully kept records of the history of Germantown show no exciting events except for their momentous antislavery protest. On April 18, 1688, the Germans of Germantown assembled in a planned meeting and issued their solemn protest in writing against slavery. "They condemned slavery in the strongest terms and set forth its evils in the most eloquent language. It was composed in the English language and signed by Garrett Hendricks, Francis Daniel Pastorius, Dirk Op den Græff, and Abraham Op den Græff. It was the first protest against slavery ever issued in this country, and in force of language leaves nothing to be wished for."[26] In scheduled meetings for a period of 17 years, only a few trivial offenses are recorded. The court, which met every six weeks, often adjourned early for there was no business to discuss.

Francis Daniel Pastorius, born in 1651 in Sommerhausen in Franconia, Germany, initiated the German immigration to North America. As the first mayor of Germantown, Pastorius also held the office of justice of the peace, city registrar, and was a member of the general assembly of Pennsylvania. "His literary activity during his life was very great. He wrote in the German, English, French, Italian, Dutch and Latin

8. Quakers Migrate to Penn's Colony and Delaware Valley

languages, mostly however in English. We have poems from him in all these languages; further, books on Arithmetic, Geometry; Latin, French and English grammars; Treatises on Agriculture, Botany, Laws, Theology, Ethics, History, Natural History and Church History.... The most important and best known is his *Full Geographical Description of the Province of Pennsylvania.*"[27]

The story of the founding of Germantown, Pennsylvania, by German-speaking Mennonites is told by the Pastorius mentioned above. Written in 1700, Pastorius's account, excerpted below, most likely was sent to Germany to induce new settlers[28]:

> The German society commissioned myself, Francis Daniel Pastorius, as their licensed agent to go to Pennsylvania and to superintend the purchase and survey of their lands.... Upon my arrival I applied to the governor, William Penn, for warrants.... William Penn laid out the city of Philadelphia between the two rivers Delaware and Schuylkill ... the Delaware is deep enough so that the largest vessels can come up close to the bank, which is about a stone's throw from the city ... on the 24th day of October 1685, I, Francis D. Pastorius, with the wish and concurrence of our governor, laid out and planned a new town, which we called Germantown.... I have also obtained 15,000 acres of land for our company, in one tract, with this condition: that within one year at least thirty families should settle on it.... The air is pure and serene, the summer is longer and warmer than it is in Germany, and we are cultivating many kinds of fruits and vegetables and our labors meet with rich reward.... Although this far distant land was a dense wilderness ... there is much cause of wonder and admiration how rapidly it has ... advanced ... the first part of the time we (obtained) provisions from the Jerseys for money and at a high price, but now we not only have enough for ourselves but a considerable surplus ... of the most needful mechanics we have enough now: but day laborers are very scarce, and of them we stand in great need. Of mills, brick kilns, and tile ovens, we have the necessary number.
>
> Our surplus of grain and cattle we trade to Barbados for rum, syrup, sugar and salt. The furs, however, we export to England for other manufactured goods. We are also endeavoring to introduce the cultivation of the vine, and also the manufacture of woolen cloths and linens, so as to keep our money as much as possible in the country. For this reason we have already established fairs to be held at stated times, so as to bring the people of different parts together for the purposes of barter and trade, and thereby encourage our own industry and prevent our little money from going abroad.
>
> The inhabitants may be divided into three classes (1) the aborigines, or, as they are called, the savages; (2) those Christians who have been in the country for years and are called old settlers (3) the newly arrived colonists of the different companies.
>
> 1. The savages or Indians ... have straight black hair which they cut off close to the head, save one tuft which they leave stand on the right side. Their

children they anoint with the fat of bears or other animals, so as to make their skin dark.... Their huts, or wigwams, they make by bending down several young trees and covering them with bark.... They use neither tables nor chairs nor furniture of any kind except perhaps a single pot or kettle to cook their food.... I once saw four of them dining together in great enjoyment of their feast. It consisted in nothing more than a pumpkin simply boiled in water, without salt, butter or spice of any kind. Their seat and table was the bare ground, their spoons were seashells, wherewith they supped the warm water, and their plates were the leaves of the nearest tree, which, after they were done their meal, they had no occasion of washing or any need of carefully preserving for future use.... They have no idols, but adore one great, good spirit, who keeps the devil in subjection. They believe in the immortality of the soul, and, according as they have lived in this world, do they expect a reward or punishment in the future.... They are in the habit of painting their faces with various colors, and the women as well as the men are very fond of tobacco.

2. The earlier Europeans or old settlers. There never had the proper motives in settling here; for instead of instructing the poor Indians in the Christian virtues, their only desire was gain, without ever scrupling about the means employed in obtaining it. By these means they have taught those natives who had dealings with them nothing but deception and many other evil habits, so that there is very little virtue or honesty remaining on either side.

These wicked people make it a custom to pay the savages in rum and other liquors for the furs they bring to them, so that these poor, deluded Indians have become very intemperate, and sometimes drink to such excess that they can neither walk nor stand. On such occasions they often commit thefts and other vices.

Pastorius's account of life in Pennsylvania served its purpose—attracting hordes of German Quaker and Mennonite emigrants from the war-torn Rhineland to Germantown.

Pastorius writes of these days: "It can not be written enough, nor impressed enough on in the minds of our wealthy descendants, in what poverty and want, but also in what Christian cheerfulness and untiring energy and industry Germantown was begun. Before the cold weather had fairly set in, every family was safely housed." The emigrants were mostly mechanics, such as tailors, shoemakers, carpenters, locksmiths, especially weavers, but all understood farming also, as is the custom in small country towns in Germany. Their industry was so great that one year after their arrival they offered linen, hosiery and cloth for sale at their store in Philadelphia, which belonged to the Frankfort company and was in charge of Pastorius, and which linen, hosiery and cloth was manufactured by them out of flax and wool raised by them. They soon became renowned for the quality of their goods, and in a book, entitled: "A Short Description of Pennsylvania," published by Wm. Bradford as early as 1692, George Frame sings in rhymes of Germantown:—"The German town, of which I spoke before, Which is at least in length one mile or more, Where lives High-German people and Low-Dutch, Whose trade in weaving linen cloth is much; There grows the flax," &c.[29]

8. Quakers Migrate to Penn's Colony and Delaware Valley

By 1690, the Quaker and Mennonite sects split. German immigrants from the southwest region of Germany founded Skippack in 1702 and Oley and Conestoga, Pennsylvania, in 1709. Most early German immigrants came from the southwest region of Germany: the Rhineland, Württemberg, Baden and German Switzerland.

Although the major German immigration to America began with Pastorius in 1683 at the Germantown settlement in Penn's Colony, smaller and sporadic groups of individuals and families came to America later. For example, in 1705 several German Reformed families emigrated from Wolfenbuttel and Halberstadt, went to Rhenish Prussia and on to Holland where they embarked for New York and then settled in German Valley, Morris County, New Jersey.

One of the largest migration waves of Germans occurred in 1709 when German Protestants fled political disorder and economic hardship in their Palatine area. Making their way to Holland and then to England more than 2,000 Palatine German immigrants debarked and settled in America, mainly New York in 1710. By 1710 the increase in German immigration to Pennsylvania was also significant. "Between 1727 and 1775, approximately 65,000 Germans landed in Philadelphia and settled in the region while some German immigrant landed in other ports and moved to Pennsylvania. The largest wave of German immigrants occurred between 1749 and 1754."[30]

The principal reason for German emigration from their homeland to America was devastation of the Rhineland by European wars. Ever since the division of Charlemagne's vast empire, the Rhine Valley was a dividing line between what gradually became the very different French and German cultures of the 1700s. By then, frequent wars were fought between the two. At first the conflicts involved dynastic rivalries and religious differences. The armies, mostly mercenaries, were paid for by ever-increasing taxes until, near the end of the century, conscription was used to fill the ranks. This was the last straw.

Greatly exaggerated accounts of life in America circulated by ship's agents, and land speculators added to the exodus.[31] The exodus was so huge and ongoing that by the year 2010, the U.S. government census showed that more American citizens trace their ancestry back to Germany than to any other nation.

The ethnic makeup of Pennsylvania and the Delaware Valley was diverse. In 1685, the population of Pennsylvania was 9,000. Swedes and Finns who had established the short-lived colony of New Sweden supplied food for the new colonists. Mennonites, mostly linen weavers, settled Germantown; Welsh Quakers settled 40,000 acres of fertile farmland west of Philadelphia and founded the communities of Radnor and Haverford. English Quakers of the Free Society of Traders stocked a general store in the city of Philadelphia and organized whaling and fishing in the Delaware Bay area. They built brick kilns, tanneries and glassworks.[32]

In the Delaware Valley, West Jersey, Pennsylvania and the future colony of Delaware unified into a single economic province and a single cultural area.[33] By the end of the 1600s a majority of English-speaking settlers in the Delaware Valley were Quakers and Quaker sympathizers. Doubling every generation, by 1750 there were 250 meetinghouses for Quakers. They had become the third-largest denomination in the British colonies; Congregationalists with 465 churches predominated, and the 289 Anglican churches came in next.[34]

Eventually Germans, migrating from the Rhineland in western Germany, outnumbered the English and Welsh Quakers in Pennsylvania. Even Benjamin Franklin questioned why the Palatine farmers should "be suffered to swarm into our settlement." Franklin spoke with alarm that "Pennsylvania, founded by the English, (will) become a colony of the aliens who will shortly be so numerous as to Germanize us, instead of our Anglifying them, and will never adopt our language or customs any more than they can acquire our complexion."[35] By 1766 Franklin seems to have softened his opinion, describing Germans as "a people who brought with them the greatest wealth—industry and integrity, and characters that have been superpoised [sic] and developed by years of suffering and persecution." He then estimated that Pennsylvania was home to 60,000 to 70,000 Quakers, and more lived nearby in western New Jersey, northern Delaware, and northern Maryland. Other people living among Quakers—especially a large percentage of Philadelphians—were un-Friendly, showing no sympathy for Quaker beliefs. There were also many Anglican settlers, especially in southeastern counties for which Philadelphia had become the intellectual and commercial center.[36]

Amazingly, the cunning Benjamin Franklin found a way to establish a militia in the peace-loving, war-opposed Quaker colony of Pennsylvania. Franklin wrote and published a pamphlet entitled *Plain Truth* to revive the governor's failed attempt to legislate a military presence in the Quaker colony of Pennsylvania prior to the French and Indian War. Franklin's pamphlet inspired the people to form a volunteer militia and organize themselves into companies and regiments. It prompted

8. Quakers Migrate to Penn's Colony and Delaware Valley

women to sew patriotic banners bearing mottos and present them to the companies. The old fox even devised a lottery to finance the building of a battery, supplying it with cannons that he obtained from Boston and England and, finally, New York.

At first Governor Clinton of New York refused to lend cannons to Franklin for Philadelphia, but at a banquet, under the persuasion of "great drinking of Madeira wine"—which was the custom in those days—the governor conceded 18, 18-pounder cannons for defense of the battery at Philadelphia.

Upon his return to Pennsylvania Franklin published pamphlets in both German and English proclaiming a fast with prayers for peace. The leaflets enlisted the help of the clergy to sway their congregations to support the militia. Surprisingly, a great number of Quakers "tho' against an offensive war, were clearly for the defensive." Franklin wrote that many Quaker Friends of Pennsylvania gave money for the king to use and did not ask how the money was applied. The heavily Quaker Assembly could not grant the governor money to buy gunpowder since it was an *ingredient of war*, but they did appropriate money for bread, flour or other grain. When the governor interpreted *other grain* as meaning gunpowder, Pennsylvania's Congress did not object. In like manner, when the colony's congress appropriated money for a fire engine, Franklin proposed buying a "great gun, which is certainly a *fire-engine*."[37]

Both William Penn—himself part Dutch—and George Fox, founder of the Society of Friends, frequently made preaching missions to Holland and Germany. There they actively recruited Dutch and German Quaker colonists to join English Quakers in the Delaware Valley.

The Quakers encouraged and partially financed large numbers of the early emigrants from western German states. After 1715, many non–Quaker emigrants from western Germany arrived in Pennsylvania. In 1752, the German population of Pennsylvania was an estimated 90,000.[38] By 1775 Germans composed one-third of the Pennsylvania population; the Scots-Irish comprised roughly one-fourth. "French Huguenot and Jewish settlers, together with Dutch, Swedes, and other groups, contributed in smaller numbers to the development of colonial Pennsylvania."[39]

The Mason-Dixon Line was drawn to separate Pennsylvania and Maryland. By royal authority two surveyors—Charles Mason and Jeremiah Dixon—were sent to fix the boundary between Penn's Colony and Lord Baltimore's existing colony of Maryland. Four years later, on October 9, 1767, the 233-mile-long Mason-Dixon Line survey was finished. In years to come, the Mason-Dixon Line would separate the slaveholding states from the free.

War, hunger and persecution drove Germans, Swiss and French immigrants to New York, North Carolina and Virginia. These oppressed people also continued to pour into Penn's Colony. Of course there were both Quaker and non–Quaker German-speaking settlers in Pennsylvania. The Pennsylvania Germans often were called "Pennsylvania Dutch," although they were not Dutch at all. The term Pennsylvania Dutch resulted from mispronunciation of the German word *Deutsch* which in translation means "German." Pennsylvania Germans (erroneously called Pennsylvania Dutch) were German-speaking immigrants who settled primarily in southeastern Pennsylvania. Pennsylvania German is a language spoken at home. It is a mixture of various German dialects, English and High German which was spoken in the highlands of southern Germany. High German was used in Amish worship services. These "Pennsylvania Dutch" had fled the war-torn area of the Rhineland and settled primarily in Lancaster County of southeastern Pennsylvania and other interior counties.

Some refugee Germans, like other continental Europeans, could not pay their way in full.[40] Instead they signed a contract agreeing to repay or redeem the loan of passage money. Often bringing their whole family, they came under better circumstances than the usual English indentured servant. When they could not pay, impatient ship captains sold their contract to the highest bidder. Since their time of service was limited by contract, they were not slaves, yet they had little freedom, and families were often separated. These German immigrants of the mid–1700s were known simply as "redemptioners." They were from the poor of the German states of Baden, Württemberg (Württemberg was formerly also spelled Würtemberg and Wirtemberg) and the Palatinate. Land agents herded them "aboard ship by promises, threats, and trickery ... and sold off to colonial purchasers on whatever ... terms could be got." They went chiefly to "Pennsylvania, Maryland, Virginia and South Carolina."

About German indentured servants, the *Pennsylvania Staatsbote* published the following article on January 18, 1774:

> There are still 50 or 60 German persons newly arrived from Germany. They can be found with the widow Kriderin at the sign of the Golden Swan. Among them are two schoolmasters, mechanics, farmers, also young children as well as boys and girls. They are desirous of serving for their passage money.

8. Quakers Migrate to Penn's Colony and Delaware Valley

The contract which these unfortunates who were "desirous of serving for their passage money" had signed with the ship captain was called an indenture, and they were known as "indentured servants."

Isn't it amazing that in spite of shipwreck, rotten food, vermin, sickness, people continued to come by the thousands? Of course conditions did improve. By 1876 nearly all the immigrants came in large steamships which took only seven, to twelve days to cross, instead of that number of weeks in a small sailing vessel, as heretofore. But even these furnished no pleasure cruise for steerage passengers.

[For steerage passengers] there is neither breathing space below nor deck room above, and the 900 steerage passengers crowded into the hold ... are positively packed like cattle, making a walk on deck when the weather is good, absolutely impossible, while to breathe clean air below in rough weather, when the hatches are down, is an equal impossibility. The stenches become unbearable, and many of the emigrants have to be driven down; for they prefer the bitterness and danger of the storm to the pestilential air below....

The food, which is miserable, is dealt out of huge kettles into the dinner pails provided by the steamship company. When it is distributed, the stronger push and crowd.... On the whole, the steerage of the modern ship ought to be condemned as unfit for the transportation of human beings.[41]

An estimated "half of the immigrants who arrived during the colonial era were [indentured servants] contract laborers—obligated to an employer for a term of years in return for the cost of their transportation. Nor did all of them have even the security, such as it was, of a contract or 'indenture.'"[42]

"Often times urban German immigrant women worked for the native-born Americans. These immigrants adapted to American ways, but also left impressions of their own culture with the American born. Women who worked as domestic servants, were often times considered a 'good catch' by a German man because they understood American culture better, and this knowledge helped the man to assimilate better and deal better with American men."[43]

The Pennsylvania Germans developed the rich Pennsylvania farm country, rotated their crops, practiced their innate thrift and diligently pursued hard work. By the time of the American Revolution, Lancaster County had developed not only the Pennsylvania long rifle adapted from the German hunting rifle but also the Conestoga wagon, forerunner of the smaller prairie schooner used by pioneers in their westward migration.[44]

In 1776 more than 100,000 German immigrants lived in the American colonies; most were Patriots, fighting for American independence.[45] German immigrants often formed their own communities; many did not speak English. German was still spoken in North Carolina's Rowan County in the 1800s and in Virginia's Poor Valley of Washington County until the early 1900s and in Wythe County, Virginia, until World War I. The Wythe County Courthouse retained a German interpreter until 1937.

Quakers attracted people from every social and educational background because they were committed to equality, social welfare work, peace, improving race relations and prison reform. They were persecuted and ostracized because they refused to take oaths, serve in the military, or pay taxes to support the established church. Quaker speech was considered impertinent in 17th-century England where the word "thou" was used when speaking to a person of lower class. The word "you" was used when conversing with equals or superiors. But Quakers used "thee" and "thou" instead of "you" to express their egalitarianism, even to high public officials and to the king. They substituted numbers in reference to days of the week and months of the year since the conventional names of weekdays and months were rooted in paganism. For example, Thor for whom Thursday is named derives from the Norse god of storms, thunder and oak trees, while January comes from Janus, the two-faced Roman god who looks two ways through gates and doorways and from the past into the future.

Impassioned Quakers sometimes interrupted church meetings by rushing in and urging the congregation to leave the steeple house and join the living church. As Quaker membership and persecutions increased, prisons overflowed with Friends. George Fox survived eight imprisonments and suffered many beatings. Quakers called themselves Friends but did not object to the appellation "Quaker," which began as a derogatory term and implied that believers quaked while listening for the voice of God to speak with them.[46]

Aside from their strict pacifism, Quakers also were known for their emphasis on education for the young. Within a year of Penn's landing aboard the ship *Welcome*, he, as Lord Proprietor, and his council took action to open a school in Philadelphia. The Friends' Public School was incorporated in 1697. The corporation consisted of 15 Quakers who were "the Overseers of the Public School founded in Philadelphia at the request, cost and charges of the People called Quakers."[47] The institution taught the poor gratuitously. Others paid part of the cost of their children's education. It was open on the same terms to all religious groups.

Quaker concern for the fair treatment of Native Americans paralleled their condemnation of slave ownership. The first known public protest against slavery was on the 18th of April 1688 when the Quakers of Germantown, Pennsylvania, met and condemned slavery as immoral. They sent a record of their solemn antislavery protest to their monthly meeting at Philadelphia. It was signed by Garrett Hendricks, Francis Daniel Pastorius, Dirk Op den Graeff and Abraham Op den Graeff. But it was 1780 before all Quakers in good standing had freed their slaves. By then, "Friends (Quakers) had taken such a firm stand against slavery that they were not longer able to come into economic competition with their neighbors who utilized slave labor."[48]

The Friends' pacifism made them unpopular. Those who would not pledge allegiance to the American cause faced punishment, confiscation of property and exile. The Friends' refusal to furnish financial support for the military or to contribute to military service in any way kept them out of the Revolutionary War. Quakers disowned Nathaniel Greene, George Washington's favorite general, because he was not a pacifist. Quakers expelled American flag maker Betsy Ross for eloping with John Ross, son of the assistant rector of Philadelphia's Christ Church.

The Quaker migration continued from 1675 to 1725 from the North Midlands of England and Wales to the Delaware Valley and Penn's Colony. The most alluring impetus for Quaker migration was launched under the leadership of William Penn.

William Penn traveled with George Fox throughout England, where he found "thousands of Quakers and other non-tolerated Protestant sects eager to emigrate." Penn preached to thousands in the lowlands of Germany in their native tongue. Because his mother was Dutch and his father was English, he spoke Dutch, German and English. Before Penn acquired his colony in America, he made two visits to Germany, one in 1671 and the second in 1677. He "became well known through the peculiar religious tenets he advocated and attempted to spread. Later, as the owner of Pennsylvania, Penn spared no efforts to attract colonists from Germany. Not only did he write full descriptions of the Province where lands were almost given away, but political and religious toleration was proclaimed as the very cornerstone of his new government. Many of these attractively written brochures are still extant to show us how great were the efforts to arouse the spirit of emigration."[49]

In rural America the Amish, a Protestant group rooted in the Anabaptist movement, live primarily on farmlands of Pennsylvania, Ohio and Indiana. The term "Anabaptist" means that they perform only adult baptism freely chosen by both males and females, usually in their teens. For this practice, as well as for their refusal to serve in the military,

Amish and all Anabaptists in German-speaking areas of Europe were persecuted. Initially almost all Amish in America derived their income from farming. Amish farmers still plow and harvest with the horse rather than the tractor, and their families ride in a horse-drawn buggy rather than the automobile. Today their large families of six or more children have reduced the available farmland supply; hence most Amish are now engaged in small enterprises or employed as relatively unskilled workers in rural and small-town businesses owned by Amish or non–Amish employers. But they carefully keep the modern technology used at work away from their homes.[50]

Amish women give birth only at home aided by a midwife. Treasuring faith and family, the Amish are God-fearing, family-centered people. Their austere self-denial celebrating God's gift of life requires Bible reading and silent prayer twice daily. The Amish are strictly governed equally by the Bible and the Ordnung. The Ordnung (a German word for Order) is an unwritten set of rules and regulations which, for the Amish, dictates plain clothing, beards, uncut hair, horses and buggies and the bishops deciding whether to allow bicycle riding or to disallow women to wear smocks over their dresses. Both the Amish and the Mennonites obey their respective Ordnung. Mennonites share similar beliefs with the Amish but, unlike the Amish, Mennonites embrace technology and electrical devices and do not separate from the world.

Impressions of modern-day Amish life are recorded by a midwife writing in the *Wall Street Journal*. She describes hardworking rural people with weather-beaten faces and swollen ankles living almost without electricity. They live in barns, sheds and basements of unfinished homes lit by lamplight, warmed by woodstoves and watered by windmills pumping into kitchen sinks, but only when the wind stirs. Living rooms often shelter orphaned lambs or a box of chirping chicks. Often there is the stench of sweat-soaked, ragged clothes, chamber pots and outdoor toilets. Their yard is strewn with tubs, a washboard and reams of clotheslines. Mice sometimes scurry across the floor, and flypaper filled with flies hangs from the ceiling. The people work hard but relax and play. Their lives are untarnished by the broader culture. They welcome, tease, tell stories, overfeed and cherish guests. "The fruit of the Amish way of life is that it keeps its people better focused on what truly matters—faith and family...[D]o we really need the fear of hell driving us before we can make time to be with one another and enjoy the magnificent world God created for us?"[51]

9

German Protestants Migrate to Colonial America

Contemporaneous German Reformed leader Michael Schlatter estimated the German population of Pennsylvania in 1752 to be 90,000. The three primary Protestant Christian denominations among Pennsylvania Germans during the first half of the 18th century were the United Brethren (Moravians) led by Count Nicholas Ludwig von Zinzendorf, the Lutherans led by Henrich (Henry) Melchior Mühlenberg, and the German Reformed organized by Michael Schlatter. Most of the Palatines in Pennsylvania belonged to the German Reformed Church, which was akin to the Lutherans and similar in religious doctrines to the Presbyterians.

The Moravians, under Zinzendorf, settled mainly in the Lehigh Valley of northern Bucks County in 1738–1739. By 1762 there were about 1,000 Moravians in Pennsylvania.[1] The Moravian Church traces its roots to ancient Bohemia and Moravia (the present-day Czech Republic, also known as Czechia whose capital city was then and is now Prague). Through the influence of Greek Orthodox missionaries, many in these countries converted to Christianity in the mid–800s. Even though they translated the Bible into their common language and developed a church ritual, Bohemia and Moravia gradually fell under the ecclesiastical jurisdiction of Rome. Some Czechs, especially common people and students, protested several practices, especially the selling of indulgences of the Roman Catholic clergy. Their chief spokesperson was Jan Hus, a professor of philosophy and rector of the University in Prague. After a long trial, the Council of Constance convicted Hus of heresy and burned him at the stake in 1415.[2] Hence the foundation of the Moravian Church was laid by Jan Hus, a Bohemian Catholic priest and martyr who died trying to reform his church.

Determined not to let the reformation of the church die, followers of Hus organized the Unitas Fratrum (Unity of Brethren), the forerunners of the Moravian Church, in a Bohemian village east of Prague in 1457. The ideals and sacrifice of Hus richly influenced the teachings of German nobleman Martin Luther, who began his Lutheran reformation 60 years later.

Moravians advocated for a general reformation of the church. In essence, Moravians wanted to abolish all sacraments except baptism and the Lord's Supper. They sought "the dissolution of all monastic orders and the repudiation of the doctrines of the mass, purgatory, confession, relics, image worship, and the efficacy of good work."[3] The burgeoning Moravians were isolated as repudiators and would have fizzled out completely except for the idealistic Count Zinzendorf.

Zinzendorf (1700–1760) was born in Dresden, Saxony (Germany). Both Zinzendorf's grandmother and his future wife were devout Pietists, stressing personal faith, emotion and feeling in religion rather than rigid confessionalism of Lutherans. Pietism was a reform movement originating in 1675 within German Lutheran Christianity protesting the religious formality and orthodoxy observed by the Lutheran Church. "The most important factor in German Lutheranism just prior to the emergence of Pietism was its rigid confessionalism."[4]

Zinzendorf's grandmother controlled her grandson's schooling. After studying law at Wittenberg, Zinzendorf purchased his grandmother's estate near the community of Herrnhut. Fleeing legal prosecution under Catholic authority, the tenants of the estate were religious refugees from Bohemia and Moravia. Their religion was Unitas Fractrum or United Brethren, who were the theological ancestors of the Moravians of the 18th century.[5] Together with these Protestant refugees, the nobleman Zinzendorf founded the Moravian Church on his estate in 1722.

Zinzendorf held that the sine qua non of faith was the belief in the "divinity of the suffering God-man who freely chose to die for humanity's sins." Faith in the divinity of Christ was the "individual's sole duty of obligation. Christ himself would initiate justification and impart saving grace. Since Christ suffered death on the cross for all persons, every individual could be saved on the merit of His sacrificial act."[6] "Once Christ entered the soul, sin was cleansed away." In order to rest assured of eternal reward, one needed only to say: "I believe." Zinzendorf believed that the essence of sin and evil was disbelief in the Lord Jesus Christ as manifested by careless indifference, estrangement, neglect towards Him or enmity and rebellion against Him.

Soon there was friction in the community of Herrnhut between local Lutherans who stressed confessionalism and Zinzendorf's refugee Moravians who practiced a more personal religion and with whom he sympathized. Trying to generate harmony between the two religions, Zinzendorf became an ordained Lutheran minister. When his mission failed, he was exiled from Saxony for 11 years.

Moravians are a denomination of Protestants, and one goal of their ministers was to unite Protestant churches. Many other German and Protestant leaders condemned not only the Moravian idea of uniting Protestant churches but also the Moravian acceptance of women preaching and holding religious offices. At age 37, Zinzendorf was named a Moravian bishop. As bishop he sent missionaries to many parts of the world to promote an ecumenical (worldwide) union of all churches. Each denomination, whether Lutheran, Reformed, Catholic or whatever, could retain its doctrinal and denominational distinctiveness. He established "new congregations in other parts of Germany, the Netherlands, England, the Baltic States, and the West Indies and New York and ... the largest of all his missions was Bethlehem, Pennsylvania."[7] Moravians founded Bethlehem and Nazareth, Pennsylvania, in 1741.[8]

Even earlier, however, the Moravians, fleeing religious persecution in Bohemia, established their very first settlement in North America in Savannah, Georgia, one year after Lutherans first arrived there. The Moravian settlement was founded in 1735 when Augustus Gottlieb Spangenberg, a disciple of Zinzendorf, sailed with ten Moravian men and a multitude of German-speaking Swiss immigrants on the ship *Two Brothers* to Savannah. Soon these pioneer Moravians were joined by a group of 24 Moravian men and women debarking from the ship *Simmons*. Their inordinate number of loudly preaching and proselytizing clergy drew large crowds at every port. Other ship passengers were John and Charles Calvin and Georgia's Governor James Oglethorpe. Moving to Georgia was part of the worldwide, proselytizing Moravian missionary campaign which included Africa, India, the Caribbean, North America, Greenland and most of Europe. Spreading the church to all continents, Moravian Brethren became the most successful Protestant missionaries. Therefore, when 41 Moravians including a dozen preachers and missionaries moved to Georgia, they were closely watched by Georgians as well as Europeans. John Wesley came to Savannah with a group of Moravians in 1736, but he failed in his effort to reconcile Moravians with Lutherans who bitterly and vehemently opposed the Moravian proselytizing clergy.

The Moravians moved from Georgia to Pennsylvania in 1740–1741 because Zinzendorf not only wanted to convert Native Americans in the City of Brotherly Love. He also intended to begin an ecumenical [worldwide Christian unity] movement among Germans who lived there. But the German Lutherans in the Shenandoah Valley resisted, refusing to allow Moravians to impose their order on all Germans. When the ecumenical experiment failed, Zinzendorf established himself as head of the Lutheran Church in Philadelphia in 1742. "This was intolerable to Lutheran pietists in Halle (a town in the German State of Saxony) who despised the Moravians for their extreme spiritualism [belief in communicating with the souls of the dead], predestinarian teachings [that God foreordains salvation of the soul], militant expansionism, and for the pompous behavior of their count."[9]

The Unitas Fratrum Church (Moravian Church), however, believed that what made a Christian was not doctrine or what he or she believed, but that a person lived his or her life according to the teachings of Jesus Christ. These first Moravians were described as "people who have decided once and for all to be guided only by the gospel and example of our Lord Jesus Christ and his holy apostles in gentleness, humility, patience, and love for our enemies."[10]

The Halle leadership sent Henry Melchior Mühlenberg, a young Lutheran minister who also disliked the Moravians and Zinzendorf, to Pennsylvania. Mühlenberg felt threatened by the "left wing of pietism which emerged in the Moravian Church." He was afraid that Moravian influence would ultimately triumph and erase any traces of genuine Lutheranism in Pennsylvania. Mühlenberg's mission was to undermine Zinzendorf's ambitions, his proselytizing and mystic spiritualism. Mühlenberg also planned to organize the Lutherans of that colony along Pietist lines that would be acceptable to the Halle leadership. While Zinzendorf was proselytizing, exuberant missionaries reached out to the Indians of Pennsylvania and tried to draw Lutherans into the Moravian Church; his antagonist, Mühlenberg, attempted to discipline Germans and bring them back into the Lutheran fold.

Mühlenberg, the father of colonial American Lutheranism, was born and baptized in 1711 in the German village of Einbeck in the Duchy of Hanover. It was in this place in 1714 that Mühlenberg's contemporary, the Duke of Hanover, was born. The duke became George I, the first Hanoverian King of England, and succeeded Queen Anne, the last Stuart monarch. When Mühlenberg and future King George I were growing up, Hanover still showed signs of the devastation of the Thirty Years'

War (1618–1648) when Catholics and Protestants had slaughtered each other.[11]

Mühlenberg's father was a middle-class brewer and cobbler. When Henry Mühlenberg was 12 years old, his father died and Henry found work to augment his family's income. Resuming his education at age 18, Mühlenberg studied the organ, clavichord and mathematics. He sang in the school choir to supplement his income. He acquired a broad knowledge of Latin and Greek, later learned French and Hebrew, and attended classes in theology and philosophy.

Henry Mühlenberg was ordained as a Lutheran minister in Leipzig in 1739 and assumed pastoral duties in Saxony near Herrnhut, the center of Count Zinzendorf's Church of the United Brethren which Mühlenberg denounced. In 1741 Mühlenberg accepted the call of the Lutheran Church to the United Congregations of Philadelphia, New Hanover and New Providence. On his voyage to Pennsylvania he brought with him a Pietistic theology which would profoundly influence American Lutheranism. "Pietism invaded all four great Christian Churches, Lutheran, Reformed, Church of England and Roman Catholic." Among German Lutherans it was known as Pietism. Dutch Reformed called it precisionism; the Anglicans knew it as Puritanism; Roman Catholics called it Jansenism. Pietists developed no common set of doctrines, but there were elements common to all Pietists. Chief among these was a meaningful relationship of the Christian believers with God, which resulted in feelings of contentment. The believer developed a personal commitment to a moral life. "The individual lived in God and God indwelled in him or her."[12]

"Although Muhlenberg and Zinzendorf can be described today as Lutheran pietists, they differed significantly in their attitudes towards authority. Muhlenberg can be described as an organization man while the count ignored authority-whether family, church, or government.... Neither Muhlenberg nor Zinzendorf knew much about Pennsylvania, the variety of religions there, or the Lutheran congregations. Zinzendorf thought that the divisions of Christendom were a scandal and he staged a series of ecumenical conferences in Pennsylvania to bring some a unity of the 'Church of God in the Spirit' even while denominational structures remained distinct.... Muhlenberg saw these Moravians as attempting to subvert Lutherans. The result was a series of bitter disputes that required the courts to decide the legal basis for ownership of church property."[13]

The definition of Pietism has changed over time. At first, the Pietist movement, which originated in Germany, attempted to reform the Protestant churches of Germany. The well-received book *Pietism in Germany and North America 1680* edited by Strom, Lehmann and Melton points out that authors of American religious history, for the most part, have dealt with Pietism in a limited manner, even silence, by failing to list the word *Pietism* in the index of the majority of their literature. This is surprising, given that *The Harper Collins Dictionary of Religion* defines Pietism as "A movement in German Lutheranism that began in the seventeenth century ... in reaction to the emergence of Protestant Orthodoxy." The dictionary also points out that Pietism's influence went beyond Lutheranism: "After the seventeenth century, it helped shape much of English Puritanism, French Quietism and Methodism."[14]

Breaking the perceived silence, in 1972, Sydney E. Ahlstrom's influential book, *A Religious History of the American People*, presented a chapter titled "The German Sects and the Rise of Pietism." In it Pietism was called a "revivifying" force in the 18th-century Protestantism of Europe and America as exemplified by Dunkers, Moravian Brethren and Schwenkfelders. He also mentioned the sway that continental Pietistic sects held over John Wesley and the founding of American Methodism. And yet, Pietism played only a minor role in Ahlstrom's total text. Many other well-regarded religious texts of the 20th century fail to mention Pietism, although Pietism is the common spiritual quality of countless sects, among them Methodists, the Moravians, the Dunkers, the Huguenots, the Church of the Brethren and the Mennonites.[15]

Immediately upon arriving in Philadelphia, Mühlenberg, still weak from the seasickness of the stressful voyage from Saxony, clashed with Count Zinzendorf in an icy-fiery theological debate before the Philadelphia Lutheran Congregation. Under Zinzendorf, women were equal to men. Deaconesses shared duties equally with deacons in serving in the highest offices of the Moravian Church. A covenant of virgins was developed as single sisters vowed to live only for the savior. As soon as Zinzendorf died, however, a group of churchmen decided to severely limit the role of women as board members and in worship services. Spangenberg, who had been a top Moravian leader under Zinzendorf, was one of the leaders in reorganizing the Moravian Church after Zinzendorf's death. Spagenberg diminished the role of equality for women, even that of his own wife as well as the daughter of Zinzendorf.

In 1937–1938 the Moravian congregation at Watertown, Wisconsin, invited the "Conference of Spiritual Descendants of John Hus" to meet at their church. An executive board as well as a committee of 23 people from various religious affiliations was formed to organize the conference. The conference gathered 170 attendants from 16 different religious bodies, all of whom traced their roots back to John Hus. The conference pointed out that "John Hus was a religious reformer who ... declared the principles of religious freedom, and wanted the people to be able to read the Bible and other writing in their own languages."[16]

In 2007 an inventory of the papers in the Moravian Archives from the 1937 conference found that "Today, the following churches trace their origins to [John] Hus: the Moravian Church on the estate of Count Zinzendorf, the Evangelical Unity of Czech Moravian Brethren in North America, which occurred after emigration to the New World, the Czech Brethren Evangelical Church in Prague, the Bohemian and Moravian Brethren churches, and the Baptist, Congregational, Lutheran, Methodist, Presbyterian, and other religious groups."[17]

"Recently the Moravian Church and the Evangelical Lutheran Church of America entered into a full communion agreement. Wagner, a Lutheran pastor and professor at the Moravian Seminary, examines the origins of the split between the two denominations symbolized by a meeting in 1742 between the founder of the Moravians, Count Ludwig von Zinzendorf, and Heinrich Melchior Mühlenberg, the pastor most influential in shaping American Lutheranism. The book's underlying theme ... is that even in the 1740s the differences were marginal and that unification requires neither denomination to repudiate its heritage."[18]

Today the Northern province of the Moravian Church in America is headquartered in Bethlehem, Pennsylvania; the Southern province is headquartered in Winston-Salem, North Carolina. A plaque at the Old Salem Visitor Center, Winston-Salem, North Carolina, notes: "The Moravian Church traces its beginnings to the martyrdom of Jan Hus in 1415.... A remnant of Hussites established a church and called themselves the Unitas Fratrum, or Unity of the Brethren. By the 1730s they were known to the English-speaking world as the Moravians."

One ritual of the Moravian Church is the Christingle, a religious tradition that began as a children's Christmas service at a Moravian Church in Germany on December 20, 1747. Carols were sung, and the minister read verses handwritten by the children to celebrate the birth of Christ. Each child then received a Christingle to take home through the dark. Characterizing the world, the Christingle was an orange holding a glowing candle representing Christ, the light of the world, surrounded by nuts, raisins and sweets stuck onto cocktail picks symbolizing God's bounty. At the base of the orange "world" was a red ribbon surrounding crinkled red paper signifying the blood of Christ that was shed for all people on the cross at Calvary. Moravians have carried the custom of the Christingle service to each part of the world including Labrador, Pennsylvania, Tibet, the Caribbean and South Africa. This Christmas custom has been widely adopted by churches of other denominations.

10

France vs. England Conflict
Phase I Glorious Revolution

The brochures sent out by William Penn inviting immigrants to his colony were a godsend to German-speaking peoples who were uprooted by the expansionistic policies of French King Louis XIV. It was the ongoing friction between France and England that ousted Germans from their homes in the Rhineland and drove massive numbers of disenfranchised religious groups to Penn's Colony as well as to other American colonies where immigrants were welcomed and needed. The conflict between France and England lasted 75 years (1688–1763) and was divided into four phases.

The 75 years of strife between France and England in Europe began with the "Glorious Revolution" and ended with the Seven Years' War, known in America as the French and Indian War. This struggle for balance of power would redraw the map of Europe. France and England were on opposite sides in all four confrontations. In each conflict on the European continent, Britain supported whatever coalition of powers in Europe "opposed the ambition of the mighty France."[1]

All four European phases of the 75-year-long conflict were accompanied by corresponding French versus English wars in America. The concomitant American wars were named for whichever monarch happened to be on the throne of England at the time. In all four American wars, France allied with Native Americans to fight against British colonists and their Native American allies. France and England were vying against each other for dominion over the North American continent.

In 1667 (20 years after the Peace of Westphalia ended the Thirty Years' War and 20 years before Britain's "Glorious Revolution") an aggressive and imperialistic Louis XIV decided to extend the boundaries of France to what he considered to be its natural physical geographic limits—the Rhine, the Alps, the Pyrenees and the sea. First, since the Dutch controlled the Rhine, they must be subdued and brought back into the Catholic faith. By controlling tributaries of the Rhine, France would monopolize German commerce. Louis's memoirs reveal that his plan for wars offered "A vast field where great occasions might arise for distinguishing myself. Many brave men whom I saw devoted to my service seemed always to be begging me to offer them an opportunity for valor.... Moreover, since I was obliged in any case to maintain a large army, it was more expedient for me to throw it into the Low Countries than to feed it at my expense.... Under pretext of a war with England I would ... begin more successfully my enterprise in Holland."[2] So he made war on the Dutch, and, in the process, Louis XIV devastated the Palatinate.

At that time the Dutch Republic (United Provinces, the Netherlands) had the largest carrying trade in the world. Transporting timber from the woodland shores of the Baltic, carrying grains from Poland, and shipping vast quantities of salted herring for market, Dutch ships outnumbered the combined fleets of England, France, Germany, Portugal, Scotland and Spain.[3]

In an attempt to reduce the powerful Dutch Empire, Louis's army advanced along the Rhine. The desolation of the Thirty Years' War was renewed, surging into the Netherlands. But the march was stopped short by an avalanche of water when the Dutch deliberately opened the dikes and flooded the land bordering the Holland province. The angry Dutch mob blamed the Netherlands ruling class for not blocking the French incursions into their homeland. That's why the Dutch people demanded restoration of the House of Orange. By popular demand, 22-year-old William III, Prince of Orange, was appointed stadtholder (head of state or king) of the Dutch Republic in 1672.

William III's father, William II of Orange, former captain general (ruler, stadtholder) of the six provinces of the Netherlands, died shortly before William III was born. William III, therefore, received the hereditary title, Prince of Orange (or Orange-Nassau), from his German-born ancestral grandfather, William I "the Silent" (1533–1584), who inherited the French principality of Orange as well as property in the Netherlands. After founding the House of Orange-Nassau, William the Silent led the Dutch revolt against Spanish rule. He fought against Spanish occupation and won freedom of religion for Protestants. The revolt resulted in independence for the United Provinces. Thus William I the Silent, the first Prince of Orange, is known as Father of the Netherlands.[4]

10. France vs. England Conflict

As supreme commander of the Netherland forces on land and sea, Stadtholder William III assembled an army and expelled the French enemy troops from Dutch soil. Yet the day of Dutch domination of the European economy and politics was over. Soon after William III became stadtholder, the French King Louis XIV offered peace in return for money and land cessions. But William advised his countrymen: "Rather let us be hacked to pieces than accept such conditions." He counseled patient and courteous negotiations with the English to check French aggression. One problem was that for two years England's King Charles II (r. 1660–1685), while professing loyalty to the Anglican Church, had actually been accepting bribes from Louis to turn England toward Catholicism.[5]

Religious tolerance dominated the political scene of England's Charles II. Charles's foreign policy teetered between alliances with the Dutch and with the French. He secretly signed the 1670 Treaty of Dover with France in which he covertly declared himself a Catholic and assured Louis XIV that England would side with the French against the Dutch. In return he received subsidies from France. Charles could not announce his Catholicism openly because Parliament contained a large Anglican majority. Instead, he issued a Declaration of Indulgences to suspend English penal laws against Catholics and nonconformists.[6]

More followed. To maintain his Protestant credentials, Charles had endorsed the marriage of his Protestant niece Mary—daughter of his Catholic brother, the future King James II—to William of Orange, stadtholder of the Netherlands. Charles had no legitimate children, therefore no heirs to the throne. James was next in line.

Dutch born William III of Orange then had two connections with England's Royal House of Stuart. His mother was the daughter of Charles I. His wife, Mary, as the daughter of England's James II, was his first cousin. William, a Calvinist Protestant, was concerned about his father-in-law's Catholicism. He was also determined to protect the Dutch province against Louis XIV's expansionism. James II succeeded Charles I to the throne of England.

Anglicans were passively resistant when their new King, James II, sought freedom of worship and the right to hold public office for Catholics. In 1687 the Protestant Parliament objected to the king's appointment of Catholics to academic, military and political positions. The English Parliament feared a standing army led by Roman Catholics in England and protested against it. James then prorogued Parliament and ruled without one. He looked for a Parliament that would remove the Test Acts which prohibited Catholics from holding public office and forbade the king's appointments of Catholics to his privy council.

It was hoped that James would be succeeded by his Protestant daughter, Mary Stuart, who was married to the Dutch Stadtholder, William III. But in 1688 when James's second wife, a Catholic, gave birth to a male heir, anxiety about popery intensified. The birth of a son to James II threatened to establish a Roman Catholic dynasty unless Anglicans intervened.[7]

Panic about popery during the reign of the Stuart kings in England prompted a group of Englanders to rise up in revolt against James II (r. 1685-1688). The revolt grew into what became known as the "Glorious Revolution" (1688-1689). In essence, the Glorious Revolution occurred when England's Catholic King James II was ousted and replaced by his Protestant daughter Mary and her Dutch husband, William of Orange.

The anxiety had increased in 1685 when Charles II was succeeded by his openly Catholic brother, James II. Historian Edward Vallance[8] noted that popery meant not only a hatred of the Catholic Church but fear that Catholics were plotting to overthrow the Anglican Church and State. It reflected the belief that British religion and political systems would be replaced by Catholicism and that England would become a satellite state under the control of an all-powerful and tyrannical Catholic monarch.

When members of the British peerage contacted William III of Orange to oust their king, William already had military plans in place to invade England and bring the British Isles into his war against Louis XIV. William's Dutch flotilla of 1688 was four times the size of the Spanish Armada of 1588, and it struck on nearly the same day that the Spanish had attempted to invade a century earlier. James's British army was larger, but desertions, defections and anti-Catholic rioting in cities and towns throughout England convinced him to flee. James II took refuge in the court of Louis XIV at Louis's Palace of Versailles.

On November 5, 1688, Protestant England welcomed the invasion of William of Orange. His incursion into England during the "Glorious Revolution" was called the "Bloodless Revolution" in England, but there was bloodshed in Scotland and Ireland.

The next year British Parliament enacted the 1689 English Bill of Rights which declared that James II had attempted to destroy the Protestant religion and abdicated the government. It also gave Parliament power over royal succession: No Roman Catholic could succeed to the throne of England. Future kings would have to subscribe to the Test Acts which forbade anyone from holding office until he accepted the Protestant religion. The English Bill of Rights prohibited taxation without parliamentary consent and denied the right of the Crown to wage war except with parliamentary consent. William declared that he would not protect Britain unless he shared the throne equally with his wife, Mary.[9] Agreeing, Mary pledged her full obedience to William and desired only that he would obey the command of "Husbands, love your wives," alluding to William's liaison with his mistress, Elizabeth Villiers, Mary's best friend.[10] William III (reigned 1689–1702) and Mary II (reigned 1689–1694), prince and princess of Orange, were declared King and Queen of England, Scotland and Ireland. The bill decreed that after they were deceased, the royal power of these kingdoms would go to the heirs of the body of Princess Mary or, in case of default, to her sister, Princess Anne of Denmark, and the heirs of her body.[11] William did not mind relinquishing the reduced powers of the British Monarchy as described in the English Bill of Rights because one of his "main reasons for accepting the throne was to reinforce the struggle against Louis XIV. William's foreign policy was dominated by the priority to contain French expansionism."[12] It was partly through the efforts of William of Orange and his fight against the forces of Louis XIV that colonial America did not become a French-speaking country.

An influx of skilled craftsmen from the Netherlands, Northern Germany and France accompanied William and Mary to England. Some migrated to America. With them arrived a refinement in cabinetmaking: walnut and ebony veneers, floral motifs, and the turned leg sometimes ending in a scroll foot.

The Glorious Revolution involved political and economic changes: The Revolution was a multilayered movement. It involved: (1) the ousting of Catholic King James II followed by the succession of Protestant William and Mary to the British throne; (2) the changing of England from an agrarian to a manufacturing society; (3) the shifting of Britain's focus from empire-building to "active political and military engagement" with Continental Europe; and (4) a relaxing of the Church of England's policy on religious intolerance and persecution.[13]

The first European phase of the 75-year-long war between England and France (War of the Grand Alliance preceded by the Glorious Revolution) was initiated by the French King Louis IV's expansionist ambitions, which took French troops into the Rhineland, the gateway to the Netherlands. Louis's ultimate goal in this phase was to overpower the Netherlands, a prosperous economy and homeland of Prince William of Orange.

Preceding the War of the Grand Alliance (1688–1697) Louis built the best army in Europe and prepared to attack the Huguenots, the Rhineland, the Netherlands and any prince or people who blocked the path of French expansion.[14] The Rhineland was part of the Habsburg territories governed by Holy Roman Emperor Leopold I (1640–1705), whose imperial residence was in Vienna, Austria. Leopold was Louis XIV's first cousin.

Leopold had inherited Austria from his father in 1657 and had become Holy Roman Emperor in 1658 at the age of 18.[15] At the time, Leopold's Austrian state contained what are now Austria, Czechia (the Czech Republic), Silesia and a slice of Hungary; its power was only 10 percent that of France. Leopold more than doubled Austria's size and power. Although Leopold was strongly Catholic, peaceful, and not personally aggressive, he supported the Protestant Dutchman William III in order to protect the western third of his empire from takeover by France. Skilled in putting together military and political coalitions, Leopold I co-organized the League of Augsburg to stop Louis's imperialism.[16]

Formed in July 1686 the League was a coalition of the Catholic Emperor Leopold I and the Catholic Prince Elector of Bavaria, joined by the Protestant Great Elector of Brandenburg, the Protestant King of Sweden, and the Protestant Stadtholder William III of the Netherlands. Having recently defeated the Turks, Leopold I was still monitoring their retreat, but his imperial troops were now free to fight France on the western front of his Holy Roman Empire.

Louis XIV, instead of invading Holland as William III expected, decided to invade the Rhineland before Leopold could deploy imperial troops to block the French frontier. Destruction of the Rhineland would damper Leopold's food foraging to feed his army. Louis's move into the Rhineland pushed the United Provinces into supporting William's conquest of England.[17] When he became King of England, William III persuaded the English Parliament to finance troops to fight France. King William then personally led his army and "carefully built up the Grand Alliance."[18] Under William, England then joined the Holy Roman Empire, Spain and the Netherlands, Denmark and Savoy in the first Grand Alliance. Each pledged to defend its members against the aggressor. Nearly all the nations of Europe joined in common defense against France's Louis XIV and his expansionist plan to invade the Lower or Palatinate (the Pfalz) east of Luxembouorg in southwest Germany along both sides of the Middle Rhine River. It was the rest of Europe against France.[19]

Troops of the Grand Alliance marched into the Rhineland to prevent France from drenching the area with Protestant blood. The war drove nearly 500,000 Germans from their homes, resulting in a mass migration of Germans to Penn's Colony.[20] Louis XIV not only uprooted Germans, but his persecution of the Huguenots (middle-class French Protestants) caused them to flee, taking with them their skills and savings.[21] His refusal to let them colonize Louisiana drove thousands of Huguenots to add "their considerable talents and wealth to the resources of English America."[22]

In the War of the Grand Alliance, Anglo-Dutch fleets won more maritime victories than did the French. Capturing one French colony after another, England remained ruler of the seas.

On land, the French repeatedly routed William. William countered, repeatedly rallying with a fresh army and replenished supplies. In England, the huge cost of William's war led to the founding of the Bank of England in 1694 as well as to parliamentary committees to scrutinize Crown expenditures and to a bureaucracy to manage the national budget. In France, exhausted in body and spirit from heavy taxing to finance Louis's wars, the economy of the starving and diseased French people verged on collapse. One town official echoed a lament typical of many French municipalities: "This town, formerly rich and flourishing, is today without any industry.... There were formerly manufactures in this province but today they have been abandoned.... Agriculture was infinitely more flourishing twenty years ago."[23] As the war wore on, William, too, was strapped for money. England's Parliament—suspecting that his passion for war was at least partly driven by his desire to protect his homeland—repeatedly refused to fund his troops.

When Louis at last saw that his victories were draining the lifeblood out of France, his diplomats endeavored to make peace. They made known Louis's willingness to withdraw support for James II and recognize William III as King of England. On September 20, 1697, the Peace of Ryswick (near The Hague) ended the War of the Palatinate with England, Holland and Spain. A supplemental peace treaty was signed the next month with Leopold's empire.

The War of the Grand Alliance restored the balance of power against French aggression. But all the chief ministers of state in Europe knew that the treaty was only a truce. The bigger war—the War of Spanish Succession—would begin when the childless and sickly Spanish King Charles II died without an heir apparent.

11

Phase II: War of Spanish Succession
Queen Anne's War

Phase II of the 75 years of conflict between France and England consisted of the War of Spanish Succession (known in America as Queen Anne's War) forcing the great exodus of the Palatines, which is addressed in the next chapter. Below is a summary of those wars.

On his deathbed, the intellectually impaired[1] Spanish King Charles II, the last Habsburg King of Spain, bequeathed all of Spain and its territories to his great-nephew, 17-year-old Philip, Duke of Anjou, who was born into the Bourbon dynasty. In November 1700, Louis XIV, King of France, announced publicly that his grandson, Philip, Duke of Anjou, would succeed Charles II as King of Spain.

Philip was "quietly and cheerfully received as king in Spain."[2] His grandfather Louis said to him, "Be a good Spaniard—that is now your first duty; but remember that you were born a Frenchman, and maintain unity between the two nations; this is the way to make them happy, and to preserve the peace of Europe."[3] The teenage Frenchman, Spain's King Philip V, who spoke no Spanish, was the first of the Bourbons to sit on the Spanish throne.

In 1701 Louis XIV, patriarch of the House of Bourbon, tried to bring Spain under the control of the Bourbon dynasty. Louis's aggression led to the conflict known in Europe as the War of Spanish Succession (1701–1713), and in America as Queen Anne's War (1702–1713). The War of Spanish Succession has been called the First World War of modern times, with fighting in Spain, Italy and Germany as well as at sea and in America.

In the War of Spanish Succession—the second phase of the 75 years of strife between England and France—England and her allies, including Emperor of the Holy Roman Empire, the Catholic Leopold I of the Habsburg dynasty, tried to prevent the Catholic Louis XIV of the Bourbon dynasty from establishing a powerful new Bourbon empire. This would happen if the French and Spanish monarchies were allowed to combine.[4]

The House of Bourbon rivaled the House of Habsburg as one of the most important ruling houses of Europe. Over the centuries, members of the Bourbon dynasty who descended from Louis I, duc de Bourbon, became monarchs of France.

When the childless and intellectually impaired Spanish Habsburg King Charles II died, the Habsburg Holy Roman Emperor Leopold I (r. 1658–1705) and the Bourbon French King Louis XIV held equally valid claims to the Spanish throne. This dual claim of Leopold from Austria and Louis from France was important since Spain was the largest empire in the world with possessions in the Philippines, Italy, Sicily and North and South America.

Habsburg Holy Roman Emperor Leopold I (b. Vienna 1640; d. Vienna 1705), a German (Habsburg) prince, opposed establishing the Spanish Bourbons because it achieved a virtual union of Louis XIV's formidable France and Spain, the world's greatest imperial power. The House of Habsburg (also called the House of Austria) had long ruled the Holy Roman Empire as well as the Spanish Empire. And so Leopold contested Philips's appointment by the intellectually impaired Charles II, whose 30-year reign had been ineffective. Leopold based his objection on a rudimentary autopsy of the body of Charles II which showed the following results: "a very small heart, lungs corroded, intestines putrefactive and gangrenous, three large stones in the kidney, a single testicle black as coal, and his head full of water."[5]

England's King William III agreed with Leopold's objection in order to curb Louis's aggression. William, who initially congratulated Philip on his accession to the throne of Spain, soon decided along with Parliament that the escalating power of France must be limited. The English knew that the controversy was not merely between Catholic and Protestant or Bourbon and Habsburg but about which country would dominate the seas, Europe's colonies and world trade. On the other hand, Louis perceived that "the whole splendor of his reign now hung in the balance, and that the dispute over Spain had become a contest for continents."[6]

Maritime powers of England and Holland opposed the unification of Spain with either France (under Louis XIV) or Austria (under

11. Phase II: War of Spanish Succession

Leopold I) because the union would be too powerful at sea. England, the United Provinces of the Netherlands and the German principalities—whether for religious, dynastic or commercial reasons—wanted neither Louis's France nor Leopold's Austria to control the vast realm of Spain. Either scenario would topple the balance of power. Nevertheless, one government after another recognized Philip, Duke of Anjou, as King Philip V of Spain. The powers who at first acknowledged Philip as king, however, then joined in an alliance to dethrone him. Europe feared French expansion and power.

The first act in the War of Spanish Succession occurred in 1701 when Louis occupied Spanish Netherlands (present-day Belgium). The principal powers of the Grand Alliance—England, the United Provinces of the Netherlands, and Austria—then prepared for war. Many other nations joined these three. The only allies of France were Spain, Bavaria, Cologne and, for a year, Savoy. Spain, however, was a liability requiring French forces for protection. Furthermore, the Spanish colonies could not defend themselves against Dutch and English fleets.

England under King William III allied with the Netherlands and the Holy Roman Empire under Leopold I of Austria (King of Hungary, Croatia, and Bohemia) to form a second Grand Alliance to preserve the balance of power in Europe. The alliance was joined by nearly all European countries west of Poland and the Ottoman Empire.

William III ruled alone for eight years after Mary II died of smallpox. In February 1702, William was killed in a fall from his horse. Consequently, Mary's Protestant sister Anne, the second daughter of the exiled Catholic King James II, became Queen of England from 1702 to 1714.

The Catholic Louis XIV refused to acknowledge the Protestant Anne as Queen of England, although even Gulliver, from Jonathan Swifts' *Gulliver's Travels*, declared that he "did reverence and esteem her more than any of the human race." Anne was not considered brilliant. And yet her stable and prosperous reign was spectacular. A diligent business woman, she was well respected and listened to by her ministers. After winning battle after battle on the continent, Anne's English armies finally "broke the power of Louis XIV's France."[7]

Queen Anne was a key power in persuading the parliaments of Scotland and England [including Wales] to create the 1707 Treaty of Union which united the two kingdoms—England and Scotland—into "one kingdom by the name of Great Britain." The treaty created "the one, unified, parliament of Great Britain."[8] Until that time—although

England, Ireland and Scotland had been united under one Crown since the time of James I—these kingdoms had been unable to achieve governmental union. (It would be almost a century later that the Acts of Union of 1800 would blend the parliaments of Great Britain and Ireland to form the United Kingdom of Great Britain).

Two months after plump and amiable Queen Anne acceded to the British throne, Europe was plunged into the War of Spanish Succession. Anne promoted a skilled strategist and diplomat, the tall, handsome and ruddy-faced Englishman John Churchill, Duke of Marlborough, to the rank of supreme commander of the English army.

English General Marlborough (John Churchill) together with his able ally, Austrian General Prince Eugene of Savoy, working under the Holy Roman Emperor Leopold I were the two principal generals fighting against the French. Of Italian ancestry, the French-born Prince Eugene—a dark-complected, thin-faced, big-nosed little man with an abundant wig—had been rejected by Louis XIV for the French army. Despite that, Eugene became not only an Austrian general but one of the best soldiers of his time. His victories against the Turks brought Hungary into the Austrian Empire. Together Marlborough and Eugene won many memorable victories over the French under Louis XIV.

The War of Spanish Succession was fought in Northern Europe. Austria's acquisition of the Southern Netherlands (Belgium) acted as a buffer against French invasion of the Low Countries.[9] Louis attempted to eliminate Leopold's Holy Roman Empire by capturing its capital, Vienna. English General Marlborough intercepted French and Bavarian troops on the banks of the Danube near Blenheim, a village in Bavaria. Although the War of Spanish Succession dragged on from 1701 to1713, its final outcome was decided in August 1704 by two main battles: One was Marlborough's and Prince Eugene's Blenheim victory which saved the city of Vienna; the other was the capture of the rock of Gibraltar by an Anglo-Dutch fleet. Marlborough's triumphs at Blenheim and at Ramillies (in what is now Belgium) two years later, coupled with further British successes at Gibraltar and Minorca, raised Britain's banner to new heights as a major power in continental politics and a strong competitor in Mediterranean and overseas markets.[10]

The treaties of Utrecht in 1713 and Rastatt in 1714 settled the map of Europe for 26 years, just as the treaties of Westphalia had settled the map of Europe for a couple of decades after the Thirty Years' War. Both cases established a balance of power between the Hapsburg and Bourbon dynasties. A balance of power between France and England in

11. Phase II: War of Spanish Succession

America was also established and would hold until the Seven Years' War (known in America as the French and Indian War). By ending years and years of war between Britain and France, the Treaty of Utrecht ushered in an era of prosperity, increasing trade between Britain and America.[11]

Holland and France were the chief losers in the War of Spanish Succession. The Dutch gained territory but lost sea power. The Dutch "could no longer match England in shipping, seamanship, resources, or war; its victory exhausted it and began its decline."[12] France lost a million lives, sea power and her economic prosperity. France was bankrupt. Although France kept her nominee, Louis's grandson Philip of Anjou, on the throne of Spain, she failed to preserve his full empire. Before he was recognized as king of Spain, Philip V was required to renounce all rights to the throne of France.[13] That's because the will of Charles II was recorded "with the proviso that the crowns of France and Spain should never be united under one head." France (Spain's ally) fell into bankruptcy and lost territory, ceding Gibraltar, Milan, Minorca, Naples, Sardinia, Sicily, and the Spanish Netherlands. France also granted Great Britain exclusive rights to the African slave trade in Spanish America.

The winners of the War of Spanish Succession were Austria on the continent and England at sea. On the continent Austria held Milan, Naples, Sicily and Belgium.

Even though Leopold's Austrians—the Holy Roman Empire of the Habsburgs—did not capture the Spanish throne, Austria did become the strongest force on the continent of Europe.

England gained control of shipping on the seas and world trade: She controlled Gibraltar in Spain and Port Mahon in Minorca. England also won Newfoundland and Nova Scotia. Attaining affluence at the end of the war, England's colonial merchants built mansions, furnishing their grand houses in the "latest style," which by 1730 was the Queen Anne Style in America, a style already popular in Britain.

The War of Spanish Succession intensified international hate: Germany could not forget that France devastated the Palatinate and precipitated the mass departure of the Palatines; France remembered Marlborough's gory victories at Blenheim; Spain resented having Gibraltar in alien hands. Each nation waited restlessly for revenge.

Louis XIV—"the magnificent and un-mourned king"—died in 1715 "to the great relief of Protestant Europe and Catholic France." His 72 year reign had begun in "the glory of martial triumphs" and literary masterpieces. At his worst, Louis XIV was a despot who purged and tortured the Huguenots. Louis's continued efforts to dominate Europe and North America nearly bankrupted France with his many wars. Louis's defects are chiefly known "from the second period (1683–1715) of his reign when bigotry had narrowed him, and success and flattery had spoiled him." His belief that he was ordained by God to rule France was supported by the "half-conscious belief of the people in the divine right of Kings."[14] He empathized more with individuals than with nations. He made war on the Dutch and devastated the Palatinate. His love of glory, aggression and his appetite for grandeur alienated his people,[15] and his reign ended with their impoverishment. He taxed them to destitution to pay for his self-indulgence, his wars, luxuries and extravagant buildings. But he gave France "an orderly government, a national unity, and a cultural splendor that won for her the unquestioned leadership of the Western world ... and France, which lives on glory, has learned to forgive him for almost destroying her to make her great."[16]

12

The Great Exodus of the Palatines and Conrad Weiser

The War of Spanish Succession—like the War of the Grand Alliance and the Thirty Years' War before that—again devastated the Rhineland region and destroyed what little was left by the previous marauders. The remaining German people were in the direst poverty. Now, even the few well-to-do were just as poor as their poorest neighbors. With homes destroyed and fields uncultivated, they had nothing. Nature further afflicted the half-starved and destitute people in the winter of 1708–1709 with intense cold. Many inhabitants froze to death. The combination of the extreme and prolonged winter of 1708–1709 (the most severe winter in 500 years) and the destruction of contending armies drove thousands of Germans from their homes in Manheim at the confluence of the Rhine and Neckar rivers, and from Heidelberg, Worms and Speyer.

After the wars of Louis XIV had laid waste to the Palatinate and to its surrounding lands and after the rough winter of 1708–1709 had ruined the crops, the pretentious rulers of small principalities attempted to emulate the grandeur of Louis XIV's court and maintain their own luxurious lifestyle by imposing heavy taxes on the impoverished population. The resulting desire of the deprived masses to evacuate their homeland and seek a new life was further influenced by their religious environment. The government of the Palatinate was Catholic and most, but not all, of the emigrants were Protestant. There was infringement on Protestant Church property and interruption of Protestant Church services. To obtain permission to leave the country, however, a citizen must be debt free. That's why many sacrificed everything in order to leave.[1]

Earlier, in 1708, before the bitter winter began, Joshua von Kocherthal, a German Evangelical (Lutheran) preacher, set out intending to lead a relatively large colony of 21 families (54 persons) to America. He led his group of Palatines through the Low Countries and across the sea and arrived in London totally impoverished. Queen Anne allowed each immigrant a stipend of one shilling per day and decided what to do with them. When the Palatines objected to the climate in the West Indies, the queen sent them to the place of their choice, New York. Departing aboard an English vessel on April 28, 1708, the Germans were accompanied by New York's newly appointed governor, Lord Lovelace. The Board of Trade showed the makeup of this colony to consist of ten men, ten women, 21 children and a number of unclassified others. Among the newcomers were one joiner, one smith and the rest farmers. The colonists also received tools. As a foreign clergymen, Kocherthal received no salary, but he was given 20 pounds for books and clothes. Kocherthal and his 53 companions founded Neuburg (now Newburg) on the Hudson at the beginning of 1709.

Exaggerated reports of the welcome and of the religious freedom offered by the agents of Penn's Colony reached the Palatines in 1708–1709. The starving people who had barely escaped freezing to death rose en masse, literally by the thousands, and reached the nearest seaports the best way they could. The great exodus of the Palatines was the largest emigration of colonial times from any country to America. Other causes of this great expatriation of home-loving Germans were many and varied. The 1701–1713 War of Spanish Succession devastated Württemberg which, next to the Palatinate, sent the most emigrants to America. Stuttgart, a vineyard and orchard capital city in the German state of Baden-Württemberg, was invaded and plundered for three days[2] by the unopposed devastations of French General Villars (Claude-Louis-Hector, Duke de Villars), Louis XIV's most successful general at that time.

When the first shiploads of emigrants reached England, Queen Anne's Protestant government set up a thousand tents removed from the tower of London and opened British warehouses and barns for lodging. The government placed the foreigners as quickly as possible. Nearly 4,000 were sent to Ireland. If these Germans did not actually establish the Irish linen industry, they at least gave it the impetus to make it the most important textile industry in that country.[3] Volunteer committees collected donations from private benefactors to feed these German refugees. On the invitation of authorities from Ireland, 821 families, or

12. The Great Exodus of the Palatines and Conrad Weiser

3,073 persons, were sent to that country in late 1709 to early 1710. Six hundred fifty were sent with Christoph von Graffenried to North Carolina in January 1710.

Even though there was little work and bread was dear, the English raised money and provided food for these German and Swiss refugees who were waiting to sail to Germantown, Pennsylvania. Some migrated to Pennsylvania Tulpehocken ("Land of Turtles") region. A total of 68,872 Germans immigrated to Pennsylvania within the next 56 years. Many of the Roman Catholics were returned to their homeland, while more than 3,000 Protestants were sent to the New York colony. Some became established as tar manufacturers for the Royal Navy.[4]

The massive migration of Germans erupted between April and October of the year 1709 when a steady flow of 14,000 Germans sailed down the Rhine to Holland on their way to the Port of London. The Rotterdam government partially financed their move. And the hospitable English government, which also wished to curb the expansion of Louis XIV, provided several ships for their transport. The Germans expected their impromptu departure to lead them to the "Islands" of Pennsylvania and Carolina.

"During the months of May and June, 1709, the citizens of the city of London were astonished to find the streets of that metropolis swarming with men and women of an alien race, speaking an unknown tongue and bearing unmistakable indications of poverty, misery and want. It soon became known that about 5,000 of these people were sheltered under tents in the suburbs of the city. Additions were almost daily made to their number during June, July, August and September, and by October, between 13,000 and 14,000 had come."[5]

Because the exodus came mainly from the Palatinate as well as from many other principalities bordering both France and Germany, all of these emigrants were called Palatines. The term "Palatine" became synonymous with the word "German." Even the emigrants from the Upper Rhine and not from the Palatinate were labeled Palatines. Two Lutheran ministers reported that most of these emigrants were farmers, vinedressers and craftsmen. A list made out in May recorded 460 husbandmen and vinedressers, 95 craftsmen and five schoolmasters.

Alarmed by the massive loss of population, the Elector Palatine of the Rhine and other German officials attempted to stop the emigration in December 1709 by imposing an order of death and property confiscation for any native attempting to exit the homeland.[6] Regardless of the consequences, a constant stream of German colonists followed

Kocherthal.[7] Transporting German immigrants in the summer of 1710 during Queen Anne's reign, 12 ships sailed from England to New York. Four hundred immigrant widows and orphans had been bound out as servants and remained in New York City. Almost 3,000 others were to be sent up the Hudson to produce naval stores such as pitch, tar and turpentine from the timber. They were to settle on the Hudson not only to supply naval stores but also to act as a barrier against the Indians and to promote the fur trade. The Palatines understood that after they had worked long and hard enough to pay off their debt, each would receive 40 acres of land. The operation would be under the auspices of New York Governor Robert Hunter.

Upon docking in New York, only 2,227 of Hunter's party of 3,000 still survived. Against Hunter's wishes the Board of Trade had designated their destination to be the Mohawk and Hudson rivers. After deciding that the Mohawk pines were not suitable for extracting pitch and tar to furnish naval supplies, Hunter chose the Hudson. There he purchased 6,000 acres of land, divided 1,800 Germans into groups and settled them in five different villages. Eight years later, by August 1718, there were 499 persons on the east side of the Hudson River and 422 on the west, with no account given of widows and orphans.

"The settlement on the Hudson was a wasteful experiment. The English Government expended large sums of money without profit. Governor Hunter had the care of the Germans added to his other administrative difficulties in New York, and the Germans lost time and energy in a profitless settlement.... The settlers complained that the land on the Hudson was barren ... it is probable that the discontent of these colonists' conditions in New York and their report to Germany assisted in turning the tide of later German immigration to Pennsylvania."[8]

Just before leaving England, the German immigrants had heard about the 93-mile-long Schoharie, a tributary of the Mohawk River. A story was circulated among them that four Indians in an audience with the queen had presented Her Majesty with lands on the Schoharie. Unfortunately, the Indians were not chiefs and had no authority. Nevertheless a few German families believed that their future prosperity was rooted in Schoharie. In the winter of 1712, 50 families led by John Conrad Weiser made their way from the Hudson to Schoharie. One hundred more families followed. When the Schoharie venture failed, Weiser led the group to Pennsylvania. The whole scheme seems to have been too zealously pushed by men of little integrity who had much to gain from the colonists. At least one ray of light shone through these dark

12. The Great Exodus of the Palatines and Conrad Weiser

days for the Germans. It was John Conrad Weiser's son, Johann Conrad Weiser, Jr., who became fluent in the Mohawk language and acted as a mediator in future negotiations between the Six Nations and the residents in Pennsylvania.

The following quote is perhaps an apt preface for a biographical sketch of John Conrad Weiser and his son Conrad Weiser:

> Given a slot of ground, with poverty and hunger to boot, and the German will turn the desert into a garden. This is characteristic of his nature, which we see exhibited almost daily.[9]

John Conrad Weiser, Sr., was born and grew up in the town of his ancestry, Grossaspach in the county of Backnang in the ancient electorate (duchy) of Württemberg, which was part of the Rhine (Lower) Palatinate. His family home was a stone mansion standing directly over the town magistrate's office. Earning his living as a baker in his youth, his hard work and relentless drive led to his success in the position of an American esquire and a corporal in the military service. John C. Weiser's wife, Anna Magdalena Uebele, was also a native of Grossaspach in Württemberg. Her name lives on in her descendants there, although she died on May 1, 1709, when she was 43 years old and pregnant with her 16th child. She was survived by her husband and eight children. Not quite two months later, on June 24, widower John C. Weiser Sr., moved away, taking eight children with him: 13-year-old Conrad Weiser, Jr., Conrad's three older sisters, and Conrad's four younger siblings—numbering three brothers and one sister.

Later, Conrad Weiser (Jr.) wrote in his memoirs about his uprooting and that of his father, brothers and sisters. In two months the grieving Weiser family reached London, England, along with several thousand Germans whom Queen Anne supplied with food and other necessities. On Christmas Day 1709 the Palatines embarked on ten ships with 4,000 other immigrants sailing to America. It would be almost impossible to exaggerate their misery and suffering during the voyage. And yet, young Conrad "did not forget to magnify the kindness of Providence" and "give thanks to the Lord, for his mercy endureth forever."[10]

It was the Weiser family's understanding that Queen Anne had acquired from Mohawk chiefs a tract of land to be patented to the Palatines for building their homes, schools and churches. The location of the land was where Newburgh on the Hudson and New Windsor, New York, now stand. Weiser was convinced, however, that Robert Hunter, Governor of New York, and Robert Livingstone, a wealthy landlord of the province, "artfully and wickedly changed the course and destiny of the unsuspecting colony." These "conspirators" moved the Germans, not to Schoharie, the place the queen had promised, but to Livingston Manor, assuring them that they would own property there. Each family of immigrants was then charged an annual ground rent, and each person was expected to pay passage money.

Here in the German-Moravian town of Livingston Manor, explained the junior Conrad Weiser, we were to burn tar and cultivate hemp to defray the expenses incurred by Queen Anne in bringing us from Holland to England and from England to America. Conrad continued, "The grounds were to have been a free gift, and their passage was to have been a free passage likewise. It was simply an outrage."

While the colony toiled collectively, inside the mind of each member a rebellion was seething, ready to boil over under the leadership of a local magistrate, Conrad's father, Corporal John C. Weiser, Sr.

In the Spring of 1713, determined to emancipate the Palatines from the servile conditions at Livingston Manor, John Conrad Weiser the elder was the first of seven deputies to depart Livingston Manor on the Hudson and travel to talk with the Mohawks of Schoharie, 48 miles west of Albany. His mission was to revive the generous offer made by the friendly chiefs in England. Meanwhile the majority of the desperate Germans left their village homes on the Hudson and awaited the report of the deputies.

By November 1713 the Mohawks met with the Germans in Albany and agreed to open their valley to the Germans for a fee of $300. Also, in November at Albany, Chief Quagnant (Guinant) of the Six Nations of the Iroquois Confederacy [which included the Mohawk, Oneida, Onondaga, Cayuga, Seneca, Tuscarora], while negotiating with John C. Weiser, developed a fondness for the teenaged Conrad Weiser. The trustworthy chief asked Conrad's father if he could take his son to live with the Mohawks. Conrad was happy to go with the Mohawk chief. The boy, who still missed and grieved for his deceased mother, had been unhappy at home ever since his new stepmother, a German immigrant, apparently much younger than her new husband, had entered the household in 1711.

The elder John C. Weiser's motherless children began leaving home from the day of their father's second marriage. His eldest daughter married and remained in the homestead at Grossaspach in Württemberg. Another daughter married in America and moved away from home in Livingston Manor. Two sons were bound out by the governor of New York to a man in Long Island. Weiser's youngest son died at age six.

After negotiating with the Mohawks in November and sending his son Conrad to live with them, John C. Weiser—leader of the colony at Schoharie—and his second wife moved along with 150 other impoverished families to the Six Nations at Schoharie in the spring of 1714. Pooling their meager resources—a horse here, a cow there, a harness—the families broke ground and planted enough corn for the next year. Barely surviving a year of hunger by eating wild potatoes, ground bean pods and juniper berries, they obtained, on credit, a bushel of meal here and another there from as far as 40 miles away. Those family members left behind waited sorrowfully and tearfully for the foragers-borrowers to return, but often they returned without any food at all. Meanwhile, the teenaged Conrad was determined to make the best of his abrupt introduction to the daily life of an Indian.

Although there was a scarcity of provisions among the Indians, the now 16-year-old Conrad, like the Indians, survived cold, hunger, thirst and inadequate clothing. At times the boy hid in the bushes and lived in fear of being murdered by the often intoxicated Natives. Conrad was an apt student under Chief Quagnant. His tuition lasted eight months, and this "Indian experience was the college in which his qualifications developed." Lying in ambush and competing in footraces developed his lungs, bone and muscle and gave him the stamina to endure subsequent marches over trails for miles and miles. He became familiar with Indian life, Indian manners, ways and habits, their instincts, likes and dislikes and their language. By the time he returned to his father's house, Conrad understood much of the Maque (Mohawk) language. In eight months, with around-the-clock struggle seven days per week and without any time off, Conrad had acquired the equivalent of a college degree in Iroquois culture and language. Conrad was now "prepared to serve as benefactor to two races, for a period of nearly fifty years."[11]

But he did not immediately find his niche as a diplomat. Upon completing his unique introduction to life among the Mohawks under the auspices of Chief Quagnant, Conrad, like the majority of his fellow German immigrants, was employed in agriculture. He lived in a Mohawk village about eight miles south of Schoharie until 1729. Pursuing his path as a self-made man, he continued to study and became a schoolmaster. On the subject of matrimony, Conrad said, "In 1720, while my father was in England, I married my Anna Eve; and was given in marriage by the Reverend John Frederick Haeger, Reformed clergyman, on the 22nd of November, in my father's house, at Schoharie."[12] For many years oral history had it that Conrad Weiser's Anna Eve was most likely a Mohawk Indian maiden. The convincing evidence seemed to be that no surname for her has even been found and that Conrad and Anna Eve's children had bronze-colored skin and straight, raven-colored hair.

Years later, however, the following notes written by German-born Henry Melchior Mühlenberg were found in an old edition of the "Hallische Nachrictem" and seem to solve the mystery of Anna Eve's ethnicity. Mühlenberg, the principal organizer of American Lutheranism, wrote: "Our young interpreter (Conrad Weiser) remained in Schoharie. In 1720 he entered the state of matrimony with a German person of Evangelical parentage and begat two sons and two daughters." Mühlenberg married Conrad and Anna Eve's older daughter, Anna Maria Weiser.[13]

Because of Conrad Weiser's enduring friendship with the Iroquois that began when he lived among the Mohawk for eight grueling months, he became a volunteer interpreter for the Council of Pennsylvania and several Indians. In 1731 the top Indian ambassador of the time, Oneida Chief Shikellamy, who lived in the Native American town of Shamokin, found Conrad in the area of Tulpehocken where he, Anna Eve and their young children had lived for two years. Chief Shikellamy, who spoke Oneida and a little English, persuaded Conrad to accompany him to Philadelphia to meet Pennsylvania Governor Gordon. The governor became acquainted with and approved of Conrad, whose first language was German, second language was Mohawk and third was English. At Shikellamy's request, the provincial treasurer paid Conrad Weiser 40 shillings for his freewill services as interpreter.

In 1732, the year in which George Washington was born, the Iroquois invited Conrad Weiser to act as interpreter for their first official meeting in Philadelphia. The introduction of Conrad at the Philadelphia powwow opened the door for Conrad's work as interpreter-negotiator of Pennsylvania between the Iroquois and English nations.

It happened this way: In August 1732 the Six Nations sent word to the New York governor that they would like to open wider channels of communication between Indians and the American colonists. When the Iroquois suggested employing Shikellamy and Conrad Weiser as negotiators, they gave "the faithful and honest" Conrad a belt of wampum, a leather string threaded with white and violet oblong shell-beads. A string of wampum is not only ornamental but also symbolizes friendship and that the person holding the belt is speaking the truth. Later,

12. The Great Exodus of the Palatines and Conrad Weiser

the governor's council presented Conrad with the sum of £12 (12 pound sterling) "for accompanying ... the Indians ... and for having been extremely useful in framing an initiatory treaty with them."[14]

By the treaty of 1732, Conrad Weiser and Chief Shikellamy were appointed as official negotiators between Pennsylvania and the Six Nations. The Indians called Conrad a "faithful and honest, good and true man who has always spoken their words and our words—not his own."[15] Within three years Conrad Weiser, the mediator, stepped from the shadows of relative obscurity into the limelight of an official and historical character.

Between 1732–1736, not only Pennsylvania but Virginia, Maryland and New York engaged Conrad Weiser in all important negotiations between the provinces and the Six Nations. Conrad arranged many important treaties and prevented many bloody outbreaks.

Conrad's first great mission came in 1737 when he was chosen to relay a message from Governor Gouch of Virginia to mediate and make peace between Virginia, the Six Nations, the Cherokee, the Catawba and others. After careful instruction, Conrad carried the message on a long journey. Leaving Tulpehocken, Pennsylvania, in February he made his way through dangerous wilderness without road or path for 500 miles and successfully negotiated at Onondaga, the Six Nations meeting ground in New York. As will be seen in subsequent chapters, Conrad Weiser would lead a long, productive life in America. He became a successful farmer, businessman and churchman who supplemented his income by knowing Indian ways and serving the Pennsylvania colony and sometimes the colonies of Maryland and Virginia as an interpreter-negotiator between settlers and the Iroquois.[16]

In 1732 "The first German-language newspaper, *Philadelphische Zeitung*, was published in the United States. German publishing flourished in Philadelphia and in smaller communities such as Ephrata, Pennsylvania."[17]

It was John Peter Zenger, a future newspaper publisher, who was one of the most prominent persons connected with the Palatine settlements in New York. In 1710, 13-year-old Zenger, who was born in the city of Rumbach in the Rhineland-Palatinate of western Germany, immigrated to New York City. There he was an indentured servant for eight years as an apprentice to William Bradford, a pioneer printer. The youthful Zenger, who along with 400 other German immigrants had remained in New York City, learned to operate the printing press and developed a feel for editorial work as Bradford's assistant. After serving his indenture, Zenger established his own printing business in 1726. His paper, the *New York Weekly Journal*, founded in 1733, published many scathing attacks on New York's corrupt British Royal Governor William Cosby, who rigged elections and allowed an enemy country to explore New York Harbor. Zenger, as publisher, was held accountable for the truth of the articles and arrested for libel in 1735. At that time libel was defined as any derogatory statement made against a royal government official. When Zenger refused to reveal the names of the authors of the news articles, their identity remained anonymous, and Publisher Zenger was imprisoned for ten months. At trial Zenger's brilliant Philadelphia defense attorney, Andrew Hamilton, a native of Ireland, demanded that the prosecution prove that the articles were false. The defense further argued that the jury was competent to decide the truth of the printed statements in the newspaper. At home, Zenger's wife Anna kept the printing press rolling. Her editorials and reports led to the expulsion of the first jury because its jurors were on Governor Cosby's payroll. Anna's efforts replaced the biased jury with one made up of the publisher's peers. The judge advised the jury to convict Zenger of printing the articles, a charge that he had never denied. In less than ten minutes the colonial jury, despite the judge's instructions, decided that Zenger's accusations were based on fact and returned a verdict of not guilty.[18] "It is important to note that the Zenger case did not establish legal precedent in seditious libel or freedom of the press. Rather, it influenced how people thought about these subjects and led, many decades later, to the protections embodied in the Unites States Constitution, the Bill of Rights and the Sedition Act of 1798."[19]

Catherine Weissenfels, another history-making German immigrant, came as a redemptioner from the Palatinate to New York where she met William Johnson, "an exceptionally capable intercultural diplomat" and a rich man with family political connections to Britain that allowed him to wield great influence on the other side of the Atlantic.[20] During the French and Indian War, the British king conferred a baronetcy and knighthood upon William Johnson for his brilliant diplomacy as superintendent of the Iroquois and other Indian Nations and as commander of an expedition of Mohawk warriors and provincial soldiers from New England and New York.[21] Before he was knighted, Johnson lived in the Mohawk Valley when he first met and fell in love with the 16-year-old indentured Catherine Weissenfels, who was a maid in the household of two Phillips brothers. William Johnson purchased Catherine's contract. She would bear him three children. After he was knighted and when she was on her deathbed, he married her, thus legitimizing their progeny and obtaining for his wife the belated title of Lady Catherine Johnson in the eyes of the Church and of the world. A narrow wedding band bearing the date of their marriage was found buried with Sir William Johnson many years later.[22] Their son, John, was also knighted and received the title of "Sir." Their two daughters married prominent New Yorkers. Widower Sir William Johnson then married the famous Native American Indian, Molly Brant, whose younger brother Joseph Brant became Sir William's protégé and a chief of the Mohawk Nation.

13

Phase III: War of Austrian Succession

King George's War

"The Austrian ruler Maria Theresa (daughter of Charles VI) derived her main foreign support from Britain, which feared that, if the French achieved hegemony in Europe, the British commercial and colonial empire would be untenable. Thus, the War of the Austrian Succession was, in part, one phase of the struggle between France and Britain."[1]

In Phase III of the conflict between France and England, King George's War was waged in America, while its counterpart, the War of Austrian Succession (1740–1748), was ravaging Europe. On one side of the War of Austrian Succession, Maria Theresa's Austria allied with Britain, the United Provinces and Russia. On the other side, Frederick the Great's Prussia allied with France, Bavaria, Spain, Sweden and Saxony. Frederick's Prussian allies sought to exploit the War of Austrian Succession in order to acquire Habsburg possessions for themselves and diminish Austrian power. Britain wanted to prevent France from overrunning the Austrian Netherlands (now Belgium) and also to protect Hanoverian territory since British King George II was the Elector of Hanover.[2] And so, the War of Austrian Succession was a struggle between France and England because England sided with Maria Theresa of Austria, while France sided with Frederick the Great of Prussia.

Nearly all the powers of Europe were involved. Southwest Germany, the Low Countries and Italy were the battlegrounds of France and Austria. The War of Austrian Succession is also known as the First Silesian War. Silesia was located mainly in today's Poland, with smaller parts in the Czech Republic and Germany. It was four centuries earlier, in 1335, that Silesia became a province of the Bohemian Crown (the

Czech Kingdom) and was passed down with that Crown to the Austrian Habsburgs in 1526. Silesia was still controlled by the Austrian Habsburgs when, in 1740, Frederick the Great of Prussia began his attempt to seize the Silesian province from the would-be Holy Roman Empress Maria Theresa. The War of Austrian Succession challenged a female's right to Habsburg lands. Specifically the war contested the right of Maria Theresa to succeed her father Charles VI as Holy Roman Emperor, King of Bohemia, Hungary, Croatia and Serbia and Archduke of Austria.

The title of emperor passed down through several generations of Habsburgs, a German family who once controlled great parts of Europe including Spain and the Spanish Netherlands (Belgium). Through the years, their holdings decreased until, in the 1740s, the only real power of the Habsburg emperor was over Austria, Hungary and Bohemia (Czechoslovakia). Parts of the original Bohemia, Moravia, and Silesia make up today's Czech Republic. At the time of the War of Austrian Succession, Austria had a population of 6,000,000; the Hungarian population was 2,000,000. Owned by nobles and the Church, the land was divided into enormous estates and tilled by serfs who paid hefty revenues which were used to build palaces and monasteries and patronize music, architecture and art. Vienna was the acknowledged center of the Western world in music. Maria Theresa's father, Holy Roman Emperor Charles VI, the King of Austria and the last male Habsburg ruler, loved music only next to his daughter Maria Theresa, who sang the principal operatic role in one of his many lavish and costly performances in Vienna. In 1736, 18-year-old Maria Theresa married Francis Stephen, Duke of Lorraine and later Duke of Tuscany.

In 1740, Austria's Habsburg Emperor Charles VI died without a male heir; he had long had his heart set on having his eldest daughter, Maria Theresa, inherit his throne, including the title Holy Roman Empress. But the ancient Salic law applied to Austria and prohibited the succession of females. Most German kings agreed to abandon the ancient law and accept Charles's pragmatic sanction to allow his daughter to succeed him, but King Frederick II of Prussia did not accept the change. Maria then became archduchess of Austria and queen of Bohemia and Hungary, and her husband became co-ruler and carried the title Emperor. Maria became empress then, not in her own right but because she was the wife of the emperor. Her husband, however, showed neither concern nor capacity for affairs of state, and the full burden of government fell on her. When she inherited the empire, she was four months pregnant with Joseph II, the son who would succeed her. Maria Theresa "had all the charms of womanhood as well as royalty; fine features, brilliant blue eyes, rich blond hair, grace of manners and movement, the zest of health, the animation of youth." Even though her intelligence and her character were superior to these charms, they seemed inadequate to solve the problems that confronted her.[3]

When several Europe nations challenged the plan of her succession, King Frederick II Hohenzollern, Frederick the Great, king of the Prussian province of Germany, plunged all of Europe into the War of Austrian Succession. With his well-trained army, an overflowing treasury and a desire to gain a reputation, Frederick, a brilliant military tactician, would make Prussia the foremost military power in Europe.

Frederick of the Hohenzollern dynasty sought to expand the German states by invading Habsburg territory. He thought that, since Maria Theresa was young, weak and female, now was the time for his highly qualified army to assert the House of Brandenburg's long-standing claim to the Austrian Province of Silesia. Rich in natural resources including coal and salt mines, copper, zinc and lead, silver, kaolin, limestone, chalk, gypsum and marble, Silesia was located mainly in today's Poland, with smaller parts in the Czech Republic and Germany. When Maria refused to recognize Frederick's claims, 30,000 soldiers of Frederick's army crossed the border into Silesia and started the First Silesian War.[4]

At that time German power was in the hands of the princes of the numerous German states including the Kingdom of Prussia, the most powerful German state of all, and whose capital was the city of Berlin. Frederick the Great's Prussian predecessors had seized enough land from Sweden to declare themselves kings. Frederick, who was born in Berlin and whose mother was the sister of British King George II, wanted to reform the German states. As a child, Frederick had been cruelly abused, both emotionally and physically, by his demanding, military father who imprisoned him because he objected to Frederick's relationship with another boy. He forced Frederick to stand at his prison window and witness the beheading of his teenaged friend. When Frederick succeeded his father, however, he abolished the practice of torture and ensured that peasants received equal justice with their landlords. Frederick the Great strengthened the military "to make Prussia the mightiest of all German states, and destroy Austria's imperial power."[5] After he confiscated Silesia and made it a province of Prussia, he then spent most of his life fighting Empress Maria Theresa's relentless attempt to regain her province.

13. Phase III: War of Austrian Succession

The deeply religious Maria Theresa was not weak! Not only was she the mother of 16 children, but she was a formidable opponent for Frederick and a good "mother" for her country. Introducing reform into Austria, she encouraged tolerance and education. She chose the ablest advisors to help her fight Frederick. She even won French sympathy for her cause and sealed the friendship by giving her 14-year-old daughter, Marie Antoinette, in marriage to the future Louis XVI of France. Eventually Prussia's Frederick the Great was surrounded by enemies on all sides—Austria, Sweden, France and Russia.

The War of Austrian Succession (as well as King George's War in America) ceased abruptly with the signing of the Peace Treaty of Aix-La-Chapelle in 1748. Aix-La-Chapelle is French for Aachen, a city in western Germany near the Dutch and Belgian border. Britain and France were the principal powers in negotiating the treaty at the peace conference of Aachen, which ended eight years of fighting. Prussia was not a party to the treaty-making process. Among the treaty's several provisions, Habsburg heiress Maria Theresa was guaranteed the right to Austrian lands. The Habsburgs, however, were weakened by the granting of Silesia to Prussia. By granting Silesia to Frederick the Great, "Both Britain and France were trying to win the friendship of Prussia, now clearly a significant power, for the next [European] war."[6] The history of Silesia, as described above, typifies the ever-changing boundaries of German states. In 1945 Silesia became part of Poland.

King George's War (1740–1748) occurred in Phase III of the struggle between Great Britain and France for mastery of the North American continent. It was the American counterpart to the European War of Austrian Succession. Previously, no major Anglo-French battle had been fought in the New World. King George's War was different because battles between England and France occurred in the New World as well as in Europe, Asia and Africa. In America, during King George's War, England captured Fort Louisbourg on Cape Briton Island. This site was significant since it controlled the mouth of the St. Lawrence River. By screening traffic on the St. Lawrence waterway, England cut off French access to the fur trade coming from Quebec and Montreal. Because France could no longer ship French trade goods to Canada, England then, instead of France, became a major trading partner with American Indians in Ohio Country.

In King George's War the British allied with the Six Nations of the Iroquois Confederacy (also called the People of the Longhouse) who lived in New York between the Hudson and the St. Lawrence rivers and Lake Erie. The Six Nations were made up of the Mohawk, Oneida, Onondaga, Cayuga, Seneca, and Tuscarora. Opposing the British allied Iroquoian-speaking Six Nations, France allied with the Wabanaki (People of the Dawn or People of the East) Confederacy which was a coalition of five Algonquian-speaking tribes of the northeastern seaboard. The Wabanaki tribes were the Abenaki, the Penobscot, the Maliseet, the Passamaquoddy, and the Mi'kmaq. Their ancestral homeland was Acadia, which stretched from Newfoundland, Canada, to the Merrimack River Valley in New Hampshire and Massachusetts. Each of the Wabanaki tribes retained its own political leadership but collaborated with each other on broader issues such as diplomacy, war and trade. During King George's War, the Wabanaki banded together to counteract Iroquois aggression.

When the St. Lawrence River was blocked, English traders gained influence because the French could no longer ship trade goods from across the Atlantic directly to Montreal and Quebec. Not only that, but France also could not exchange steel-edged weapons, firearms and ammunition for pelts and hides with the Native Americans of the Ohio River Valley. Trade between Europeans and Native Americans had begun when fishermen who came ashore along the North Atlantic to dry their fish developed a lucrative enterprise—trading inexpensive knives, axes, pots and woolen cloth for beaver pelts that could be sold in Paris for a good profit. When beaver hats became a fashion necessity in Europe, the fur trade led to the first French settlements in New France at Acadia and then Quebec.

Native Americans in the Ohio Country were under the authority of the Six Nations of the Mohawk Valley in New York. That's why conferences about European trade with Native Americans were usually held in Albany, New York, near the Mohawk Valley. Once the St. Lawrence was blocked, however, Pennsylvania traders as well as Native American groups in the Ohio Valley attempted to bypass the influence of the New York governor as well as the Six Nations. Ohio Valley tribes were represented by two Native American half-kings: one was an Oneida leader known as Scaroudy; the other was a Mingo leader called Tanaghrisson (Tanagrisson). Logstown's head sachem, Half King Tanaghrisson—a Catawba by birth and a Seneca by adoption—was an emissary of the Iroquois Confederacy and was authorized to speak on behalf of the Mingo (western Seneca) and other Ohio Indians. Any agreement he made, however, was not binding until it was ratified by the Onandago, a tribe of the Iroquois (Six Nations) based in the Mohawk Valley of New

York. Iroquois headmen were usually called "king," but because the Ohio Valley hunters and warriors, having lost the long-ago Beaver Wars and therefore had no permanent council fire, Tanaghrisson's authority was limited—his decisions were not binding but subject to approval by the Six Nations, hence his *Half King* title.[7]

A valuable asset to colonial America during King George's War was the German-born negotiator Conrad Weiser, who been uprooted from the Palatinate by the War of Spanish Succession and fled to America where he learned the customs and language of the Iroquois while living with the Mohawks. Though Conrad was constantly busy as interpreter-negotiator between the Pennsylvania Germans, Iroquois and English-speaking people in America, he did not neglect his own home and neighborhood. In 1741 he was commissioned as justice of the peace for Lancaster County, Pennsylvania.

In April 1748 representatives of the colony of Virginia asked Weiser to distribute gifts among the Indians of Ohio Country to try to win them away from the French and over to the British as trading partners. In the same year, he negotiated the Treaty of Lancaster between the Iroquois tribes and the colonial government of Pennsylvania. Weiser was an essential part of the treaty process because, while no major officials in the colonies could understand the language of the Iroquois, he could both understand and speak several Iroquoian dialects. The treaty enabled the colony of Pennsylvania to expand its Indian trade to the Mississippi River.

At first, in April, the Ohio Indians, via the Lancaster Treaty, granted only Pennsylvania the rights to land and trade. At another conference, in July 1748—after Conrad had smoothed the way—an amended Lancaster Treaty gave rights to the Maryland and Virginia colonies as well as to the Pennsylvanians. The July 1748 Lancaster conference also established a "Chain of Friendship between Pennsylvania-Ohio River groups (including 'Twightwee' or Miami), separate from Covenant Chain created between the New York-Six Nations."[8]

In 1749 Weiser was a key player in establishing the borough of Reading, Pennsylvania, and three years later, of Berks County. In Reading, on Penn Square, he established the first general merchandise store in the community. He also participated in forming the first Lutheran congregation in Reading. It was the Trinity Lutheran Church, and Conrad crafted a 13-stanza German hymn for its dedication.

Earlier, Conrad Weiser—who even as a teenager had prayed and praised God—had made a radical change in his religious life. It happened when another important mission opened up in the form of Count Zinzendorf who arrived in America in 1742 to preach to the Indians and establish Moravian communities in Bethlehem, Pennsylvania. Zinzendorf coaxed Conrad to accompany him to Bethlehem to interpret and preach to the Indians. Weiser said, "This is the man whom God hath sent, both to the Indians and the white people, to make known his will to them." Shortly thereafter, Conrad accompanied Zinzendorf to Shamokin where he was "enraptured over the success of the Gospel among the Indians."[9]

Conrad suggested several ways for missionaries to convert Indians to Christianity: to live among them and learn their manners and customs and also to become familiar with Indian tunes and melodies in order to use music to convey the Gospel to them. Conrad Weiser spent three months at Tulpehocken instructing missionaries from Europe in the Mohawk language in order to preach to the Six Nations of the Iroquois.

Ongoing bickering over boundary lines of Acadia (Nova Scotia) and northern New England, plus differences over control of the Ohio Valley, led to continual bloody border raids aided by Indian allies on both sides. Neither mother country supplied adequate military aid for the costly and hopeless struggles. The capture of Louisbourg in Nova Scotia, Canada, on Cape Breton Island in 1745 was the most important victory for New Englanders. To complicate matters, however, the struggle was inconclusive because, although the Treaty of Aix-la-Chapelle ended both the American and European fighting and mutually restored the conquered territory, it failed to settle boundary disputes between France and England over control of the Ohio River Valley. Both nations claimed modern-day Ohio, Pennsylvania, West Virginia, Kentucky, Illinois and Indiana. No wonder that in 1754 war between France and England broke out again. This time it was simply called the French and Indian War in America. Europe called it the Seven Years' War.

14

Phase IV

French and Indian War and Bouquet's Royal Corps

> Brethren, the governor of Virginia and the Governor of Canada are both quarreling about lands which belong to us
> —Mohawk Chief Hendrick, during the French and Indian War

The fourth and final phase of the 75-year intercolonial strife between England and France was known in America as the French and Indian War (1754–1763). It was during this war that Americans began calling themselves "Americans" rather than "Colonists."[1] This conflict was crucially important to American history because it played a major role in precipitating the American Revolution. Although Benjamin Franklin's "Join or Die" political cartoon published in the Pennsylvania Gazette on May 9, 1754, tried to persuade the colonies to unify in order to strengthen their fight against the French, the colonies remained divided. Franklin and others had submitted a plan for the colonies to unite—"Join or Die"—for their own defense, but the British government opposed—even feared—the idea of united colonies. Later Franklin opined that if the colonies had been allowed to unite according to his Albany plan, then the colonies would have been strong enough to defend themselves against France and "there would then have been no need of troops from England; of course the subsequent pretence for taxing America and the bloody contest it occasioned, would have been avoided."[2]

In the end Britain reasoned that her disunited British colonies in America failed to do their part in winning the war. Consequently, to recover the cost, the British imposed taxes on the colonies by declaring the Stamp Act in 1763. The subsequent riots and protests over taxation without parliamentary representation, as well as resentment of the

British Monarchy, began the chain of events that would soon lead to American independence.[3]

Unlike the first three phases of the 75 years of conflict that started in Europe, Phase IV—the French and Indian War (1754–1763)—began in America. When the nine-year-long war spread worldwide, it became known in Europe as the Seven Years' War (1756–1763) or the Great War for Empire pitting Great Britain against France not only in eastern North America and the West Indies but also in Central Europe, on the Mediterranean Sea, and on the Indian subcontinent.

The disagreement preceding the French and Indian War centered on a territorial dispute regarding the Upper Ohio Valley. British claims were based partly on the 1744 Lancaster Treaty mediated by German-born Conrad Weiser, official translator for the colony of Pennsylvania. At Lancaster the Six Nations of the Iroquois Confederacy released to English commissioners of Maryland, Pennsylvania, and Virginia "all right and title to the land west of the Alleghany Mountains, even to the Mississippi, which land—according to tradition—had been conquered by their forefathers"[4] who long ago had won the Beaver Wars against Ohio Country Indians and other Indian groups.

The French and Indian War involved at least four competitors vying for dominance of the North American continent: One was New France, a Catholic empire which depended on trading muskets and ammunition for furs and pelts with their Indian alliances. New France arched westward from the Gulf of St. Lawrence to the Great Lakes, the Mississippi River and then southward to the Gulf of Mexico.

Another competitor was the British colonies, a Protestant empire based on farming settlements and transatlantic commerce and confined to the North American area east of the Appalachian Mountains. The British needed Ohio Country for colonial expansion.

A third competitor was the Iroquois League who, for more than a century during and after the Beaver Wars, had fought to exercise dominion over other native peoples.[5] The Iroquois tribes struggled to maintain and expand their territory and serve as middlemen between other Native American tribes and the French in order to corner the fur trade in the area.

A fourth faction was composed of 3,000 Ohio Country Indians who called Ohio Country their homeland. Tribes of Wyandot, Maumee, Shawnee, Miami, Mingo, Delaware, Ottawa and Chippewa—living near the site of present-day Pittsburg—sought independence from Iroquois dominance. *Ohio Country* meant the territory of North America in the

Upper Ohio Valley, north of the Ohio River, south of Lake Erie, and west of the Appalachians. It encompassed the present-day state of Ohio, northwestern West Virginia, western Pennsylvania and eastern Indiana.

A fifth dynamic, the Cherokee and other powerful tribes of the South, chose sides and played decisive roles later in the war. During the French and Indian War the Indian population of northeast America was about 175,000. The British colonists numbered 1 million and there were 70,000 settlers throughout New France.

The war began when the British attempted to foil the French plan to construct a chain of forts from Quebec to Louisiana and thus eliminate westward expansion of Britain's American colonies. Virginia Governor Dinwiddie received explicit instructions from London signed by King George II himself: If the French were found building forts on English soil, they should be asked to depart peacefully. Otherwise, they were to be forced off at gunpoint. On October 31, 1753, Dinwiddie commissioned Major George Washington, the 21-year-old proprietor of Mount Vernon, to deliver the ultimatum to Fort Le Boeuf, a French fort located in the disputed territory just south of Lake Erie. It was this explosive letter bearing the affixed seal of the Colony of Virginia that ignited the French and Indian War.[6]

Washington volunteered his services as special envoy and, though inexperienced, was chosen to negotiate with the French. His journal entry reports that he left Williamsburg the same day and rode to Fredericksburg. Stashing the king's instructions into his saddlebag, he rode alongside packhorses and seven men who were hired to do the heave-ho grunt work of hauling weapons, provisions, baggage, and tents. The next day Washington employed Jacob Van Braam, who had served as a soldier in the Dutch and British armies and as a translator of French.[7] Though born in the Netherlands, Van Braam had acquired a superficial knowledge of the English and French language and would serve Washington frequently in the capacity of interpreter.[8]

Washington's mission was to gather intelligence from the Six Nations of the Iroquois and coax them to provide an escort to Fort Le Boeuf. In the Iroquois council house it was decided that Half King, two other old chiefs, and a young warrior would join Washington's party. Washington's party rode to the French fort at Venango and ate dinner with the French fort commander. Except for Half King, the Indians met with the Delawares. Half King met with the French. Then the entire group, accompanied by four French soldiers, rode toward the next French fort.

After six days riding through rain and heavy snow, Washington and his Indian chief and warrior escort arrived at Fort Le Boeuf. Washington showed the message to the elderly, very professional French commander. After waiting for the commander of the next fort to join them, Washington showed them the letter and asked for a reply, which he received in writing.

Having accomplished his mission, Washington arrived at Williamsburg on January 16, 1754, dismounted and handed Virginia Governor Dinwiddie the French reply to the governor's ultimatum. The French defiantly refused to withdraw from Ohio territory and vowed to destroy every Virginia settlement they found there.

Washington gave Dinwiddie more specifics. The disturbing news was that the French surreptitiously disclosed "their absolute design to take possession of the Ohio" and revealed military secrets about building forts at strategic points along the Ohio.[9] Washington's report was published in London. For his efforts the 22-year-old Washington was promoted to Lieutenant Colonel.[10]

The British established a private land company, the Ohio Company, and insisted that the area be kept open for trade. The French, who believed that the British were trying to claim territory, immediately countered by building a string of forts along the Ohio River and attempting to oust any British colonist already settled in the Ohio River Valley.

Virginia Governor Dinwiddie ordered Lt. Colonel Washington to lead a force of 200 militiamen into the Ohio Valley to complete the construction of a British fort already under construction there. Meanwhile, the French had already claimed and completed construction of the British fort and renamed it Fort Duquesne. Not deterred, Washington built Fort Cumberland, a supply storage house and base of operation for the Ohio Company, located at the mouth of Wills Creek, a tributary of the Potomac River. And then Washington marched on to the Great Meadows located about 18 miles east of present-day Uniontown, Pennsylvania, which is 46 miles southeast of Pittsburg.

While Washington's detachment camped at Great Meadows, Christopher Gist (Geist) approached on horseback to sound the alert that the French were nearby. Gist, a frontiersman and surveyor of German (and not British)[11] ancestry, was the first non-Native American explorer of Ohio Company. Silverheels, Half King's fleet-footed messenger, brought the same alarming news. Warned of the impending attack, Washington plunged into the pitch-dark night and followed Silverheels to Half

14. Phase IV

King's camp. Arriving by morning's light, Washington, with 40 men and Half King's handful of warriors, attacked the French camp, which had posted no sentries. Washington's militiamen and Half King's warriors struck, firing a volley at the sleeping fort. It was peacetime; war had not been declared. But the Mingo Indians and Washington's 40 Virginians slaughtered many French soldiers, including the camp's commander, Ensign Joseph Coulon de Villiers Sieur de Jumonville. Half King's warriors scalped the dead.[12]

After the surprise attack, the slaughter, Washington mounted and rode back to Great Meadows with his prisoners. Soon afterward, when the position opened, Washington was promoted to colonel and assumed full command of the Virginia regiment.[13]

Anticipating French reprisal, Washington constructed a small, circular, palisaded fort beside a couple of shallow ditches flanked by earthwork berms tall enough to protect kneeling riflemen. He named his stronghold Fort Necessity.[14]

On June 2, 1754, Washington was joined by Half King, who brought 100 warriors plus their wives and children. The next week the remainder of the Virginia regiment arrived, bringing Washington's total to 293 officers and men. Feeding his growing army posed a major challenge, especially when a company of regular British troops joined them from South Carolina.[15]

Washington and Half King rode to intermediary Christopher Gist's plantation for a three-day meeting with Ohio delegates of the Six Nations. Half King had tried to persuade the Iroquois to ally with the English, but the French had the upper hand. The Iroquois (Six Nations) Council at Onondaga told their Ohio brothers that the Iroquois had decided to stay neutral.[16] Washington and Half King returned to Great Meadows.

The French captain who was building Fort Duquesne at the Forks of the Ohio (now Pittsburgh) prepared to counter Virginia's forays into Ohio Country. This captain organized a retaliatory expedition led by Francois Coulon de Villiers, the older brother of the slain Jumonville. The French, bent on revenge, outnumbered the English two to one. Advancing in three columns across Great Meadows toward Fort Necessity, the French paused, fired a volley, and advanced again. Washington's men avoided the frontal assault by taking cover in shallow trenches surrounding the fortress. The French stormed the fort on July 3, 1754. After nine hours of battle fought in heavy rain, Washington surrendered Fort Necessity.[17] De Villiers called a cease-fire. The Dutch interpreter Van

Braam accepted an invitation to enter the French camp and negotiate terms of surrender, which Washington and Mackay signed. The French raised the fleur-de-lis over the fort as Washington and his men withdrew, still retaining their baggage and weapons, except their nine swivel guns. The French burned the fort and returned to Fort Duquesne.

The Battle of the Great Meadows (Fort Necessity) was the first battle of the French and Indian War. For Washington it was his first defeat and the "only time he ever surrendered to an enemy."[18] The Ohio Valley was left in the possession of the French. Stunned by the French victory and disgraced in the eyes of the Delaware, Shawnee, and Iroquois, Half King returned to his village where he died a few weeks later. Meanwhile, the western tribes began switching their loyalties to the French.[19]

All England was astir with news of Washington's defeat in a minor skirmish known as the Battle of the Great Meadows. All-out war began the next year with Braddock's campaign.[20]

British Major General Edward Braddock served as commander in chief of all the British and Colonial military units in North America.[21] In April 1755, two months after his arrival, Braddock divulged his campaign strategy to the royal governors. Braddock's objective was unequivocal: Drive the French from Ohio Country, seize Fort Niagara, capture Crown Point, destroy Fort Beauséjour and occupy Fort Duquesne.

Colonel William Johnson, the recently appointed general superintendent of Indian affairs for the whole of British North America, was assigned the mission of providing Iroquois warriors to protect Braddock's army. He needed to insure the safety of British troops proceeding toward Lake Champlain through the wild to the northern border, which swarmed with the French and their Algonquin allies. Johnson was also to assemble a provincial army and attack Crown Point, New York.

Oneida Chief Scarouady (Monacatoocha), Half King's successor, arrived on the scene with a party of warriors, their wives, and children. The normally desolate area now swarmed with nearly 3,000 redcoats, colonials and Indians. Braddock prohibited giving rum to the warriors and forbade the warriors from "selling" their women to the soldiers, a custom that usually brought Indian husbands plenty of money.[22]

The arrogant Braddock alienated almost all his Indian allies. He refused to recognize any rights of Indians to Ohio Country. He considered them completely subject to Crown rule. Shingas, the leader of Ohio Valley Delawares and second only to Half King, left immediately to join the French. "He looked upon us as dogs," said Scarouady.[23] One night around a campfire Scarouady's band, bodies painted red and black, performed an ancient ritual: drums beating, wild dancing, tomahawks raised, and knives flashing in the firelight. Later, however, when the march got under way, the Indians, at first numbering about 50, had dwindled to a half dozen plus the sullen Scarouady and his son.

"About the middle of June ... the two Regiments from Ireland, some independent companies and the provincial troops ... began to move from Fort Cumberland"[24] toward Fort Duquesne. General Braddock had badly underestimated the threat posed by the enemy's Indian allies. He and his men were unprepared for Indian-style warfare. His army marched in a typically organized English manner. Leading the way were 300 axmen cutting trees, building bridges and clearing a 12 foot road for supply wagons and the heavy artillery. The line of march extended four miles.[25] Benjamin Franklin persuaded Pennsylvania Quaker farmers to provide Braddock with 150 wagons and 259 packhorses.[26]

Marching *rum-tum-tum* to the beat of a British drum through the great tangle of woods, the scarlet columns of Braddock's platoons and their few remaining Indian allies approached Fort Duquesne at the Forks of the Ohio River where the Allegheny and Monongahela rivers converge. The tall miter caps of the grenadiers were conspicuous targets for the French and their Indian allies—waiting and watching and poised to attack.[27] The British forded the Monongahela River, unaware that they were surrounded.

Major General Braddock's army marched to within ten miles of Fort Duquesne but then were attacked and routed. Braddock was wounded on July 9, 1755, in the Battle of Monongahela and soon died, wrote George Washington in a letter to his mother:

> We were attacked by a party of French and Indians, whose number ... did not exceed three hundred men; while ours consisted of about one thousand three hundred well-armed troops, chiefly regular soldiers, who were struck with such a panic that they behaved with more cowardice than it is possible to conceive. The officers behaved gallantly, in order to encourage their men, for which they suffered greatly, there being near sixty killed and wounded; a large proportion of the number we had.
>
> The Virginia troops showed a good deal of bravery, and were nearly all killed; for I believe, out of three companies that were there, scarcely thirty men are left alive.... In short, the dastardly behavior of those they call regulars exposed all others, that were inclined to do their duty, to almost certain death; and, at last, in despite of all the efforts of the officers to the contrary, they ran, as sheep pursued by dogs, and it was impossible to rally them.
>
> The General was wounded, of which he died three days after.... I luckily escaped without a wound, though I had four bullets through my coat, and two horses shot under me.... I am, honored Madam, your most dutiful son.[28]

In the July 9, 1755, Battle of the Monongahela Braddock's defeat was total. The spoils of war lay on the battlefield alongside scalped bodies of British soldiers. In addition to cannons and gunpowder there was easily enough booty to arm France's allies, the Indians.[29] Estimates vary. One postulates that Braddock's force of 1,500 British and American troops were routed by an enemy force of 500 Indians (Ottawa, Miami, Huron, Delaware Shawnee and Mingo) and 30 French colonial troops.[30]

The Cherokee might have shortened the French and Indian War, but they refused to send warriors to assist Braddock, who treated them as inferiors, not allies. Braddock's defeat "brought over all Indians of the Northwest to the French side, caused the Six Nations to waver in their long-standing allegiance to the British, threw back the effective English frontier hundreds of miles and exposed new settlements to a series of devastating Indian attacks." Thousands of settlers in the Shenandoah Valley of Virginia lost all they had and were lucky to escape with their lives.[31]

After Braddock's defeat, Ohio Indians began to raid settlements on the western borders of Pennsylvania and Virginia. Fear stalked the frontier. The pioneers who lived along the Wilderness Road in Virginia's Holston Valley had been doing fairly well, but after Braddock's defeat, Shawnee Indians ravaged settlements and drove hoards of frightened settlers east, out of the Great Appalachian Valley, and kept them out for several years. Despite these battles, Britain, however, did not officially declare war on France until mid–May 1756. Less than a month later, in early June 1756, France declared war on Britain. Tension between France and Britain for domination of Europe was not new. This time, however, the struggle was not about claims to thrones or who would control Europe. It was about who would rule the other continents of the world. The French and Indian War merged into a global war when the German expansionist-reformist Frederick the Great of Prussia "launched military operations against the Austrian Empire."[32]

The direction of both the Seven Years' War in Europe and the nine-year-long French and Indian War in America changed dramatically in 1758. That's because George II appointed William Pitt the Elder as Britain's secretary of state and prime minister. Relishing the new appointee, Frederick the Great declared "England has long been in labour, but at last she has brought forth a man."[33] Pitt recalled Lord Loudoun who spent most of his energies in "getting ready to begin" and replaced him with the stolid Jeffery Amherst as commander in chief of military forces in America. The Great War Minister, Pitt, chose able men to carry out his grand strategy: He would subsidize Britain's ally, Frederick the Great, to fight the French in Europe, but "send no more English troops to the European continent." Pitt's principal objective was to oust the French, occupy Canada and open up the American West—Ohio Country—for colonial expansion.[34]

Pitt's "lean, tall, commanding figure, combined with a Roman beaky nose and hawklike eyes ... overwhelmed all onlookers.... He looked everywhere and saw everything."[35] In late 1757 he employed his theatrical demeanor and organ-like voice in his effort to end the worldwide war, which then extended from India in the East to America in the West. He believed that holding "North America was critical for England's global domination."[36] He called his *system ... a grab bag of strategies*" for waging war against France.[37] Because the French army and its powerful allies could not be defeated on the continent, Pitt chose America—where the French and Indian War was already underway—as his battleground. His strategy was to reduce France's power on the continent by taking away her colonies around the world.[38]

With his aggressive personality, his passion for reading Cicero, the "golden-tongued orator," and having the confidence of his countrymen, William Pitt invigorated the lethargic spirit of England. He made The Union Jack "supreme in every ocean."[39]

Pitt replaced many incompetent generals and admirals "with younger men upon whom he could rely.... By taking the initiative in every quarter of the globe Britain prevented the French from concentrating their forces, confused their plan of campaign, and forced them to dissipate their strength."

Turning his attention to the American war, Pitt studied maps and sent dispatches to governors and generals, "but supervision at a distance of three thousand miles was almost impossible in the days of sail."[40] The voyage to America took at least two and sometimes four months in either direction.

When the war between France and England broke out in 1754 and involved two continents, Parliament resolved to raise a German-speaking regiment or corps named Royal Americans. The proposed corps would consist of four battalions containing 1,000 men each. "It was proposed to fill the ranks of this regiment by enlisting Protestant German and Swiss settlers in Pennsylvania and Maryland, who for the most part were unable to speak or understand the English language."[41]

The history of the French and Indian War is largely identical with the history of early German settlers in Pennsylvania, said historian

Henry Melchior Mühlenberg Richards, who married the German-born interpreter Conrad Weiser's daughter. "They [Germans] did not do all the fighting but they did most of it." They alone treated the American Indian with unfailing justice. But they did far more than that. Like the Palatines Conrad Weiser of Pennsylvania and Count Zinzendorf, "Where others met him [the Native American] with a musket in one hand and a bottle of rum in the other they [German-Americans] took the Bible."[42]

A contemporaneous historian, Henry Smollett, in speaking of these German and Swiss settlers, wrote: "As they were all zealous Protestants and in general strong, hardy men accustomed to the climate, it was judged that a regiment of good and faithful soldiers might be raised out of them, particularly proper to oppose the French; but to this end it was necessary to appoint some officers, especially subalterns, who understood military discipline and could speak the German language; and as a sufficient number of such could not be found among the English officers it was necessary to bring over and grant commissions to several German and Swiss officers and engineers. But as this step ... could not be taken without the authority of Parliament, an act was now passed for enabling his majesty to grant commissions to a certain number of foreign Protestants who had served abroad as officers or engineers to act and rank as officers or engineers in America only."

Henry Bouquet, who was a Swiss mercenary, and his good friend Frederick Haldimand from a relatively poor German family were appointed lieutenant colonels of the new, unique regiment of four battalions, the 62nd Foot (Royal American Regiment of Corps) soon to be renamed the 60th. These two leaders, Bouquet and Haldimand, then selected subordinate officers, especially for the artillery and engineer departments of the newly formed 60th. The Act or Parliament specified that 50 of these officers might be foreign Protestants while the enlisted men were to be raised from the American colonies, largely from German and Swiss settlers in Pennsylvania.[43]

When Bouquet sailed to America in the summer of 1756, the year after English General Braddock's disastrous defeat, military matters in America were lethargic until William Pitt took the helm with a firm grip and changed the direction of the war. Pitt arranged for New Jersey, New York and New England to aid the Northern campaigns against the French. Pennsylvania and the Southern colonies were to join the conquest of the West and finish the work that Braddock had so miserably failed to do three years prior. In 1758 Pitt stipulated that England would provide arms, ammunition and tents to aid the colonies in financing the war. Delighted with aid from England, Pennsylvania, furnished 2,700 troops for the expedition against Fort Duquesne.[44]

General John Forbes, a Scots officer in the British Army, commanded the Fort Duquesne campaign. The Swiss mercenary, Lieutenant Colonel Henry Bouquet, was Forbes's second in command. Bouquet brought regular forces—four companies of his 60th Royal American Regiment—from South Carolina to take charge of the First Division. George Washington commanded the Second Division of 2,600 Virginia troops.

Many of the men in Bouquet's Royal American Regiment were recruited among the Germans living in Pennsylvania. Montgomery's Scottish Highlanders marched alongside Bouquet's Germans of the Royal Regiment. Bouquet, wishing to avoid the pitfalls that had triggered Braddock's defeat, was a keen observer of the woods and Indian ways in warfare. Every day Bouquet exercised his men among the trees and underbrush of the wilderness according to his own innovative technique and trained them to engage in combat with the Indians by combining knowledge of the frontiersman with that of a trained soldier. Several years later at Quebec City, General James Wolfe would use the motto "Swift and Bold" to describe the courageous and disciplined action of the 2nd and 3rd battalions of the 60th Royal Regiment. There it was demonstrated that the "plan to train frontiersmen to fight in the Indian manner of skirmish and ambush, and to supplement them with experienced foreign officers had molded the regiment into soldiers capable of combining the qualities of a scout with the discipline of a trained soldier."[45]

While General Forbes remained behind, contracting supplies and organizing his army, his second in command, Colonel Bouquet, pushed his troops forward toward Fort Duquesne, which was located at the Forks of the Ohio (now Pittsburg, Pennsylvania) and was held by the French. Along the way, Bouquet decided that instead of traveling Braddock's old road, which was filled with loose and sharp stones, Forbes's army should cut a new path. Even though the new trail would zigzag over the mountain, it would be shorter by many miles than the old road. George Washington, who had worked hard building Braddock's Road and now commanded Virginia and Maryland forces under Forbes, objected. But Forbes agreed with Bouquet, whose Royal American Regiment and Pennsylvanians then began constructing Forbes Road and its supporting forts to guard supplies and troops traveling the road. Later, both Braddock Road and Forbes Road would provide a path for farmers to reach Ohio Country and for migrants to settle near military posts along the way.[46]

By November 25, 1758, Bouquet had held conferences with the Delaware Indians and soon calmed the frontier borders between the pioneer settlers and Indians. Four thousand settlers who had fled following Braddock's defeat now returned home while Bouquet with Royal Americans composed largely of recruits from the German and Swiss settlers from Pennsylvania and Maryland garrisoned the forts and posts from Philadelphia via Carlisle, Bedford, Fort Pitt, Lake Erie and Sandusky to Detroit. These Royal Americans held the outposts of civilization in the midst of sometimes savage men for seven years while Pennsylvania German farmers secured the route between posts.

As part of Pitt's overall plan, a British naval and land expedition of a predominately colonial force captured Fort Frontenac, a French trading post on Lake Ontario in Canada at the origin of the St. Lawrence River. The collapse of the Frontenac warehouse and distribution point cut off communications between French colonists in Montreal and Quebec. French fortresses in the Mississippi and Ohio valleys lost their source of supplies.[47] Fort Duquesne was now doomed to fall not only because its routes for supplies and reinforcements were blocked but also because the ongoing Easton conferences with Delaware tribes were ending the French alliance with Ohio Indians. Encouraged, the Forbes Expedition resumed its victorious march toward the Forks of the Ohio.

The Treaty of Paris (also called the Peace of Paris) was signed in Paris on February 10, 1763, by representatives of Great Britain, France and Spain. Portugal explicitly agreed with these proceedings. The treaty officially ended both the nine-year-long French and Indian War in America and the Seven Years' War in Europe. At the peace conference, France conceded territories to the British. The newly gained region opened the way for American westward expansion into the Mississippi Valley.

Ships passenger lists from 1727 to 1776 supported the idea that European wars were a major cause of German immigration to America. During the War of Austrian Succession (1740–1748), only a few emigrants were able to escape their war-ravaged homeland and sail to American colonies, which were also involved in an ongoing, intermittent Anglo-French conflict. Following the signing of the Treaty of Aix-la-Chapelle which ended both Europe's War of Austrian Succession and its corollary, King George's War in America, German immigrants crowded the ships sailing to America. In almost all cases since 1727 the lists contained the name of the ship, the shipmaster and the names of ports from which the ships sailed. From the years 1727 to 1741 the passengers were labeled "Palatine," except in 1740 one ship's list was labeled "Palatines and Switzers." From 1742 to 1748 the passengers were called "Foreigners." But in 1749 the lists became more detailed and specified "Foreigners" from several places including Wirtemberg (Wirtemberg is also spelled Württemberg), Alsace, Zweibrücken, Nassau, Hanau, Darmstadt, Eisenberg, Swabia, Mannheim, Durlach, Rittenheim and more. From 1740 to 1753 passengers were categorized according to their religion: Calvinists, Mennonites, Catholics, etc. During the Seven Years' War in Europe, there was almost no immigration from 1756 to 1763.

The immediate outcome of the French and Indian War and its corollary, the Seven Years' War, was a crushing British victory that made Great Britain the world's leading colonial power. In a capsule the Seven Years' War, which Sir Winston Churchill called the First World War, was a major conflict in which "France, Austria, Saxony, Sweden, and Russia were aligned on one side against Prussia, Hanover, and Great Britain on the other. The war arose out of the attempt of the Austrian Habsburgs to win back the rich province of Silesia, which had been wrested from them by Frederick II (the Great) of Prussia during the War of the Austrian Succession (1740–1748). But the Seven Years' War also involved overseas colonial struggles between Great Britain and France."[48] The war involved every European great power of the time except the Ottoman Empire, spanned five continents and affected not only Europe and the Americas but also West Africa, India, and the Philippines.

In the mercantile age of the Seven Years' War, the "most successful mercantilistic powers," Britain and France, pushed each other to the brink of worldwide war. In North America, the French built a chain of forts from Quebec to Louisiana to thwart the spread of British colonies.[49] Royal Americans—German and Swiss soldiers—held the outposts of civilization bordering Ohio Country for seven years while Pennsylvania German farmers secured the route between posts.

Not only that, but the two countries, Britain and France, constantly bickered over the disputed Sugar Islands as well as the West African slave trade. In India, friction between the British and the French East India tea companies created an explosive situation. England's failure to curb the French Navy and her subsequent loss of Minorca intensified the ferocity between the two powers.

In 1758 William Pitt became England's secretary of state as well as her prime minister. Pitt changed the direction of the war by focusing Britain's objective on defeating France by winning the American West and conquering Canada.[50] Under Prime Minister Pitt, England's decisive victory over France in both North America and India led to a peace agreement. The Treaty of Paris 1763, signed by Britain, France, Spain and Portugal, left France and Spain looking for revenge. The opportunity for France to get even by tipping the scales of power in the opposite direction would come when France aided America in the War of Independence against Great Britain.

15

Pontiac's War, Bouquet's Regiment and the Delaware Indians

"Whole Indian Nations have melted away like snowballs in the sun before the white man's advance. They leave scarcely a name of our people.... Where are the Delawares? They have been reduced to a mere shadow of their former greatness."
—Dragging Canoe 1775 oration at Sycamore Shoals

In 1763 the Treaty of Paris ended the French and Indian War: France then ceded all French lands in North America to the English. When their French support departed colonial America, the French-allied Indians feared that British settlers would swarm into the Great Lakes region and settle Ohio Country which the Native Americans claimed as their homeland and hunting ground. Ottawa Chief Pontiac formed a coalition of Indian tribes to counter the anticipated onslaught of settlers into Indian homeland. But before looking at Pontiac's War, it is helpful to know the story of Lenape Chief Teedyuscung's effort to protect his people, the Eastern Delawares, from being pushed out of Pennsylvania into Ohio Country. Lenape was a tribe of the Eastern Delaware Indians. Teedyuscung's story blends with Pontiac's War and Chief Pontiac's struggle against Colonel Henry Bouquet, commander of Fort Pitt, and his 60th Royal American Regiment, which was made up mostly of Germans, Swiss and German-American frontiersmen.

British General Edward Braddock's 1755 defeat, in one of the first battles of the French and Indian War, had emboldened the Ohio Country Indians—the Shawnee, Mingo and Western Delaware tribes to attack settlers along the Pennsylvania and Maryland frontiers. They killed 1,500 farmers, took 1,000 prisoners and terrorized hundreds of thousands of pioneers. By 1758 the western counties of Pennsylvania,

Maryland and Virginia had lost half of their population. Many captive children were adopted. Some women captives married warriors and became "white Indians." Grown men who were considered dangerous were slain. Younger male prisoners had cash value. Most were bought by the French to work as farm laborers and artisans.[1]

Teedyuscung's Eastern Delawares who had been pushed out of Pennsylvania's Delaware Valley (today's Philadelphia area) were now confined to the Wyoming area of Pennsylvania's Susquehanna Valley. Traders fled Pennsylvania, leaving the Eastern Delawares without a market for their furs and without much-needed supplies. To make matters worse, crops on the banks of the Susquehanna failed. When the governor of the province refused to provide the Delaware with trade goods and guns for hunting, Eastern Delaware Chief Teedyuscung could not prevent his young braves from taking up the hatchet, ransacking frontier villages and capturing hostages in the same way that their French-allied Indian kinsmen, the Western Delawares, in Ohio Country were doing. Seeking food and safety Teedyuscung led his warriors and their prisoners to Iroquoia in the Mohawk Valley of New York. Sir William Johnson, British superintendent of Indian affairs in the North, urged the Six Iroquois Nations to tell Teedyuscung to stop raiding the frontier. At that point, Teedyuscung could see a potential benefit in negotiating for peace between Pennsylvania colonists and Ohio Country Delawares. If the Eastern Delaware Chief Teedyuscung could put an end to the frontier plundering by the Eastern Delawares as well as that of Ohio Valley Western Delawares, he might then persuade Pennsylvania Governor William Denny to set aside a permanent sanctuary for the Delaware Nation in Pennsylvania.

Teedyuscung found support for his plan among Quakers of the anti-proprietary Friendly Association. The Anti-Proprietary Party was one of the two main political parties in Pennsylvania at the time. Its counterpart, the Proprietary Party, was similar to England's Tory Party, while the Anti-Proprietary Party was more like the Whig Party. Though William Penn himself was a Quaker, his sons headed the Proprietary Party. "The Proprietary Party believed in the prerogatives of the king, the nobility, and other leaders of society, as well as the necessity of hierarchy in society. Its members were generally men of wealth who believed that their rank and class (popular concepts that Benjamin Franklin scorned) set them apart from the lower sort."[2] As a populist, Franklin agreed with the common people. Although Quakers agreed that some degree of social hierarchy was necessary, both they and Franklin were more egalitarian. The Quaker's Friendly Association was formed in 1756 to regain and preserve peace with the Indians. Quakers objected to legislative appropriation of money for military use as well as to the mercenary policies of the Penn family. Benjamin Franklin, although a non–Quaker, was one of the leaders of the Anti-Proprietary forces of the Friendly Association that continued to challenge the non-taxpaying Penn family's control of the province. Franklin had told the Pennsylvania Assembly that he was at odds with the hereditary governor "respecting the exemption of his estate from taxation."[3] The Penn family raised troops, built forts and encouraged frontier folk to set fire to Indian villages. They also offered bounty for Indian prisoners and Indian scalps.

The non-sanctioned Easton Agreement of 1757[4] materialized when the Friendly Association worked through a refugee Oneida Half King who contacted Chief Teedyuscung and urged him to meet with Governor Denny at Easton, 50 miles north of Philadelphia. Denny wanted peace, but he did not want to alienate the Penn family, who had appointed him governor. Denny worked with the Friendly Association to finance gifts for the meeting with Teedyuscung in return for the chief's promise to bring Ohio Delawares to a peace conference the next year at Easton. The 1757 Easton conference was a great success. In the treaty Teedyuscung promised peace between Eastern Delawares and Pennsylvania. He also agreed to continue negotiating for peace with the Ohio Delawares and to encourage them to ally with the British Colony of Pennsylvania against the French. Governor Denny, in return, pledged to subsidize the Eastern Delawares (to be underwritten by the Friendly Association) and to create a refuge for the Delawares in Pennsylvania's Wyoming Valley.

While planning his assault on Fort Duquesne, General Forbes realized that one reason for Braddock's defeat was his lack of Indian allies. Forbes also knew that any diplomatic move involving the Ohio tribes must be mediated by Sir William Johnson, the sole officer of the Crown who was authorized to conduct Indian affairs in the North. Forbes knew that Johnson had deep ties with the Iroquois. He was also aware that the 1757 Easton Treaty between Governor Denny and Chief Teedyuscung was of dubious legitimacy because Johnson and the Iroquois had not participated in its negotiation. Thus Forbes cultivated the friendship of both Teedyuscung and Denny. When Teedyuscung invited Pisquetomen, an eminent Western Delaware chief, to come to the Wyoming Valley for peace talks, Forbes pressed Denny to negotiate directly with the chiefs with, or without, Johnson. He assured the governor that making peace with the Ohio Indians was his highest priority. Forbes then circumvented Johnson's objection by appealing to the newly appointed Commander in Chief of British forces Major General James Abercromby, who was both Forbes's and Johnson's superior. After some hesitation, Denny sent a Delaware-speaking Moravian preacher with Pisquetomen to Ohio Country with an invitation to negotiate directly with Pennsylvanians to make peace at the conference at Easton in October 1758. Meanwhile, Col. Henry Bouquet, Forbes's commander in the field and his regiment of Germans and Swiss, continued cutting the Forbes Road to the French-controlled Fort Duquesne at the Forks of the Ohio River.

The Iroquois, as usual, claimed that the Wyoming Valley and Ohio Country (much of which would soon become the Northwest Territory) were theirs by virtue of conquest and that other tribes lived there only

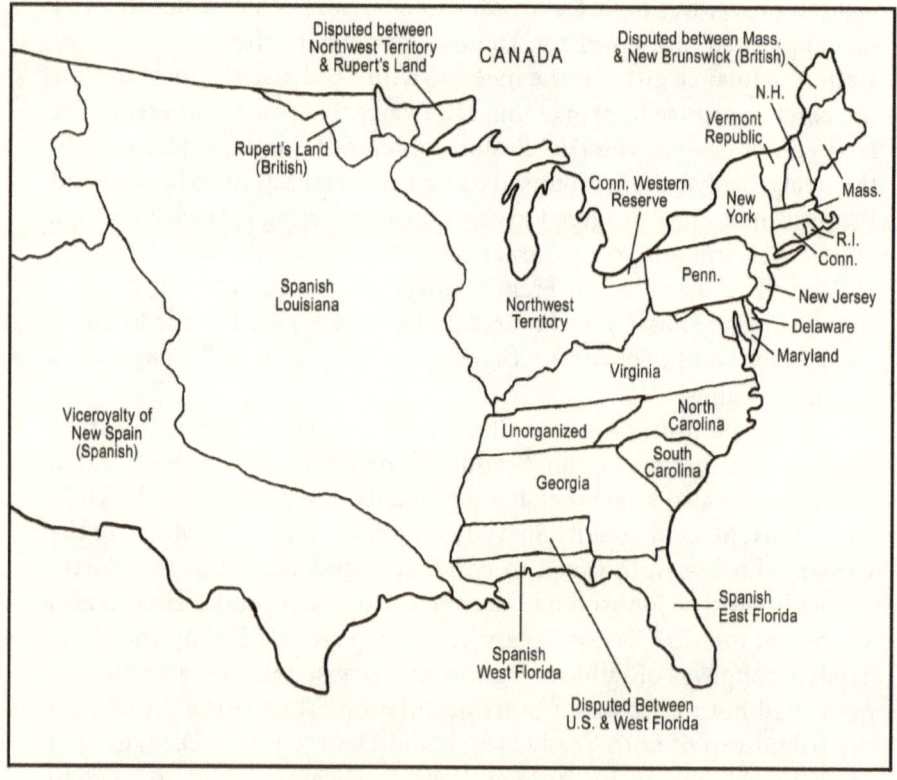

States and Territories of the future United States of America, 1760 CE, showing the Northwest Territory which incorporated most of the former Ohio Country.

with their approval. Thus, the Iroquois were furious with Teedyuscung's insistence that he was the king of the Delawares and an independent spokesperson for them.

More than 500 Natives from 13 Indian Nations attended the 1758 Treaty Conference at Easton, Pennsylvania. Among them were Teedyuscung's Eastern Delawares, Pisquetomen's Ohio (Western) Delawares, Shawnees and representatives from other Ohio tribes as well as the Six (Iroquois) Nations. White participants were Governor Denny of Pennsylvania and the governor of New Jersey, who co-sponsored the conference. George Croghan, who was Sir William Johnson's chief deputy of Northern Indian Affairs, was there and so were members of the Friendly Association. All were pursuing different interests, and all agreed to make peace with the British colonies.[5]

The Western Delaware Chief Pisquetomen pledged that the chiefs would sever their alliance with the French and that English captives would be released. In return Governor Denny—on behalf of the Penn family—agreed that the province would henceforth deal directly with the Ohio Delawares and no longer recognize the authority of the Iroquois over them. Denny also promised that in the future white farmers would be forbidden to settle on lands west of the Alleghenies and that a trading post would be opened at the Forks of the Ohio. Because the Ohio Delaware Chief Pisquetomen was dealing directly with Denny and the Pennsylvanians, Teedyuscung was no longer needed. Pisquetomen had undercut Teedyuscung's bargaining power. With Chief Teedyuscung's clout diminished, the Six Nations reasserted their dominance over the eastern chief's people in the Wyoming Valley of Delaware. The Iroquois, however, could not regain power over the Ohio Indians because Governor Denny had agreed to deal directly with Pisquetomen as the Ohio Indian spokesman.

When go-betweens brought news of the Easton Treaty to Indian towns of the Ohio River Valley, the French realized they could no longer depend on Indian support. This news coupled with the fall of Fort Frontenac, which had cut off their source of supplies, persuaded the French to abandon Fort Duquesne.

While Forbes's army was constructing Fort Ligonier, Bouquet—on his own authority—planned a coup de main hoping to quickly end the campaign. He sent Major James Grant with a detachment of 800 to reconnoiter Fort Duquesne. Francois-Marie Le Marchand de Lignery, a master of guerrilla warfare who had commanded Duquesne ever since Braddock's defeat, had been harassing Forbes's road and fort builders with his hit-and-run tactics. He knew, of course, that Grant was advancing toward the Forks. On September 14, 1758, Lignery's French and Indian forces surrounded Grant's 800. A third of Grant's troops were killed, wounded or taken prisoner. Grant himself was captured and transported to Canada.

But on November 7 when the cheering news of the Easton Treaty reached General Forbes whose army was constructing Fort Ligonier, the general wrote letters to the Ohio chiefs, embracing them as friends. Forbes was even happier to hear that Canada's major supply center, Fort Frontenac, a French trading post at the headwaters of the St. Lawrence River, had fallen to the British and that the main body of French troops, now lacking access to crucial supplies, had pulled out of Fort Duquesne. Encouraged because only a reduced force of 300 shoeless, half-naked troops now garrisoned Fort Duquesne, Forbes hurriedly left Fort Ligonier and resumed his march to the Forks. In November as the Forbes Expedition neared the fort, they heard a huge explosion. The French had detonated 60 barrels of power under the fort. The only remaining artifact from Fort Duquesne is a cannonball bearing a fleur-de-lis emblem.[6]

Although Pitt had planned successful military expeditions to win the war against France, he also incurred enormous debt. When the terminally ill Forbes wrote to Pitt from the site of Fort Duquesne, he reported that he had named the place in Pitt's honor. It is the first reference to the site as *Pittsburgh*. By the time Pitt received the letter several months later, Forbes was already buried in Philadelphia. A permanent fort was soon built. By late 1759 Fort Pitt became one of the largest English strongholds in North America. But it violated the 1758 Treaty of Easton, which had promised to build a trading post but to eliminate military forts on Indian lands. This fort was obviously larger than a trading post. Delaware Chief Pisquetomen asked what "ye general meant by coming here with a great army." It was becoming clear that the British seldom honored treaties made with Native Americans.[7]

Whereas most frontier fortresses were built of logs, Fort Pitt was made of brick. After two years, the huge fort covered 18 acres and was surrounded by a moat and a drawbridge. Its redbrick walls enclosed a bowling green, a deer park, King's Garden, and vegetable garden. All that remain today are a bricked area and the moat.[8]

The Forbes Road, "with way stations not more than a day's travel apart,"[9] created a direct route for Pennsylvanians to travel from Philadelphia to the Ohio Valley. Today, between Harrisburg and Pittsburgh,

15. Pontiac's War, Bouquet's Regiment and the Delaware Indians 143

there are many Forbes Road historical markers that trace the footprints of General John Forbes's army.

American colonies celebrated the Treaty of Paris, which declared peace between France and England. After 75 years of war, the treaty finally settled the question of boundaries in North America between the English and the French. However, when the French withdrew from the western frontier, the Indians lost their trading partners. The French had treated Native Americans with respect as equals. The English, on the other hand, simply wanted to take their land.

Ottawa Chief Pontiac's War[10] began in April 1763, at about the same time that Teedyuscung—the watchdog of the Wyoming Valley of Pennsylvania's Susquehanna River—was burned to death when his cabin was set on fire. It was speculated that the unidentified arsonist murdered him and then torched his house. He was drunk on rum provided by the Mingo (Western Seneca). After Teedyuscung's demise, the Susquehanna Company—a land-speculating syndicate hoping to develop the Wyoming Valley of Pennsylvania—competed with the Delawares, the Iroquois and the Penn family for control of the area. New Englanders soon began flocking into the now-unguarded Wyoming Valley. They brought livestock, built houses, planted crops and constructed forts. In October Captain Bull, Teedyuscung's son, led a war party of Delawares to avenge his father's death. They killed ten of the Yankee intruders, captured the rest and drove them upriver to a Lenape-Delaware village in northern Pennsylvania.

At about the same time that assassins lit fire to Teedyuscung's cabin, Northwestern Indians recognized their peril.[11] Consequently, Ottawa Chief Pontiac (Obwandiyag) formed an alliance of Northwestern Indian Nations to defend their lands.

In the council of April 27, 1763, held a few miles south of Detroit, Pontiac—the charismatic sachem of the Algonquin Nation's Ottawa Tribe (his father was an Ottawa, his mother a Chippewa)—urged Ohio Country tribes to rise up against the settlers. Rallying Ottawa, Delaware, Shawnee, Muncee, Wyandot, Seneca, Potawatomi and Ojibwa tribes to the cause, Pontiac's coalition went on the warpath. In an attempt to push the colonists back east across the Appalachians, he began targeting and reclaiming western outposts that the French had surrendered to the English.[12]

The fighting ignited by Ottawa Chief Pontiac quickly spread from northern Michigan to the Ohio Valley and from the Susquehanna to the Mississippi rivers.

Pontiac's outrages against colonists and British forts were encouraged by Neolin, an Indian religious prophet who preached a change in lifestyle to his followers, urging them to give up liquor and trading for ammunition with the British and to return to making their traditional weapons, the bow and arrow for the hunt and for defense.

On May 7, 1763, Pontiac's Ottawa, Potawatomi and Huron nations unsuccessfully attacked British garrisons at Fort Detroit. Joined by the Chippewa, Pontiac's band laid siege to Fort Detroit on May 9. Although they captured relief convoys and killed and imprisoned British soldiers, Pontiac's followers could not penetrate the fort itself. However, surrounding forts in Michigan, Indiana and Pennsylvania did fall.

In June Pontiac's supporters staged a game of lacrosse as a ruse to gain entrance to Fort Michilimackinac in what is now Mackinaw City, Michigan. As the English soldiers gathered to watch the game, the players grabbed their tomahawks and stormed the unguarded citadel. Its occupants were slaughtered and the fort laid to ashes. The strong Indian resistance astonished the government and the colonists.

In July Pontiac extended his blockade of Fort Detroit and won a brilliant victory at the Battle of Bloody Run.[13] Pontiac's victory happened when a relief convoy led by Amherst's aide-de-camp, Captain James Dalyell, reached Fort Detroit in July 1763. Dalyell, who was the conceited son of a baronet, brought very few provisions but a gluttonous desire for glory. His convoy included a variety of companies he had picked up along the way from the 55th, 60th (Royal American Corps containing many Germans and Swiss) and 80th regiments. Three days later, against the advice of his superior officer, Dalyell led a sortie of 247 men out of Fort Detroit to attack the Indians in Pontiac's camp. Dalyell had clout because of his family connections and closeness to Commander in Chief of British Army Forces, Jeffery Amherst. Within an hour Dalyell led his men directly into Pontiac's ambush at a creek now called Bloody Run. Several British troops were wounded or died. A hundred were captured. Shot dead in battle, Dalyell's heart was cut out and his head impaled on a pole at Pontiac's camp.

Fort Pitt—a gateway to western expansion—was also under siege but did not fall, although Pontiac wiped out many other forts. Wielding tomahawks, scalping knives and fire, Pontiac destroyed all but three British posts in the West and massacred more than a thousand settlers on the Pennsylvania, Maryland, Virginia frontiers. Pontiac's War was one of the most successful Indian wars ever fought against Europeans.[14] Thousands of Pennsylvania and Virginia pioneers fled Pontiac's fury, and many migrated South to populate the frontiers of Carolina and Georgia.

Amherst proposed to solve "the problem of the interior" by spreading smallpox among the Indians. When Delaware warriors approached Fort Pitt and demanded its surrender, its commander, following the orders of Amherst, invited them to a conference. He then handed the unsuspecting Indians an infected handkerchief and two blankets oozing with scabs and pus from the fort's smallpox-ridden hospital.[15] Amherst's evil germ warfare did not succeed. He remained clueless concerning the effects of curtailing the policy of providing presents, guns and food to the Natives and blamed their uprising on the French.

Every fort west of Detroit had fallen to the Indians by the first of July 1763. By the end of July, Pontiac's besieging force grew to 900 warriors from a half dozen Indian Nations.[16] Only the great forts that functioned as central distribution posts—Fort Niagara, Fort Pitt and Fort Detroit—withstood the sieges. Fort Pitt awaited the relief column of Colonel Bouquet. Meanwhile, the Native Americans waited in vain for the hoped-for return of the French who treated them as equals in trade and did not establish settlements on Indian hunting grounds.

By mid–July, Colonel Henry Bouquet had assembled his regiment of 460 troops for the relief of Fort Pit. His troops came from the German-American and other provincials and the German and Swiss mercenaries of the Royal American 60th and from Scottish Highlanders of the 42nd and 77th regiments, plus a unit of rangers. In addition to provisions, Bouquet needed to assemble cattle, horses, wagons and teamsters. Provincials were recruited to replace troops that dropped out and to garrison forts along Forbes Road. To his dismay, he proceeded slowly because he needed to drop off redcoats, food and ammunition to reinforce forts along the way. Upon reaching Fort Ligonier, he had fewer than 400 men to march the 40 miles to Fort Pitt. Twenty-five miles from Fort Pitt on August 4, 1763, while moving through the rolling hills and forests near Bushy Run Creek, the exhausted and extremely thirsty soldiers of the relief column, anticipating a drink of cool water from the creek, ran instead into a trap. Abruptly struggling for their lives, they were fighting off Shawnees, Delawares, Mingos, Wyandots, Ottawas and Miamis. Bouquet's troops surrounded their packhorses and cattle and tried desperately to defend against the Indians and survive the intense heat and their almost unbearable thirst. Forced by darkness to halt the fighting, Bouquet developed a plan overnight during the cease-fire. According to Bouquet's plan, when the battle resumed the next morning, two of his companies of light infantry faked retreat. When the Indians took the bait, broke from cover and advanced, two companies of Bouquet's men fired a volley and charged with bayonets. Two more companies advanced from the perimeter. Outmaneuvered and disorganized, the Indian warriors fled into the woods. Bouquet's men rushed to Bushy Run for water. Afterward the Indians lifted the siege of Fort Pitt, not because they lost the encounter at Bushy Run but because they needed to prepare for the winter's hunt. It was a costly victory for Bouquet. The Indians had nearly exterminated him.

Losing one-fourth of his men but winning the August 5–6, 1763, Battle of Bushy Run, Bouquet went on to break the siege of Fort Pitt. He thus restored the line of communication between the Ohio Country frontier and eastern settlements.[17]

Frontier historian Francis Parkman called the narrowly won, two-day engagement at Bushy Run "one of the best contested actions ever fought between white men and Indians." The British victory led to the eventual defeat of Native Americans' unified attempt at resistance to colonization. Failing to protect their homes and their hunting grounds from colonial expansion, "the Indians never recovered their status as strong independent nations and were constrained to accept a peripheral role in the new America."[18]

A brief recapitulation of Henry Bouquet's military service reflects that he was a professional Swiss officer and a competent and professional military leader. He served from 1756 to 1765 in the British Army in the Royal American (60th) Regiment, also known as the King's Royal Rifle Corp, which became one of the most renowned corps of the British Army.[19] The regiment was recruited in Germany and from German colonists in North America. Bouquet participated in three major campaigns in North America. In addition to serving as second in command to Brigadier General John Forbes in securing the French Fort Duquesne (Fort Pitt) during the French and Indian War, and winning accolades in the 1763 Battle of Bushy Run in Pontiac's Rebellion, Bouquet led another expedition in 1764 in Pontiac's War against the Delaware and Shawnee Indians in the Muskingum River Valley in Ohio and ended the Indian uprising without having to fight.[20] His success in the Ohio expedition enabled westward expansion of British settlements. Promoted to the rank of brigadier general, Bouquet was assigned command of the Southern District of North America headquartered at Pensacola, Florida. There, he caught yellow fever and died in September 1765.

By July1763—before the Battle of Bushy Run—Native Americans

had driven out most of the settlers from the land of the western waters. Colonel William Preston (land developer Patton's adopted son) of Southwest Virginia wrote, "All the valleys of Roanoke River and along the waters of the Mississippi are depopulated, except"[21] for a few families who hold out in five or six fortresses along the New River. The little stronghold that Preston had built sheltered 87 people, 20 of them armed, on guard against Indian attack that they knew would surely come.

Pontiac's depredations forced the British to rethink their policies for dealing with Native Americans. Previously the British recognized no Indian rights to lands west of the Blue Ridge. In response to Pontiac's War, they concocted the Royal Proclamation of 1763. News traveling across the ocean by ship between England and America, however, required weeks or even months to reach the other side.

The French and Indian War had nearly bankrupted the British government. In order to make peace with both northern and southern Native Americans and prevent another war as costly as the French and Indian War, Britain's Parliament in October 1763 enacted the Proclamation of 1763. One section of the proclamation forbade English settlements west of the Blue Ridge unless these settlements were on lands negotiated by the king's agents and Native Americans. The proclamation virtually closed the frontier to colonial expansion. Therefore, colonists were prohibited from settling in parts of the Great Appalachian Valley and Ohio Country.

The Proclamation Line of 1763 corresponded roughly to the summit of the eastern chain of the Appalachian Mountains from Massachusetts to Georgia, delineating the 13 colonies from Indian territory. This imaginary line also roughly corresponded to the Eastern Continental Divide. Specifically, the proclamation forbade white settlements "beyond the sources of rivers that flow into the Atlantic."[22] For the first time Britain, by way of the proclamation, recognized the American Indian claim to the western waters—that is, all those lands drained by rivers flowing west, such as the New and the Holston, toward the Gulf of Mexico. In addition to mollifying the Indians, Parliament expected the proclamation to benefit Britain in another way: to confine American settlements to the east, keeping colonists and their tax money under the watchful eye of the Crown rather than having pioneers moving west across the mountain, out from under British control.

Bounty lands were offered as an incentive or reward to men who performed military service during the French and Indian War. The acreage granted depended on the serviceman's rank and was subject to conditions of cultivation and improvement. Field officers were awarded 5,000 acres each; captains received 3,000; staff officers 2,000; noncommissioned officers 200; and privates 50 acres. However, the area in which the land was available was closed by the Proclamation of 1763, so it was not until 1779 and after that the bounty was actually awarded.[23]

The King's Royal Proclamation further provided protection for American Indians. Reserved for Indian use were all the lands lying west of the Proclamation Line. The purchase, settlement or possession of any property within the reserved land by private persons was strictly forbidden. Any land that the Indians wished to sell was to be purchased in the name of the king and mediated by the colonial governor or another government agent.[24]

By blocking the frontier from colonial settlement, the King sought to soothe the fear of the Indians and avert another costly war. Colonists, however, who had fought the French and Indian War in order to expand their colonies into Ohio Country—the land between the Appalachians Mountains and the Mississippi River—ignored the new rule.

Even George Washington considered the law as a mere ploy to appease the Indians. He believed that the road to American prosperity lay in developing western lands. He viewed the proclamation as shortsighted and unworkable. He urged veterans from the French and Indian War to encourage Virginia's Governor Botetourt to honor his commitment to award chunks of western lands to veterans. "Not only did Washington exploit his position to pin down prime real estate for himself, but he bought up rights surreptitiously from needy veterans to enlarge his holdings."[25]

Washington's desire to acquire land and slaves was shared by most Virginia planters. He petitioned Virginia's Governor Dunmore (1771-1776) for 5,000 acres of Ohio Country as provided under the section of the Proclamation of 1763 that rewarded French and Indian War veterans.[26] Upon learning that the British had ruled that the land grants promised to French and Indian War veterans by the proclamation would be limited to British regulars, Washington remarked: "I conceive the service of a Provincial officer as worthy of reward as regulars and can only be withheld from him with injustice."[27] The militia veterans had no intention of relinquishing their entitlements. Totally ignoring the Proclamation of 1763, settlers as well as longhunters continued to cross over the line.

The proclamation fueled American discontent. Its significance in angering colonists was on par with "taxation without representation" in planting seeds for the upcoming American Revolution.[28] Acting as if the king had not rescinded their patent, Dr. Thomas Walker of the Loyal Land Company continued to survey and sell the company's 800,000 acres as if the proclamation did not exist. (See endnote for elaboration.)[29] Meanwhile, Pontiac's War continued.

By 1764 Bouquet's 1,500 regular soldiers of the Royal American Regiment and colonial militiamen had moved into Ohio Country and put an end to Pontiac's War. Trade with the Indians resumed. Chief Pontiac finally made peace in 1766. After Pontiac surrendered, real estate broker Dr. Walker advertised throughout the region that all settlers who had been driven off land they had bought from his Loyal Land Company should return to that land, reclaim it and resettle it, or else he would resell it.

Since British Commander in Chief Amherst would not agree to restore the practice of gift giving to the Indians, Sir William Johnson worked with the British Board of Trade to have him recalled. By dispensing with Amherst, Johnson was able to persuade the Six Nations of the Iroquois to ally with the British and thereby weaken Pontiac's position. The Six Nations then could once again claim dominion over the Indians of Ohio Valley, and Pontiac's power would be broken. Once home, Amherst was not hailed as the conqueror of Canada but blamed for Pontiac's Rebellion.

Pontiac's influence dwindled after leaders of the western tribes turned on him. In 1769 he was assassinated—clubbed and stabbed in the back—by a Peoria Indian. This happened at the French trading center in Cahokia, the oldest European settlement in Illinois[30] and onetime centerpiece of the ancient Mississippian culture.

16

Germans and Scots-Irish Migrate to Virginia

Hite vs. Fairfax

In 1717 Quaker and German-speaking merchants of Penn's Colony first noticed the surge of immigrant ships that began crowding into the Delaware River. These first ships heralded a mass migration of families numbering more than 250,000 emigrants from North Britain pouring into the city of Philadelphia over the next half-century. Like their social diversity, the religion of these newcomers from Northern Britain was varied. Those from Scotland and Northern Ireland were mostly Presbyterian with only a few Roman Catholics. The English were mostly Anglican with a sprinkling of other Protestant sects.[1]

As streams of Scots-Irish (or Scotch-Irish as most Americans say[2]) immigrants continued to flow to the American colonies in the 18th century, some settled in New Hampshire. Some went to New York, but most traveled beyond the German communities of eastern Pennsylvania and settled on mountain ridges or in the valleys of the Appalachians.[3]

By 1775 Germans composed one-third of the Pennsylvania population; the Scots-Irish composed roughly one-quarter. "French Huguenot and Jewish settlers, together with Dutch, Swedes, and other groups, contributed in smaller numbers to the development of colonial Pennsylvania."[4] Around the time of the American Revolution one-fifth of white Virginians were German speaking. At that time one-seventh of America's colonial population were Scots-Irish.

To reiterate briefly, the story of Germans in Virginia began in the early 1600s on the eastern shore in Jamestown and in adjacent Tidewater sections of Virginia. The Virginia Company of London recruited a handful of skilled workman, German glassmakers and three German carpenters, to build houses in Jamestown and settle in the new colony.

But, like most of the early Jamestown newcomers, they died. The cause of death is unknown. Next, German sawmill workers willingly immigrated from Hamburg to the Virginia Tidewater, but they didn't make it either. The sawmill wrights had to move upstream into dangerous and unfriendly Indian lands to find swiftly moving water to turn their waterwheels and power their saws. All but one sawmiller died, and the lone survivor sailed back to England.

The first German settlers arrived inland in the Shenandoah Valley of the Blue Ridge Mountains (part of the Appalachian chain) of Virginia in 1714. At that time 42 iron ore miners from the northwestern Siegen region of Germany settled in the Rappahannock River Basin of Central Virginia (present-day Orange County). Next, in 1717, Governor Alexander Spotswood bought 100 indentured servants from Baden-Württemberg and put them to work in Spotsylvania County of Northern Virginia. In 1721 a smaller third group of relatives of earlier German immigrants settled in Culpeper County in Northern Virginia. By the 1740s German architecture, log cabins and two-story "bank" barns dotted the landscape of the northern Shenandoah Valley. Bank barns were built on a slope or hill so that both floors were at ground level. By 1780, 28 percent of the white population living between Strasburg in Shenandoah County and Harrisonburg in Rockingham County were Germans.

When the German Jost Hite was granted many thousands of acres in the Shenandoah Valley, he sold most of his land to other Germans in 100- to 500-acre farm plots. For a while the Germans and Scots-Irish immigrants moving south from Pennsylvania shared the northern part of the Shenandoah Valley. The Germans preferred to cluster together around church, community and family. On the other hand, although the Scots-Irish were clannish and family oriented, they moved frequently. They soon moved farther west along the Great Valley Road and became the Indian fighting pioneers of the New World frontier, which was so similar to the border country between Scotland and England, the Old World they had left. The Scots-Irish did not intermarry with the English or the Irish Catholic for at least two generations. Likewise, the Germans, although they acculturated readily, married other Germans.

In Virginia, the British Lord Thomas Fairfax and the German settler Baron Joist (Jost) Hite commenced an argument that resulted in a lawsuit. The dispute happened after the English Civil War, when Charles II became king of the restored English monarchy in 1660 and granted over 5 million acres of Virginia land to seven loyal subjects who had supported him in exile. The grant, known as the Northern Neck Proprietary (or land grant) encompassed Virginia's portion of what is now known as the Delmarva Peninsula in addition to all the land between the Rappahannock and Potomac rivers, the Chesapeake Bay and a great portion of the Shenandoah Valley. Lord Thomas Culpeper, who was the son of one of the loyal seven, began to acquire the entire Northern Neck Proprietary. At Culpeper's death, his daughter, Lady Catherine Fairfax, inherited the proprietary and bequeathed it to her son Thomas Fairfax.

Fairfax visited Virginia in the 1730s to inspect, clear and cultivate his immense hereditary estate of more than 5 million acres (more exactly 5,282,000 acres). When he relocated to America in the 1740s, he became the only member of the British peerage (nobility) to reside in colonial America. Fairfax himself served as county lieutenant and justice of the peace of his proprietary. When pudgy, middle-aged Fairfax found his domain dotted with homesteads, he hired agents and built a land office. He then began demanding quitrent, saying—in essence—this is my property and you must pay a land tax or I will deed the property you're living on to someone else. Most settlers, squatters and speculators paid the rent.

Among those who objected to the Fairfax quitrent demand was Baron Jost Hite, a German native of Strasbourg who had embarked for America in his own vessel in 1709.[5] Jost Hite partnered with two Dutchmen, Isaac and John Van Meter who had moved from the Hudson in 1730 and obtained a 40,000-acre patent from Virginia's royal governor on condition that they would settle 200 German families on the ceded land. Hite and Van Meter canvassed German settlers in the North and enticed them to move South to Virginia. In 1732 Hite moved his family and 16 other families from Pennsylvania to a location just south of present-day Winchester. There Hite, an honest, taciturn, and wise executive, founded the first white settlement west of the Blue Ridge.[6]

"This settlement of Hite's may be considered as the entering wedge which started the great movement of the Germans from Pennsylvania into Maryland and Virginia."[7] Pleased with the movement of settlers into Maryland, Lord Charles Baltimore further encouraged settlers to move into his province. His extremely liberal offer of land with no rent to be paid for three years and afterward to limit the rent to one cent per acre per year attracted many immigrants.

Hite's stone house in the Shenandoah Valley of Virginia stood on the Indian Trading Path that became the Great Wagon Road of Virginia. Refusing to pay the quitrent to Lord Fairfax, who disputed Hite's ownership of the land, the willful, old German sued Fairfax in a court battle which would go on for decades and wouldn't be settled until long after both litigants were dead.[8]

Fairfax employed 16-year-old George Washington to survey his holdings west of the Blue Ridge. Washington's diary, "A Journal of My Journey Over the Mountains," includes the following entry regarding Baron Hite and tells how the court case ended:

> Jost Hite (d. 1760) was born in Strasbourg, Alsace and emigrated to America about 1710, settling first in the vicinity of Kingston, N.Y. About 1716 he moved to Pennsylvania and in 1731 purchased a tract of nearly 40,000 acres from John and Isaac Van Meter in what soon became Frederick County, Va. In 1732 he moved to his Virginia lands with 16 other families of settlers. He was a member of the first Frederick Parish vestry. Hite was one of the leading land speculators and developers in Frederick, eventually settling families on a tract amounting to 94,000 acres. His land purchases involved him in a dispute with Lord Fairfax over ownership of his grants. The case continued in the courts for 50 years and was settled in Hite's favor in 1786, 26 years after his death. Frederick Town is now Winchester, Va.[9]

German men who spoke American Indian languages were often entrusted with important and hazardous missions to negotiate and conclude treaties with Native Americans. Two kinds of treaties were negotiated between the English colonies and the Indians of North America. One was a treaty of amity—friendship between nations—the other concerned ownership of land and its transfer.[10]

The chiefs of the Six Nations of Iroquois esteemed Conrad Weiser as a trusted friend who spoke their language. In 1748 Sir William Gooch, lieutenant governor of Virginia, commissioned Weiser to negotiate the armistice Treaty of Logstown. Weiser also negotiated a defensive alliance with the Cherokee and Catawba. Six years later, at the beginning of the French and Indian War, Weiser negotiated between deputies of seven colonies and chiefs of the Six Nations to form an alliance between the English and the Six Nations against the French.

In 1751 another distinguished German, Christopher Gist (Geist, Guest), of Frederick, Virginia, was appointed agent of the Ohio Company. Two years later, when Major George Washington was assigned the dangerous mission by Virginia Governor Robert Dinwiddie to deliver a protest to the French commander on the Upper Ohio, demanding French withdrawal from the Ohio Valley, Washington chose Christopher Gist to be one of his companions.

When hostilities between Virginians and the French began, the surrounding German settlements on the frontier suffered greatly from assaults by the Indian allies of the French.

Much credit for achieving the 1763 Treaty in which the French gave up all of their American Territory, including the Upper Ohio region, was attributed to the Prussian-born Moravian Missionary Christian Friedrich Post. Having learned Indian languages and customs and married an Indian woman, Post—standing on the battlefield within firing range of a French cannon in full sight of Fort Duquesne—persuaded the Indian warriors surrounding him to break with the French.

Another German, Captain Adam Stephan, a medical doctor at Shepherdstown, Virginia, from 1747 until 1754 organized German volunteers near Harper's Ferry and led them to fight along with Washington at the Battle of the Great Meadows, Fort Necessity and at General Braddock's disastrous defeat. Stephan later was given command of Fort Cumberland. German Ensign Carl Gustav Splitdorf and Lieutenant Edmund Wagner also fought with Washington and were killed in battle at Great Meadows. Colonel Wilhelm Drake, who immigrated as a child from Germany, served in Braddock's campaign and later became a colonel.[11]

German immigrants were widespread in all directions in the Virginia colony. George Washington held German colonists in high esteem. Having received 10,000 acres of the Ohio Valley for his service in the French and Indian War, Washington purchased additional large tracts of land on the Kanawha and Greenbrier rivers. He hoped to settle his estates with Germans. He envisioned financing German transportation from Holland to his estates, providing the immigrants with food and exempting them from rent for four years until their crops became profitable. But these dreams would be interrupted by the American Revolutionary War.

17

Germans in Colonial Maryland, the Carolinas and Georgia

Certainly not all early German immigrants settled in New York and Pennsylvania and spread to Virginia's Shenandoah Valley. German societies also sprang up in Baltimore, Maryland; Charleston, South Carolina; New Bern, North Carolina; and Savannah, Georgia.

Maryland welcomed not only Germans but all religious sects. The plan for the colony of Maryland, which was known for its nondiscriminatory policy, originated in 1632 when England's Catholic King Charles I granted a royal charter to George Calvert, the 1st Baron Baltimore (or 1st Lord Baltimore), to establish a colony as a refuge for Catholics. Maryland was named for the king's wife, Queen Henrietta Maria. After George Calvert died, his son Cecil Calvert, the 2nd Lord Baltimore, implemented his father's plan and founded the Province of Maryland in 1634. Calvert's Maryland colony not only tolerated all religious sects but welcomed all denominations as equals.

The Calvert proprietary governors of Maryland managed their colony well. And yet, because it accomplished George Calvert's dream of making Maryland a haven not only for Catholics but for all Christians, Calvert's colony soon attracted an unhappy mix of Puritan, Catholic and Anglican factions.[1] England's Glorious Revolution of 1689, which ousted England's Catholic King James II, ended Maryland's religious freedom. Though the Catholic Calvert family continued to govern Maryland competently, James II's successors, the Protestants William and Mary, took the colony from them. In an attempt to have the colony restored, Benedict Calvert, the 4th Lord Baltimore, renounced Catholicism and joined the Church of England in 1713. George I soon returned Maryland to the Calvert family, who now were Protestants, loyal to the Church of England.[2]

In 1710 when the Maryland House of Delegates noticed that several

Palatines were coming into their province as settlers, the delegates "desirous to encourage those poor people in their industry ... resolved that those Palatines with their Servants shall be free from paying any publick, County, or Parish Levy or Charge."[3] But this action failed to entice many Germans to move to Maryland.

It was not until the latter part of the 1700s that the larger migration occurred and Germans moved in great numbers to Maryland. The cause was the indifference of the Pennsylvania Quakers to the safety of the Germans on the frontier. Quakers opposed war of any kind. But the Palatines provided a barrier against hostile Indians. A long list of petitioners, including land speculator-developer Jost Hite, from the borderlands of the wilderness frontier made known their need for arms and ammunition to protect their women and children. The petition was presented to authorities and the governor of Pennsylvania. All the people in power ignored the request. That is when the Germans living on the Pennsylvania frontier realized that the Quakers of Pennsylvania were unconcerned about the attacks of the Indians and the safety of inhabitants of the frontier, who provided a buffer between the colonists and Native Americans. The peace-loving, nonviolent Quakers simply would not provide arms and ammunition to protect German settlers from Indian attack. Hence many Germans moved to other colonies.

In 1732 immigrant Carl Wistar wrote a letter from Philadelphia warning his fellow Germans of the hazardous voyage and subsequent hardships they could expect if they survived the difficult exit from the Fatherland and the subsequent immigration to America. His letter noted that several years before, Pennsylvania was a fruitful, sparsely inhabited country where German emigrants were cordially welcomed since the wilderness required intensive labor. Hardworking emigrants could easily earn enough to buy land. But now, since thousands of Germans as well as the English and Irish had settled in Pennsylvania, that part of the country was crowded, and all who sought land had to go far into the wilderness where the purchase price was higher.

Wistar emphasized that the voyage from Germany to America was perilous. The previous year one ship of 150 passengers was tossed around for six months and more than 100 starved to death. The survivors ate rats and mice. The cost of a mouse was high. Those who reached land were required to pay the entire fare for both the living and the dead. The story of death at sea and sickness upon arrival happened repeatedly, vessel after vessel. The letter continues:

"Every person over fourteen years old, must pay six doubloons

17. Germans in Colonial Maryland, the Carolinas and Georgia 157

(about 90 dollars) passage from Rotterdam, and those between four and fourteen must pay half that amount. When one is without the money, his only resource is to sell himself for a term from three to eight years or more, and to serve as a slave. Nothing but a poor suit of clothes is received when his time has expired. Families endure a great trial when they see the father purchased by one master, the mother by another, and each of the children by another. All this for the money only that they owe the Captain. And yet they are only too glad, when after waiting long, they at last find someone willing to buy them; for the money of the country is well nigh exhausted."[4]

Maryland grew slowly. The first settlers plowed and planted a narrow strip along the Chesapeake Bay in the Tidewater area from which the shipping of their cash crop, tobacco, was relatively easy. Tobacco was cultivated instead of corn and other food crops because tobacco was the only medium of exchange. All debts were paid by tobacco. In 1733, about a century after its founding, Maryland's taxable inhabitants, including all males above the age of 15, was only 32,470. About this time German settlers began to migrate into Maryland from Pennsylvania. By 1756 Maryland's population had grown to 130,000, and most of these newcomers were Pennsylvania Germans. In 1760 southeastern Pennsylvania and western Maryland were home to 50,000 Germans, the largest ethnic group in these areas. By 1790 the Maryland backcountry counties of Frederick, Washington, and Allegheny contained 86 percent of all Maryland Germans. "Germans made up 50 percent of the white population and 44 percent of the total population in those counties."[5]

A Pennsylvania German (Dutchman) named Cornelius Comegys (Commegys) was one of the first of the German settlers in Maryland. At that time there was little if any distinction between the terms *Dutch* and *German*. In fact, the term *German* was rarely used, and the designation "Dutchman" was indiscriminately applied to all members of the Teutonic race. After first arriving in Pennsylvania, Comegys had resettled and lived in the Delaware Colony and then moved to Maryland around 1661. He was naturalized on July 22 of that year. Very little is known about Comegys except that he received a patent for 150 acres in Cecil County, Maryland, in 1666 and another patent for 350 acres of land in 1669. Ten years later, when two Labadists visited Maryland, they found that Comegys owned a large farm. His first wife, Wilhemintye, had died, and his new wife was an English woman. His son was then in the process of purchasing a nearby farm.[6]

The most distinguished German who lived in Maryland around

that time was Augustine Herman (Heermans), a surveyor and skilled mapmaker. Born at Prague, Bohemia, Herman entered the service of the Dutch West India Company (WIC) and came to New Amsterdam, where he attained prominence and married a relative of the colony's director, Peter Stuyvesant. In 1660, Herman received a grant of 4,000 acres of land to be selected wherever he liked. He chose his tract on the Elk River. Early in the following year, having bought the land from the Indians, he settled and named his land Bohemia Manor. Herman immediately went to work drawing a map, which was completed in 1670. It covered not only Maryland but the whole section of country between North Carolina and the Hudson River in New York. In acknowledgment of receipt of the map Herman was informed that "His Lordship had received no small satisfaction by the variety of that mapp." Herman was naturalized by an act of assembly on September 17, 1673. It was the first act of this kind passed by the assembly.[7]

Augustine Herman filled various offices in the colony of Maryland. He took an active part in the quarrels arising over the boundary between Maryland and Pennsylvania, and his Bohemia Manor farmhouse was chosen in 1682 as the place of meeting for Lord Baltimore and Governor Markham, of Pennsylvania, to discuss the question of the Maryland-Pennsylvania boundary. It was also on Herman's land that a Labadist colony was established.

The Labadists were one of several communal groups of Mystics who established themselves temporarily in colonial America. In Maryland they settled on Herman's land. The Labadists were a Pietistic sect founded in Germany about 1669 by Jean de Labadie. They emigrated about the same time as the Krefelders (aka Crefelders) who founded Germantown, Pennsylvania, in 1683. Although this body of Labadist emigrants came from Friesland, a northern province of the Netherlands, their leader P. Sluyter (whose original name was Peter Vorstmann) was a German from Wesel, now a city and district in North Rhine-Westphalia, Germany. Among this sect were many Germans, who like the Krefelders, hailed from the borderland between the "High and Low Dutch." Sluyter, along with a man named J. Dankers, who changed his name from Jasper Schilders, explored Maryland for a place to settle. Keeping their identity secret lest their association with the "Bush People" (as Labadists in Wienwaert were called) should be discovered, they finally chose a tract in Herman's Bohemia Manor on the Chesapeake Bay at the junction of the Bohemia and Elk rivers.

William Penn said that the Labadists were "a plain, serious people and came near to Friends as to silence in meeting, women speaking, preaching by the Spirit, and plainness in garb and furniture."[8] About 20 years after the community was founded, a Quaker preacher visited and described Labadist life as quiet, industrious and religious. The Labadist sect, however, did not survive long. The cause of their demise is unknown.

Another band of strange Mystics comprising 40 men (including hermits), women and children set sail at Rotterdam toward Philadelphia. However, they arrived at Bohemia Manor Landing in Maryland about ten years after the Labadists settled there. The community was nicknamed "the Woman in the Wilderness" from an allusion to the Bible Book of Revelations, Chapter 12: Verse 14. The last survivor of this brotherhood expired in 1765. This group, soon after setting foot in Maryland, had made their way to Germantown and from there into the wilderness. Every night throughout its history this eccentric group of Mystics sent observers to the top of their common house, which housed a schoolroom, to spend the night watching for the second coming of Christ.[9]

The Mason-Dixon Line separated Penn's and Lord Baltimore's colonies. The line was established by royal authority to settle border disputes. Two surveyors—Charles Mason and Jeremiah Dixon—were sent to fix the boundary between Penn's Colony and Lord Baltimore's existing colony of Maryland. Four years later, on October 9, 1767, the 233-mile-long Mason-Dixon Line survey was finished. In years to come, the Mason-Dixon Line between Maryland and Pennsylvania would separate the slave states from the free and the South from the North.

The Carolinas

The gigantic Carolina Colony was carved out in 1629. English King Charles I (r. 1625–1649) established the colony stretching from just south of—but not including—Roanoke Sound (now Albemarle Sound) and extending to Spanish Florida. He named the entire province *Carolina (Carolana)* for himself and granted it to Sir Robert Heath, an English lawyer and judge, making him the first Lord Proprietor of Carolina. Heath's attempt to attract Huguenots failed, and further attempts to colonize were interrupted by the English Civil War.

The first settlements in the vast Carolina Colony (province) grew up on the Atlantic Seaboard around Roanoke Sound on the Outer Banks of what is now North Carolina. When John White's Lost Colony, one of the first English settlements in North America, vanished in 1590 from Roanoke Island at the southern tip of Roanoke (now Albemarle) Sound, other settlements sprang up in the area. In 1655, Nathaniel Batts, a fur trader-explorer, opened a trading post on the western end of Roanoke Sound. It became the first permanent settlement in Carolina because it was located in that part of Virginia which—a decade later—the Crown would assign to the Carolina Colony.[10]

Charles II (r. 1660–1685), the son of the beheaded Charles I, having been in exile during the English Civil War, became a popular king after the monarchy was restored. Although his reign would become increasingly repressive in later years, Charles II, known as the "merry monarch" because of his hedonic lifestyle, had no intention of literally losing his head by repeating his father's mistake of taxation without parliamentary consent. Greedy for gain, however, he hoped to fatten England's coffers from abroad by developing plantations and proprietary colonies.[11] Unwilling to depopulate England to establish the colony, Charles II expected to draw settlers from existing colonies and to attract persecuted Protestants from Continental Europe. Charles II gave proprietary grants for six of the original 13 colonies, although he had no particular proprietary policy. He allowed the colonies to "grow any old way, which in the long run made them strong."[12]

In 1663, Charles II voided his father's Carolina patent to Heath "because the conditions on which it was granted had not been fulfilled."[13] He then divided Heath's proprietorship into eight parts and granted it to English noblemen adventurers who had helped restore the monarchy.

Two years later, Charles II enlarged the Carolina grant by adding the Roanoke Sound (Albemarle) Settlements of Virginia to North Carolina. The new northerly latitude passed halfway between the Chesapeake Bay and the Albemarle Sound and gave both Virginia and Carolina a major waterway on the Atlantic Ocean.

The revised southern border of Carolina reached far down into Spanish Florida. It engulfed the Florida panhandle and the Spanish Settlement of St. Augustine and spread slightly south of present-day Daytona Beach. Carolina's western border shot "in a direct line, as far as the South Seas." At its largest, the province of Carolina included today's North Carolina, South Carolina, Georgia, Alabama, Tennessee, Mississippi and parts of Florida and Louisiana. The king dictated that the Carolina charter would include: "The fishings of all sorts of fish, whales,

17. Germans in Colonial Maryland, the Carolinas and Georgia 161

sturgeons and all other royal fish. Moreover all veins, mines and quarries as well as discovered, and not discovered, of gold, silver, gems, and precious stones, metal and any other thing found, or to be found, within the Province."[14]

The Lords Proprietors were absentee owners who attempted to govern the Carolina Colony from a distance. Not one, with the possible exception of Virginia Governor William Berkeley, ever visited Carolina. Until Charles II made his grant to the eight Lords Proprietors, Virginians had spoken of "Carolana" as "South Virginia," just as the province of Maine was once called "North Virginia."

Henry Phillips and his wife were the first Quakers (Friends) known to settle in North Carolina. Fleeing persecution in New England, the newly converted Phillips family arrived in northeastern Carolina (now North Carolina) on the banks of Albemarle Sound across from the Virginia line in 1665. Carolina welcomed Quakers, while New England Puritans persecuted Quakers by imposing heavy fines, ear cropping, tongue boring, public stripping, whipping and even hanging. Governor William Berkeley's Virginia Anglicans were also intolerant of Quakers but less harsh than Puritans since Berkeley only imprisoned and fined Quakers. On the other hand, Carolina's eight Lords Proprietors (including Virginia's Governor Berkeley) encouraged and welcomed Friends in Carolina. In the nascent colony of Carolina only Catholics and atheists were barred. The Lords Proprietors were more interested in quitrents and profit from sugar, ginger, indigo, cotton, wines and whale oil than in religion. That's why the young colony of Carolina guaranteed Quakers and all settlers (except Catholics and atheists) the rights of Englishmen.

The northern part of the expanded Carolina Colony—the settlements on Albemarle Sound which Charles II had sliced off Virginia and spliced onto North Carolina—was renamed Albemarle County for one of the eight Lords Proprietors, the Duke of Albemarle.[15] Many of the 500 inhabitants of the Albemarle Sound area, having moved there when it belonged to Virginia, were unhappy—at least at first—to find themselves now under the colonial charter of the Carolina Colony. The secluded Albemarle Sound region had been a haven for runaway slaves and for debtors to escape taxes. These transplanted families, like most Virginians, were former indentured servants and other poor whites. They had been nudged south by the low prices paid for their only cash crop, tobacco, and by the increase of Negro slavery. They had no desire to plow the large Virginia tobacco plantations which were cultivated by slave labor. The independent pioneers had moved to Albemarle in what they believed to be the coast of southern Virginia where they could earn a living by working very hard on their own small tobacco farms. It was intense, monotonous work—plowing the fields, hand planting the tobacco slips, hoeing the weeds, picking off the harmful insects, harvesting the long, heavy stalks, hanging them to dry over hot fires, removing and folding the cured leaves. They bypassed Parliament's export duties by piling their cash crop into small vessels and slipping through the shallow waters of Albemarle Sound.[16]

German immigrants moving in the mid–17th century were the first settlers to arrive in the central part of the Carolina Colony. The earliest Germans settled in Friedens Lutheran Community of Guilford County. The Moravians, coming a little later, turned westward and founded the Salem (Wachovia) settlement.[17]

The first German known to step onto Carolina soil was Johann Lederer, a physician and pioneer-explorer whom Virginia Governor William Berkeley commissioned to cross the Blue Ridge, look for a water route to the Orient, and open up trade with Native Americans. With a Susquehanna Indian Guide, Lederer reached Yadkin Ford near Spencer, North Carolina, and the Catawba River probably near Rock Hill, South Carolina. After Lederer explored Carolina in 1670, there was a great influx of Dutch (German) people, mostly Lutherans, into the colony. Concomitantly a great number of German Lutherans disappeared from New York.[18]

In 1710 New Bern, North Carolina, benefited by the efforts of Baron Christoph von Graffenried, born in the canton of Bern, Switzerland. A leader of Swiss and German Protestant colonization in North America, Graffenried invested in the Georg Ritter Mining Company, which intended to employ indigent Swiss and Swiss Anabaptists of Pennsylvania and Virginia to mine silver deposits. Graffenried broadened the company's plans by including many victims of the War of Spanish Succession. These were the poor Palatines who had fled the devastated Rhineland to find refuge in the tent camps of Queen Anne's England on the Thames River. The Ritter Company then purchased from the Carolina Lords Proprietors 19,000 acres of land on the Neuse, Trent and White Oak rivers in what is now North Carolina. The purchase included the future site of New Bern at the site of Chattoka, an American Indian town. The Lords Proprietors then gave Graffenried the title "Landgrave of Carolina and Baron of Bernburg."[19] Graffenried alone purchased 5,000 acres and then, to avoid hostilities, he paid Native Americans for the same lands that he had already purchased from the Carolina proprietors.[20] With a surveyor he laid out in a cruciform pattern the little town of New Bern where he would settle the craftsmen. The farmers would live on farmland in outlying areas. It was rough going for the colonists: In all, about 100 Swiss and 600 Palatines left Europe for New Bern. In 1710, nearly all of the Swiss arrived; however, only about half of the Palatines survived the journey to New Bern. Still others were killed during the Tuscarora Indian Wars of 1712–1715,[21] which nearly destroyed the settlement around New Bern, while others moved to Governor Spotswood's colony in Virginia. Baron Christoph von Graffenried was captured, confined for five weeks by the Tuscarora and then let go unharmed. He returned to Bern, Switzerland, in 1713 to manage his father's estate.

> North Carolina Historic Marker C-10:
> BARON CHRISTOPH
> VON GRAFFENRIED
> ———...———
> was a citizen of Bern,
> Switzerland. Led Swiss
> and Palatine immigrants
> to N.C. where in 1710
> he founded New Bern.

After Sir Walter Raleigh's first English settlement, Roanoke Sound on the Outer Banks of North Carolina failed in the 16th century, German activity in 18th-century North Carolina began, as described above, when New Bern, the second-oldest town in North Carolina, was founded by Baron Christoph von Graffenried in 1710.

In an attempt to find inhabitants for South Carolina, the absentee owners, the Lords Proprietors, hired three English vessels in 1669 to carry English colonists from Barbados—the easternmost Caribbean Island—to settle southern Carolina. The next year, these English colonists from Barbados founded the Carolina village of Charlestown in what would become South Carolina. Captain Joseph West, commander in chief of the fleet of three vessels, became perhaps the most prominent South Carolina settler between the years 1669 and 1685. The Charlestown area developed faster than northern Carolina because of its natural harbor and its trade with the West Indies.

In 1712 Queen Anne split Carolina into two colonies—North and South Carolina. When North Carolina and South Carolina became separate colonies, North Carolina received its own governor. Until the time of separation there usually was a governor in Charlestown for the lower settlements and a deputy governor for the northern settlements.[22]

In 1728, King George II purchased all the Carolina land owned by seven Lords Proprietors. The eighth part still belonged to George Carteret, former governor of the Isle of Jersey. John Carteret, the Earl of Granville, inherited his father's one-eighth, which consisted of a strip 66 miles wide (from north to south) beginning at Hatteras and extending westward to the Pacific. Thus Lord Granville's grant (the Granville District) embraced 66 miles of the northern portion of North Carolina's entire width as well as the site of the future overmountain settlements of Watauga and Nolichucky in East Tennessee Country, the birthplace of the state of Tennessee and across to the Mississippi and beyond.[23]

Upon their purchase the Carolinas became royal colonies—Georgia was still part of Carolina at the time. King George II sent George Burrington to North Carolina in 1731 as its governor. Not only the governor but also all his various officials were appointed by the king. The king then established a two-house Parliament: the Upper House of 12 members and a 35-member Lower House.[24]

In 1740 Waxhaw Indians, decimated by smallpox, abandoned their lands in present-day Union County, North Carolina, and joined the Catawba. "The vacated lands were then settled by German, English, Scottish, and Welsh immigrants.... The small number of settlers remaining, after losses due to disease, war, and the hardships of the ocean voyage, intermarried with residents of other nationalities, and the Swiss-German community blended into the population at large. Their family names, however-including Metz (Metts), Kernegee (Kornegay), Eibach (Ipock), Mueller (Miller), and Kuntz (Koonce)-are still prominent in eastern North Carolina."[25]

The first German-speaking immigrants were brought to South Carolina in 1732 to settle the new township of Purrysburg. From that time forward, almost until the Revolution, there was an intermittent but fairly rapid influx of Palatines and German-Swiss, or Switzers. German settlers came to Orangeburg and Amelia in 1735–1737. Next were Germans who settled New Windsor and Saxe-Gotha in 1737. Afterward, in 1744, a fifth group moved into the Fredericksburg Township. Around 1745 Germans moved from Pennsylvania into the Upper Dutch Fork around present-day Pomaria. Soon there were Germans in lower Dutch Fork, on the north side of Broad and Santee rivers, as well as at Port Royal, Monck's Corner, and elsewhere. The *South Carolina Gazette* files show the frequent arrival of immigrant ships carrying passengers for several of the German settlements, including the German colony in Charlestown which was established in 1734. Germans also migrated from Pennsylvania and other colonies. By 1752 there were an estimated 3,000 German settlers in South Carolina.[26]

"In 1748 people of German descent began migrating in large numbers from Pennsylvania and resettled throughout the western Piedmont. In 1755 Salisbury was founded as the county seat of Rowan County which was created from Anson County in 1753 to accommodate increasing numbers of German and Scots-Irish settlers in the area. By 1775 the total population of North Carolina was 250,000. At that time 10 to 30 percent of the backcountry (Piedmont) was of German descent. In 1775 the first German Baptist (Dunker) congregation in the state formed near Muddy Creek in present-day Forsyth County."[27]

Georgia

Georgia was formed in 1732 when King George II carved the colony out of South Carolina by dividing South Carolina at the Savannah River. He granted a royal charter for Georgia to English General James Edward Oglethorpe and a corporation of 21 persons for 21 years. The Savannah River still forms the boundary between South Carolina and Georgia.

From its inception, Georgia was a unique proprietary colony, existing not for the benefit of the owners but for the people. Oglethorpe neither asked for nor received a monetary reward for his services. By this charter, Oglethorpe established a polyglot colony in America to give "the worthy poor" of England, as well as oppressed people throughout much of Europe, a new start. Religious toleration was proclaimed for all except Catholics. "Jews quickly arrived, followed by Protestants from Salzburg, Moravians from Germany and Highlanders from Skye." Missionaries, notably John Wesley, soon began their ministering work.[28] Georgia was the last of the 13 colonies to be established. The king wanted to provide employment for Britain's poor, to set them to work cutting timbers, planting crops of indigo, rice and wheat, and producing resources that could be sent back to England. He also expected the people of Georgia to defend the colonial frontier in the South.

Educated at Oxford, English army officer and philanthropist Oglethorpe felt great compassion for the plight of small debtors in English prisons. He conceived the idea of releasing small debtors from prisons on condition that they immigrate to the new colony. Setting sail from England aboard the ship *Anne* were Oglethorpe, a doctor, a preacher and 114 colonists. After landing in Charlestown, they proceeded to scout for a place to settle. On February 12, 1733 (now celebrated as Georgia Day), Oglethorpe's contingent arrived at Yamacraw Bluff (the present-day site of Savannah). They were warmly welcomed by the Yamacraw, a small band of Lower Creek Indians. This tribe had migrated north from the village of Apalachicola on the Gulf of Mexico.

In hope of befriending the Native Americans, Oglethorpe endeavored to protect them from unscrupulous white traders. What's more, he took Chief Tomochichi and his family to London to meet the king. The purpose of the trip was to ensure Creek allegiance to Britain.

"The colony was not to be confined to the poor and unfortunate. The trustees granted portions of five hundred acres to such as went over at their own expense, on condition that they carried over one servant to every fifty acres, and did military service in time of war or alarm. Thus the materials of the new colony consisted of three classes: the upper, or large-landed proprietors and officers; the middle, or freeholders, sent over by the trustees; and the servants indented to that corporation or to private individuals."[29]

"Religious toleration was proclaimed for all except Catholics." Next, after the English debtors, came Jews and Protestants from Salzburg, Germany (in present-day Austria), Moravians from Central Europe and Highlanders from the Isle of Skye, Scotland. Intrigued by this diverse, multilingual community, a number of dedicated missionaries, including John and Charles Wesley, came to practice their ministry.[30]

Georgia eventually began producing the wines, silks, and spices that England once imported only from foreign lands. The new colony not only supplied luxuries for England, but—as anticipated—it acted as a barrier protecting wealthy plantations in South Carolina from Spanish and French incursions.

When Oglethorpe arrived in Georgia in 1733, its only English occupants were stationed at Fort King George, a mile east of present-day Darien, Georgia. Having brought a large military force, Oglethorpe established Fort Frederika on St. Simon's Island. Built on a bluff amid sprawling live oaks hung with Spanish moss, Fort Frederika soon became the largest British fortification in North America. Standing on land also claimed by France and Spain, it defended the British presence in Georgia.[31]

In 1734 Oglethorpe welcomed Protestant immigrants who had

17. Germans in Colonial Maryland, the Carolinas and Georgia 167

been ousted from their homeland in Salzburg. In the 18th century, the archbishopric of Salzburg was a semi-independent territory of the Holy Roman Empire, ruled by an ecclesiastical prince who had both secular (worldly) and priestly authority. In 1731 the powerful Catholic archbishop of Salzburg issued an Edict of Expulsion which, over the next three years, uprooted more than 20,000 Protestants who were mostly Lutheran peasants and farmworkers. The expulsion marked the culmination of two centuries of ongoing attempts to re-Catholicize the territory.[32] Most of these outcasts settled in East Prussia and Holland. Others accepted an invitation extended by England's sympathetic Hanoverian King George II to settle in his American colony of Georgia. The House of Hanover was a British royal house of German origin. Its first monarch, George I, was born in the city of Hanover, a former state of Northwestern Germany which became an electorate of the Holy Roman Empire. The father of George I was a German duke, and his mother, Sophia, was born in the Palatinate. King George II also was born in the city of Hanover. George III was the first Hanoverian king born in England and the first to speak English as his native tongue. George's wife, Queen Charlotte of Mecklenburg, was a German princess of part-African descent.

Accepting the king's invitation, Protestants who were expelled from Salzburg in 1731 began immigrating to America.[33] The first group of 300 Salzburgers, "sailed from England to Georgia in 1734, arriving in Charlestown, South Carolina ... then proceeding to Savannah.... They were met by James Oglethorpe, the founder of the Georgia colony, who assigned them a home about twenty-five miles upriver in a low-lying area on Ebenezer Creek. Subsequent ships brought the rest of the original exiled Salzburgers, as well as other European settlers from German-speaking nations who also became identified generically as Salzburgers." These Salzburgers founded Ebenezer, Georgia, and established Jerusalem Church, which would become the Jerusalem Evangelical Lutheran Church. Their qualities of piety, modesty and industriousness led English authorities to consider Germans as model colonists. But their fierce independence and "mistrust of secular authority isolated them from the rest of the Georgia colony."[34]

When the original settlement of Ebenezer failed because it was too far inland, Governor Oglethorpe gave the group a new location. "New Ebenezer" was built on high bluffs above the Savannah River. Partly because they agreed on prohibiting slavery, the Salzburgers had a good relationship with the trustees. Funded by the trustees, these Germans built the first water-driven gristmill in the Georgia colony. They built stamping mills for rice and barley and ran two sawmills nearby. Ebenezer's lumber was a valuable product for the Georgia colony. The Salzburgers also established the first Sunday school in Georgia in 1734 and the first orphanage in 1737. "By 1752 the Salzburgers had expanded north of Ebenezer Creek to establish the Bethany and three other minor settlements."[35]

In 1752, almost 20 years after founding the colony, its trustees—as agreed—turned Georgia back to the Crown. Royal governors, in some respects, were more powerful than the king. That's because the British Monarchy had lost its veto power over Parliament. In contrast, the colonial governor could summon the colonial assembly or dissolve it whenever he liked. He could also veto its acts. The Crown governor carefully juggled his duel roles: carrying out the instructions of England's king and Parliament and yet managing the colony to the satisfaction of the colonial legislature that paid him. Each colony had a legislature, usually with two branches. The governor served two masters, the one who appointed him and the other who paid him.[36] The inhabitants of the new Crown colony of Georgia numbered roughly 3,000. As the population grew, it spread, mainly along the Savannah River between Savannah and Augusta. There were Salzburgers from Austria in New Ebenezer and Savannah, Scottish Highlanders at Darien, and New England Congregationalists at Sunbury and Midway.[37]

18

The Great Wagon Road and the Carolina Road

In the last sixteen years of the colonial era southbound traffic along the Great Philadelphia Wagon Road was numbered in the tens of thousands. It was the most heavily traveled road in all America.[1]

"Nearly 43 million Americans, about 1-in-6 U.S. residents, identified their ancestry as German in the Census 2000.... The ports of departure for immigrants from Germany were either Bremen, Bremerhaven, Cuxhaven or Hamburg. The ports of arrival for most immigrants from Germany were Philadelphia, New York, Baltimore and New Orleans."[2]

Many of the early immigrants, searching for sufficient farmland, moved to rural southeastern Pennsylvania near Philadelphia. Others traveled farther west beyond the Susquehanna River and south into Maryland. As more and more immigrants flooded into Philadelphia, many German-speaking peoples overflowed into the Great Appalachian Valley. By the 1730s they crossed the Potomac River and settled in the northern valley of Virginia.

The Great Philadelphia Wagon Road, which stretched through the Shenandoah Valley of Virginia and then branched southeast into the Carolina Road and west into the Wilderness Road, played a key role in populating and developing the interior—Piedmont and the western frontiers—of Virginia, North Carolina, Tennessee Country and Kentucky. It soon became the most important long wagon road in America.[3]

The Great Philadelphia Wagon Road originated in the mind of Virginia's Governor Alexander Spotswood. Searching for more land to expand the Virginia colony, Spotswood organized an expedition in August 1716.[4] Tapping a group of explorers, men he later dubbed "Knights of the Golden Horseshoe," about 50 in all, the governor and

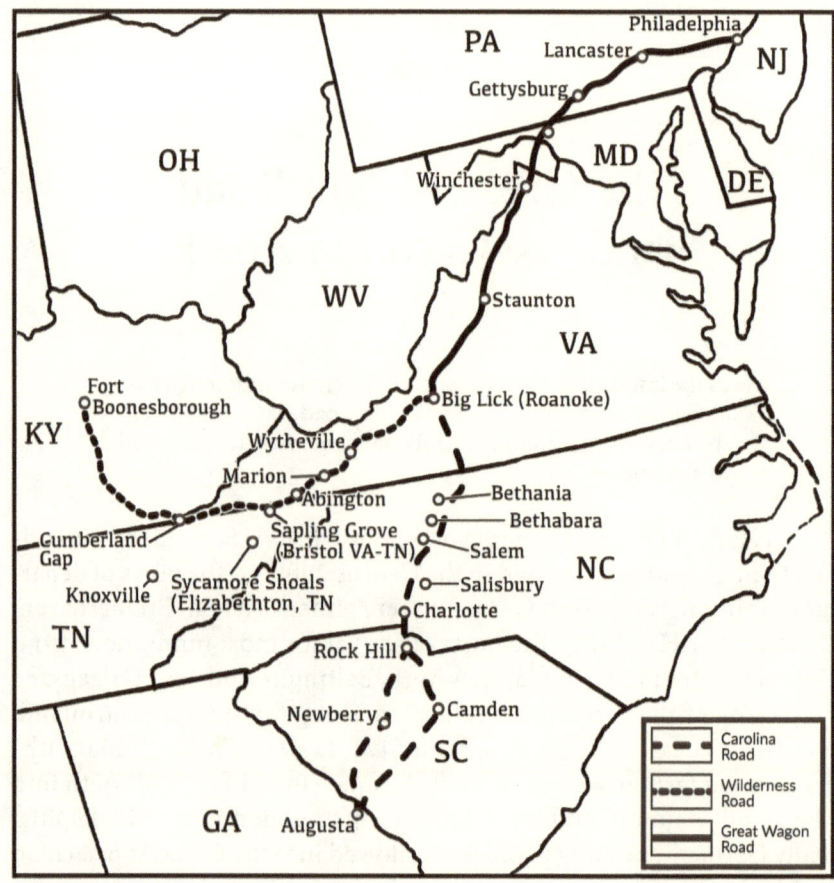

The Great Wagon, Carolina, and Wilderness Roads. The section of this map outlining the Wilderness Road was based partly on the *History of Southwest Virginia and Washington County* by Lewis Preston Summers and partly on the journal written by Lt. Governor Henry "Hair Buyer" Hamilton, whose nickname, "Hair Buyer General," came from his policy of paying Britain's Indian allies for the scalps of settlers. He armed American Indians at Fort Detroit with 8,640 knives and sent them scouting for prisoners and scalps. Over a ten-month period he received 55 prisoners and 210 scalps. Hamilton, a British lieutenant governor of the province of Quebec as well as a British superintendent of Indian affairs, was captured at Fort Sackville at Vincennes, handcuffed and transported under guard via the Wilderness Road (that is, through the Cumberland Gap). He entered Powell's Valley, crossed Clinch River and the North Fork of the Holston River and "breakfasted at Colonel Shelby's Plantation now in Sapling Grove" (now Bristol, TN). He then traveled via Abingdon to Roanoke. Leaving the Wilderness Road at Roanoke, Hamilton then was taken to Richmond, Virginia, and "layd in Gaol at Williamsburgh."

party accompanied by four Meherrin Indian guides left from the governor's palace in Williamsburg, Virginia, and proceeded westward on horseback through what is now Augusta County. Climbing to the crest of the Blue Ridge chain of the Appalachian Mountains, the Spotswood party caught their breath and then lost it again as they peered down upon the breathtaking beauty of the Shenandoah Valley and River in Northwestern Virginia.

The valley comprised a hardwood forest, including chestnut trees, stretching east to west and "varying from thirty to eight miles in width," from the Blue Ridge range to the Allegheny range of the Appalachians. From north to south the valley extended "some seventy miles in length,"[5] reaching from the Potomac River on the Maryland-Virginia border at Harper's Ferry to the James River near what is now Roanoke, Virginia. The Shenandoah Valley followed the course of the Shenandoah River and beyond.

After drinking to "King George's health and the royal family's health at the very top of the Appalachian Mountains" and descending the western slope into the lush Shenandoah Valley, the explorers pitched camp on the banks of the scenic Shenandoah River which Spotswood christened "Euphrates," burying "a bottle with a paper enclosed on which he writ that he took possession of this place in the name and for King Geo.1st of England." Then the fledgling knights finished the christening in the following manner, as one of the "knights," John Fontaine, described in his journal: "We had a good dinner, and after it we got the men together, and loaded all their arms, and we drank the king's health in champagne and fired a volley, the Princess's health in Burgundy and fired a volley, and in claret and fired a volley. We drank the Governor's health and fired another volley. We had several sorts of liquers, viz. Virginia Red Wine and White Wine, usquebaugh, brandy, shrub, rum, champagne, cavory, punch water, cider, etc. We called the highest mountain St. George and the one we crossed over Mount Spotswood."[6]

Looking at the river, Spotswood envisioned the Great Philadelphia Wagon Road and resolved to colonize this fertile and beautiful valley. Many future settlers of Spotswood's Shenandoah Valley were German-speaking people migrating from Pennsylvania.

Their inter-colony journey began when a long list of Germans on the Pennsylvania frontier requested guns and ammunition from the Quakers to protect their families against Indian attack. They signed a petition, which was ignored by the peace-loving, anti-war Pennsylvania authorities. Palatine (German) families then began caravanning from

Pennsylvania south and west to other colonies. One of the petitioners, Jost Hite, as mentioned in the last chapter, moved to Virginia. Governor Spotswood, excited about these desirable immigrants, established a colony for them at Germanna in the Shenandoah Valley of Virginia where he founded an ironworks to employ them. Although this colony failed, these ingenious and industrious Germans moved to other parts of Virginia.

By constructing the Spotswood Ironworks, the governor had enticed not only German but also Scots-Irish immigrant workers to move southward from Pennsylvania into the Great Valley of Virginia. These pioneer ironworkers and farmers occupied the frontier and thus protected the Tidewater region from threats of both the Indians and the French. As Germans spread west in Pennsylvania from Philadelphia to Lancaster, which became home to many Amish people, plentiful land and cheaper property prices drew Germanic peoples, as well as the Scots-Irish, even farther along the Great Indian Warpath into Virginia.

Created by the Five Nations of the Iroquois, the Great Indian Warpath—forerunner of the Great Philadelphia Wagon Road—was used for both trade and war. It stretched from the land of the Five and then Six Iroquois Nations in New York's Mohawk Valley to the Great Appalachian Valley of Virginia. One branch turned southwestward at Big Lick (Roanoke) and ran through the New and Holston river valleys—the land of the Western Waters—to the capital of the Cherokee Nation at Chota in Tennessee country. Another prong of the Great Indian Warpath turned southward at Big Lick. It was the most direct route into the Carolinas for the Iroquois to raid the Siouan-speaking Catawba.[7] The earliest settlers sought permission from Native American tribes to build roads through their hunting grounds. These efforts led to three treaties which opened the western Virginia frontier for settlement: the 1722 treaty of Albany, the 1744 Treaty of Lancaster with the Six Iroquois Nations, and the 1752 Treaty of Logstown with the Delaware and Shawnee.[8]

By this series of treaties the English, German and Scots-Irish pioneers acquired permission to expand the Great Indian Warpath into a wagon road which became known as the Great Philadelphia Wagon Road. It was an inland road paralleling the coastal King's Highway (Postal Road).

The Great Philadelphia Wagon Road became the principal highway of communication, trade and migration through the backcountry after the Lancaster Treaty of 1744 was signed. At Lancaster the sachems (top chiefs) and lesser chiefs of the Six Nations of the Iroquois Confederacy met with English commissioners of Maryland, Pennsylvania, and Virginia. In exchange for 400 pounds, the Iroquois, mediated and translated by German-born Conrad Weiser, gave up "all right and title to the land west of the Alleghany Mountains, even to the Mississippi."[9] Iroquois tradition claimed that the Six Nations owned, by right of conquest, the territory won by their forefathers in the 1640-1701 Beaver Wars.

Like the Great Indian Warpath, the Great Wagon Road split at Roanoke: the western artery continued as the Wilderness Road which was constructed gradually through the Great Valleys of Virginia and Tennessee and finally through the Cumberland Gap into Kentucky. The Southern artery slowly developed as the Carolina Road and eventually stretched 700 miles to reach Augusta and Charlestown.[10]

The Germans and Scots-Irish who had flooded into Penn's Colony overflowed. Before long, the German language could be heard from Pennsylvania to Georgia. The Scots-Irish who settled farther west in the Valley of Virginia, the Piedmont and the interior of the Carolinas became "the cutting edge of the frontier."[11]

The most important impetus for movement down the Great Indian Path and the Great Philadelphia Road after 1725 was the increasing cost of arable land in Pennsylvania. Settlers moved south because the price of land patents and quitrent (land tax) in Lord Granville's district of North Carolina was considerably lower.[12] The tight reins of Quaker authority also played a role. In 1746 during King George's War, the British issued a proclamation to each colonial governor from New England to Virginia. They were requested to raise a large number of troops for the conquest of Canada. The purpose was to rid Canada of French control and to erase French influence over frontier Indians.[13] Since the Carolinas were excluded from the levy, the risk of military conscription could be avoided by moving into the Carolinas. A North Carolina governor described immigrants flocking into his state:

North Carolina colonial Governor Gabriel Johnson informed the Board of Trade, on February 15, 1751, "inhabitants flock in here daily, most from Pensilvania and other parts of America, who are overstocked with people and some directly from Europe, they commonly seat themselves toward the west and have got near the mountains."[14]

Danish-born immigrant Morgan Bryan, who led settlers into North Carolina, was one of the first builders of the Carolina Road. Sailing from Denmark, Bryan immigrated to Ireland, crossed the Atlantic

Ocean to Lancaster, Pennsylvania, and settled in a Quaker community. Although Bryan was not a Quaker, he led a group of Quaker Friends down the Great Indian War Trading Path in 1730 and built a settlement in the Shenandoah Valley near present-day Winchester. Fifteen years later Bryan moved his French-born wife, Martha Strode Bryan, and their eight children along the Great Indian Path to Big Lick (now Roanoke), a salt lick on the Roanoke River, and settled where the river cut through the Roanoke Gap in the Blue Ridge Mountains.

In 1748 Bryan, again leading a group of Quaker Friends through the Shenandoah Valley, traveled by wagon train to Big Lick, drove through the Roanoke Gap and then continued along Indian and buffalo trails into North Carolina. Sometimes they removed the wheels and carried their wagons in pieces to the top of a ridge. Bryan and the Quakers spent three laborious months clearing the trail through the Shenandoah Valley of Virginia, making their way through Roanoke Gap and then widening the Indian path to begin developing the Carolina Road. Bryan's contingent settled near the Shallow Ford crossing of the Yadkin River about 15 miles west of present-day Winston-Salem. There, near Shallow Ford, the Quakers established another Bryan's settlement, which was northwestern North Carolina's first center of population.[15] Soon, two other population centers were built almost simultaneously in northwestern North Carolina: the Irish settlement and the Davidson Creek settlement.

Before 1750 there were at least 43 inhabitants of the Yadkin-Catawba Basin of Lord Granville's domain. By 1751, at least 82 families inhabited the Piedmont between the Yadkin River (near today's Winston-Salem) and the Catawba River (near Charlotte). In the mid–1750s, North Carolina Governor Arthur Dobbs noted that only a few persons who moved inland into the backcountry were poor. Most backcountry settlers were rich planters from the North. Many were Quakers or Scots-Irish who had prospered during their several decades of living in Pennsylvania and Maryland. The majority of settlers on the northwestern Carolina frontier were Scots-Irish Presbyterians or German Lutherans. There were also significant numbers of English, Welsh, Quakers and Baptists. And yet the North Carolina frontier had neither an Anglican nor a Catholic Church prior to 1768.[16]

The Moravians first began migrating to North Carolina in 1753. This was three years after Parliament declared the Moravian Church "an

Opposite: **Main areas of German settlement in the Thirteen Colonies.**

18. The Great Wagon Road and the Carolina Road

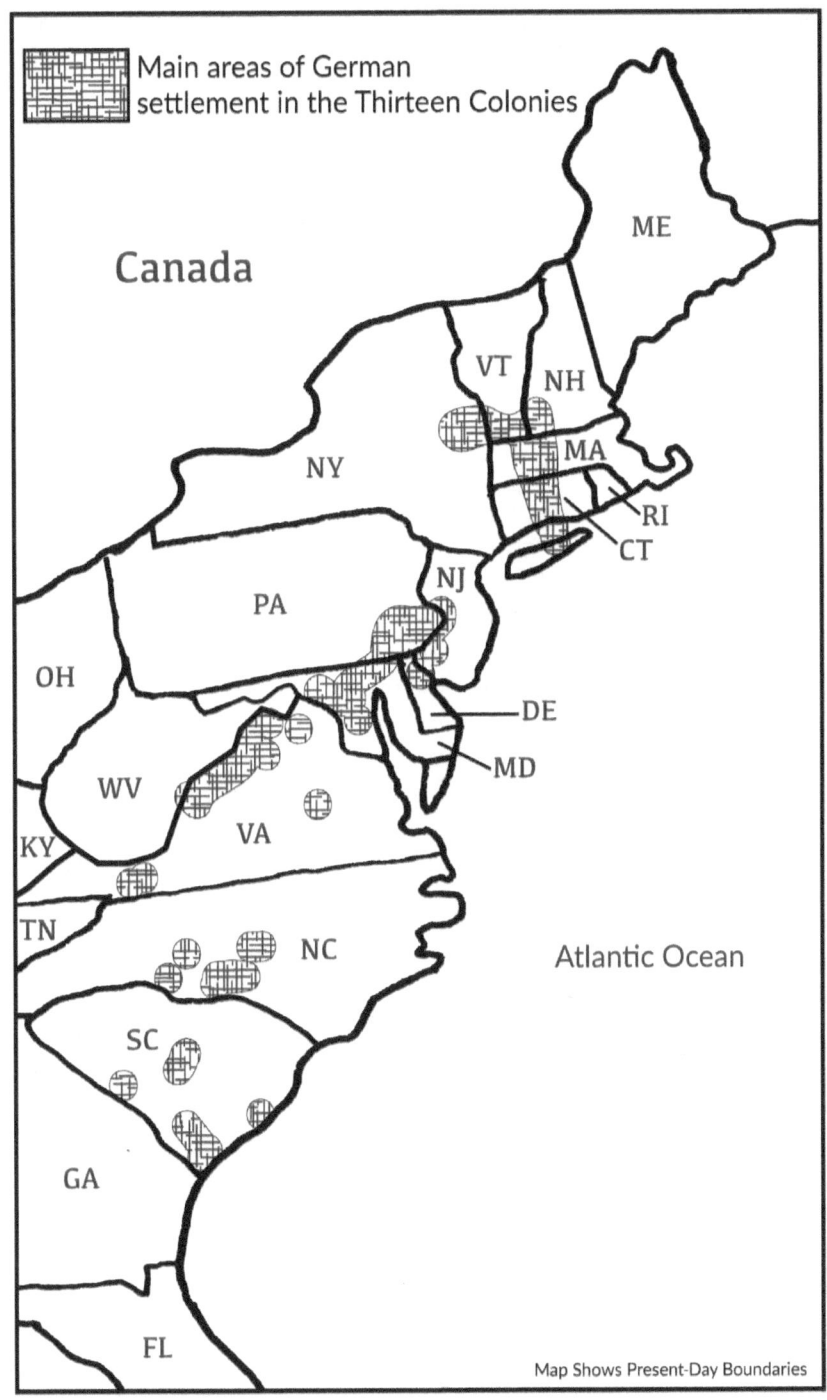

ancient Protestant Episcopal Church,"[17] giving the Church legal status equal to the Church of England. The next year, 1751, Lord Granville, the last remaining Lord Proprietor of the Carolina Colony, offered to sell 100,000 acres of his vast Carolina grant to the Moravian Count Zinzendorf. The North Carolina land, a broad plateau of wilderness between the Dan and the Yadkin rivers, was selected by Bishop August Gottlieb Spangenberg. This is how, as more Moravian immigrants poured into Pennsylvania, the sect acquired a large tract in North Carolina and chose to name it *Wachovia*. It was the site of the future city of Winston-Salem.[18]

Two months after the Church acquired the deed to Wachovia, 15 unmarried Moravian brethren, calling themselves "Unitas Fractrum" (United Brothers), began their six-week journey from Pennsylvania. They followed Morgan Bryan's route on what later became the Carolina extension of the Great Philadelphia Wagon Road. One of the single Brothers recorded in the group diary that they "spent two nights and a day while their wagon, which awaited them, was made three inches narrower, it having been found that it was too wide for the normal track in the road."[19] About a half mile off the Great Road as it ran through the forest of Wachovia on its way to Shallow Ford, the Brothers founded the hamlet of Bethabara in November 1753. This was the birth of the Southern province of the Moravian Church. That evening as the brethren held the first love feast in Wachovia, they were surrounded by howling wolves.

Within two years, married couples and singles flocked in to settle this outpost on the western frontier. They soon built a palisade to protect against Indian attacks. Over the next two decades Moravians established a Brother's House, a meeting house, store, pottery, brewery, tavern, and tannery. After Moravians sold some of their land to finance the construction of Salem, several English-speaking settlements also grew up in the predominately German-speaking land of Wachovia.[20] The Moravians' goal was to build a central town with offices, trades, and schools—a hub "from which to carry on missionary work among the Indians."[21] During the French and Indian War, the two forts at Bethabara served as defensive and supply centers for the Catawba Indian allies of the British.[22] Although Wachovia was not attacked by the Cherokee, the Wachovians overcame their aversion to bearing arms and began carrying guns for self-preservation. When peace came, they put down their guns and sent missionaries to the Cherokee.[23]

19

Quaker and German Longhunters and the Wilderness Road

I am no Statesman. I am a Woodsman—Daniel Boone[1]

Immediately following the French and Indian War, the outbreak of Ottawa Chief Pontiac's War (1763–1766) displaced thousands of Pennsylvanians and Virginians.[2] Fleeing their homes, many of these refugees migrated South on the Carolina Road to the friendly and safer frontiers of Carolina and Georgia.

The Carolina Road, a major north-south thoroughfare, played a key role in bringing settlers from Pennsylvania to the Carolina frontier. It became a gateway for immigrants traveling to Piedmont, Carolina. Swinging through present-day Winston-Salem, Salisbury and Charlotte, North Carolina, the Carolina Road crossed into South Carolina at the site of the Waxhaw settlement. Near present-day Camden, South Carolina, the road split. Eventually one branch spread to Augusta, Georgia. The other reached the port city of Charlestown, South Carolina, when merchants paid for a connection to their city.[3]

Among the settlers along the Carolina Road was the famous excommunicated Quaker from Pennsylvania, Squire Boone and family. The Boones mingled easily with folk of various religious and ethnic backgrounds since, before the Boones moved to North Carolina from Oley Valley, Pennsylvania, their homestead was within a five-mile radius of "Germans, Swiss, French Huguenots, Welsh and English Quakers, Irish, Swedes—about a dozen different groups. The spirit of the people was reflected in their religious associations."[4] When the Boone family moved to the Carolina Road, their neighbors were William Linville and his wife, Elinor, who was the daughter of one of the first builders of the Carolina Road, Morgan Bryan. In 1756 Squire Boone's son, longhunter and trailblazer Daniel Boone, married Rebecca Bryan, granddaughter of the road builder Morgan Bryan who was born in Denmark, came to America and befriended a group of Quakers. Another of Boone's Yadkin Valley neighbors, German-American Christopher Gist (Geist), an Ohio Company explorer and surveyor, had guided George Washington through Ohio Country during the French and Indian War. One of Christopher's sons, Nathaniel Gist, accompanied Daniel Boone when he named Wolf Hills (Abingdon), Virginia, on his way to Kentucky. Nathaniel Gist was said to be the father of Sequoyah, inventor of the Cherokee alphabet.

On the Virginia frontier, while surveying in the wilderness, Dr. Thomas Walker, a physician and land speculator, encountered a few of the earliest pioneers. Many had German ancestry. Stephen Holston (Anglicized from Holstein) and James Burke held land by "corn rights." According to Virginia law, planting an acre of corn entitled a settler to claim 100 acres surrounding that crop.[5] Stephen Holston was a longhunter, one who went on hunts that lasted for many months at a time, usually from October until March or April. Stephen's father may have been Henry Holstein, son of Matthias Holstein, a German Dane.[6] Stephen led a small group from his cabin at the head spring of the Middle Fork of the Indian River downstream to Natchez country on the Mississippi River. The Indian River, as well as a nearby mountain, soon bore his name, becoming Holston River and Holston Mountain.[7]

In 1753 James Burke planted his acre on a flat Appalachian Mountain peak in a ten-mile-wide spot now known as Burke's Garden or "God's Thumbprint" in Tazewell County. Burke's Garden, Virginia's highest valley, was named for a fine crop of potatoes that grew up at a campfire site where Burke had thrown out potato peels the preceding year. Burke's community soon became an outpost of German immigrants who settled in the backcountry frontier. By the 1990s, the site supported a short-lived Amish neighborhood in the heart of Appalachia.

A German immigrant, Samuel Stalnaker, an explorer-trapper, settled in the Valley of Virginia in 1732. Stalnaker was a Dunkard, one of the German Baptist denomination who called themselves "the Brotherhood of the Euphrates." They had migrated from Pennsylvania. Dr. Walker described them as "an odd set of people who make it a matter of religion not to shave their Beards, ly on beds, or eat Flesh, though at present, in the last they transgress, being constrained to it, as they say, by want of sufficiency of Grain and Roots, they having not long been seated here. I doubt the plenty & deliciousness of the Venison & Turkeys has contributed not a little to this."[8] "They don't baptize either

Young or Old, they keep their Sabbath on Saturday.... They are very hospitable."[9]

Dr. Walker first met Stalnaker in 1748 "on his way to the Cherokee Indians." The two met again in 1750 when Walker and Ambrose Powell, for whom Powell Valley is named, "helped him raise his house."[10] Stalnaker's "house" (cabin-trading post) was located on the Middle Fork of the Holston River at the present site of Chilhowie, Virginia. In 1755 it was Virginia's farthest western settlement.[11]

Heinrich Adam Herman (Harman), a German immigrant who settled on the New River around 1750, had a large family of boys. All these boys were said to be great hunters and Indian fighters. Some of them, including Jacob Harman and several others, were longhunters.

Hamilton's "The Long Hunters" from *Historical Sketches of Southwest Virginia* recognizes that hunters and groups of hunters were familiar figures on all the frontiers in pioneer days but argues that organized and publicized long hunts and longhunters originated on the Southwest Virginia frontier on the Holston River near present-day Chilhowie. Most of these longhunters lived either on the Clinch River or the Holston, although a few lived on the New River.[12]

The period after the Cherokee War of 1759–1761 is known as the "decade of the Long Hunters."[13] Their hunting ground was the uninhabited land paralleling the Great Indian Warpath west of the Blue Ridge through the Great Appalachian Valley (the Shenandoah, the Roanoke River, New River, Holston River, and Tennessee River valleys) to the Little Tennessee River at Chota. The capital of the Cherokee Nation, Chota, was located 35 miles south of present-day Knoxville at Fort Loudon. Crunching for long hours through autumn leaves, carrying a knife, shouldering a rifle, sloshing across knee-deep streams, bushwhacking through underbrush, climbing steep snowcapped Appalachian ridges and emerging in springtime into a forest of redbud trees fragrant with blossoms, the longhunter blazed trails, looked for passages through mountain gaps and mentally mapped the geography as he pursued game.

Longhunters were the first to penetrate the wilds of Tennessee and Kentucky which then were "the West."[14] Unique to Southwest Virginia, the longhunter was a woodsman, explorer and adventurer, an immigrant, mainly of English, Scots-Irish, German or Scandinavian ancestry. Meat from the hunt fed his family. Hides and pelts shipped to the British market supplemented the meager income earned from his farm, which was managed by his wife during the long weeks he was away from home.

The American Revolution would abruptly stop his trade with Britain and therefore end the era of the long hunt.

To avoid frightening the animals and to escape the ferocity of the Indians, longhunters seldom hunted in parties larger than two or three. These unsung explorers of the wilderness knew its topography and gave their names to its rivers, streams, gaps, salt licks and mountain valleys long before 1750, when surveyor Dr. Thomas Walker made his trip to the Ohio. Called by the itch for adventure, the love of the hunt and the earnings from leather and fur, the longhunter weathered raw winters, illness and hunting accidents: He risked being scalped by the Indians whose land he robbed and later cleared and tilled.

Elisha (Elijah) Wallen, prototype of the longhunter, was an easy-going, chunky, dark-skinned, rough-featured backwoodsman. Living east of the Blue Ridge near Martinsville, Virginia,[15] he met other woodsmen at a point on the New River near the site of Fort Chiswell near Wytheville, Virginia, which was a familiar gathering place for longhunters.[16] Quite successful in the fur trade, Wallen began organizing hunts in 1761, explored as far as the Cumberland River, and named Wallen's Ridge (south of today's Big Stone Gap) in 1762.[17] Leading longhunters through the Cumberland Gap into Kentucky in 1763, Wallen was followed by others, including Daniel Boone, the son of Quakers, who made his first trip across the gap into Kentucky six years later.

In 1769, 20 or more woodsmen followed Elisha Wallen on his great hunt into Tennessee and Kentucky. These longhunters rendezvoused in June on the New River eight miles from Fort Chiswell. One member of Wallen's party was Caspar (Gaspar) Mansker who spoke with a heavy German accent. Mansker's emigrant parents had embarked from a Dutch port. Germans living near Holland often sailed on Dutch ships. Caspar was born aboard ship on the way to America. He became a longhunter and survived 25 years of Indian Warfare on the frontier. Like most long hunts, Wallen's great hunt into Kentucky was a dangerous one. On this trip, Mansker was "luckier than most: He kept his scalp."[18] He attributed his escape from scalping to his pet rifle, Nancy. When an Indian faked a wild turkey gobble to draw the hunter into the open, Mansker took the bait and stepped forward. As soon as the Indian came into range Mansker declared that Nancy wanted to speak to him, and she did so "with fatal effect." Caspar Mansker swore that he never would have killed the Indian, "It was the act of Nancy, his pet rifle."[19]

Among those known to be in Wallen's original hunting party was Michael Stoner, a good woodsman, truthful and reliable. Michael

19. Quaker and German Longhunters and the Wilderness Road

Stoner's real name was George Michael Holsteiner, a stout, humorous German who spoke broken English and was one of the best marksmen on the frontier. This is the same Michael Stoner who, at the onset of Dunmore's War against a Shawnee Alliance of Indian Nations, was sent into Kentucky with Daniel Boone to warn surveyors that the Indian War had started. When Fincastle County Lieutenant William Preston wrote to Captain William Russell of Castles wood (Castlewood) concerning the safety of the surveyors, Russell answered on the 26th of June 1774: "I have engaged to start immediately, on the occasion, two of the best hands I could think of, Daniel Boone and Michael Stoner, who have engaged to search the country as low as the Falls (Louisville) and to return by Gasper's Lick on Cumberland and through Cumberland Gap."[20] Boone and Stoner trekked 800 miles on their 62-day journey through the wilderness to bring the rod and chain dragging surveyors to safety.

Judge Richard Henderson hired Stoner as a hunter for the Transylvania Land Company in 1775 and awarded him a tract of land on what came to be called Stoner's Fork of the Licking River near Daniel Boone's original claim. Stoner stayed in Kentucky but sold his original tract to Henry Clay.

Daniel Boone's good hunting buddy, Michael Stoner, worked with him in 1775 in extending the Wilderness Road. At first the Wilderness Road stretched only from Big Lick (Roanoke) to Patton's settlement at Draper's Meadow on the New River. During the summer of 1760, Colonel William Byrd built Fort Chiswell on the New River at present-day Wytheville to protect the lead mines. He then broadened the path from the New River to Long Island on the Holston River (Kingsport, Tennessee). This turned most of the Warpath—that part from Fort Chiswell to Sapling Grove (Bristol TN-VA)—into a road wide enough for wagons. This widened path was an extension of the Wilderness Road—the western branch of the Great Wagon Road of Virginia.

The Transylvania Company's 1775 negotiations with the Cherokee at Sycamore Shoals, North Carolina (now Elizabethton, Tennessee), led to the Transylvania Purchase, which included most of Kentucky and Middle Tennessee. The company hired Daniel Boone to mark out a road. Guiding a work crew of 30 woodsmen, Boone extended the Wilderness Road from Long Island of the Holston into Kentucky. The stout and jolly German, Michael Stoner, was a member of Boone's bushwhacking team, cutting the Wilderness Road through the Cumberland Gap to Boonesborough, Kentucky.

"In later years," said Nathan Boone in an interview with Lyman Draper, "he (Michael Stoner) hunted in Missouri and stopped at our house; through good circumstances Father was at home. Once an old neighbor of Stoner's from Kentucky came here and said to Stoner, as a ruse to get him to go home, that in Kentucky people thought he was dead, and his wife was engaged to be married again in the near future. The next morning Michael Stoner packed off for Kentucky."[21]

Boone's road crossed the North Fork of the Holston and passed through Moccasin Gap and then Cumberland Gap into Kentucky. It was a heavily trodden route by which thousands of emigrants went west. "No single trail was more significant in the westward spread of English colonization than the Wilderness Road of Virginia, Tennessee and Kentucky.... It was the lifeline which saved the Northwest for the young republic."[22]

A bevy of settlers—some guided by George Rogers Clarke—followed Boone to Boonesborough, which was chosen as the capital of the Transylvania land that had been purchased from the Cherokee. Benjamin Logan, a big, good-looking Scots-Irish frontiersman, and his company of men from Wolf Hills joined the group at Powell's Valley and traveled with them for a while. But Logan soon split with the group. Logan then blazed a trail westward from Boone's Trace and built Logan's Fort at Crab Orchard, Kentucky. By July 1775, both Boone's and Logan's forts had attracted large groups of settlers. The perilous journey of so many settlers streaming in "successive caravans ... moving westward ... along a lonely path ... to a wild and cheerless land" is described by Chief Justice Robertson of Kentucky:

> Behold the men on foot with their trusty guns on their shoulders, driving stock and leading packhorses; and the women, some walking with pails on their heads, others riding with children on their laps, and other children hung in baskets on horses, fastened to tails of others going before, see them encamped at night expecting to be massacred by Indians; behold them in the month of December ... the "hard winter" traveling 2 or 3 miles per day frequently in danger of being frozen or killed by the falling of horses on the icy and almost impassable trace.[23]

Pioneers from the Watauga settlement traveled over the Wilderness Road, through the Gap into Kentucky and then turned south into Middle Tennessee where they founded a settlement at French Lick (now Nashville) on Christmas Day 1779.

The Virginia Assembly appointed commissioners in 1779 to explore all paths on both sides of Cumberland Gap and mark a road to Kentucky. They were to clear it, make it convenient immediately for packhorses, and judge the practicability and cost of eventually turning it into a wagon road. The resulting 1781 Kincaid-Calloway road plan expanded Boone's Trace and became the official Wilderness Road.

As the wilderness pushed farther and farther west, the name "Wilderness Road" began to apply to different points on the frontier until the road gradually faded away. Only a few historic markers remain to point the way across the Old Wilderness Road route from Fort Chiswell to Abingdon, Virginia, to Bristol and Kingsport, Tennessee, and through the Cumberland Gap into Kentucky and beyond.

Back East, immigrants kept pouring into Penn's Colony and other ports along the Atlantic Seaboard.

20

American Revolutionary War Soldiers of German Descent

After suffering in London and on the ocean, many Germans found the home they wanted in the wilderness of Pennsylvania. These immigrants were loyal to England during the French and Indian War and fought as Americans in the Revolutionary War because they loved their new homeland. Many of those who came by way of Philadelphia had their own peculiar religious beliefs. Since they were constantly persecuted in the land of their birth, they sought religious freedom on the Pennsylvania frontier where they worshiped God unmolested. They refused to be driven away by Native American tribes "Or even the savage though he were daubed from head to foot with war paint."[1]

Conrad Weiser, a famous German immigrant who became fluent in the Mohawk language, studied English and acted as a mediator-interpreter in negotiations between the Six Nations and the residents of Pennsylvania. As a Pennsylvania citizen, he founded and helped organize the Lutheran Church at Reading. He also acted as a magistrate and a soldier and organized a militia to defend the Pennsylvania frontier. His sons Philip and Samuel joined their father's militia group. Conrad's youngest son Benjamin served in the American Revolutionary War, as did most of Conrad's grandsons.[2]

Another German soldier who served as a general in the Revolution (1775–1783) was Baron von Steuben, a flamboyant and dominant figure at Valley Forge. Friedrich Wilhelm Ludolf Gerhard Augustin Baron von Steuben was not really a baron. He was a tough, quirky mercenary "who liked to decorate himself with sonorous names."[3] A former Prussian army captain and aide-de-camp to Frederick the Great, Steuben—with his "drooping face, ample double chin and almost comical pomposity"[4]—came to America carrying a letter of introduction to Congress and to George Washington. The embellished letter was written

20. American Revolutionary War Soldiers of German Descent

by Benjamin Franklin and Silas Deane, American emissaries to France. Washington recommended that Congress appoint Steuben major general and inspector general of the Continental Army. Both Washington and Steuben were intent on creating a professional army.

Steuben brought to Valley Forge his Prussian discipline and the tactics necessary to build such a top-notch army. Sweating under his full military regalia, he was the stereotypical disciplinarian. So meticulously did Steuben instruct Washington's officers that every one of his 100 trained officers was able to teach each threadbare man under his command and turn him into a professional soldier.

Beloved by the troops this delightful showman, with a greyhound trotting by his side, drilled the Continental Army eyeball to eyeball, yelling and swearing in German and French. When the trainees could not understand him, the baron commanded his aide to curse at them in English. Teaching his "School of the Soldier" from dawn to dusk, Steuben relied on interpreters—one was Lt. Colonel Alexander Hamilton, future first secretary of the treasury—to translate his ideas from German-accented French to English. Performing in a Grand Review before the French ambassador and dignitaries of Congress, he paraded his class, celebrating with grace and precision the new Franco-American alliance. "In the brilliant sunshine of a spring morning, they marched in perfect columns, quickly and precisely unwound into two parallel lines, and fired three rolling volleys of musketry to salute their awe-struck guests."[5] As the first inspector general of the United States Army, Steuben introduced new firing drills and regulations and monitored camp sanitation. During the winter of 1777–1778, while he was at Valley Forge, he wrote the basic plan for his *Regulations for the Order and Discipline of the Troops of the United States*, also known as the Blue Book.

The drillmaster's practice ground, near the center of the camp, was a showplace for his grand parade of precision-trained troops. General von Steuben's imposing bronze figure commands attention there even today.

Steuben appeared again as an important figure in 1781 when General George Washington assigned Major General Marquis de Lafayette to capture the traitor Benedict Arnold in Virginia. Lafayette was to reassemble his troops and join Steuben, military commander of Continental and State Militia forces in Virginia. Lafayette and Steuben together launched a Virginia campaign to stop Arnold.

Friedrich the Great, Steuben's role model, amazed Europe by lifting

Prussia from a minor German state to the most powerful province of Germany. Even though Frederick the Great never voyaged to America, he instilled into Steuben the ability to drill and discipline an army. But not all of Frederick's contributions were direct. George Washington adopted another of Frederick's most important lessons, which was the secret to the survival of the Continental Army: "He kept his army intact, no matter how small, as a viable threat to the British. After crushing defeats, and sometimes facing overwhelming odds from three adversaries, Frederick always managed to scrape just enough together to outmaneuver and outlast his enemies. Perhaps no other general in history other than Washington, who learned from Frederick, was so adept at this feat."[6]

"Frederick's greatest achievement was perhaps the creation of effective government bureaucracy, which became the model for the nineteenth century, and laws establishing religious and social freedoms, which were fundamental in defining the concept of liberty."[7]

Revolutionary War General George Washington served as first president of the United States from 1789 to 1797. Because his bodyguard was suspected of treasonable intent, the group was dismissed and replaced by a new bodyguard composed mainly of Germans supported by a troop of German cavalry. Not only that, but 12 German soldiers escorted Washington to Mt. Vernon when he retired. Later, when the ex-president died, Congress directed his funeral procession to wend its way from Congress Hall to the German Lutheran Church where General "Light Horse" Harry Lee delivered an eloquent oration.[8]

Another valorous American patron of German heritage was General Nicholas Herkimer who served in the Revolutionary War in the Mohawk Valley Battle of Oriskany. Born in New York, Herkimer was a first-generation American of German heritage whose parents were from the Rhenish Palatinate (Rheinpfalz). When he heard that the British were blockading Fort Stanwix, the critical portage point on the Mohawk River in New York, General Herkimer gathered Patriot militia and allied Oneida scouts to reinforce the fort's defense. Upon learning that Herkimer was marching, British Colonel Barry St. Leger detached Sir John Johnson and Mohawk Chief Joseph Brant and directed them to ambush Herkimer's men before they could reinforce Fort Stanwix. Johnson led the Royal New York Regiment while Brant led Loyalists of several Iroquois Nations of the Mohawk Valley.

Brant skillfully set a trap for Herkimer's militia and Oneida

Patriots. The ambush was set in a ravine at Oneida Creek near the Oneida Indian village of Oriska (now Oriskany, New York), a few miles east of Fort Stanwix. En route to the fort, Herkimer led 600 patriot soldiers, 15 wagons and 200 rear guardsmen down the slopes of the fateful ravine. They were suddenly ensnared in the Battle of Oriskany. In a blaze of musket fire, the Indian Loyalists attacked Herkimer's troops in the gorge. Herkimer's right leg was shot through, his horse killed from under him. Patriots carried Herkimer up the hill where, sitting on his saddle under a tree, he organized his remaining men in a circle for defending in all directions. The Fort Stanwix commander aided the dying Herkimer and his militiamen by sending a sortie to create a diversion. The patriot sortie raided the British-American Indian campsite, taking prisoners and wagonloads of booty. It was a civil war: Whigs fought Tories; brother shot brother; Iroquois tribes attacked each other. More than three-quarters of Herkimer's militia either died or were seriously injured; Herkimer died within days after his leg amputation. British losses were far fewer than patriot losses.

Hessian soldiers played also a prominent role in the American Revolution. Thirty thousand German troops, "Hessian Soldiers," were hired by the British to fight as Loyalists against Patriots in the American Revolutionary War. First landing at Staten Island in August 1776, "The Hessians came in entire units with their usual uniforms, flags, weapons and officers."[9] They made up a quarter of the British fighting force in America. Hessians came mainly from Hesse-Cassel (Hesse-Kassel), a mid-size German state located between the main part of Prussia and the Prussian provinces of Westphalia in western Germany. Some hired soldiers (mercenaries) came from other parts of Germany which, at that time, was not a unified country but a conglomeration of individual states sharing a common language and culture. Soldiers for hire were the major export of the province of Hesse-Cassel. The fee paid for Hessian soldiers by Britain to the state of Hesse-Cassel allowed the state's prince to keep taxes low and public spending high. He was then financially able to oversee public works projects, administer a public welfare system and encourage education. Training as a soldier was compulsory for those drafted by the state. So German soldiers, mercenaries, were conscripts not volunteers. All deserters were executed.

When Hessian boys turned seven, they were required to register for military service. Some of the registered were exempt. Others were forced into service at any time between ages 16 and 30. The Hessian army instilled iron discipline using the threat of brutal punishment. "Officers were well-educated, promotion was by merit and soldiers took pride in serving their prince and their people."[10] Military service paid wages higher than farmwork and provided economic benefits for the soldier and his family. An accepted way for Hessians to supplement their wages was through the sale of captured military plunder as well as from plunder confiscated from civilians.

Hessian soldiers included hussars, three artillery companies and four battalions of grenadiers. Usually mustachioed, a hussar was a member of a European light-cavalry unit used for scouting. The infantry was made up of sharpshooters, musketeers and fusilier who were armed with smoothbore muskets. The Hessian artillery shot three-pounder cannons. Hessian commanders refused to take soldiers who were criminals or sick back to Germany.

The Hessians' first Revolutionary War engagement was in the Battle of Long Island. They also fought in the Revolutionary War battles at Fort Washington, White Plains, Savannah, Trenton and Guilford Courthouse.

Americans encouraged Hessians to desert and blend into the large German-American population. Continental Congress offered 50 acres of farmland and some livestock to individual Hessian soldiers to encourage them to desert. (Fifty to 800 acres of land were offered to British soldiers, depending on rank, to encourage British troops to desert.)

Of the 30,000 Hessian mercenaries hired by the British, "as many as 5,000 remained in America after the end of the hostilities."[11] Over 6,000 died from illness or accident; 1,200 were killed in action. More than 17,300 returned home to Germany. Many Hessian deserters remained as farmers and married into German families. Eventually, their progeny blended with other ethnic groups and became thoroughly Americanized. One such soldier was John Henry Bisaner, whose parents lived in Göttingen, a city in Lower Saxony Germany. Born May 10, 1758, in Germany, Bisaner stated that while studying for the ministry, he ran away from school and boarded a ship carrying Hessian soldiers to America. When his ship anchored at Charlestown, South Carolina, he jumped overboard and made his way to Lincoln County, North Carolina.

The following genealogies illustrate that immigrant Germans tended to congregate with other German-speaking people and marry each other rather than choose a mate who did not speak the same language. After deserting a ship carrying Hessians, Bisaner received a state land grant which was recorded in the 1790 census as well as the North Carolina State and Colonial Records, Vol.20. There in Lincoln County in 1788, he married Catherine Haas, daughter of Simon Hass and wife, Susannah Wittenburg. John Henry Beisener (Bisaner) recorded his last will and testament in 1843 in Catawba County, North Carolina, and was buried at Ore Bank Lutheran Church. According to article 46 of the Heritage of Caldwell County, North Carolina, John Henry and Catherine Haas Bisaner's son Simon Pinkney Bisanar was born in March 1806 in Burke County, North Carolina, and died in Caldwell County, North Carolina. Simon accumulated 875 acres, built a gristmill on Silver Creek in 1834 and had a large inventory of livestock, produce, molasses, honey and wood. He donated the first organ to Bethany Church and is named on the first deed of the church. Simon's wife, Rachel Starnes, was a daughter of Revolutionary War soldier Joseph Starnes, a Patriot of the Battle of Kings Mountain. Joseph Starnes's father, Joseph Starnes, Sr., was born in the 1720s at German Flats, New York, in the Mohawk Valley, moved to a farm on the Smith River in Virginia and was killed in battle with Indians in Boonesborough, New York. Joseph Starnes, Sr.'s immigrant father, Frederick Starnes, was born in the Palatinate ca. 1700, while Joseph's immigrant mother (Frederick's wife) Mary Baker Goldman was born in the city of Mannheim in the German state of Baden-Württemberg.

Records show that the descendants of John Henry Bisaner (b. Germany 1758) married German-speaking spouses for more than a century after he landed in America. Finally, one of Bisaner's documented descendants, James Romulus ("Rom") Wike of North Carolina, broke with tradition and married a Scots-Irish woman named Nellie Ferguson in 1916. Their son, Sidney, continued to broaden his German roots by marrying a woman whose earliest American ancestor was Englishman Peter Brown, a Pilgrim who came to Plymouth Colony on the 1620 *Mayflower*. Branches of her ancestry also were rooted in the Puritan Massachusetts Bay Colony and Berkeley's Anglican Jamestown, Virginia colony. Her family's DNA evidence also claims Native American ancestry, the timeline of which coincides with oral family history of the Wicocomico tribe of the Powhatan Confederacy.

North Carolinians, like residents of other states throughout the 1700s and onward, experienced improved methods of transportation which broadened their option to move from one state to another. Virginia and Carolinians often went to Kentucky and Tennessee;

Pennsylvanians migrated to Ohio. From 1775 to 1855 the United States granted bounty-land warrants for military service, primarily to encourage volunteer enlistments but also to reward veterans for service during various wars. Early warrants were available principally in Ohio and in the Old Northwest Territory.

21

Germans Begin Migrating to Kentucky, Ohio and the Old Northwest

Until 1781 the state of Virginia claimed a huge chunk of territory on both sides of the Ohio River. To the south of the river, Virginia possessed Kentucky. Lying north of the Ohio River was Virginia's Ohio Country, also known as the Northwest Territory, now called the Old Northwest. The development of the Old Northwest began in 1781 when the state of Virginia, nudged by the state of Maryland, began its process of ceding its territory northwest of the Ohio River.

Back in 1775, Judge Richard Henderson signed the Transylvania Purchase Agreement with the Cherokee. The Transylvania Purchase included all of Kentucky and much of Middle Tennessee. Henderson hired trailblazer Daniel Boone to extend the Old Wilderness Road and "mark the road to Kentucky."[1] Henderson soon led pioneers along Boone's New Wilderness Road through the Cumberland Gap to establish Fort Boonesborough in the new land which Henderson named Transylvania.

The following year, the settlers became disgruntled with some of Henderson's business arrangements. Virginia Militiaman and Surveyor George Rogers Clark, encouraged by discontented Virginians and some Kentuckians, conducted a general meeting at Harrodsburg, Kentucky, in 1776. At the convention Clark and John Gabriel Jones were elected as representatives of the unhappy Transylvania people to travel to Williamsburg, Virginia, and petition the Virginia Assembly to dissolve Transylvania and declare Kentuckians citizens of Virginia. At that time Governor Patrick Henry, the newly elected first governor of the State of Virginia, also favored making Kentucky a county of Virginia. It was late in the fall session of 1776, said Clark, when the Virginia Assembly established a new county by the name of Kentucky.[2]

In 1778 George Rogers Clark, having garnered the approval and support of Governor Henry and the Virginia Assembly, led a militia from Virginia's Kentucky County and entered the Old Northwest Territory. These Kentucky militiamen won victories at British-held Kaskaskia, Cahokia, and Vincennes. That's how Clark temporarily broke the British-Indian alliance in the Old Northwest and won the accolade "Conqueror of the Old Northwest." But he could not hold onto it; he was continuously on the defensive in Detroit, Kentucky, and Ohio Country. It was not until the close of the Revolutionary War that Kentucky, Illinois, and much of the territory of Ohio in the Old Northwest were in American hands.

The fact that Virginia ceded the land lying north of the Ohio River to the U.S. government was confirmed in Paris in 1783 at the signing of the Peace Treaty ending the American Revolutionary War. The United States Congress accepted Virginia's cession in 1784. This new acquisition of 265,878 square miles[3] of raw wilderness doubled the size of the United States. It was still called the Northwest Territory, or "Ohio Country," and contained four of the five Great Lakes. It would be carved up into five states: Ohio, Indiana, Illinois, Michigan, Wisconsin, plus part of Minnesota. A plethora of Indian Nations—the Wyandot, the Delaware, the Ottawa, the Chippewa, the Potawatomi, the Sauk, the Ojibwa, the Shawnee and others—would belligerently and determinedly defend this land which was their homeland, their hunting ground and the source of their livelihood.

Quaker longhunter Daniel Boone and German pioneer Ebenezer Zane (Zahn) were among the first to cut traces through the Appalachian forest wilderness. Boone blazed the way to Kentucky. Zane carved the path through Ohio Country which opened the way to the Northwest Territory, or the present-day East North Central states.

The Confederation Congress officially created the Northwest Territory by passing The Northwest Ordinance Act of 1787. "The following three principal provisions were ordained in the document: (1) a division of the Northwest Territory into 'not less than three nor more than five States'; (2) a three-stage method for admitting a new state to the Union—with a congressionally appointed governor, secretary, and three judges to rule in the first phase; an elected assembly and one nonvoting delegate to Congress to be elected in the second phase, when the population of the territory reached 'five thousand free male inhabitants of

Old Northwest Territory (Ohio Country) and Zane's Trace.

full age'; and a state constitution to be drafted and membership to the Union to be requested in the third phase when the population reached 60,000; and (3) a bill of rights protecting religious freedom, the right to a writ of habeas corpus, the benefit of trial by jury, and other individual rights. In addition the ordinance encouraged education and forbade slavery."[4]

Virginia born Ebenezer Zane, one of the "German founders of Wheeling,"[5] Virginia (now West Virginia), and his two brothers Silas and John as well as his teenaged sister, Betty, played major parts in opening wide the gate to the Old Northwest. Born in Zanesville, Ohio, and descended from this family was Zane Grey, one of the greatest storytellers of the American West. In addition to the Zanes, many other Germans founded communities in Ohio. As reported by the German-Americans of Cleveland Memory Project, "Frederick Post and David Zeisberger, Moravian missionaries from Pennsylvania, and pioneers Conrad Weiser, John Heckewelder and Ebenezer Zane were some of the first Germans to explore and establish settlements in Ohio back in the late 18th century."[6]

In March 1786, a year before the Northwest Ordinance was passed, a group of ten or more veteran officers of the Continental Army who would call themselves the Ohio Company of Associates met at the popular Bunch of Grapes Tavern in Boston. Their purpose was to organize the settling of the wilderness land known as the Northwest Territory west of the Alleghenies and north of the Ohio River that had been ceded to the nascent United States government. The purpose of the Bunch of Grapes meeting was to form a company to purchase lands in Ohio from the federal government and establish the first settlement there.

So the Ohio Company of Associates[7] was a group of private investors who acquired acreage from the federal government to settle the Northwest Territory. The company was led by General Rufus Putnam, a colorful military engineer of Revolutionary War fame. Putnam was a straightforward man, standing nearly six feet tall, who always made an effort to partially shield from view his unsightly right eye disfigured in childhood. A man of integrity with sound common sense, Putnam, as leader of the Ohio Company of Associates, was powerfully aided by the Rev. Manasseh Cutler, a fellow Ohio Company investor. Cutler, as chief spokesman for the Ohio cause, acted as go-between for the company's dealings with Congress.

Manasseh Cutler, with three doctorate degrees—divinity, law and medicine—was a widely read man of infinite curiosity who prepared that part of the Northwest Ordinance banning slavery. Preceding his travels to Ohio Country, Cutler, an avid naturalist, particularly treasured his lengthy dialogue with Benjamin Franklin pouring over Franklin's heavy, lavishly illustrated tome on botany called *Systema Vegetabilium* written by the famous Swedish naturalist Carolus Linnaeus. Cutler described Franklin as "a short, fat, trenched old man in plain Quaker dress, bald pate, and short white locks, sitting without his hat under the tree"[8] and extending a welcoming hand. Cutler was equally fascinated by the conversation and gardens of America's first native-born botanist William Bartram who explored the American Southeast to record the region's plants, animals, and customs of Indian peoples. Later, Dr. Cutler visited several notables in the fields of science and medicine, including making rounds through Philadelphia Hospital wards with Dr. Benjamin Rush and his entourage of medical students. The rounds included checking through the cells of the raving insane. Cutler was impressed that, contrary to most physicians of his day, Dr. Rush treated the mentally ill with exceptional kindness.

After negotiating with Congress in New York and hobnobbing with notoriety in Philadelphia, Cutler traveled to Ohio. At times traveling in a high-wheeled sulky—a two-wheeled, single-seat horse cart—or riding horseback or floating on a barge down the Ohio River, he traveled the country to the site of the future settlement of Marietta. The Ohio Company selectively approved settlers for the new land. The first Ohio non-native settlers were American Revolutionary War veterans and their families, who received land grants in compensation for their military service. The first settlement founded by the Ohio Company was Marietta, Ohio, established in 1788 at the junction of the rivers Muskingum and the Ohio, which the Indians called "O-Y-O, Great River."[9] Marietta gained fame for its ancient Indian mounds which the pioneers carefully preserved. Later, Marietta, surrounded by huge hardwood trees—beech, sugar, maple, ash, elm, sycamore—would become famous for its high-quality shipyards.

Even before Ohio Country was settled, the Northwest Ordinance was forceful and clear on the matter of education, decreeing that "schools and the means of education shall be forever encouraged." Following through on the idea of education, the first settlers of the new land immediately sought funds to found a university.

Gradually, with hard work, the first row of crude huts which stood in fields of mud on the frontier in what would become Marietta were turned into comfortable cabins and then into houses with glass windows. For several winters the woods surrounding Marietta were bare of game because the Indians had slaughtered much of the wild game in an attempt to starve the settlers and drive them out of Ohio. The starving time began in September 1789 when flour was in short supply. Those who had milk divided it with their neighbors, especially those with children. There was little sugar and molasses and no bread. An outbreak of the dreadfully morbid, often fatal measles infection occurred in November, followed by cases of the even deadlier and more debilitating smallpox virus, notorious for its unsightly and permanent scarring.

Notwithstanding the hardships, Germans were attracted to Marietta when they were made aware of the settlement by two men in particular. One was Major Johann Zeigler who was stationed at Fort Harmar at the confluence of the Ohio and Muskingum rivers near Marietta. Later Zeigler would be elected the first mayor of Cincinnati, Ohio. The other, John Heckewelder, was the son of a German missionary. Knowledgeable about Indian culture, Heckewelder acted as interpreter of Indian languages and worked with General Putnam to draw up a treaty with the Indians. Heckewelder's logs and journals, published in certain German provinces of Europe in 1797, drew scores of Germans to the American land of opportunity, employment and freedom. Many came through Wheeling, Virginia, and then traveled down the Ohio River on flatboats, canoes and steamwheelers. In the mid–1800s Germans became the predominate immigrants to the Marietta area.

Although the Jewish population of Marietta remained small, two German brothers, Charles and Samuel Coblenz were among the 19th-century's earliest Jewish immigrants to arrive in Marietta. They established a dry goods store there in the 1840s.

In the 1860s German immigrants as well as first-generation Americans of German ancestry of Marietta fought against slavery in the American Civil War.[10] By that time Marietta had become a major escape route for runaway slaves. On the opposite side of the state, to the west, Cincinnati, also a haven for refugee slaves, was home to a diminutive, five-foot-tall famous American author, Harriet Beecher Stowe. For 17 years Harriet lived in Cincinnati and gathered stories from black servants about human suffering. Based on these stories, her *Uncle Tom's Cabin* published in 1852 was an astounding literary and political sensation, widely sold both in America and England. "It would be said Mrs. Stowe made more converts to antislavery with her book than all the preachers and lecturers combined."[11]

Because America considered Germany as the most educationally efficient nation in the world, the state of Ohio sent Harriet Beecher Stowe's husband, Calvin Elvis Stowe, to Europe to learn about Prussian schools. Stowe observed the "organization of their curriculum and how Prussian teachers moved beyond mere rote learning to engage the student's higher faculties such as imagination and judgment." Stowe concluded, "If it can be done in Prussia, I know it can be done in Ohio.[12]

"Between 1880 and 1920, the population of Marietta nearly tripled, mainly due to German immigration. By 1905, German merchants dominated the shopping area of the first two blocks of Front Street. Otto Brothers and Strecker Brothers built regionally significant businesses in the developing shopping area of Putnam Street."[13]

Back in 1784, at President George Washington's request, the United

21. Germans Begin Migrating

States Congress authorized Colonel Ebenezer Zane and his brothers to bushwhack Zane's Trace from Fort Henry at present-day Wheeling, West Virginia, through the wilderness of Ohio Country in order to open the way for settlement. Shawnee Indian Guide Tomepomehala helped Zane plot the trace. It was only a narrow path along an ancient Indian trail, "a tight fit for a fat horse"[14] and not accessible by wagon. And yet thousands of settlers including many of Germanic heritage migrated to Ohio from Pennsylvania during the late 1700s and early 1800s. They traveled from Pennsylvania along Zane's Trace from Wheeling, Virginia (now WV), and southwestward through Ohio, ferried across the Ohio River and disembarked at Limestone (now Maysville, Kentucky).

In February 1803 Ohio became the 17th State of the Union. It was the first state established in the Northwest Territory. Later, in 1803 the extensive Louisiana Territory west of the Mississippi was purchased from France and explored by experienced soldiers Meriwether Lewis and William Clark. This newer, vaster Louisiana Territory then became the Northwest Territory, while Ohio Country became the *Old Northwest*.

Along Zane's Trace Germanic people settled in communities such as Lancaster which Ebenezer Zane founded in 1800. "In Lancaster, Ohio, Zane's Trace crossed the Hocking River. German settlers used the road for their westward travels, many arriving from Pennsylvania. The Trace provided the way for such a large population of German settlers that by 1809, Lancaster was publishing a German language newspaper, *Der Ohio Adler*."[15] Zane's Trace was broadened in 1804, a year after Ohio became a state. The trace was then a road, wide enough to accommodate the Conestoga wagon which Pennsylvania German settlers had designed and built. Many Germans traveled along Zane's Trace in the 1820s and 1830s, found jobs constructing the region's numerous canals, and built many communities throughout the state.

In October 1811 the ship *New Orleans*, the first steamboat on western waters, departed from Pittsburg. With paddle wheel creaking and smokestack puffing, the ship paddled down the Ohio, stopped briefly at Marietta, chugged on to the Mississippi and—linking America's interior like nothing before—arrived in New Orleans. The entire 2,000-mile-long voyage was made in just two weeks. A succession of steamboats followed, carrying produce, supplies and passengers. "The age of steam had arrived on western waters."[16]

Fort Laramie, a frontier trading post, became a predominately German community which inhabitants named New Berlin. In the early

1800s, viewing America as a kind of promised land, German-speaking Ohioans tried to hold onto their German heritage by publishing German-language newspapers. In the 1830s Cincinnati, especially a Cincinnati neighborhood known as Over-the-Rhine, emerged as an important center of German culture. "German immigrants escaping political oppression, religious persecution, and economic depression found the route to Cleveland more accessible upon the opening of the Ohio Canal in 1833 and later with the railroads in 1848–49. Many of them settled on [Ohio] farms in Newburgh, Independence, and Parma."[17] The European Revolutions of 1848 caused many German "Forty-Eighters" to immigrate to America's Old Northwest. An anti-German uprising erupted at Over-the-Rhine in 1855, but the German neighborhood's armed militia barricaded Vine Street and successfully repelled the mob after three days of fighting.

22

The Revolution of the 1848-ers

The Revolutions of 1848 were widespread uprisings of middle- and working-class people across many nations of Europe. Rebelling against monarchal rule, both the bourgeoisie and the plebeians attempted to establish new leadership in which the common man, like the aristocracy, would have a voice in government.

In Germany, the Revolution of 1848 forced thousands upon thousands of German "Forty-Eighters," to immigrate to the United States of America. The upheavals arose from a multitude of causes in the Fatherland: hunger, misery, unhappiness, hatred, and a bitter sense of oppression coupled with an obsession—the vision to "cure the ills of mankind and help create a utopian society."[1] Inspired by the success of several preceding French Revolutions, Germans, like their neighbors, also began taking up arms against their government. The German Revolution of 1848 was their most forceful uprising.

The first French Revolution which motivated Germans to rebel erupted in 1789. It evolved into years of fighting in Europe, continued as the Napoleonic Wars and ended in 1814. "The Holy Roman Empire dissolved in 1806 under the impact of Napoleon. Its fall removed an obstructing ... agent of German unity; it cleared the way for a progressive German nationalism, the desire to create a modern unified German state."[2] After Napoleon's abdication and exile and his French troops evacuated German soil, the German people reorganized their 300 separate German kingdoms that had been disbanded during Napoleon's heyday. Germans created a German Confederation composed of four independent cities and 35 German-speaking states. Prussia and Austria were the largest of these states. But Prussia, ruled by the powerful King Frederick William IV, was by far the strongest state of this federation.[3]

In 1815 European states sent ambassadors as delegates to create the

Congress of Vienna, Austria. Attended by all the major European powers, the Congress was dominated by Prussia, Russia, Britain, Austria, and France. The purpose of the Congress of Vienna was to settle the Napoleonic Wars and reorganize Europe. A conservative Austrian statesman, Prince Klemens von Metternich, was elected chairman of the Vienna Congress. Through the ensuing years, a widespread series of liberal and national demonstrations against the restored monarchial governments cropped up all across Europe, but Confederation Chairman Metternich and his aristocratic allies managed to put down the insurrections and restore conservative rule. Conservative ideology held that "legitimate and desirable change came about through slow, gradual historical evolution, not by violent and dramatic revolution.... Conservatives worked for change in the sense of returning a revolutionary society to its 'old order' and to preserving traditional institutions such as dynastic monarchy, aristocratic privilege, and the church."[4]

Influenced by the second French Revolution, also known as the French Revolution of July 1830 or July Days, German rioters in 1832 demanded national unification of German states and a liberal constitution. The sole effect of the 1832 German riots, however, "was to enable Chairman Metternich to persuade the members of the confederation again to declare their support for conservative principles and to agree on further measures of repression."[5]

It was about this time, however, that at least one German emigrant escaped repression and became an entrepreneur in the land of the free. Christian Frederick Martin migrated to New York City in 1833. Born in 1796 in Markneukirchen, Saxony, Germany, Martin studied guitar building in Vienna while working under Karl Kuhle. By later working in the shop of Johann George Stauffer, he gathered designs which he used in developing his own scroll-shaped headstock, metal machine tuners, guitar body outline and the pin bridge. After immigrating to New York City, Martin designed a guitar known for its superior craftsmanship and tone. It was a "Distinctly American form of the guitar that would shape all subsequent acoustic guitar making in the United States."[6] His company, C.F. Martin & Co., became world famous, and his company continues to this day to manufacture acoustic guitars in Nazareth, Pennsylvania. Consequently, the German guitar together with the Scots-Irish fiddle and the African banjo form the backbone of traditional Country and Western Music in America today.

Back in the German Fatherland, however, the idea of liberalism did not go away. "Liberalism's chief aims were the liberation of the economy from state intervention and the establishment of representative government, mainly in the form of constitutional monarch," a monarch whose powers were limited by a constitution.[7] Liberalism, which originated in the Age of Enlightenment, was an ideology which guaranteed to each citizen inalienable rights. Among these were freedom of speech, freedom of press, freedom of religion, separation of church and state, freedom of trade, the establishment of a militia, and the protection of habeas corpus (a writ requiring a person under arrest to be brought before a judge or into court). "The enlightenment held that it was rational that everyone should be given the freedom to demonstrate their talents and abilities. It would be detrimental to the state for all those individuals who possess talent not to be permitted to participate in the political process due to their birth."[8]

The conservative aristocracy in Germany, however, did not support this liberal ideology. Liberalism, instead, was embraced by a new middle class created by the Industrial Revolution. The middle class, in general, was made up of well-educated persons, professors, students, bankers, merchants and other professionals. The middle class believed that since the German Kaiser (emperor) and other noblemen had not earned their position, but were simply born into the upper class, they did not deserve to be in power. The middle class were nationalistic, loyal and devoted to their country and took great pride in German culture. The middle class objected to the working class having too much power since they believed the working class lacked the talent to have a voice in government.

In 1840, the new king of the powerful state of Prussia, Frederick William IV, a romanticist, relaxed censorship and became tolerant toward teachers and writers who had been censured for their liberal views. The king seemed to loosen his hold over his subjects even though his conservative views helped spark the Revolution of 1848. In response to the king's temporary leniency, a variety of Prussian political activities began to revive. Eventually, however, King William's belief in the divine rights of kings proved incompatible with liberalism.

The persisting political unrest was complicated by an economic depression which began in 1846. In addition to the deepening economic depression, political conditions among Germans varied widely by 1847. In towns, artisans and apprentices were burdened by restrictions on their professional freedom. In the country, peasants in the south and west and in German provinces of Austria wanted to be freed from their remaining feudal obligations. Among the intellectuals, lawyers, professors and students advocated for freedom of speech, trial by jury and a representative form of government.

The far-reaching revolution of the 18 Forty-Eighters first exploded in Paris in February 1848. It was an outcry against autocratic authority and feudal privilege. Similar insurrections broke out in the major European cities of Vienna, Milan, Berlin, Budapest and throughout the Habsburg Empire and in the numerous Italian and German states. Minor differences existed among revolutionary movements since each country had its own local concern. But in general the patterns were the same. "To their leaders, the uprisings symbolized a triumph of the rationalism of the Enlightenment and a realization of the dreams of poets and intellectuals who championed a cosmopolitan humanitarianism based on natural law and the inalienable rights of man which transcended all national and racial boundaries."[9]

As a result of the Paris Revolution of February 1848, a republic replaced the monarchy in France and guaranteed men the right to vote and the right to work. Hope for a similar outcome spurred uprisings in Germany and throughout Europe. Following successful demonstrations in Bavaria, Vienna and Berlin, one after another government yielded, promising to adopt a constitution and appoint liberal ministers. In March, Metternich, who was still chairman of the Congress of Vienna Confederation, was forced to resign and go into exile. Workers and artisans in Berlin, capital of the Brandenburg province of the Kingdom of Prussia, demonstrated again and won further concessions from Prussian King Frederick William IV, who not only withdrew troops but saluted the corpses of those rioters who were killed in the street fighting. He granted a constitution to the Confederation in 1848 and revised it later.

There was a strong rise of liberalism which entailed: consent of the governed; equality before the law; limited government; individual rights to work, and the right of all adult males to vote; freedom of speech, freedom of press and freedom of religion; replacement of hereditary privileges; and abolishment of absolute monarchy. "National unification, individual freedom, greater economic opportunities, and popular self-government were the watchwords of a long-overdue revolt against the censorship, espionage, repression, militarism, and special privilege which marked the Age of Metternich. A new era of democracy and enlightenment seemed about to dawn throughout western Europe."[10]

Prompted by widespread and diverse political opinions, liberal leaders in individual German states met and discussed their liberal and national views. Infighting among these politically inexperienced nationalist and liberal leaders divided and weakened the revolutionaries. Such internal bickering of the revolutionaries and the inability of the middle class and working class to unite and work together allowed the conservative powers to recover strength, regain authority and rescind their most liberal reforms. The liberals of the bourgeoisie (middle class) who wanted to overthrow conservative rule and to have a voice in government needed the muscle of the proletariat (working class) and liberal students to revolt. But many workers, in the economic downturn of 1845–1847, had lost their 14-hour day of backbreaking jobs. Hunger was rampant. The workers' feeble, weakened attempt at revolt was met in the streets by Prussian troops of the conservative, monarchical rulers.

In the 1830s a new ideology called socialism sprang up in Germany but did not immediately gain popularity. It was defined by Karl Marx, Freidrich Engels and the Communist Manifesto written in 1848. In a socialist society everyone was equal, devoid of class. This would happen when the working class rise up and take control. The idea terrified both the aristocrats and the middle class.[11]

By March 1851, political reform in Europe was almost back to where it had been before the outbreaks of 1848. It was apparent that the Revolution of 1848 had failed. The old constitution of 1815 was restored unchanged. "It was as if the revolution of 1848 had never happened."[12]

The European Revolution of 1848 caused 10,000 disillusioned German "Forty-Eighters" from the Fatherland to become citizens of the United States of America. These political refugees came to New York Harbor after spending two weeks on steamships or much longer on sailing vessels. They came with sadness for their homeland but filled with great hope for building a utopian society in America, creating an ideal place, perfect in law, government and social conditions.

The stream of refugees continued. In 1850 Philadelphia had the fourth largest German-born population in the United States and from 1900 to 1950 had the third-largest German-born population after New York and Chicago.[13] Due to the unresolved discontent of the Forty-Eighters in Europe, "The decade of the 1850's produced a net immigration larger in relation to the existing population than any other decade in American history.... In states like Wisconsin, the increase among the German element was 225.4%, as compared with a total increase of all foreign-born in that state of only 154.4%."[14] The United States provided sanctuary for 60,000 German Forty-Eighters, some of whom feared reprisal by restoration authorities in Europe or even faced criminal charges such as high treason.

A considerable number of expert German engineers immigrated to America in the 19th century. One was John August Roebling, who graduated from the Berlin Royal Polytechnic School, settled in Pittsburgh, Pennsylvania, and began manufacturing iron and steel cables, which, he found, could be used in bridge construction. Using the first suspension wires ever seen in America, Roebling engineered the construction of the bridge over the Alleghany River at Pittsburgh. He also erected what was considered "one of the wonders of the world," the suspension bridge across the Niagara River. Roebling then drafted plans for the Brooklyn Bridge across the East River in New York City. The actual building of the Brooklyn Bridge was supervised by his son, Washington Augustus Roebling.[15]

However, most German immigrants who preceded the Forty-Eighters were mainly farmers, workmen and traders. But this diverse group of Forty-Eighters, these passionate lovers of freedom who came to America after they failed to establish a republic in Germany, found positions of leadership in the community where they implemented their ideals of liberty, humanitarianism and public, secular education for all. They contributed to American culture in areas of architecture, sculpture, theater, arts, crafts, music, the press and literature.[16]

Most of the German Forty-Eighters who came to America were well educated. Some were graduates of military academies in Europe. Others were doctors, former university professors, writers and editors. Many were military veterans of the failed Revolution of 1848. Having firsthand knowledge of fiefdoms, serfdoms and indentured servitude, many of these Forty-Eighters were very supportive of Abraham Lincoln. Most Germans who settled in the North and Old Northwest liked Lincoln's antislavery stance in the 1860 presidential election in which pivotal issues were slavery and states' rights.

23

German Influx

Indiana, Illinois, Michigan, Wisconsin and Minnesota

As American settlers gradually moved west from the Tidewater toward the Piedmont and then over the mountains, the Northwestern lands that stretched north of the Ohio River and west of Maryland and Pennsylvania became America's wilderness. Those backwoods lands, the Old Northwest, comprised all of today's Midwestern states of Ohio, Indiana, Illinois, Michigan and Wisconsin plus a portion of Minnesota. Eventually, as the population expanded westward, the Old Northwest became the new Middle Region of the United States.

Ohio was granted statehood in 1803, Indiana in 1816, Illinois in 1818, Michigan in 1837 and Wisconsin in 1848. Just as Germany played a greater role than any other nation of Western Europe in populating the United States, German-speaking peoples constituted the largest non-English-speaking group of settlers. In the century between 1820 and 1910 nearly 5.5 million German-speaking pioneers arrived. Most of these newcomers settled in the Old Northwest.[1]

Indiana

After the Revolutionary War, when the United States won independence from Britain in 1783, most of Indiana was considered to be property of American Indians. However, Indians ceded to the U.S. government land in extreme southern Indiana between 1800 and 1810 and again in 1838 when the State of Indiana forcibly removed the Potawatomi people to Kansas. That's when Kentuckians and other southern Americans moved in to occupy desirable Indiana land before very many international immigrants arrived.[2]

Overflowing Ohio into Indiana from 1840 to 1870, Germans were the major immigrant group to settle in northern Indiana, where they played an important part in turning a thriving trading post located on an Indian trail into the industrial city of South Bend. Simultaneously the thrifty, debt-hating, industrious Germans helped transform the outlying wilderness into fertile farmland. Following is a sample letter, one of hundreds sent back to friends and family in Germany by these German-American newcomers:

"If you come here to America…. Maud and I will put you up until you have a job and can get on your feet. Here is a clipping we cut out of a newspaper as we left Germany. It was printed by one of the big railroads here in the Midwest of the United States of America. 'Open land, work for all who are willing to work; a higher standard of living for all, religious freedom political democracy, social equality, and a second chance for the young' Your friend Karl."[3]

One catch was that it was technically difficult for Germans to exit their country. In the 1840s and 50s only Germans who were financially solvent could afford to obtain an emigration visa (the Auswanderungspatent) which permitted a person to depart Germany. This presented a problem because many people were leaving German-speaking lands. Hence the housing market was flooded, and it was difficult to sell houses, farms and businesses in order to become solvent. Not only that, but the prospective emigrant had to resolve all back taxes, fulfill all military duties (or pay a fee to be excused from them), procure a birth certificate, possess a good character reference from a church, and then wait many weeks to receive the visa. Additionally, once emigrants renounced citizenship they were not allowed to reenter the country in poverty.

Between 1820 and 1914, 100 million letters were sent from the United States to Germany. These letters, which were sent to European Germans from resident German-Americans, rather than from agents, advertisements or periodicals, were circulated in German newspapers and books. Prompting "chain migrations," these letters were a major motivation for emigration. An 1864 letter written by Johann Wolfgang from South Bend, Indiana "stressed the equality and independence everyone enjoyed, which were in stark contrast to the oppressive semi-feudal social system under which his readers suffered in Germany":

"All men are equal here and no one thinks that he should have greater respect shown him or that he should enjoy some higher rank than his neighbor." No one had to cheer public officials as one had to do in Germany, since they all are "sovereign citizens who recognize no superior but God." He concluded that "everyone is filled with enthusiasm, especially a German who hears all this for the first time. It seems impossible to him that there is really a country on earth where the worth of the individual is so recognized, and it is to him a delight to hear people say, 'Thank God, I, too am an American.'"[4]

By 1850 at least one-eighth of the population of Indianapolis had come from the German states. However, there is good reason to believe that a large percentage of the people of Indianapolis who had come from the Mid–Atlantic states such as Pennsylvania and Ohio were also of German stock. In Indianapolis German immigrants found both abundant work and affordable land which, in many cases, could be bought directly from government land offices. The rapidly developing Midwest needed artisans, skilled workers, professionals, laborers and farmers. German farm families were quite familiar with crop cultivation and needed little or no orientation for an agrarian way of life.[5]

And yet, in 1880 only 7.8 percent of Indiana's residence were foreign born, compared to 23 percent in Illinois and 14 percent in Ohio. Even now, Indiana has a higher percentage of people who have moved from the American South than any other Midwestern state. Politically, culturally and linguistically Indiana is the most southern Midwestern state.

In the last half of the 1800s Germans began gravitating from farms to Indiana cities. Germans then accounted for 14 percent of the population of Indianapolis, where instruction in German became available in public schools. Skilled German workers were recruited by industries in Fort Wayne whose population grew to be 80 percent German. Long-established Amish communities lived separately from other Indianans of German extraction. That's why the year 2000 U.S. Census showed that a German dialect called Pennsylvania Dutch was spoken at home by almost 8,000 Indiana residents.[6]

Illinois

The following letter was written in Red Prairie, Illinois, by a German immigrant, Herbert J. Keiser, to a friend in Germany. His migration was difficult: a 52-day transatlantic voyage and a 16-day trip by steamer up the Mississippi River from New Orleans. Keiser was one of thousands of German and Irish immigrants who left adverse economic and political conditions in their homelands in the late 1840s and early 1850s in pursuit of happiness and prosperity in America. Dated March 6, 1852, Keiser wrote the following letter[7]:

> We thank God, and we are glad that we are here, here in the country of love and of peace, of freedom and abundance. We wish this high happiness to all our brothers longing in body and spirit in East-Friesland, who are alarmed about their livelihood in the future.
>
> Our ship was riding at anchor at the river Weser, perhaps half an hour distant from Bremerhaven, until Sept. 8, 1851, in the forenoon at 10:30. Then it sailed in a strong and not very favorable wind into the ocean. Almost everybody was immediately seasick, and vomiting, similar to drunkenness. They usually laugh, however, because they know that it doesn't mean very much and will soon be over.
>
> In the evening the helmsman announced that the ship was leaking and had 8 feet of water in the hull. This was an inexplicable matter in the case of a new ship. All able men were called on deck, and ten men had alternately and unceasingly to pump water with four pumps. Six feet of water remained in the ship. At daybreak, a leak was found in the oblique lead tubes of the toilets into which the stupid new cooks had thrown bones, and since they had been blocked, pounded them with large iron bars and so caused the leak. The leak was immediately repaired, the ship was pumped out, and seasickness faded away.
>
> The ship sailed as quickly as an arrow through the channel and so near passed England's coast that we could clearly see the houses in the streets illuminated with gas light. Everybody was in good health again and gay and cheerful. On the 13th we saw still to the right the chalky hills of England and to the left the city of Calais in France.
>
> Always quickly forward. On the 15th we passed a passenger ship which had left the harbor eight days ahead of us: From the 15th to the 19th there was a very strong wind in the Spanish sea so that we all, except my wife, again took seasick for a day. A bride from the village Giften near Hildesheim gave birth to a son on the 19th.
>
> We sailed quickly forward, so that we, on the 22nd, had already covered half of our trip. Our captain avoided the trade wind, and he hoped to complete the whole trip in about 30 days. But it did not go that way. On the first of October there came a calm which lasted for nine days, so that we did not sail forward but came backward daily about two English miles. The whole surface of the ocean looked like a sheet of glass, so quiet and still. We now had beautiful, very hot weather so that everybody went barefoot and sweated day and night, dressed only in a shirt.
>
> On the 10th the wind increased, and we encountered a ship with the name of "Phoenix" from Bremen which wanted to sail from Peru to Baltimore. It hoisted the emergency flag, whereupon we put alongside. It had been on the way for 160 days and the food was gone. Our ship provided it to them gratuitously. On the 11th one child died, 24 weeks old, born in Stuttgart, in Wuerttemberg. Later, on the 17th, another died, 17 weeks old, born in Hessencassel. Upon request of our captain, I delivered the funeral oration while the corpses were being dropped into the ocean.

On the 14th of October we saw the island of Puerto Rico through the telescope, far away. On the 16th we saw to the left the island of Santo Domingo with its high mountains which towered over the clouds and on the 17th to our right the island of Cuba.

We sailed from Cuba's eastern tip, passed by Cuba and through the Gulf of Mexico ten days until the evening of the 26th, when we arrived at the mouth of the Mississippi. Here, a thunderstorm moved up from the west. The captain, who hoped to be able to stay near the coast during the storm, let the ship sail at night very quickly under full sails 30 German miles back again into the gulf, and we had to sail until the morning of the 28th before we again reached the mouth of the Mississippi.

Now we saw the continent of North America, far in front of us, and we all were very glad that we had made the trip without real discomfort. A steamer came immediately and towed us over the breakers into the river, where we lay at the banks the whole day because the steamer towed three other ships. In the evening, the steamer towed four large three-masters and sailed with them to New Orleans where we arrived on the evening of the 29th at four o'clock under great jubilation and set foot on the long-yearned-for land with profound feelings of thanks and praise.

On the evening of November 1st we sailed with the steamer Glenco and captain Lee to St. Louis where we arrived on Sunday morning, the 9th of November. The farther to the North we came, the colder and colder it became, so that we really suffered from it. In St. Louis the ground was already covered with snow. The quick change of the weather, the drinking of the Mississippi water, and the poor room which we had on the steamer, beginning from New Orleans, had affected our health very disadvantageously, so that we all arrived unwell. On Thursday, the 14th, to our great joy, your father and your brother Harbert came with two wagons and took us to Red Prairie where we found the friendliest reception.

In 1852 (when the preceding letter was penned) people of German descent composed one-sixth of the Chicago, Illinois, population. Until the turn of the 20th century (immediately preceding and immediately following 1901) Germanic people constituted the largest ethnic group in the city, followed by Irish, Poles, and Swedes. (An ethnic group may be defined as "a social group whose membership is based on race, religion, national origin, or any combination of these.")[8] By 1900, one-fourth of Chicago's 470,000 population had either been born in Germany or had a parent born there.[9]

Michigan

At first, before the American Civil War, Germans came to Michigan because of political instability, religious incompatibility, crop failures, overpopulation or land scarcity in their homeland. Most immigrants also harbored more personal reasons for leaving the Fatherland. Michigan's state policy of encouraging emigration in the late 1840s increased the flow of migrants to America. But the bulk of German immigration was stimulated by chain migration. Immigrant families wrote encouraging letters about life in America to family and friends back home.

German immigration to Detroit began before 1820. And yet, even in 1837 when Michigan declared statehood, Germany still was not unified. That's why, since there was no unified German country until 1871, it is not surprising that German immigrants to Michigan in the 1830s and 40s did not list their place of birth as Germany, but instead they listed such places as Bavaria, Westphalia, Baden, Prussia, Mecklenburg and Württemberg. There were also Russian Germans. Not only were Germans diverse in place of origin, political beliefs and occupations but also in religion—mainly Catholic and Lutheran.

Many German newcomers worked to integrate, assimilate and become Americans. Other groups, however, clung to their German culture and remained isolated ethnic communities for more than a century. Because city life in Detroit and Saginaw communities could be drastically different from rural life, generalizations about Germans in Michigan can be contradictory. Nevertheless, most German-American immigrants in Michigan endeavored to create for their children and grandchildren a sense of belonging. Consequently, their hallmarks of rural conservatism, a strong work ethic and dogged persistence remain as reminders of the German immigrants. "Michigan's German settlers should be viewed as descendants of those who struggled to become Americans." To engage in ethnic sentimentality "is to celebrate a people for what they tried to escape" and "demeans the importance of what they wanted to become."[10]

Driven from the Fatherland by poverty and hoping for a new life in America, many German immigrants sailed into New York City, the key point of entry for European immigrants. Newly arrived Germans were attracted to Michigan by the completion of the Erie Canal in 1825 and the Michigan land rush in 1834. The canal made steamboat travel to the territory easy via the Great Lakes and Detroit, while the land rush resulted from the federal government removing Indians to the west of the Mississippi River. Indian removal made way for government land surveys to apportion fertile farmland to immigrants, especially in the southern one-third of the state where wheat and wool became the chief cash crops. Just as in Germany, villages and neighborhoods bound immigrants together, and Michigan's rural areas continued to share a common ethnic-religious identity. Later immigrants were skilled metal workers who were attracted by promising descriptions of northern Michigan's mineral resources, especially copper and iron ore. It was not only the burgeoning mining industry but also the prospect of forestry development that drew more and more loggers, sawyers and land speculators to the Upper Peninsula of Michigan.

In the 1830s the Michigan frontier suitable for farming was confined to only a few counties in the Lower Peninsula where the growing season was longer. Most of this land was rapidly settled. German immigration to Detroit increased following the arrival of the Forty-Eighters.

By the late 1800s Detroit had three daily German-language newspapers. While keeping German culture alive, these papers also kept Germans informed about the American way of life and helped newcomers assimilate. Employing newspapers the educated and cultured Forty-Eighters sponsored plays by German, Greek and English playwrights and provided a bridge for acculturation into mainstream Detroit society.

By the 1880s, 28 percent of the households of Detroit and 39 percent of Saginaw were headed by German immigrants. Building simple, frame, single-family houses, most of these arrivals from northeastern Germany owned their own homes. Most took factory jobs, some—moving across socioeconomic lines—found "white collar" employment. In fact, "By 1900, 17% of German heads of households in Detroit were employed in white-collar jobs."[11] Forty-three percent worked as skilled laborers, while 40 percent worked as unskilled laborers. Low-income Germans as well as Polish workers often relied on child labor—sending children between ages six and 13 to school and then putting them to work at age 14. This, of course, helped the family survive in relative comfort but also limited their children's educational opportunities and kept them in their own ethnic communities.

At the onset of World War I, when frightened, fanatical Americans attacked German families, the people of Michigan made every effort to Anglicize. In Saginaw a prominent lumberjack wrote to the school board, "It is time to cultivate the pro–American spirit. We should talk in English, read it, write it, sing it and ... teach only English in our public schools."[12] German-sounding street and town names were Anglicized; books extolling German culture were banned, and German was outlawed in elementary schools.

By 2007 Germans were the largest ancestral group in Michigan, representing over 2.6 million descendants, almost one-quarter of the state's population.

Wisconsin

Although many Forty-Eighters remained in Michigan, numerous others, as well as those pioneer families seeking farmland, bypassed Michigan's fertile, heavily populated lower counties and pushed into Illinois, Iowa and Wisconsin.

"The common route from the port of New York to Wisconsin in the 1840's and 1850's was by steamboat up the Hudson River to Albany, from there by boat on the Erie Canal or by rail to Buffalo, and finally by steam or sailboat to the port of Milwaukee," Wisconsin, on the western shore of Lake Michigan. In later years the travel time from New York to Milwaukee was reduced when rail service expanded from east coast ports to Detroit and then to Chicago.[13] By investing in equipment, supplies and minimally priced government land, these financially well-off Germans boosted the economy of Milwaukee, which was called the "German Athens" because of its many cultural institutions.

Greatly influenced by German ideas on education, Wisconsin's school system introduced the first public kindergarten to the United States in 1873. German ideas about vocational education led to the establishment of high schools for girls and boys of rural counties in 1901–1902 and to the development of the nation's first statewide adult and vocational school system in 1911.[14]

Germans were the largest ethnic group to settle Wisconsin, and they were also the most diverse. Although their regional, occupational and religious backgrounds ranged from farmers to skilled craftsmen to professionals and from Catholic to Protestants, Jews and freethinkers, they quickly became Americanized and were soon considered to be bona fide settlers rather than immigrants.

Germans established communities throughout Wisconsin, but the heart of Germanic settlements was a large rectangular area delineated at its corners by Milwaukee, Dane, Brown and Taylor counties. "By 1900 there were nearly 270,000 Germans in Wisconsin, and almost a third of all Wisconsin citizens had been born in Germany!"[15]

German immigrants entered Württemberg in three waves. The first (1845–1860) group was driven from areas of Bavaria and other southwestern German states mainly by crop failures and agricultural consolidation. These first settlers found inexpensive farmland in southern Wisconsin and the city of Milwaukee. Many of this first group of Germans were liberal intellectuals fleeing the failed revolution of the Forty-Eighters. The second wave of German immigration to Wisconsin (1865–1875) were mainly small farm holders caught by an agricultural depression that resulted from cheap American wheat flooding European markets. This second group, the small farmers, came from states such as Hanover and Westphalia in northern Europe. The third group (1875–1890), the largest and poorest, came from Prussia and Pomerania and other northeastern German states. These people were largely displaced agricultural laborers.

Besides the economy, religious beliefs drew settlers to Wisconsin. The largest religious body in the state was the Catholic Church. Next in numbers to the Catholic were the statewide Lutheran churches whose pews were filled not only with Germans but also Scandinavians, especially Norwegians. In the city of Milwaukee, however, German Lutherans were as numerous as Catholics. Of course, not all Catholics in Wisconsin were Germanic. Irish, Polish and, later, Hispanics made up a significant number as well.

Religious affiliations and churches were a basic and powerful social institution. Wisconsin immigrants from northern Germany were mainly Lutheran, while most of those from southern Germany were Catholic. "Marriages between German Catholics and Lutherans were uncommon and usually resulted in at least one family's ostracizing a child and grandchildren…. Devout German Lutherans would even utter sighs of regret when a child married outside the family's synod into a different German Lutheran synod."[16]

An influential German-speaking Swiss immigrant, the Rev. John Martin Henni, became the first Catholic bishop in 1844. As bishop, he encouraged German-speaking Catholics to leave the Fatherland and move to Wisconsin. By far, the most effective and trusted stimuli for persuading German immigrants to move to Wisconsin were the spontaneous, unsolicited letters like this one written in 1849 by John Konrad Meidenbauer from Wisconsin to his sister in Germany:

> You will next ask: Is it really good in America…? and I can give you the answer, from my full conviction…. Yes, it is really good here. I would advise my sister Barbara to come over with her intended for she can do better than in Germany. There are no dues, no titles here, no taxes … no [mounted] police, no beggars.[17]

Newly arrived German immigrants knew what a scarcity of wood meant. The immigrants who intended to build their own houses preferred dense hardwood forestland to prairie land. Those who could not afford to buy cleared land with preexisting homes chose cheap government land near an existing water supply and close to rail transportation. The immigrant needed woodland to provide fuel and lumber to build his own house, animal shelters and fences. To make this happen, clearing the land and removing stumps were backbreaking, necessary chores. But the new farmer also needed an immediate plot for a subsistence garden followed by forest-free acreage for cash crops.

German farmers knew the value of rotating crops, conserving the soil and how to enhance the fertility of gardens and fields by liberally broadcasting livestock droppings as fertilizer. There was an old German folk saying, "The manure pit is the farmer's gold pit," and another: "Where there is manure there is Christ."

In the 1850s the railroad network brought not only a plethora of displaced Forty-Eighters pouring into America, but trains also transported seaboard and European markets to Wisconsin fields and assured farmers that wheat would be their primary cash crop. Even so, new wheat-producing lands expanding northward and westward opened up and drove the price of wheat down. With much of their farmland depleted of fertility by growing wheat and plagued by wheat-destroying insects, farmers searched for new cash crops. Germans and other farmers tested hops, flax, sugar beets, sheep-raising, tobacco and sorghum. In the 1880s they achieved success in dairy farming, not by rushing to deliver fresh milk to faraway markets in Milwaukee and Chicago but rather by cheese production.

And then there was the growing beer enterprise. Whether Mrs. O'Leary's cow kicked over a lantern in a Chicago barn and started the Chicago fire in October 1871 may or may not be mythical. But it's no fairy tale that as soon as the famed fire destroyed Chicago's breweries, the local brewers of Milwaukee, Wisconsin, which became "the Beer Capital of the World," learned how to advertise and expand the market for their own beers—Pabst, Schlitz, Miller and Best. Pabst, in particular, developed containers for safely shipping and distributing the brew. The bonanza lasted for a century before "regional and local beers began to regain the market, spelling an end to the Schlitz and Pabst brands."[18]

Minnesota

Minnesota, the "Land of 10,000 lakes," is known for its waterways, which are vital to the economy of the state and the nation. Minnesota is the point of origin for the Mississippi River which runs southward, is joined by the Ohio River, and continues southward to the Gulf of Mexico. Minnesota is also the westernmost point of the St. Lawrence Seaway which flows eastward through the Great Lakes and then to the Atlantic Ocean. When the French claimed the Minnesota area in the mid-1600s, the land was home to the Ojibwa (Chippewa) and Dakota (Sioux) tribes. It became a territory of the United States through the 1783 Treaty of Paris and the 1803 Louisiana Purchase.[19] Today Germans are Minnesota's most numerous ancestry group and also its most widely dispersed and perhaps its most inconspicuous.

Although a few German immigrants came to Minnesota before it was declared a territory, most came afterward. At first, these pioneers did not come directly from Europe but from German settlements elsewhere in the United States such as Ohio, Wisconsin and Missouri where land was becoming scarcer and more expensive. They ordinarily settled on rural farmsteads. Those first settlers who came to territorial Minnesota's frontier faced the hardships of chopping wood, clearing and settling wilderness land, guarding against Indian uprisings and difficult communication while trading goods and commodities with the outside world. Soon these early settlers came directly from Europe, and later many also settled in urban communities.

Minnesota's first German resident was Eugen Gass, an educated German-Swiss who immigrated to America in 1825 and traveled to St. Louis. Twelve years later, in 1837, Gass migrated to Fort Snelling, a United States Army frontier post located at the confluence of the Minnesota and Mississippi rivers in what is now the greater Twin Cities (Minneapolis-Saint Paul) area of Minnesota. At Fort Snelling, a Mendota fur trader hired Gass to keep his books and teach his children. By the fall of 1850, there were 21 Germans among Fort Snelling's 143-man garrison.

Alexander Ramsey, Minnesota's first territorial governor, whose mother was Pennsylvania German, attracted a large number of German workers to begin colonizing the Minnesota territory: sawmillers, lumberjacks, craftsmen, a couple of doctors, and nine farmers. German-born craftsmen, merchants and other businessmen came to the new territory via steamboat. Although cheap government land was available in parts of Wisconsin, Iowa, Kansas and Nebraska, Minnesota's fertile land lying close to the Mississippi River was the greatest lure. In the days before railroads were widespread, steamboats and the river's navigable tributaries promised easy access for workmen and farmers transporting their produce to market.[20]

Friederich Schmitz from Stillwater, Minnesota (in the Minneapolis–Saint Paul Metro Area, across the St. Croix River from the state of Wisconsin), wrote a letter in 1858 to his parents in the Rhine Province. Schmitz's letter epitomized America's appeal to Germany's peasants and landless laborers, as well as to artisans who inherited ever-smaller plots of land in Germany:

> Anyone in Germany, like myself, or most of those in our village, who marries and has a family can see in advance that he is to be and remain a poor and worried person as long as he lives. And in addition he must take his hat off to anyone who has a handful more of land, scraping and bending as the custom is. That is not here. Anyone here who has nothing and is in health can support himself better than one in our village who may possibly have property to the amount of one thousand thaler [a German silver coin comparable to the American dollar].... And if one will work in this way for three or four years, he will be able to buy himself a small landed property.[21]

The transition of the farm family from cultivating scattered plots in German village fields to clearing land and growing new crops on their own expansive, 100 acre farms in America involved the intensive labor of the whole family. All family members, males and females, adults and children worked together for the family's survival. A typical Minnesota German farmer in 1875 "Cut his barley with a scythe … while his pregnant wife bound the sheaves, and his daughter was plowing behind a team of oxen by the time she was 16. Like others in the Red River Valley, he rode the wheat boom to prosperity by 1880, but it was his cautious diversification into vegetables, fruits, and firewood that enabled him to survive the farm crisis of the 1890s.[22]

"There has … been a tendency to lump all German-speaking immigrants together as German-Americans, so that Austrians, German Swiss, and the Luxemburg Germans in Minnesota were considered 'German-Americans' by non–Germans, though the immigrants themselves continued to recognize the regional and national distinctions not perceived by the dominant society."[23] German immigrants brought their regional ways with them. Regional cultural differences characterized various German states. For instance, the typical Bavarian peasant house was the chalet. In Austria, the traditional feminine dress was a dirndl worn over a white cotton blouse covered by an apron. She wore a small hat, white stockings and black shoes with buckles. Men wore gray jackets with green lapels and knee socks. Their hats were trimmed with goat beards. They danced polkas, schottisches (slow polkas) and schuhplattlers, which was a characteristic Bavarian dance in which the dancer strikes the soles of his shoes ("Schuhe") with his hands held flat ("platt"). Their songs included yodels and zither music. The friendliness and neighborliness (gemütlichkeit) was typified by their German pubs (Bierstuben or beer halls) where they fraternized over steins of beer and energetically danced the polka.

The church was the center of German community life in Minnesota. A rich devotional life, parish schools, feast days like Christmas, as well as choirs, bands and even a shooting society were developed by Catholics around their tall-steepled Gothic church.

In Minnesota "German Lutherans were as prominent but never as unified ... as their Catholic compatriots. They were not only divided from other Lutherans by ethnicity, but among themselves by differences of doctrine, liturgy, governance, and custom, and unlike Catholics had no single institutional structure to direct growth and allocate resources."[24] The first German Lutheran congregation was founded in Minnesota in 1855. Within ten years, there were five separate Lutheran synods struggling to organize Minnesota parishes. Like many Catholics, conservative Lutherans favored steepled, Gothic churches. Many conservative Lutherans kept speaking their German language and preserved their culture to protect against secular contamination. Like Catholics, Lutherans too supported parochial schools and socialized within their own church groups.

There was a rich variety of religious differences for German newcomers to Minnesota. "Germans were not just Catholics or Lutherans; they were also Baptists, Mennonites, Methodists, Moravians, Presbyterians, and Jews; and the religious ideology which they embraced colored their perceptions of the world and their relationships with other people around them."[25]

Before World War I, the German language was spoken in German homes, churches and schools. In many areas, the schools were affiliated with churches, especially the Catholic and Lutheran. Combining German and English lessons, courses were taught in German in the mornings and English in the afternoons. There were four grades in the school, which was a one-room, small building without indoor plumbing. The woodshed and water pump were in the backyard, and all the pupils drank out of the same water pail with a communal dipper. A wood-burning stove stood in the center of the room. All four grades were taught by an exceptionally strict minister. So strict was he, "The school was compared to the Prussian army: He told you to do something, and you did it, or else you got knocked under the table." Lessons were done on slates, and assignments had to be done right, or the children would be whipped or kept after school until they had the lessons letter-perfect, by heart. "This was sometimes difficult for farm-children, who had chores to do when they got home from school and then had to study at night by kerosene lamps."[26]

Although German-Americans voted, they were not usually active in community politics with the exception of the Forty-Eighters. One notable exception, however, was Prussian-born Rudolph Knapheide, who became an American citizen soon after his arrival and settled in Minnesota where he held a political office. Knapheide then helped German newcomers to St. Paul by finding them a job and living quarters until they acculturated enough to fend for themselves. The Knapheides usually kept in contact with their indentured servants after the servant was freed. Once when the Knapheides visited a former housemaid, she served them a chicken dinner. At the end of the meal, they complimented their hostess on the fine meal, to which she replied, "Yes, poor old rooster, killed him this morning, been sick so long!"[27]

24

Go West, Young Man
Louisiana, Oregon, California and Texas

Although northeastern Minnesota belonged to the Old Northwest, which was a British-American Territory, St. Paul, Minnesota, on the Mississippi River where the German Knapheides family and their former indentured servant with her poor, old chicken lived, was in Louisiana Territory.

Louisiana Territory was named by René-Robert Cavelier, sieur de La Salle, who led a canoe expedition down the Mississippi River and reached the Gulf of Mexico. On April 9, 1682, La Salle, proclaimed the whole Mississippi basin—the exquisitely fertile region watered by the river and its tributaries—for France and named it Louisiana after Louis XIV.

One of La Salle's most loyal followers was Hans, the German buccaneer from Wittenberg. When La Salle was murdered by a fellow French explorer who wanted to succeed him as expedition commander, Hans the buccaneer avenged La Salle's death by shooting La Salle's French murderer through the heart with a pistol.[1] Many Germans after Hans played important parts in developing the area.

In the first half of the 18th century, France controlled and settled the colony of Louisiana, a vast settlement in North America covering the Natchez district and the area of present-day Mississippi along the Mississippi Gulf Coast. The Louisiana Colony stretched 3,000 miles from the mouth of the Mississippi River, through present-day Louisiana, Mississippi, Arkansas, Missouri, Illinois, Iowa, Wisconsin and Minnesota.[2] French forts and settlements built along the Gulf Coast and in the Mississippi Valley included Biloxi, Mississippi, first inhabited in 1699, and Mobile, Alabama, in 1702. Natchitoches (Nack-a-tish), established in 1714, was the first permanent settlement in the present state of Louisiana. After New Orleans was founded in 1718, several settlements mushroomed farther upstream along the Mississippi. New Orleans became the capital of Louisiana in 1722.

John Law, a Scottish economics wizard and adventurer as well as a friend of the Duke of Orléans, engineered a financial scheme which, from 1718 to 1720, ballooned into what is now known as the Mississippi Bubble. The duke was a nephew of Louis XIV, whom he succeeded as interim regent of France since Louis XV was only five years old when his father, Louis XIV, died. The French duke wanted Law to help compensate for his country's reckless spending under Louis XIV.

The scheme pivoted around Law's exclusive right to develop the extensive French territories in the Mississippi Valley by enticing French people to settle there. Law sold shares of the Mississippi company for cash. But his scheme to establish French colonies along the Mississippi River failed when fur trading, silver and gold mining didn't pan out. The French settlers, disappointed in their failure to discover gold and silver and having neither desire nor aptitude for farming, returned home. The unfortunate Law's scheme led to a general stock market crash in France and other countries. The huge debt accrued by companies and banks was taken over by the French government, which raised taxes to pay it.

Attempting to make amends for the stock market crash, Law initiated an advertising blitz to entice German emigrants from distressed Switzerland and the Rhenish districts to settle the Mississippi Valley. Pamphlets printed in the German language and published in Leipzig in 1720 exaggerated the amenities of French settlements of the lower Mississippi and stimulated the exodus of at least 10,000 hard-pressed Germans from the Rhine region and the Palatinate. Their long, stressful journey was plagued by infection and tropical diseases. Of the 8,000 Germans who actually set sail from Europe in 1720–1721, only one-third disembarked in Biloxi and Mobile. A copy of the aggrandized pamphlet was discovered by a Tulane professor in a New Orleans bookstore.

When the disillusioned Germans arrived at Biloxi and Mobile, there was no accommodation for them. In a condition of semi-starvation, many immigrants died. In desperation, a flotilla of German directors approached Governor Bienville and officials of the Law company and demanded free transportation back to Europe. The conference ended when the Germans were assigned to "the rich alluvial lands on the right bank of the Mississippi about twenty-five miles above New Orleans." The district, still known as the German Coast, was already occupied by two German settlements, one settled in 1719 and the other in 1721.

Even so, life was hard. There were only seven cows to support 56 German families, and there was not a horse for ten years. "Every foot of the hard soil had to be made arable by hand labor."[3] People less industrious and of less hardy stock simply would not have endured. Since Germans produced more offspring than French, Creoles (people of mixed European and black descent) of German ancestry now outnumber the French Creoles, and many families kept their German traditions alive.

Far northwest of Louisiana lies Astoria, Oregon, the oldest American settlement west of the Rockies. Astoria was founded by John Jacob Astor, one of the most outstanding German immigrants in the building of America. Born in Waldorf near Heidelberg in 1763, Astor came to America when he was 20 years old after spending several years in London. A Quaker tanner employed him in the trade industry to work as a buyer of pelts and hides in the wilderness of New York. In 1786 the German-American immigrant began working independently as a fur trader and then founded the American Fur Company in 1809 in competition with the Hudson's Bay Company. Astor opened a branch fur supply trading post called Astoria overlooking the Columbia River near the Pacific Coast in Oregon. There, in the permanent settlement of Astoria, Astor hoisted the first American flag on the West Coast.

Another avant-garde German figure who carved a settlement on the Pacific Coast and raised the American flag there was John August Sutter. Born in Baden, Germany, on the east bank of the Rhine River to parents who hailed from Switzerland, Sutter, always proud of his Swiss heritage, received a good education and joined the Swiss military. Having fallen into bankruptcy in 1834, he left his wife and children in the care of his brother and set sail for America to regain his fortune. Soon he decided that the West Coast offered the best chance for fulfilling his vision of founding a colony on the Sacramento River,[4] so Sutter moved from New York to Missouri and operated as a successful fur trader on the Santa Fe Trail. The Santa Fe Trail originated in Missouri, crossed Kansas, branched slightly north through Colorado or slightly south through the Oklahoma Panhandle and ended in New Mexico. With cash in his pocket and his head full of dreams, he traveled the Oregon Trail on his way to the West Coast. The Oregon Trail began in Independence, Missouri, trekked through northeastern Kansas and through Nebraska, Wyoming and Idaho to end in northwestern Oregon. Sutter arrived at Fort Vancouver, near present-day Portland, Oregon. Looking for a ship to take him to San Francisco Bay, he detoured to the Hawaiian Islands and Alaska, trading profitably along the way until he arrived in Monterey, California, in 1839 and implemented his long-held ambition. From Mexican Governor Alvarado, he acquired a strip of land, 120 miles northeast of San Francisco and, with the help of Hawaiian laborers, Sutter founded the New Helvetia (New Switzerland) settlement and constructed Fort Sutter. Standing on the Sacramento River in the midst of American Indian Territory, the fort was an enormous adobe structure with walls 18 feet tall and three feet thick.[5]

He attracted settlers, broke several hundred acres of land, built a tannery, a mill and a distillery. His livestock numbered 20,000 head of cattle, horses and sheep. In 1844, on the Sacramento River he laid out the town of Sutterville, which eventually became the city of Sacramento. Sutter's vineyards and wheat crops prospered, and his fortune was estimated in the millions. Sutter declared his independence of Mexico in 1846, and, with the American invasion of Mexico, California became a territory of the United States.[6]

In 1844 Sutter's son had come to live with him, and the rest of his family followed to share in his fairy-tale life. But the fairy tale soon turned into a nightmare that tarnished his dream and destroyed his achievements. It happened one morning in January 1848 when a carpenter who was building a sawmill saw nuggets of gold in the water on the bottom of a stream and told Sutter of his discovery. Sutter verified the find and pledged his employees to secrecy, but the news spread like wildfire to San Francisco "and the gold rush was on."[7] His workers soon abandoned him to join the squatters who swarmed over his land, seeking gold, staking out claims, destroying his crops and butchering his livestock. Thousands of lawsuits were filed to dislodge the intruders but to no avail. The courts ruled against him, although the state paid him a $3,000 annuity for seven years in allowance for taxes paid by him. One-time millionaire John August Sutter, a shrewd and courageous man, was reduced to poverty. A ruined man, he died at Litiz, Pennsylvania, leaving behind him in California rivers, counties and towns to be named in his honor and a legislative hall where his portrait now hangs.

Texas German Belt

Overflowing the Old Northwest Territory as well as the original 13 colonies, Germans as pioneers, pathfinders, farmers, dairymen, weavers, miners and soldiers continued, as did other Americans, their journey across the continent, settling in all the United States of America.

24. Go West, Young Man

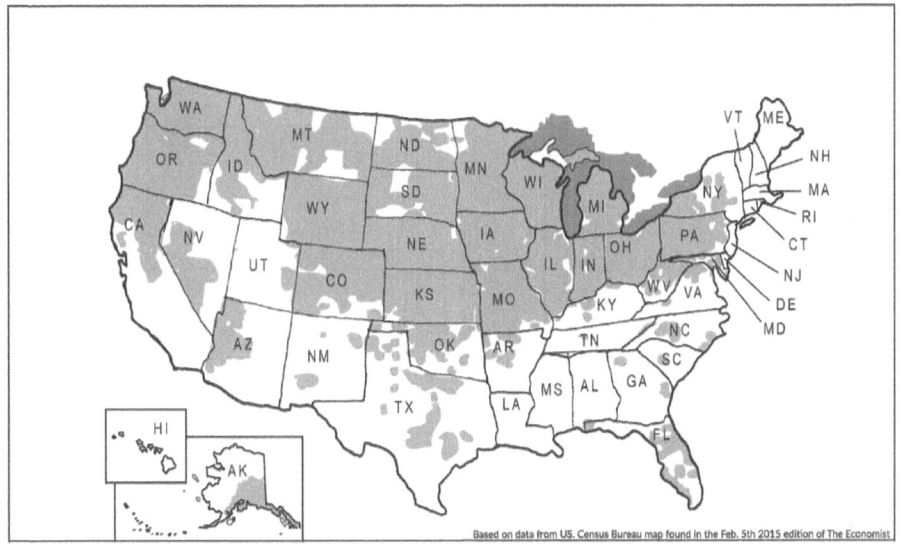

Areas of the United States where Germans are the largest ethnic group.

The major U.S. immigration ports were New York, Philadelphia, Baltimore, Boston, Galveston, New Orleans, and San Francisco.

Migrants sailed on cargo ships on their way to Philadelphia, Baltimore, New Orleans and New York to pick up wheat, tobacco, cotton or other supplies for the European market. Other than chain migrations in the 1830s and 1840s, there were sporadic, more organized efforts to colonize the New World. The largest of these was the 1843 enterprise launched by a group of noblemen to settle several thousand impoverished immigrants to the Republic of Texas. The transfer of power from the Texas Republic to the new state of Texas did not formally occur until February 1846.

The true pioneer responsible for Germans migrating to Texas and creating the German Belt was Friedrich Diercks, alias Johann Friedrich Ernst, who attempted to solve the economic, social, political or religious problems in his homeland. In 1831 Ernst applied for and received a 4,000-acre grant in south central Texas (in what is now northwestern Austin County) which would form the nucleus of his German Belt.

To entice Germans to immigrate to America, Ernst wrote letters to friends in Germany. He omitted negatives and dwelled on positives, describing fertile and rich farmland just waiting for German labor to make it productive. He painted Texas as an earthly paradise overflowing with game and fish, where there was no winter, and taxes were nil.

His letters appeared in both newspaper and guidebook and beckoned a chain emigration of Germans from rural parishes in districts of Oldenburg, Westphalia, and Holstein to find work and new homes in Texas.

The 1990 United States census shows that 17.5 percent of the total population of Texas claimed either pure or partial German ancestry. A majority settled across the south central part of the state in the patchy German Belt stretching from Galveston and Houston on the east to Kerrville, Mason, and Hondo in the west, from the humid coastal plain to the semiarid Hill Country.[8]

Even in the early 17th century, when Germans deserted their war-torn homeland, the majority turned westward towards America. Beginning as a little ripple, "The current of immigration gradually increased in volume until, between the years 1880–1884 the yearly exodus from Germany averaged nearly one hundred and seventy-five thousand."[9] Of the 2.6 million Germans living outside the empire in 1884, 2 million were citizens of America.

25

Americans of German Heritage During World War I

Until World War I German-Americans were viewed as an esteemed, much sought-after and valuable segment of American society. By and large, they had escaped the discrimination and prejudice so often heaped onto other racial and ethnic groups. But the Great World War temporarily tainted some people's perception of Germans.

Circumstances which led up to World War I arose in 1888 when 29-year-old German Crown Prince Wilhelm II (1859–1940) became both German Emperor (Kaiser) and King of Prussia. During his difficult birth in Potsdam in 1859, Wilhelm—the eldest child of Crown Prince Frederick and Victoria, daughter of Queen Victoria of the United Kingdom—sustained crippling damage to his left arm and hand which he tried to conceal all his life. His withered left arm was paralyzed and noticeably shorter than his right. He could not cut his own food. Not only that, but having both a quick mind and a quick temper, Wilhelm II did not get along with either parent. Wilhelm's father lacked stamina, and the young Kaiser's relationship with his mother was tense. Her "intellect was hopelessly at the mercy of her feelings."[1] On the other hand, Wilhelm adored his grandmother Victoria, Queen of the United Kingdom. Wilhelm was 12 years old when the German Empire was formed under the leadership of the Prussian Empire; Wilhelm then was in line to become emperor as well as king of Prussia.

Filled with nationalist enthusiasm, Wilhelm wanted to fulfill the expectations which he perceived the Prussian people had formed of their leader: to be a firm, brave, frugal ruler, just and manly, self-sacrificing and self-reliant. He was determined to increase the strength of the German armed forces, especially the navy, to carry out his imperialistic and nationalistic agenda.

During the 26 years of his reign before World War I, Kaiser

Wilhelm II, "one of the most remarkable figures in modern history,"[2] developed his German Empire with whirlwind rapidity in industry, commerce and military strength. He formed the Kaiser Wilhelm Society for the promotion of basic scientific research in which leading scientists were permitted to pursue their own research projects. The experiment would be jointly funded by industry and state. A similar version of the new academic pursuit existed in Paris at the Institut Pasteur, but nothing comparable previously was to be found in Germany.

German trade spread worldwide, and the German Navy quickly rivaled that of Great Britain. The carefully organized German Army and the country's apparent preparation for war left no doubt that Germany intended to become the dominant power in the world. Wilhelm's control extended from the Baltic and North seas to the Persian Gulf. He sought to destroy the military power of France and replace the British Empire's control of the seas. Even more widespread was Wilhelm's wish to overthrow the Monroe Doctrine and exploit countries of the New World which, at the time, were less powerful than Europe. The Monroe Doctrine was the bedrock of America's foreign policy. It expressed the intention of the United States to remain neutral in European wars and warned that if a European nation tried to interfere with a nation in the Western Hemisphere, the United States would view the move as a hostile act and respond accordingly.

The world looked at Wilhelm's ambitious accomplishments in amazement but considered his goals too grandiose to be achievable. France, Russia and Great Britain did, however, form a triple alliance to counterbalance the triple alliance of Germany, Austria and Italy that former German Chancellor (Prime Minister) Otto Von Bismarck had formed in 1882. It was then that Bismarck had drafted a secret agreement between Germany, Austria-Hungary, and Italy that if any were attacked by France, the other two would assist their assaulted partner.

After Archduke Franz Ferdinand, the heir presumptive to the throne of Austria-Hungary, was assassinated in June 1914, Austria-Hungary declared war on Serbia the next month for harboring a terrorist group that presumably had murdered the archduke. The declaration of war on Serbia gave German Empire Emperor Wilhelm II just what he was looking for: justification for waging a general European war. Germany supported Austria in declaring war upon Serbia. When Russia mobilized to defend her small ally, Serbia, Germany declared war on both Russia and Russia's ally, France. Because marching German armies forced their way through neutral Belgium to strike France,

25. Americans of German Heritage During World War I

Britain kept her pledge to defend Belgian neutrality by declaring war on Germany.

In 1914 most German-Americans were American-born descendants of earlier immigrants. Although they sympathized with relatives in the Fatherland, they were loyal Americans who wanted to stay out of the war and agreed with United States President Woodrow Wilson's stance on neutrality. But anti–German propaganda from Europe began to divide American opinion. And a German-backed, counter-campaign in the U.S. failed to squelch the growing anti–German sentiment.

President Wilson opted to remain impartial and stay out of the fray. In August former United States President Theodore Roosevelt wrote, "I am not now taking sides," and praised Germans as a "stern, virile and masterful people."[3] But before the month was over, Americans, unable to remain neutral in such an international catastrophe, did indeed take sides. They became divided emotionally into pro–Ally (backing France and Britain), pro–German, or pro-neutral.

Although Italy was a member of Bismarck's Triple Alliance of 1882, Italy was not bound to join the Central Powers of Germany and Austria. That's because the "Great War" [World War I] was a war of aggression on the part of Germany and Austria. Italy therefore denounced the German-Austrian alliance and, in May 1915, entered the war on the side of the allies—the French, Russian, Great Britain alliance.

Except for invading—brazenly marching through neutral Belgium without permission—no single act of the Germans caused greater disgust and anger than the sinking of the British passenger liner *Lusitania* in May 1915. In violation of the rules of international law and chivalry at sea, Germany torpedoed the *Lusitania* off the coast of Ireland. Among the 1,150 or more lives lost, 114 were Americans. This crisis at sea was one of the most important events that led America into the war.[4] In Germany's defense, German officials had warned the crew not to sail into a war zone since they correctly suspected that the speedy and luxurious ship, *Lusitania,* was smuggling munitions for the British.[5] But even with the sinking of the *Lusitania,* President Wilson still refused to enter the war. "Leaders like Theodore Roosevelt [who had served as President of the United States 1901–1909] clamored for war and the press took up the cry."[6]

Yet, the United States did not enter the war until 1917, when Germany proclaimed submarine war against all vessels, neutral or enemy, that were found in a war zone around the British Isles and along the coast of France and Italy. The decree was announced on January 31, 1917, when electronic communication was not as swift as it is today. So when the decree went into effect the next day, Germany sank liners and merchantmen without adequate warning.

The act of war, the sinking of ships, led the U.S. Senate and House to declare war on the German Empire. President Wilson and the secretary of state signed the formal proclamation on April 6, 1917.

On Sunday morning, July 21, 1918, the only shots fired at United States soil during World War I landed on the east coast of Cape Cod. The massive barrage of more than 100 shells was fired from two huge guns mounted on the deck of German submarine U-156. The attack was aimed at an American tugboat and the barges she towed. The tug was badly damaged, and the barges were sunk. It was "part of the German effort to sink as many ships in as little time as possible."[7]

Brendan Simms's 2019 book, *Hitler: A Global Biography*, notes that Adolf Hitler, a private of the 16th Bavarian regiment, escorted two doughboys (a nickname applied to United States soldiers during World War I) to brigade headquarters. From that day forward Hitler remained convinced that American soldiers were descendants of sturdy German emigrants to the New World whom the Fatherland had allowed to slip away. They had now "returned as avengers in the ranks of an unstoppable enemy." Stopping that unstoppable enemy, America, became Hitler's lifelong obsession. "Hitler saw America's rise as the work of Aryan [Germanic] immigrants. How could his Germany become a world power, if its best citizens left for the U.S.?" The migration of Germans who had crossed the Atlantic in the 19th century and settled in America "Made that country great," said Hitler in a speech.[8]

America's entry into World War I prompted President Wilson and the U.S. Congress to condone a "terrific propaganda drive to convert Americans from their traditional isolationism and make the people love the war and hate the enemy."[9] Prompted by the U.S. government, artists, advertisers, poets, photographers and educators bombarded the country with printed material. Although there were few private radio sets at this time, speakers at public gatherings and motion picture theaters conspired to make the Germans look depraved. Anyone who dared suggest that there were good Germans as well as bad Germans became suspect.

State laws forbade the teaching of German in public schools, and German books were thrown out of public libraries. German and Austrian musicians were forbidden to play in public. Music composed by Wagner and Mendelssohn was removed from concert programs and was not allowed to be played at weddings. Due to anti–German sentiment, local residents changed German street names. Hundreds of German names for towns, streets, parks and public buildings were changed. For example, the name of the city of New Berlin, Ohio, was changed to North Canton. Hamburg was renamed "Pershing" or "Belgium." German-Americans suspected of being pro–German were tarred and feathered.

With the outbreak of war, German ancestry became a liability. First, President Wilson warned against hyphenated Americans (such as German-Americans) whose loyalty was likely to be divided. Next, a government official warned that "every citizen must declare himself American—or traitor." "Ironically, and contrary to Wilson's opinion about divided loyalties, thousands of German Americans fought to defend America in World War I, led by German American John J. Pershing, whose family had long before changed their name from Pfoerschin."[10] United States General Pershing commanded the American Expeditionary Force (AEF) in Europe during World War I.

Furthermore, President Wilson proclaimed all German citizens "alien enemies."[11] He (the president) also barred German-Americans from living near military bases, airports, port towns and Washington, D.C., the nation's capital. They were fingerprinted and required to disclose their bank accounts and property to an alien property custodian. German citizens in America who were noncompliant and those who were considered potentially dangerous were confined to internment camps for the duration of the war. Some 2,300 employees of German passenger and merchant ships were confined to Fort McPherson, Georgia; about 1,400 academics, journalists, business people, artists and all other suspects were incarcerated at Fort Oglethorpe, Georgia. Fort Douglas in Utah housed 500 prisoners of war, plus 800 "alien enemies" and 200 American conscientious objectors. The CPI (Committee on Public Information) warned Americans to watch their neighbors of German descent. It's no wonder that the fear of spies and the thought of being poisoned permeated neighborhoods as well as the American psyche.

Church services using German language were disrupted. Especially harassed were Mennonites, Amish and Hutterites because not only were their members German, but they were also pacifists, opposed to the military. Their pacifism was unjustifiably mistaken for pro–German sympathies.

The shutting down of German-language newspapers ended the

German-American press's influence in American politics. Mob action forced school children to sign pledges not to use any foreign language, forced the kissing of the American flag and the singing of the National Anthem. Mob action lynched a German native in Illinois who was suspected, but not proven, to have stolen dynamite. A jury found the 11 hangmen not guilty. Numerous German businesses changed the names of their companies to prove their loyalty and to stop customers from boycotting their products.

The United States' weighty entry into the war, plus severe German shortages of men as well as materials from years of trench warfare, led to Germany's military collapse in 1918. Wilhelm, the last German Kaiser (emperor) and Prussian king, was forced to abdicate and went into exile in the Netherlands. He had hoped to regain status when Führer Adolf Hitler came into power, but that did not happen.

In summary, World War I (First World War or Great War) was fought between 1914 and 1918. It was an international, extraordinarily gory conflict of butchery, bloodshed, killing and devastation. The Great War pitted the Central Powers—mainly Germany, Austria-Hungary, and Turkey—against the Allies. The Allies were mainly France, Great Britain, Russia, Italy and Japan, joined by the United States in 1917. The carnage ended at the Paris Peace Conference with the Treaty of Versailles, in which Germany acknowledged that it was solely responsible for causing the war. The treaty, which essentially redrew the map of Europe, was signed on June 28, 1919, and took effect on January 10, 1920. However, many Germans felt that the treaty was too severe and failed to comply with it.

Back in 1918 America, when the sale of sauerkraut dropped, its name was changed to "liberty cabbage" or "pickled vegetable." The Federal Food Board realized that the consumer felt unpatriotic to buy products with German names. That's why "hamburgers" became "liberty sausage" and "Bismarck pastry" became "American beauty." German shepherds became "Alsatian shepherds," and dachshunds were called "liberty pups." Not only did German businesses change their company names, but they often Anglicized their family names.[12]

Propaganda—United States Government propaganda—erased German culture during World War I.[13] President Wilson attempted to rally Americans to support the war by dividing the country. He instilled his own prejudice, intolerance, fear and hatred of immigrants, especially Germans. This xenophobia and nativism shattered the lives not only of recent immigrants but of families of German descent who had been productive, valuable and loyal patriots of America for several generations.

It was not only in America but also in Britain that family names were changed. This is the story of why the Germanic surname Saxe-Coburg-Gotha for the British royal house was changed to House of Windsor: When Queen Victoria died in 1901, the royal house took the Germanic surname of her consort Prince Albert of Saxe-Coburg-Gotha. Victoria and Albert's eldest son, King Edward VII (Bertie) was the only sovereign of that dynasty to reign in Britain. "At the height of World War I, when German xenophobia had reached boiling point, Edward VII's son, King George V (1910–1936) changed the family name to the more English sounding House of Windsor."[14]

Frederick Trump, 21st-century American President Donald Trump's grandfather, was born in the village of Kallstadt, in the Palatine part of Rhineland-Palatinate, a district in western Germany. It was the same village where Henry J. Heinz, founder of the Heinz Tomato Ketchup Company, was born. Trump immigrated to the USA in 1885 and made his fortune during the Yukon gold rush in Alaska. There he established several hotels "that doubled as brothels.... The story that he [Frederick Trump] came from Sweden appears to have been an attempt by the family to obscure their origins amid popular anti–German feeling in the US following the First World War. According to the New York Times and the Boston Globe, Donald Trump's father made repeated attempts to hide his German roots."[15] Prompted by the anti–German feeling in the United States following World Wars I and II, not only the Trump family but countless other Americans with German heritage considered it prudent to conceal their German ancestry.

In the years after World War I, families with Germanic ties thought of themselves only as Americans. Many of their ancestors had served as soldiers or patriots in the American Revolution. Many more Germans had fought on both sides of the American Civil War. But during and after World War I, many Americans of German heritage either suppressed or did not know or did not tell their children about their German roots.

26

World War II German Rocket Scientists Immigrate to USA

127 Exceptional Men[1]

BY JAMES EVANS LYNE

At the close of the First World War, the Treaty of Versailles was intended to limit the probability of a future conflict. A large part of the document involved very specific constraints which were placed on the number and types of weapons that Germany was allowed to maintain. German artillery, for example, was limited to a total of 504 guns, including both heavy and light mortars and field artillery pieces. These numbers represented only a tiny fraction of the thousands of similar weapons that had been deployed during the Great War.

The relevant sections of the treaty, however, are striking in that they seem to ignore the possibility of future technical developments. Germany was able to use this oversight to devise some of the most infamous weapons of the Second World War, the Vergeltungswaffee or Retribution Weapons, better known as the V-1 and V-2 rockets. Despite the destruction they caused during the war, the technical advances achieved during the development of these weapons have had profound and far-reaching consequences, including the spectacular success of the American space program in the 1960s, enabled to a great extent by a small group of German rocket engineers who immigrated to the U.S. at the close of the war.

German work in rocketry initially developed, however, not as a tool of warfare, but from an outpouring of public interest in the possibility of space travel. This interest was first sparked by the 1923 publication of Herman Oberth's seminal book *Die Rakete du den Planetenraumen* (The Rocket into Planetary Space) and was later reinforced by the 1927 film, *Frau in Mond* (Woman in the Moon). Societies of amateur rocket enthusiasts sprang up in several German cities, including Berlin, Frankfurt, Breslau and Hanover. The most prominent of these was Verein fur Raumschiffahrt (V f R), established in Berlin in 1927 and headed by Oberth himself. Within about two years, membership had grown to over 800, including one Wernher von Braun, a tall and handsome young man, only 19 years of age.

Using private funding and proceeds from the sale of tickets for public demonstrations, these groups made substantial progress in the development and testing of liquid-fueled rocket engines. In the spring and summer of 1931, V f R conducted a series of test flights to progressively higher altitudes from its facility in Reinickendorf on the outskirts of Berlin. The following year, the test site was visited by several members of the Army Ordnance Corp, including Captain Walter Dornberger and Colonel Kurt Becker. The latter was not only a military officer but had literally "written the book" on ballistics.

Due to public safety concerns and financial difficulties, V f R was dissolved in 1934. Several prominent members of the society, including von Braun and Walter Riedel, went to work for Dornberger with the Army Weapons Department, first at Kummersdorf and later at Peenemunde on the Baltic coast. No longer a shoestring effort, the facility at Peenemunde eventually grew to a staff of over 5000, with von Braun as the technical director and Dornberger, now a major general, in charge of the overall effort. At these facilities and elsewhere, a variety of weapons was being developed for the war, including surface-to-air, air-to-air, and ballistic missiles. The German high command had great hopes that these devices could reverse the increasingly adverse course of the war. However, financial support was sporadic and depended on Hitler's whims. At one point in March of 1943, von Braun and several of his key staff members were arrested by the SS on the suspicion that their interests lay more in the development of a means of space travel rather than in supporting the war effort of the Third Reich. Von Braun was even accused of intending to fly to England with technical details of the project. The group was released only after Dornberger drove to Berlin and personally intervened with the SS. As a result of these delays and the inherent technical difficulty of the projects, many of the weapons only came into active use late in the war.

Supposedly fielded as retribution for allied bombing of German cities, the V-1, also known as the "buzz-bomb," was a subsonic, winged cruise missile developed by the Luftwaffe (air force), which could be launched either from aircraft or from an inclined launch rail on the ground. While the guidance system was very advanced for its day, it lacked the accuracy of modern systems, resulting in a great deal of randomness in the impact site; this enhanced the weapon's psychological effectiveness since no one in the greater London area could feel secure from the threat. Over 10,000 were deployed against England and Belgium in 1944 and 1945, causing more than 6,000 deaths. The V-1, however, was essentially a flying bomb, using an airbreathing, pulsejet engine rather than a rocket. It flew at a fairly low altitude and therefore was subject to both antiaircraft fire and to intercept by Royal Air Force fighters. As a result, over time, they became somewhat less effective, as the British developed improved countermeasures.

The V-2 was a much larger missile, 12,500 kg compared to the 2,150 kg of the V-1, and developed by the German Army in direct competition with the Luftwaffe's V-1. It launched vertically using a liquid oxygen-ethanol engine and flew to an altitude of approximately 80 km (50 miles) before descending towards its target at a very steep angle. Upon impact, it was traveling in excess of 1,700 miles per hour. Because of its steep approach and very high velocity, there was no warning before impact and no opportunity to take cover or attempt to shoot it down.

It was initially planned that V-2s would be fabricated at Peenemunde, but a massive air raid by the RAF in August of 1943 damaged the facilities and killed several hundred personnel, including both civilian employees and slave laborers. While not as successful as had been hoped, the attack delayed the program by perhaps two months and caused production to be moved to an underground facility 250 miles to the southwest in Thuringia. At this huge facility, work was largely carried out by forced labor from the nearby Milltebau-Dora concentration camp. Over 3100 V-2s were launched between September 1944 and March 1945, primarily targeting London and Antwerp and killing in excess of 4,500 persons, including 567 in a single blow, when a missile landed on an Antwerp cinema.

As the war was drawing to a close, it became increasingly apparent that the west and the Soviet Bloc would become engaged in a dangerous power struggle after the defeat of the Axis powers. The potential role of critical German technology in that struggle was obvious. Moreover, the well-known intent of the Allies to divide Germany after the war, coupled with conditions on the ground, made it clear that the Soviets were likely to control the Peenemunde area. Aware of the Allies' plans, von Braun met with several of his closest colleagues in January of 1945, and they unanimously decided that, when necessary, they would move their group into an area that would eventually fall under American, rather than Soviet, control. This decision was facilitated by the fact that, in the chaos of early 1945, von Braun had received several sets of conflicting orders as to how he should proceed. Starting in February, and following the orders of Hans Kammler, the SS officer in charge of the V-2 program, the move began, with thousands of personnel and family members heading southwest from Peenemunde, along with an extensive array of equipment and documents. They traveled by train, barge and truck, initially to the area around Nordhausen, where, acting on orders from von Braun, Dieter Hunzel and Bernard Tessmann hid tons of critical documents in an abandoned mine. Then in early April, Kammler ordered a second move, this time involving only 400 men, to a location farther south, near the Austrian border. By early May, this key group was scattered among small lodges in Oberammergau, with von Braun, Dornberger, and others staying in Haus Ingeburg, a comfortable ski resort in Oberjoch. Both American and French forces were in the area, and fearing capture and possible execution by French Algerian troops, on May 2, the group dispatched Magnus von Braun, Wernher's younger brother and the group's most fluent English speaker, riding a bicycle on a mission to find the Americans and surrender the crown jewel of German technology.

Meanwhile, Allied leaders had drafted a list of German scientists they hoped to capture, which, oddly enough, was largely based on a partial document found in a toilet at Bonn University. This document was originally compiled for the Third Reich by Walter Osenberg as a list of scientists, engineers, and technicians who were deemed both technically useful and reliable. And at the top of the Americans' "Wanted List" was Wernher von Braun.

Magnus made contact with the American forces and explained the situation as well as he was able. Luckily, the first GI he met was of German descent and spoke a bit of the language. Although the Americans doubted his story, they took him to Lt. Charles Stewart, a nearby counterintelligence officer, who was also skeptical and feared a trap. However, Stewart provided safe passage papers for Magnus to return and get several of the group's key people for questioning. Magnus soon returned with his brother, Dornberger, Hans Lindenberg (the chief propulsion engineer for the V-2), and three others. It quickly became apparent to the Americans that this was no ruse, and within a few days, the

Germans were being interviewed by Dr. Richard Porter, the manager of Project Hermes, an American effort to develop long-range missiles.

Although Peenemunde had fallen to the Soviets, the V-2 production plant at Mittelwerk in Thuringia was, for the time being, in American hands. However, under the terms of the Yalta Conference, that would soon change, and the territory would come under Soviet control. Realizing that their opportunity was fleeting, staff of the U.S. Army Ordinance Department, led by Colonel Holger Toftoy, began the process of removing 100 V-2 missiles for transport to America, with the plan to test them at the remote White Sands Proving Ground in the desert of New Mexico. Dubbed Special Mission V-2, this effort was greatly complicated by the fact that the missiles were not assembled until shortly before launch. As a result, individual components had to be gathered rather than complete missiles. Nevertheless, by May 22, the move began, with the spoils of war filling over 300 railcars bound for Antwerp, where they would be loaded onto ships for America.

In the meanwhile, Major Robert Staver of the Ordinance Department began searching for technical personnel still in the Mittelwerk area. Through these contacts, he found the vast trove of V-2 documents hidden in the mine some weeks earlier by Tessman and Hunzel. The removal of both the documents and the missile components was done sometimes without the knowledge and at other times over the strenuous objections of the British. During the early weeks of June, the search continued for German rocket engineers who preferred to leave with the Americans rather than fall into Soviet hands. By June 20, almost 1,000 had assembled in Nordhausen, where a mass evacuation to the American zone was arranged for the engineers and their families.

Over the next few weeks, Staver and his superiors in the Ordnance Department received approval from senior figures including the U.S. Joint Chiefs of Staff and Eisenhower to begin the transfer of essential German personnel to the U.S. under the auspices of Project Overcast (later known as Operation Paperclip). The objective was not only to speed America's progress in long-term missile research but also to use the Germans' technical expertise to develop weapons that could hasten the defeat of Japan. Initial plans were to bring over a relatively small number of men on a temporary basis—perhaps six months to a year—and return them to Germany after learning as much from them as possible. Their families were to remain in Germany in housing provided by the U.S.

The V-2 components that had been confiscated at Mittelwerk were

26. World War II German Rocket Scientists—JAMES EVANS LYNE

sent ahead and arrived via rail and truck at White Sands during August of 1945, a scant four months after Hitler's death. Then the exodus began, with von Braun and six others flying to the U.S. on a military transport in September. Three more groups followed by ship, with the last of them reaching White Sands in late February of 1946. The entire contingent totaled 127 men.

Despite the initial intent to send the group back after a short period, their expertise in the complex new technology of rocketry proved indispensable. For the next several years they worked not only on the assembly and launch of V-2s at White Sands but also consulted with American industry from California to New Jersey on the design of new missiles. Their work was instrumental both in the early launches of primates in 1948 and 1949 and in the development of the first two-stage American rocket, the Bumper. This vehicle initially flew in 1948, using a V-2 as the first stage, with a WAC Corporal mated to the top as the second stage. Altogether over 60 V-2s were launched, the vast majority from White Sands but one from the deck of the U.S. aircraft carrier *Midway* and two more from Cape Canaveral (under the Bumper program). In one case, the guidance system failed, and the V-2 arced to the south, flying over El Paso and crashing just south of Juarez, Mexico. Fortunately, no one was killed, and the diplomatic fallout was minimal.

The first year in the U.S. was difficult for many of the Germans. The landscape of the American West was strikingly different from their home, the technical work was done on a very limited budget, their families remained behind in Europe, and many Americans were untrusting and suspicious of their motives. Finally, in November of 1946, 13 months after the arrival of the first technical staff, family members were allowed to join them, and the following month, the first press interviews of the rocket designers took place. Despite the military nature of their work at White Sands, many of the Germans maintained an enthusiasm for space exploration, and by early 1949 von Braun was giving press interviews and talks to army brass about the possibility of orbiting space stations and trips to the Moon. A few of the group, including Walter Riedel, one of the chief propulsion engineers for the V-2, left and took positions with North American Aviation, where they continued important development work, leading to engines that would see extensive use not too many years later.

In early 1950, the entire team was moved from White Sands to Redstone Arsenal in Huntsville, Alabama, where future army missile development was to take place. This was a welcome change for many, since the area was green and hilly, much more like their homeland than the New Mexico deserts. A large group chose to build homes in a German enclave on Monte Sano, a beautiful hill on the east side of town, rising about 1,000 feet above its surroundings and affording commanding views of the city, the surrounding countryside, and the arsenal. The newcomers, however, did not sequester themselves but integrated into the community, joining the local chamber music group, building an observatory atop Monte Sano, founding a new Lutheran church with its own scout troop, and participating in other civic activities. Walter Wiesman even became president of the local Junior Chamber of Commerce in 1952, less than three years after arriving in town.

Over the next few years, the Paperclip team continued developing missiles for the army, spurred on initially by the conflict in Korea as well as by the early stages of the Cold War. Their work in Huntsville included the development of the single-stage Redstone missile, a V-2 derivative, powered by a series of engines developed at North American Aviation with technical guidance from Riedel's group. The Redstone and its derivatives would come to play a critical role in America's military and civilian space programs, launching the nation's first satellite, its first astronaut, and its first missile-borne nuclear warhead.

While White Sands had served well for short-range missiles, it was inadequate for longer range testing. That would require a much larger unpopulated area, since common sense precluded missile test flights being done over people's homes. The solution was to follow Jules Verne's lead and launch from the Florida coast, with the rockets flying seaward. To make this possible, in 1952 Kurt Debus, the former director of flight testing at Peenemunde, was sent to Cape Canaveral, where he supervised the design, construction and operation of the necessary facilities. July 24, 1950, saw the first launch, with the two-stage Bumper #8 traveling 200 miles and reaching a peak altitude of just over 16 kilometers.

Meanwhile, scientific interest was growing in Earth-orbiting satellites. The potential benefits of such a project had been understood and discussed for many years, with Hermann Oberth, Konstantin Tsiolkovsky, and Robert Goddard, the three giants of early rocketry, all advancing the idea. Their ambitious vision was finally within reach due to the technical developments of the last few decades.

The organizing committee of the International Geophysical Year supported these plans at a meeting in Rome in October of 1954 and called for the launch of scientific satellites during the upcoming IGY

(July 1957 through December 1958). This international call spurred both the United States and the Soviet Union into action. A proposal supported by the National Science Foundation was approved by President Eisenhower, and in July of 1955 the announcement was made that the USA planned such a launch. In the same month, Oberth himself joined the team in Huntsville.

The army, navy, and air force all sought to lead the effort, and a group headed by John Hagen of the Naval Research Laboratory was selected, beating out von Braun's Huntsville team. The reasons for the choice of the navy's Vanguard program seem to be somewhat uncertain; some authors claim that there was a reluctance to divert the attention of the army and air force from the development of military ballistic missile technology, while others state that the use of German engineers to conduct such a high-profile program would have been politically embarrassing so soon after the war. Still other sources contend that since the NRL was viewed as a civilian rather than a military organization, the Soviets were less likely to object to the satellite flying over their territory. Von Braun himself later wrote that he did not fully understand the reason for the choice, especially since his team would have been able to place a satellite in orbit within a few months.

Unfortunately, the Vanguard program suffered numerous setbacks, with substantial cost overruns and a delay of the orbital launch, which originally was intended to take place in the spring of 1957. Nevertheless, the program achieved some success, with a suborbital flight using a one-stage vehicle in December of 1956 and a second using a two-stage booster to reach an altitude of 121 miles in May of the following year. The gradual progress of Vanguard, however, was suddenly interrupted by the Soviet Union's successful launch of Sputnik on October 4, 1957. The psychological impact on the American public was enormous. Signals from Sputnik—simple beeps—were widely rebroadcast on American radio, and in some locations, the satellite itself could be seen with the naked eye as it passed overhead. Although the public was generally alarmed at the implications of a Russian satellite flying over their homes, Eisenhower took a somewhat different view, since it meant that the Soviets accepted the concept of "open skies," or the right of nations to use satellites to overfly another country's territory without causing disputes. This was important to the development of the top secret American spy satellite program known as Corona.

On November 3, 1957, the Soviets managed a second successful launch, this time carrying an 1,100 pound spacecraft with a live dog and a television camera. Spurred on by the Russian success, the Vanguard team attempted a launch on December 6, intending to place a three-pound radio beacon into orbit. The vehicle exploded after lifting only a few feet into the air, blowing the satellite a short distance from the pad, where it proceeded to transmit signals and earned itself the nickname Kaputnik.

The Soviet success with Sputnik and the reaction of the American public finally led the government to give the go-ahead for the other U.S. military branches to work in parallel with Vanguard on separate satellite launch programs. In Huntsville, the newly formed Army Ballistic Missile Agency (ABMA) developed the Juno booster, a four-stage derivative of the Redstone, under the technical direction of von Braun. Simultaneously, the Explorer 1 satellite was designed and built at the California Institute of Technology/Jet Propulsion Laboratory in Pasadena. This combination proved successful, and the first American satellite was launched into orbit from Cape Canaveral on January 31, 1958. The navy followed suit, with a successful Vanguard orbital launch on March 17.

In addition to the work on orbital launch vehicles, significant efforts continued on the development of military ballistic missiles. An important milestone in this effort was the first American pairing of a nuclear warhead with a ballistic missile, accomplished using a Redstone rocket launched from the Johnston Atoll on August 1, 1958. The device detonated at an altitude of almost 80 km with a yield of 3.8 megatons. Debus supervised the launch, and von Braun traveled to Johnston to witness the event. A few months later the air force used an Atlas ICBM to orbit its first satellite, known as SCORE, and broadcast the first human voice from space—sending a recorded message from President Eisenhower wishing "peace and goodwill to men everywhere"— and an unspoken message to the Soviets that American ICBMs could target locations around the world.

Despite the military dominance of early U.S. space activities, for some time there had been discussions in political and scientific circles about establishing a civilian space program. These plans came to fruition in July of 1958 with the passage of the National Aeronautics and Space Act. All personnel and facilities of the National Advisory Committee on Aviation (NACA) were transferred to the newly formed NASA on October 1, 1958. A year later, Debus's launch operations group at the Cape, now totaling about 5,000, also joined NASA as the Launch Operations Directorate. After the Kennedy assassination, this organization was renamed Kennedy Space Center, with Debus serving as the first director.

In a separate development, in April of 1957, the von Braun team at ABMA began development work on an enormous booster known as the Saturn. The plans were for a vehicle capable of orbiting a satellite with a mass between 9,000 and 18,000 kg. The first stage was expected to produce 1.5 million pounds of thrust, 25 times that of the V-2. However, within about two years, Pentagon leaders had concluded that there was no foreseeable military application for such a large rocket, and moves had been made to eliminate the program. NASA leaders, however, believed that a very large booster would be invaluable to future civilian space programs and were very concerned by the potential cancellation of the Saturn vehicle. As a result, it was agreed that the personnel, equipment and facilities of the Army Ballistic Missile Agency would transfer to NASA, and in March of 1960, the Marshall Space Flight Center (MSFC) began operations on the Redstone Arsenal, with Wernher von Braun serving as the first center director.

In December of 1958, less than three months after its formation, NASA had announced Project Mercury, a program to launch men into space and return them safely to the ground. The first group of astronauts, known as the Mercury Seven, was presented to the nation at a press conference on April 9, 1959. In addition to the scientific and engineering purposes of the program, a clear national objective was to place a man in space before the Russians. However, once again, the Soviet Union moved first, launching Yuri Gagarin into orbit on April 12, 1961. Three weeks later, Alan Shephard became the first American to reach space, when he was lofted on a suborbital flight to an altitude of 187 km by a Mercury-Redstone Launch Vehicle (MRLV). This rocket was a version of von Braun's Redstone missile, which the Huntsville team had modified to include the Mercury capsule itself, a launch abort system, and larger propellant tanks. Additional modifications were made to reduce unnecessary complexity and improve reliability. The chimpanzee Ham had flown on a similar vehicle just three months before Shepherd. However, the single-stage MRLV was not large enough to place the capsule in orbit, and America had to wait until the much larger Atlas was ready in February of 1962 for John Glenn to fly on the nation's first manned orbital flight.

The addition of astronauts greatly complicated the entire design process for launch and space operations. Life support systems, peak acceleration levels, the effects of micro-gravity exposure on the human body and many other issues became critical. Once again German researchers played leading roles in overcoming the challenges. Former Luftwaffe physicians Hubertus Strughold and Richard Lindenberg both came to the U.S. under Operation Paperclip. They initially worked for the air force in San Antonio, where Strughold served as Professor of Space Medicine at the School of Aviation Medicine. In 1962 Strughold transferred to NASA and served as Chief Scientist of the Aerospace Medicine Division until his retirement in 1968. He is widely recognized as the Father of Space Medicine.

The next few years saw rapid development, with America's first two-man space crew in March of 1965, first extravehicular activity (EVA) less than three months later, and first in a space docking maneuver the following year. The MSFC team in Huntsville continued working on the massive Saturn launch vehicles under von Braun's leadership, and on July 16, 1969, the world was transfixed, watching as a Saturn V weighing 6.5 million pounds lifted off carrying a crew of three. Neil Armstrong and Buzz Aldrin would become the first and second men on the Moon, while Mike Collins orbited overhead in the Command Module. It has been estimated that over 600 million people watched the landing worldwide, the largest TV audience ever at that time. Over 50 years later, the Saturn V launch vehicle remains the largest and most powerful rocket ever to fly.

It is hard to overstate the contributions made by a small group of German immigrants in this crucial period of history. They certainly hastened America's access, probably by years, to technologies that were vital to defending the free world against Soviet aggression. How would history have unfolded if America had been delayed by five years in developing intercontinental ballistic missiles? Would the Cuban Missile Crisis have had the same outcome? While answers to questions like these can never be known, we do know that many aspects of modern life would be impossible without the technologies pioneered by Oberth, von Braun and others. GPS systems, accurate (or somewhat accurate) weather forecasts, international telecommunications, search and rescue activities, wildfire detection and monitoring of rogue state activities all depend on the reliable access to space enabled to a large extent by 127 exceptional men.

27

Interview with a Contemporary German Immigrant

When 19-year-old Max Herrmann left his home in Stuttgart near the Black Forest in the German state of Baden-Wuerttemberg and arrived in New York City, the only English word he knew was "hotdog."[1] But he had $200 in his pocket, the promise of a job in North Carolina and boundless enthusiasm for life in the United States of America. He would be a tool and die maker instructor for workers of the Black and Decker Corporation, the world's leading maker of power tools. When the time came for him to return to Europe, Max chose to stay in his new country and become an American citizen.

In order to improve his chance for citizenship, Max signed up for service in the United States Air Force. During his 20 years in the military, he met and married a young woman from Damascus, Virginia, and started a family. As an air force veteran, Max, his wife and their two children settled in Abingdon, Virginia, only a few miles from his wife's hometown.

Once, when this author was greeted by Max, who welcomed every customer, he was standing in front of his tremendously successful restaurant, The Tavern, possibly Abingdon's oldest building. It is just down the street from Abingdon's Barter Theater, the state theater of Virginia. At his feet, beside a lamppost, on the old handmade brick sidewalk, laid in herringbone pattern with grass poking through the seams instead of mortar, sat one of the town's whimsical wolf and pup sculptures painted by local artists. The Abingdon Wolf Project is devoted to making Abingdon a welcoming place while promoting the small business community, as well as contributing to the town's historic and artistic assets. The wolf commemorates Abingdon's original name, "Wolf Hills," so-named by Daniel Boone who encountered a pack of howling wolves rushing from a cave onto what is now Abingdon's Main Street.

The name of the painted wolf looking up at Max was aptly named, "Max."

Recently, when asked to tell about his life as an immigrant and a restaurant owner, Max said: "I have lived the American dream! When I entered the restaurant business at The Tavern, I didn't know anything about restaurants." Max, who is now a renowned restaurateur, continued: "The workers have made this place. It is what it is because of them. But I did know how to hire. I learned how to hire when I was in the Air Force." Max had entered the restaurant business, against the advice of a lawyer friend, when he was 42 years old. Over the 13 years preceding Max's arrival, The Tavern had failed as a restaurant four times. In answer to his friend's advice, Max had rebutted, "Failure is not an option for me."

The now 67-year-old gregarious and burly Max Herrmann sometimes worked as many as 90 hours per week and eventually bought the business. At first he worked seven days per week, serving lunch and dinner each day. And then he cut back, stopped serving lunch, took Sundays off and worked six days per week. He worked for 25 years until he recently sold the restaurant to 30-year-old Josh Fuller, who was hired by Max and began bussing tables at The Tavern when he was 23 and became manager a few years later under Max's ever-watchful fatherly eye. Showing the traditional paternalism of many German employers, Max said, "I could have gotten more money from somebody else, but this is not a business you just sell and step away from. I wanted to be sure that the business I have built continues to go in the direction that I want." Max Herrmann's legacy is the outstanding reputation he has built for The Tavern. He continued, "I decided to retire because in 25 years I have had only 25 weekends off work. I want Josh to manage my 25 employees and let me come back on weekdays just to walk around and talk to customers. And I want him to succeed." Max, now retired for only a few weeks, said these words as he served someone a glass of water and then picked up a dirty plate from an empty table. His work ethic is astounding. He sets a good example. Like their former German immigrant boss, his (and now Josh's) employees work nonstop with wide, wide smiles and contagious happiness. Through the years, the historic old tavern, built in 1779, has served as a tavern, post office, hospital and barber shop. Today its thick brick walls, squeaky floors, uneven tables, and fireplaces in every room radiate calm, peace and charm. Upstairs and downstairs, it is a fitting backdrop for the indefatigable Herr Max Herrmann with his kind, no-nonsense manner and his veteran's memorabilia on the mantles. His native tongue has given him a compelling way with words. Whenever he enters a room, or sits at the bar sipping a glass of wine with customers, his forceful, abrupt German dialect commands attention. And oh, yes, by the way, the food is good!

Afterthoughts: Our family ate at The Tavern one Friday in September 2019. Max wasn't there, but we told Josh that he was doing a great job as the new owner. He simply beamed and said, "I've got some big shoes to fill." And I thought, "What a good phrase to fit into *German Footprints*." Josh also said that Max Herrmann's two children grew up moving from air force base to base while Max served in the military. In that situation, Josh thought that the Herrmann children, as first-generation Americans of German heritage, had absolutely no trouble blending in.

Like Max Herrmann, countless other people of German descent, quietly, in their thoroughgoing manner, have contributed and continue to contribute valuable teamwork to art, science and business but have never sought mass control. America is tremendously indebted to German immigrants. President Theodore Roosevelt put it this way: "The Germans are not merely our brothers; they are largely ourselves. The debt we owe to German blood is great; the debt we owe to German thought and to German example … is even greater."[2]

Appendix: Chronology
The Germans in America

Published by Library of Congress Researchers, April 23, 2014, European Reading Room, Library of Congress

1608—Several Germans were among the settlers at Jamestown.

1626—Peter Minuit, a German, came to New Amsterdam to serve as the governor of the Dutch colony, New Netherland. Later he governed the Swedish colony in Delaware.

1683—Thirteen families of German Mennonites seeking religious freedom arrived in Pennsylvania; led by Franz Pastorius, they purchased 43,000 acres of land and founded Germantown, six miles north of Philadelphia.

1700s—The settling of the British colonies by small German-speaking religious groups continued. The groups included Swiss Mennonites, Baptist Dunkers, Schwenkfelders, Moravians, Amish, and Waldensians; most German immigrants belonged to the main Lutheran and Reformed churches. The central colonies received the greatest part of this immigration, especially Pennsylvania. As many as half of these immigrants came as redemptioners; that is, they agreed to work in America for four to seven years in exchange for free passage across the Atlantic. German settlers designed and built the Conestoga wagon, which was used in the opening of the American frontier.

1731—Protestants were expelled from Salzburg, Austria, in this year. They subsequently founded Ebenezer, Georgia.

1732—The first German-language newspaper, *Philadelphische Zeitung*, was published in the United States. German publishing flourished in Philadelphia and in smaller communities such as Ephrata, Pennsylvania.

1733—John Peter Zenger, who came to America as an indentured servant from the Palatinate region of Germany, founded a newspaper, *The New York Weekly Journal*; two years later he was acquitted in a landmark trial involving freedom of the press.

1741—Moravians founded Bethlehem and Nazareth, Pennsylvania.

1742—Christopher Saur, a German printer in Philadelphia, printed the first Bible in America.

1778—General Friedrich Wilhelm von Steuben, a Prussian officer, became inspector general of the Continental Army.

1783—As many as 5,000 of the Hessian soldiers hired by Britain to fight in the Revolutionary War remained in America after the end of hostilities.

1784—John Jacob Astor (1763–1848) left his village of Waldorf in Germany and arrived in the United States in 1784 with $25 and seven flutes. He amassed a fortune from real estate dealings and the fur trade and at his death was by far the richest man in the country, worth an estimated $20 million.

1790—By this date as many as 100,000 Germans may have immigrated to America; they and their descendants made up an estimated 8.6 percent of the population of the United States; in Pennsylvania they accounted for 33 percent of the population; in Maryland for 12 percent.

1804—A Protestant group from Wuerttemberg, named Rappists after their leader George Rapp, founded Harmony, Pennsylvania, a utopian community.

1814—The Rappists purchased 30,000 acres of land in Indiana and founded a new settlement, New Harmony. In 1825 they returned to Pennsylvania and founded Economy, 20 miles northwest of Pittsburgh. Other towns founded by religious groups in this period included Zoar, Ohio, Amana, Iowa, and St. Nazianz, Wisconsin.

1821—The Germanic custom of having a specially decorated tree at Christmastime was introduced to America by Pennsylvania Dutch in Lancaster, Pennsylvania. Later in the century, the Pennsylvania Dutch version of St. Nicholas, Sinterklaas, evolved into America's Santa Claus, popularized by a German immigrant and influential political cartoonist, Thomas Nast. The Easter bunny and Easter eggs were also brought to this country by German immigrants.

1829—Gottfried Duden published in Germany his idyllic account of the several years he spent as a settler in Missouri; so popular that it appeared in three editions, the book caused numerous Germans to leave for the New World.

1836—John Nepomucene Neumann (1811–1860) arrived in the United States in 1836 from his native Bohemia to work as a priest in the country's German-speaking Roman Catholic communities. He founded the first American diocesan school system and in 1852 became Bishop of Philadelphia. In 1977 he was canonized as a saint by Pope Paul VI.

1837—The German Philadelphia Settlement Society was founded and purchased 12,000 acres of land in Gasconade County, Missouri; two years later the society's town of Hermann was incorporated with 450 inhabitants.

1844—Prince Carl of Solms-Braunfels sailed to America with three ships and 150 families to settle in Texas; the following year New Braunfels, Texas, was established.

1847—The Missouri Synod of the Lutheran Church was founded by German immigrants to combat what they saw as the liberalization of Lutheranism in America.

1848–1849—The failure of the Revolution of 1848 to establish democracy caused thousands to leave Germany to settle in America; the most famous of these refugees was Carl Schurz. He later served as a Union general in the Civil War, a United States senator from Missouri, and secretary of the interior under President Rutherford B. Hayes.

1850s—Nearly 1 million Germans immigrated to America in this decade, one of the peak periods of German immigration; in 1854 alone, 215,000 Germans arrived in this country.

1856—Margaretha Meyer Schurz, a German immigrant and wife of Carl Schurz, established the first kindergarten in America at Watertown, Wisconsin.

1857—Adolphus Busch (1839–1913) left the Rhineland and settled in St. Louis, Missouri. Four years later, he married the daughter of a prosperous brewer. In addition to children, this union resulted in the founding of what was soon to become an industry giant with holdings across the country: the Anheuser-Busch Brewing Association.

1860—An estimated 1.3 million German-born immigrants resided in the United States; 200 German-language magazines and newspapers were published in this country; in St. Louis alone, there were seven German-language newspapers.

1872—The century-old privileges granted to German farmers settled in Russia were revoked by the Tsarist government, causing thousands of the farmers to emigrate. By 1920, there were well over 100,000 of these so-called Volga and Black Sea Germans in the United States, with the greatest numbers in the Dakotas, Nebraska, and Colorado. Black Sea Germans soon became known for their skill as wheat farmers. In 1990 an estimated 1 million descendants of these Russian Germans lived in America.

1880s—In this decade, the decade of heaviest German immigration, nearly 1.5 million Germans left their country to settle in the United States; about 250,000, the greatest number ever, arrived in 1882.

1890—An estimated 2.8 million German-born immigrants lived in the United States. A majority of the German-born living in the United States were located in the "German triangle," whose three points were Cincinnati, Milwaukee, and St. Louis.

1894—About 800 German-language journals were being printed in the United States, the greatest number ever. A typical newspaper was the *New York Staats Zeitung*.

1910—In this year, an estimated 2.3 million German-born immigrants lived in the United States. With declining immigration and increasing assimilation, the number of German-language publications fell to about 550.

1920—Roughly 1.7 million German-born immigrants lived in the United States; the number of German-language publications fell to about 230.

1933—The coming to power of Adolf Hitler in Germany caused a significant immigration of leading German scientists, writers, musicians, scholars, and other artists and intellectuals to the United States to escape persecution. Among them were such notables as Albert Einstein, Bruno Walter, Arnold Schoenberg, Walter Gropius, Ludwig Mies van der Rohe, Hans Bethe, Thomas Mann, Marlene Dietrich, Kurt Weil, Billy Wilder, Hannah Arendt, and Hans Morgenthau. By the end of World War II, there were some 130,000 of these German and Austrian refugees living in America.

1940—An estimated 1.2 million German-born immigrants lived in the United States.

1948—The Displaced Persons Act made general provisions for the immigration of displaced persons in Eastern Europe, including ethnic Germans, to the United States.

1950s—Between 1951 and 1960, 580,000 Germans immigrated to the United States.

1960s—Between 1961 and 1970, 210,000 Germans immigrated to the United States.

1970s—Between 1971 and 1980, 65,000 Germans immigrated to the United States.

1983—The United States and Germany celebrated the German-American Tricentennial, marking the 300th anniversary of German immigration to Pennsylvania.

1987—German-American Day was established by Congressional resolution and presidential proclamation.

1990—According to the Bureau of the Census, 58 million Americans claimed to be solely or partially of German descent. German-Americans were highly assimilated, and the use of German in the United States had declined dramatically. Some German-language newspapers continued to be published in the United States, for example, the *California Staats-Zeitung*.

Chapter Notes

Introduction

1. Churchill, *Great Republic*, 16–19.
2. Tucker, Heather, "The City and the Sea," *Archaeology*, September/October 2016. 55.
3. Wike, Monte & Noma, *The Wike Family, Descendants of Jacob M. Weik*, Colorado City, Texas, 1978.
4. "Ships' Passenger Lists," Pennsylvania Historical and Museum Commission, Commonwealth of Pennsylvania, 2019.
5. Winawer and Wetzel, "German Families," 558.
6. Conzen, Kathleen Neils, *Germans in Minnesota*, Minnesota Historical Society, 2003, 4.
7. "German Confederation," Encyclopedia Britannica 2018.
8. Winawer and Wetzel, 557.
9. McSweeney, E.F., "The Racial Contributions to the United States," from Schrader's *The Germans in the Making of America*, 6.
10. Fogleman, Aaron Spencer, *Hopeful Journey*, 1996, 1–3.
11. *Religion and the Founding of the American Republic*, Library of Congress, Exhibitions.
12. Bittinger, Lucy Forney, *The Germans in Colonial Times*, Chapter I.
13. Fogleman, *op. cit.* 4.
14. Chronology, "The Germans in America," European Room, The Library of Congress.
15. Bittinger, *The Germans in Colonial Times*, Chapter I.
16. Wittke, Carl. "Introduction," *Refugees of Revolution: The German Forty-Eighters in America*, 1–5.
17. "German-Americans, The Silent Minority, "*The Economist*," February 12, 2015.
18. Ibid.
19. Luton, Wayne, "American Immigration History from Colonial Times to the 1965 Immigration Act," 1988, http://usinc.org/wp-content/uploads/2014/02/USImmigrationhistorylutton.pdf.
20. Check, John, "Turning Swords into Saxaphones," *Wall Street Journal*, December 29–30, 2018, critiquing E. Douglas Bomberger's *Making Music in America*.
21. McSweeney, E.F., "The Racial Contributions to the United States," from Schrader's *The Germans in the Making of America*, 2, 5.
22. Chronology, "The Germans in America," European Reading Room, The Library of Congress.
23. "The Silent Minority," *The Economist*, February 5, 2015.
24. Cahan, David "Helmholze, a Life in Science," review by Peter Pesic, *Wall Street Journal*, books, Saturday/Sunday November 24–25, 2018.

Chapter 1

1. englishmonarchs.co.uk.
2. Churchill, *Great Republic*, 14.
3. *The Jewish Magazine*, March Passover 2007 Edition.
4. Lawler, Andrew, "Muslims Were Banned from the Americas as Early as the 16th Century," *Smithsonian Magazine* and Smithsonian.com, February 7, 2017.
5. Abrahams, Israel. "Joachim Gaunse: A Mining Incident in the Reign of Queen Elizabeth." *Transactions of Jewish Historical Society of England*, Vol. IV.

6. Grassl, Gary C., "Gans, Joachim," NC pedia, 1986, www.ncpedia.org/biography/gans-joachim.
7. Lawler, op. cit.
8. Morgan, *Oxford Illustrated History of Britain*, 268–272.
9. Churchill, *Great Republic*, 32–35.

Chapter 2

1. Chronology, "The Germans in America," European Reading Room, The Library of Congress.
2. Craven, Wesley Frank, *The Virginia Company of London 1606-1624*, Williamsburg, Virginia, 1957. 5.
3. Gordon, John Steele, "Entrepreneurship in American History," *Imprimis* Vol. 43 Number 2, February 2014 (a pamphlet published by Hillsdale College, MI).
4. Baker, Peggy M., "Plymouth Colony Patent," Pilgrim Hall Museum.
5. Morison, *Oxford History of the American People*, 34.
6. Thomas Jefferson Papers, Virginia Records Timeline: 1553–1743 (hereafter referred to as Jefferson Papers: 1553–1743 Timeline).
7. Churchill, *Great Republic*, 26.
8. Wilson, Woodrow, *History of the United States*, 45.
9. Speidell, "On John Smith's Trail," 45; Mann, *1493*, 58.
10. Wilson *op. cit.*, 46.
11. Lohr, Otto, "The First Germans in North America and the German Element of New Netherland," New York: G.E. Stechert, 1912; contributor, Library of Congress.
12. Schrader, *The Germans in the Making of America*, 38–39.

Chapter 3

1. Morison, *Oxford History of the American People*, 64.
2. Fischer, *Albion's Seed*, 14.
3. Gaskill, Malcolm, "The Pilgrims Are Us," *Wall Street Journal Review*, Sat–Sun November 29–30, 2014.
4. Morison *op. cit.*, 64–69.
5. Fischer, *Albion's Seed*, 57, 123, 136.
6. Morison *op. cit.*, 61, 65.
7. U.S. Library of Congress, Thanksgiving Timeline.
8. Garraty & Gay, *Columbia History of the World*, 663.
9. Schrader, *Germans in the Making of America*, 39–41.
10. Henninghausen, Louis P., "The First German Settlement in North America," Loyola Notre Dame Library, Baltimore, MD.
11. Morison *op. cit.*,110.
12. Fischer *op. cit.*, 194.
13. Gritz, Connie Green, "Quakers: A Silent Influence," an essay from *Legacy*, Reading Area Community College, accessed 7/5/2018.
14. *The New England Historical and Genealogical Register*, Volume 25, 347.
15. Fischer *op. cit.*, 194–5.

Chapter 4

1. Gordon, John Steele, "Don't Bet Against New York," *The Wall Street Journal*, Weekend. Edition Saturday/Sunday, September 19–20, 2009, Vol. CCLIV NO.68.
2. Wilson, *History of the American People*, 69, 70.
3. The Rijksmuseum Timeline of Dutch History.
4. "Dutch East India Company," New World Encyclopedia.
5. Axelrod, *Savage Empire*, 55, 56, 62.
6. Juet, Robert, *Juet's Journal of Hudson's 1609 Voyage*, New Netherland Museum Translation, transcribed by Brea Barthal.
7. Schrader, *Germans in the Making of America*, 34.
8. "A Brief Outline of the History of New Netherland," University of Notre Dame.
9. Durant, *Age of Faith*, 685.
10. Federal writers project, *New York, the WPA Guide to New York: The Empire State*.
11. Caliendo, Ralph, *New York City Mayors*, Vol. I, Part I. Xlibris, 2010, 502–3.
12. Schrader, *op. cit.*, 49.
13. Morison, *Oxford History of the American People*, 56; Henninghausen, Louis P., "The First German Settlement in North America," Loyola Notre Dame Library.
14. Hemstreet, Charles, *The Story of Manhattan*, Chapter III, published before 1923.
15. Putnam, "Dutch on the Hudson," *America's Historylands*, 97–98.
16. Gordon, John Steele, "Don't Bet Against New York," *The Wall Street Journal*, September 18, 2009.

17. Axelrod, *Savage Empire*, 75–77.
18. Jackson, Kenneth, "A Colony with a Conscience," *New York Times* Editorial December 27, 2007.
19. "1657," *Annals of America Volume I*, Chicago, Encyclopedia Britannica, 1976, 223-4.
20. Jackson, Kenneth, "A Colony with a Conscience," *New York Times* Editorial December 27, 2007.
21. *Annals of America*, 221.
22. Massachusetts Historical Society Proceedings, Vol. XVI, 1878, Boston, 241.
23. "Swedes on the Delaware," *America's Historylands*, 102.
24. *The German Exodus to England in 1709*, prepared at the request of the Pennsylvania-German Society.
25. Henninghausen, Louis P., "The First German Settlement in North America," Loyola Notre Dame Library, Baltimore, MD.
26. "Swedes on the Delaware," *America's Historylands*, 102.
27. Gordon, John Steele, "Don't Bet Against New York," *The Wall Street Journal*, September 18, 2009.
28. Axelrod, *Savage Empire*, 77.
29. Putnam, "Dutch on the Hudson," *America's Historylands*, 100.
30. *Proceedings of the New Jersey Historical Society*, Vol. III, 144, 145, 239.
31. Wynn, John Huddlestone, *A General History of the British Empire in America*, Vol. I, 202–206.
32. McMaster, John Bach, *Brief History of the United States*, 79.
33. Bittinger, *The Germans in Colonial Times*, Chapter VI "German Valley, New Jersey."
34. Chambers, Theodore Frelinghuysen, *The Early Germans of New Jersey: Their History, Churches, and Genealogies*, chapter XIV, digitized by the Internet Archive in 2010; Sache, Julius Frederick, *German Pietists of Provincial Pennsylvania*, Philadelphia, January 1, 1895.

Chapter 5

1. Kennedy, Paul, *Rise and Fall of the Great Powers*, 2–4, 32, 36, 56.
2. "The Protestant Movement," Harvard Divinity School, Religious Literacy Project.
3. Fulbrook, Mary, *A Concise History of Germany*, 37.
4. Durant, *Age of Reason*, 556; Observations by author from a tour of Prague in 2012.
5. Fulbrook, *op. cit.*, 56.
6. "Thirty Years' War," *Encyclopedia Britannica*.
7. Wells, H.G., *Outline of History*, 652.
8. Sachse, Nead Buckenham, Published by The Pennsylvania-German Society, Lancaster, PA, 1914.
9. Chambers, Theodore Frelinghuysen, *The Early Germans of New Jersey: Their History, Churches, and Genealogie*, digitized by the Internet Archive in 2010.
10. Fulbrook, *op. cit.*, 64, 65.
11. Bittinger, *The Germans in Colonial Times*, Chap. 1.
12. Durant, *The Age of Louis XIV*, 416.
13. Durant, *The Age of Reason*, 568.
14. *Ibid.*, 570.
15. Fulbrook, *A Concise History of Germany*, 60, 61.
16. Magill, Frank N., ed., *17th and 18th Century Dictionary of World Biography*, Volume 4, 838–840.
17. Gombrich, *A Little History of the World*, 247.
18. Durant, *Age of Voltaire*, 431.
19. Durant, *Age of Louis XIV*, 3.

Chapter 6

1. Durant, *Age of Reason*, 570.
2. Gombrich, *A Little History of the World*, 230.
3. Durant, *The Age of Louis XIV*, 12, 4.
4. Editors of *Encyclopaedia Britannica*, "Anne of Austria, Queen of France," *Encyclopaedia Britannica* September 21, 2011, accessed May 18, 2018.
5. Durant, *The Age of Louis XIV*, 5–12.
6. Edict of Nantes, Excerpts in English, Items 2 and 27, *Musée Du Désert Museum*.
7. Durant, *The Age of Louis XIV*, 70–72.
8. *Ibid.*, 3.
9. Durant, *The Age of Louis XIV*, 72–74; Morison, *Oxford History of the American People*, 97.
10. Fogleman, *Hopeful Journeys*, 16, 18.
11. Lutton, Wayne, "American Immigration History from Colonial Times to the 1965 Immigration Act," 1988, usinc.org.
12. Schoepperle, Katherine, "A History of German Immigration to New York in

1710," master's thesis, University of Illinois, digitalized by internet archive in 2013.
13. Durant, *The Age of Louis XIV*, 75.
14. *Ibid.* 129, 104, Book flap.
15. Perry, *Western Civilization*, 371.

Chapter 7

1. Baker, Peggy M., "Plymouth Colony Patent," Director & Librarian Pilgrim Society & Pilgrim Hall Museum.
2. Fischer, *Albion's Seed*, 207.
3. Hatch, *America's Oldest Legislative Assembly*, 20; Encyclopaedia Britannica Premium Service, s.v. "Papers of Sir William Berkeley (1605-1677)" Edited by Warren M. Billings, UNO; Tobacco.org, "A Brief History of Jamestown."
4. Morison, *Oxford History of the American People*, 85, 86, 89, 90, 91, 113.
5. Friends of Green Spring National Historic Park, "What Did Governor Berkeley Do During His Retirement, 1652-1660." Historicgreensprings.org (accessed January 15, 2012).
6. Fischer, *Albion's Seed*, 207-234.
7. Boorstin, *Discoverers*, 82.
8. Smith, Walt, "The Discoveries of John Lederer," *The Potomac Appalachian Trail Club History* Archives.
9. Cumming, W.P. 1991, "Lederer, Johann," Dictionary of North Carolina Biography.
10. Fischer, *Albion's Seed*, 207-212.
11. Historic Christ Church, Lancaster County, Virginia, http://www.christchurch1735.org.
12. Morison, *Oxford History of the American People*, 91.
13. Quoted from Jim Doggett's Web site, "Reverend Benjamin Doggett."
14. *Historic Christ Church*, christchurch1735.org.
15. Morison, *Oxford History of the American People*, 90-91.
16. Fischer, *Albion's Seed*, 234.
17. Editors of *Encyclopedia Britannica*, "The Protestant Movement," Harvard Divinity School, Religious Literacy Project.
18. Bruce, Philip Alexander, *Institutional History of Virginia in the Seventeenth Century*, Volume 1, New York, G.P. Putnam's Sons the Knickerbocker Press, 1910, 222-3.
19. Gritz, Connie Green, "Quakers: A Silent Influence," an essay from *Legacy*, Reading Area Community College, accessed 7/5/2018.
20. Fischer, *Albion's Seed*, 234.

Chapter 8

1. Morison, *Oxford History of the American People*, 126.
2. *Ibid.*
3. Smith, Robert Lawrence, *A Quaker Book of Wisdom*, Chapter I, "Silence," 3-5.
4. "Quakers in the World," quakersintheworld.org/quakers-in-actiion/166/-Rights-of-Women.
5. Story, *The Building of the British Empire*, 327-29.
6. "Charter for the Province of Pennsylvania—1681." Avalon Project Yale Law School.
7. "The Charter of Charles the second, of England, Scotland, France and Ireland, King, defender of the faith, &c. unto William Penn, proprietary and Governor of the province of Pennsylvania..."
8. Munro, William Bennett, *Government of the United States*, 4-7.
9. "Germantown Mennonite Settlement (Pennsylvania, USA)," *Global Anabaptist Mennonite Encyclopedia*.
10. "The Germans in America Chronology," Library of Congress Researchers, April 23, 2014.
11. Fischer, *Albion's Seed*, 419-429.
12. Morison, *Oxford History of the American People*, 128.
13. Fischer, *op. cit.*
14. Schrader, *Germans in the Making of America*, 34, 426.
15. Kutz, Kim, "A Battle in Quaker Pennsylvania: Reading a Document of the French and Indian War," Pennsylvania State University Libraries.
16. Axelrod, Alan, *Savage Empire*, 6.
17. Morison, *Oxford History of the American People*, 76, 126-28.
18. Fischer, *Albion's Seed*, 426.
19. Franklin, Benjamin, "Writings of Benjamin Franklin," 289-98.
20. McNeese, Tim, *American Frontier*, 10.
21. Franklin, Benjamin, *The Writings of Benjamin Franklin, Volume III: London 1757-1775* "A Narrative of the Late Massacres, in Lancaster County, of a Number of

Indians, Friends of This Province, by Persons Unknown with Some Observations on the Same," 289–98.
22. Chronology, "The Germans in America," European Reading Room, The Library of Congress.
23. Hennighausen, Louis P., "The First German Settlement in North America," Loyola Notre Dame Library.
24. Bittinger, *The Germans in Colonial Times*, Chapter III, 6.
25. Henninghausen, Louis P., "The First German Settlement in North America," Loyola Notre Dame Library, Baltimore, MD.
26. Ibid.
27. Ibid.
28. Pastorius, "Germantown," in *Annals of America*, Encyclopedia Britannica, 1: 310–14.
29. Hennighausen, Louis P., "The First German Settlement in North America," Loyola Notre Dame Library.
30. "German Settlement in Pennsylvania: An Overview," Pennsylvania Historical Society.
31. Ramsey, *Carolina Cradle: Settlement of the Northwest Carolina Frontier, 1747–1762*, 146; Rouse, *Great Wagon Road*, 21–28.
32. Morison, *Oxford History of the American People*, 128.
33. Tolles, *Quakers and the Atlantic Culture*, 117.
34. Fischer, *Albion's Seed*, 424, 422.
35. Rouse, *Great Wagon Road*, 22.
36. Pennsylvania Historical and Museum Commission, "Pennsylvania State History."
37. Franklin, *Autobiography*, 156–163.
38. Ramsey, Robert, *Carolina Cradle*, 146–148.
39. Pennsylvania Historical and Museum Commission, "Pennsylvania State History."
40. Merk, *History of the Westward Movement*, 20.
41. Huberman, Leo, *We the People*, United States, 1932.
42. *Annals of America*, Encyclopedia Britannica 2:3.
43. Rex, Brigitte A., "A Comparative Examination of German-American Women Immigrants in the Rural and Urban Areas of America in the Nineteenth Century," Presented to the American Culture Faculty at the University of Michigan–Flint, September 2001.
44. Pennsylvania Historical and Museum Commission, "Pennsylvania State History."
45. Lossing, *1776*, 186.
46. Smith, *A Quaker Book of Wisdom*, Chapter I, Silence, 7.
47. Tysen, Rae "Our First Friends, the Early Quakers," *Pennsylvania Heritage Magazine*, Volume XXXVII, Number 2—Spring 2011.
48. Ibid.
49. *The German Exodus to England in 1709* "prepared at the request of the Pennsylvania-German Society; the original of this book is in the Cornell University Library. There are no known copyright restrictions in the United States on the use of the text."
50. Fischelt, William A., "Do Amish One-Room Schools Make the Grade?" *The University of Chicago Law Review*.
51. Osterholzer, Kim Woodard, "Faith and Family Among the Amish," *Wall Street Journal*, Friday June 15, 2018, Opinion A13.

Chapter 9

1. Ramsey, *Carolina Cradle*, 147–49.
2. "A Brief History of the Moravian Church," Moravian Church in North America, North: Bethlehem, PA. and South: Winston-Salem, NC. www.moravian.org/2018/07/a-brief-history-of-the-moravian-church/.
3. Riforgiato, Leonard, *Missionary of Moderation: Henry Melchior Muhlenberg*, 78.
4. DeLashmutt, Gary, "Early German Lutheran Pietism's Understanding of Justification," an essay published by Xenos Christian Fellowship.
5. *The Pennsylvania Magazine of History and Biography* Vol. CXXXV, No. 1, January 2011.
6. Riforgiato, Leonard, *Missionary of Moderation: Henry Melchior Muhlenber*, 81.
7. "Nicolaus Ludwig, Count von Zinzendorf," Moravian College, Bethlehem, PA.
8. Chronology, "The Germans in America," European Reading Room, The Library of Congress.
9. Fogleman, *Hopeful Journeys*, 19.
10. "A Brief History of the Moravian

Church," www.moravian.org/2018/07/a-brief-history-of-the-moravian-church/.
11. Riforgiato, Leonard R., *Missionary of Moderation Henry Melchior Muhlenberg and the Lutheran Church in English America*, 18.
12. Riforgiato, Leonard R., *Missionary of Moderation Henry Melchior Muhlenberg and the Lutheran Church in English America*, 26, 27.
13. Frost, J. William, "Review of 'The Zinzendorf-Muhlenberg Encounter: A Controversy in Search of Understanding' by W. H. Wagner". *Pennsylvania Magazine of History and Biography* Vol. 127, Issue 1. 109–110.
14. Strom, Jonathan, Hartmut, Lehmann, and James Van Horn Melton, eds., *Pietism in Germany and North America 1680–1820*, Routledge, 2009, 23.
15. *Ibid.*, 24.
16. Zataveski, Theresa, "Inventory of the Papers of The Conference of Spiritual Descendants of John Hus 1937 1938," Moravian Archives, 2007.
17. *Ibid.*
18. Wagner, Walter H., *The Zinzendorf-Muhlenberg Encounter: A Controversy in Search of Understanding*, Nazareth, PA: Moravian Historical Society, 2002.

Chapter 10

1. Williams, T. Harry, *History of American Wars*, 12–14.
2. Louis XIV, *Mémoires*, as quoted by Durant, *The Age of Louis XIV*, 42.
3. Sommerville, J.P., "United Provinces in the Early Seventeenth Century," Department of History, University of Wisconsin–Madison.
4. "William of Orange, Father of the Nation," *History of Delft*.
5. Durant, *The Age of Louis XIV*, 178, 70.
6. "Charles II," The British Monarchy, royal.gov.uk.
7. "James II," The British Monarchy, royal.gov.uk.
8. This section is based on Dr. Edward Vallance's "Glorious Revolution," bbc.co.uk., taken from his book *The Glorious Revolution: And Britain's Fight for Liberty*, London, Little Brown, 2006.
9. Morgan, *Oxford Illustrated History of Britain*, 341.
10. Durant, *Age of Louis XIV*, 179, 295.
11. "English Bill of Rights, 1689," The Avalon Project, Yale Law School.
12. "Mary II, William III and the Acts of Settlement," The British Monarchy, royal.gov.uk.
13. "England's Revolution," a review of *1688: The First Modern Revolution* by Steven Pincus, Professor of History at Yale; *The Economist*, October 17–23, 2009, 97, 98.
14. Durant, *Age of Louis XIV*, 691.
15. Sommerville, Faculty History.wisc.edu.
16. "Emperor Leopold I of Habsburg Holy Roman Emperor, King of Hungary, King of Bohemia," www.government.nl.
17. Durant, *Age of Louis XIV*, 691, 692.
18. "William III and Mary II," *History of the Monarchy*, royal.gov.uk.
19. Durant, *Age of Louis XIV*, 693.
20. Ramsey, *Carolina Cradle: Settlement of the Northwest Carolina Frontier, 1747–1762*, 146.
21. Durant, *Age of Louis XIV*, 690.
22. *American Heritage Pictorial Atlas of United States History*, 55.
23. Tocqueville as quoted by Durant, *Louis XIV*, 695.

Chapter 11

1. Durant, *Age of Louis XIV*, 452.
2. Lord Chesterfield as quoted by Durant, *Age of Age of Louis XIV*, 701.
3. Louis XIV as quoted in Durant, *Age of Louis XIV*, 702.
4. Morgan, *Oxford Illustrated History of Britain*, 356.
5. "The Spanish Angle: Urological Problems of Charles II (1661–1700)," March 24, 2015, European Association of Urology, https://uroweb.org/eau15-the-spanish-angle-urological-problems-of-charles-ii-1661-1700/.
6. Durant, *Age of Louis XIV*, 704, 706.
7. Somerset, Anne, *Queen Anne* as reviewed by Allan Massie, *Wall Street Journal* Book Review November 29, 2013.
8. Articles 1 & 3, Act of Union 1707.
9. Perry, *Western Civilization* I, 371.
10. Morgan, Kenneth O., ed., *Oxford Illustrated History of Britain*.
11. Durant, *Age of Louis XIV*, 707, 714–15.
12. *Ibid.*, 714.

13. Durant, *Age of Voltaire*, 6.
14. Durant, *The Age of Louis XIV*, 14.
15. Durant, *The Story of Civilization 9 the Age of Voltaire*, 5.
16. Durant, *Age of Louis XIV*, 721.

Chapter 12

1. Schoepperle, Katherine, "A History of German Immigration to New York in 1710."
2. Bittinger, *The Germans in Colonial Times*, Chapter VIII, 14, "The Great Exodus of the Palatines."
3. "Pennsylvania-German in the Settlement of Maryland," Pennsylvania-German Society, Lancaster, PA, 1914.
4. Rouse, *Great Wagon Road*, 21.
5. "The German Exodus to England in 1709. (Massenauswanderung der Pfälzer.) Prepared at the request of the Pennsylvania-German society," Cornell University Library.
6. Schoepperle, "A History of German Immigration to New York in 1710."
7. Sachse, Nead, Buckenham Committee, "The Pennsylvania-German Society," Lancaster, PA, 1914.
8. Schoepperle, "A History of German Immigration to New York in 1710."
9. Weiser, C.S. D.D., *The Life (John) Conrad Weiser, German Pioneer, Patriot*, Reading, PA, Daniel Miller, Publisher 1876, Chapter V.
10. Ibid.
11. Weiser, Clement Zwingli, *The Life of (John) Conrad Weiser, the German Pioneer, Patriot, and Patron of Two Races*, Chapter IX, Library of Congress.
12. Ibid.
13. Richards, H.M.M., *American Historical Register*, Volume IV, March 1896–November 1896, 179, 180.
14. Weiser, Clement Zwingli, *The Life of (John) Conrad Weiser, the German Pioneer, Patriot, and Patron of Two Races*, Chapter XII, Library of Congress.
15. Ibid., Chapter XIII.
16. Weiser, Frederick S., "Conrad Weiser, Peacemaker of Colonial Pennsylvania."
17. Chronology, "The Germans in America," European Reading Room, The Library of Congress.
18. Schrader, Frederick Franklin, *The Germans in the Making of America*, Boston, MA, Stratford, 1924, 78–81; "John Peter Zenger," *Encyclopedia Britannica*.
19. "Crown v. John Peter Zenger," Historical Society of New York Courts, nycourts.gov/history.
20. Anderson, *The War That Made America*, 62–3.
21. Anderson, *Crucible of War*, 87, 92, 131.
22. Bittinger, *Germans in Colonial Times*, 56.

Chapter 13

1. *Encyclopedia Britannica*, accessed 11/2/2018.
2. National Army Museum, United Kingdom, https://www.nam.ac.uk/explore/war-austrian.
3. Durant, *Age of Voltaire*, 436.
4. Durant, *The Age of Voltaire*, 450–451.
5. Gombrich, *A Little History of the World Illustrated Edition*, 249.
6. The Editors of *Encyclopedia Britannica*, "Treaty of Aix-la-Chapelle," *Encyclopedia Britannica*, October 11, 2018.
7. Anderson, *War That Made America*, 23.
8. "Key Treaties Defining the Boundaries Separating English and Native American Territories in Virginia—The 1748 Treaty of Lancaster," virginiaplaces.org.
9. Weiser, Clement Zwingie, *The Life of (John) Conrad Weiser, German Pioneer Patriot*, 58.

Chapter 14

1. McCullough, *John Adams*, 37.
2. Franklin, Benjamin, *Autobiography*, 63.
3. Kutz, Kim, "A Battle in Quaker Pennsylvania: Reading a Document of the French and Indian War," Pennsylvania State University Libraries.
4. Irving, *Life of George Washington*, chap. 5, 18.
5. Anderson, Fred, *The War That Made America*, Prologue XXIII–XXV.
6. Chernow, *Washington*, 31.
7. Fowler, *Empires at War*, 34.
8. Boucher, John Newton, *Old and New Westmoreland Volume I*, 19.
9. Fowler, *op. cit.*, 35–36.
10. Chernow, *Washington*, 35–38.

11. Schurchi, Hermann, *History of the German Element in Virginia, Volume 2*, T. Knoh & Sons, 1900.
12. Fowler, *op. cit.*, 42, from Washington's Letter to Dinwiddie, March 29, 1754.
13. "Fort Necessity National Battlefield," U.S. Department of Interior, NPS; Chernow, *Washington*, 45.
14. Axelrod, *Savage Empire*, 180.
15. "Fort Necessity National Battlefield," United States Department of Interior, NPS; Fowler, *Empires of War*, 44.
16. Fowler, *op. cit.*, 44.
17. Summers, *History of Southwest Virginia*, 56.
18. U.S. Department of Interior National Park Service "Fort Necessity National Battlefield, Background of the Conflict."
19. Fowler, *op. cit.*, 47.
20. *Annals of America*, 2:1.
21. Axelrod, *A Savage Empire*, 200.
22. Summers, *History of Southwest Virginia*, 59, 60.
23. Axelrod, *Savage Empire*, 204.
24. Manuscript of General George Washington as reprinted in *Scribner's Magazine*, Vol. XIII, May 1893, No. 5 available online at The Fort Edwards Archive on the Web.
25. Tilberg, *Fort Necessity*, 23; Parkman, "Braddock's Defeat," *The French and English in America*.
26. National Park Service educational kit, "French and Indian War."
27. Chernow, *Washington*, 57.
28. George Washington to Mary Ball Washington July 18, 1755, Manuscript Division, Library of Congress.
29. Fowler *op. cit.*, 71–72.
30. Reynolds, Jr., William R., *Andrew Pickens: South Carolina Patriot in the Revolutionary War*, 19.
31. Morison, *Oxford History of the American People*, 163.
32. Anderson, *Crucible of War*, 171.
33. Churchill, *Great Republic*, 43.
34. Morison, *Oxford History of the American People*, 164–65.
35. *Encyclopaedia Britannica Premium Service*, s.v. "Pitt, William, the Elder."
36. U.S. History.org, *America's Place in the Global Struggle*, "The French and Indian War."
37. Anderson, *The War That Made America*, 123.
38. Peckham, *The Colonial Wars*, 155.
39. *Encyclopaedia Britannica Premium Service*, s.v. "Pitt, William, the Elder."
40. Churchill, *Great Republic*, large print 74–75, 81–82.
41. Cort, Cyrus, Col. *Henry Bouquet and His Campaigns of 1763 and 1764*, Lancaster PA, Stbinman & Hannah, Printers, 1883.
42. Richards, Henry Melchior Muhlenberg, *Historical Sketches by Henry Melchior Muhlenberg Richards Part XV*, 31.
43. Anderson, *Crucible of War*, 243.
44. Lossing, Benson John, *Harpers' Encyclopædia of United States from 458 A. D. to 1905*, Volume 9.
45. Marston, Daniel P., "Swift and Bold: The 60th Regiment and Warfare in North America, 1755–1765," master's thesis, McGill University, Montreal, March 1997.
46. Anderson, *Crucible of War*, 268.
47. Helmolt, *History of the World*, 1:450.
48. Editors of *Encyclopedia Britannica*, "Seven Years War," *Encyclopedia Britannica*, www.britannica.com, updated January 20, 2020.
49. Morgan, *Oxford Illustrated History of Britain*, 399–402.
50. Morrison, *Oxford History of the American People*, 165.

Chapter 15

1. Anderson, *Crucible of War*, 108; Anderson, *The War That Made America*, 152–59.
2. Lemay, J.A. Leo, *The Life of Benjamin Franklin, Vol. 3: Soldier, Scientist and Politician*, 235.
3. Franklin, *Autobiography*, 211.
4. This section is based on Anderson, *The War That Made America*, 158–65.
5. Anderson, *The War That Made America*, 168.
6. Anderson, *Crucible of War*, 272, 281–283; Anderson, *The War That Made America*, 170, 182.
7. Carnegie Library of Pittsburgh, "The Point: William Pitt"; National Park Service educational kit, "French and Indian War."
8. Pennsylvania Historical and Museum Commission, "Forts at the Forks."
9. Anderson, *Crucible of War*, 285.
10. Ohio History Central: "Treaty of Paris (1763)"; "Proclamation of 1763"; "Lord Dunmore's War and the Battle of Point Pleasant"; "French and Indian War";

"Pontiac"; and "Pontiac's War"; GlobalSecurity.org, "Lord's Dunmore's War"; Philadelphia Print Shop Inc., "A History of the French and Indian War"; Axelrod, *A Savage Empire*.
11. Anderson, *Crucible of War*, 534–535.
12. Axelrod, *Savage Empire*, 234–236.
13. Anderson, *Crucible of War*, 547–48; Encyclopaedia Britannica Premium Service, s.v. "Pontiac."
14. Merk, *History of the Western Movement*, 65, 68; National Park Service educational kit, "French and Indian War."
15. Axelrod, *A Savage Empire*, 238.
16. Anderson, *Crucible of War*, 535–546.
17. Commonwealth of Pennsylvania, Historical and Museum Commission, "Bushy Run Battlefield."
18. Morgan, Lisa, "Bouquet's Stand at Bushy Run," Pennsylvania Center for the Book, Spring 2010, Penn State University Libraries.
19. Summers, Jack L, and Rene Chartraand, *Military Uniforms in Canada, 1665–1970*, Ottawa: Canadian War Museum, 1981.
20. Hannum, Patrick H, Major USMC, "Henry Bouquet: A Study of Three Military Campaigns in North America, 1758–1764," master's thesis, General Staff College, Fort Leavenworth, Kansas, 1991.
21. Summers, *History of Southwest Virginia*, 78.
22. Morison, *Oxford History of the American People*, 183.
23. "The Royal Proclamation of 1763," ushistory.org.
24. The full text of "The Royal Proclamation- October 7, 1763 by King a Proclamation George R," is available at Yale University's Avalon Project website.
25. Chernow, *Washington*, 147–48.
26. Ibid., 165.
27. Ellis, Joseph J., *His Excellency George Washington*, 58.
28. Gardner, Andrew G., *Journal of Colonial Williamsburg*, Summer 2012, 45–49.
29. The House of Burgesses had passed an act in November 1753 to encourage settlement along the Mississippi River. "England's government was exceedingly eager to encourage settlement on the waters of the Mississippi and thereby strengthen their frontiers and fortify their claim to lands lying west of the Alleghany mountains." The "governor and council of Virginia renewed their grant to the loyal company in 1753," (Summers, *History of Southwest Virginia*, 52) allowing them four more years to complete surveying and settling the land. As agent of the Loyal Company, Dr. Walker began selling land at three pounds per 100 acres. By 1754, he had sold 224 two-hundred-acre tracts, many of which were soon settled. But the French and Indian War interrupted land sale activity when Indian resurgence associated with this war forced some settlements to be abandoned.
30. Fowler, *Empires at War*, 282, 283.

Chapter 16

1. Fischer, *Albion's Seed*, 613–15.
2. Not only do Americans use the term Scotch-Irish, but Queen Elizabeth I used the term in a 1573 letter.
3. Quinn, *Arthur Campbell*, 3.
4. Pennsylvania Historical and Museum Commission, "Pennsylvania State History."
5. Summers, *History of Southwest Virginia*, 41.
6. Waddell, *Annals of Augusta County, Virginia*, 23.
7. Sachse, Nead, Buckenham Committee, "Pennsylvania-German Society," Lancaster PA, 1914.
8. Kincaid, *Wilderness Road*, 38, 39.
9. Washington, George, "A Journal of My Journey Over the Mountains Began Fryday the 11th. of March 1747/8," *Founders Online*, National Archives, last modified February 1, 2018, http://founders.archives.gov/documents/Washington/01-01-02-0001-0002. [Original source: Jackson, Donald, ed., *The Diaries of George Washington*, vol. 1, 11 March 1748–13 November 1765, Charlottesville: University Press of Virginia, 1976, 6–16.]
10. Schuricht, Hermann, *The German Element in Virginia Vol. I*, Baltimore, MD: Theo. Kroch & Sons, 1898.
11. *Society for the History of the Germans in Maryland, Eleventh and Twelfth Annual Report*, Baltimore, MD: Theo Kroh & Sons, 1897.

Chapter 17

1. Garraty and Gay, eds., *Columbia History of the World*, 670.

2. *Annals of America*, Encyclopedia Britannica, 1:239, 392.
3. *Proceedings and Acts*: Jan. 1637–1747, Volume 27, By Maryland. General Assembly, 496.
4. *The Pennsylvania-German Society Proceedings and Addresses*, Harrisburg, PA, October 30, 1911, Vol. XXII published by the Society 1913, copyright 1914, 35.
5. Fogleman, *Hopeful Journeys*, 8.
6. Nead, Daniel Wunderlich, *The Pennsylvania German in the Settlement of Maryland*, Lancaster, PA: New Ear, 1914.
7. Nead, *The Pennsylvania German in the Settlement of Maryland*, Chapter II.
8. Bittinger, *The Germans in Colonial Times*, Chapter IV, "Labadists in Maryland."
9. *Ibid.*, Chapter V, "The Woman in the Wilderness."
10. *North Carolina Architects & Builders, a Biographical Dictionary*, "Bodnam, Robert (fl. 1650s)," North Carolina State University Libraries.
11. Wells, *Outline of History*, 690.
12. Morison, *Oxford History of the American People*, 94–5.
13. Williamson, Hugh, *History of North Carolina Volume I*, 65.
14. Charles the Second, "Charter of Carolina June 30 1665," Avalon.law.Yale.edu.
15. Ramsey, *Annals of Tennessee*, 40.
16. Morison, *Oxford History of the American People*, 97.
17. "The Carolina Quaker Experience 1665–1985 an Interpretation," The Library of the University of North Carolina at Chapel Hill, The Collection of North Carolina endowed by John Sprunt Hill, class of 1889.
18. Lohr, Otto, "Carolina," in *The First Germans in North America and the German Element of New Netherland*, G.E. Stechert & Co., 1912, contributor Library of Congress.
19. Dill, A.T., "Graffenried, Christoph, Baron von," in *Dictionary of North Carolina Biography*, edited by William S. Powell, UNC Press, 1979–96.
20. Collins, Donald E., "Swiss and Palatine Settlers," *Encyclopedia of North Carolina*, University of North Carolina, 2006.
21. "List of Known Persons Who Left Switzerland and Germany to Settle in New Bern, North Carolina in 1710," Compiled by Victor T. Jones, Jr. Local History & Genealogy Librarian New Bern-Craven County Public Library.
22. *Classic Encyclopedia*, s.v. "South Carolina."
23. Rea, *Washington County, Tennessee Deeds, 1775–1800*, 6, 7.
24. Brickell, John, *Natural History of North Carolina*.
25. Collins, Donald E., "Swiss and Palatine Settlers," *Encyclopedia of North Carolina*, University of North Carolina Press, 2006.
26. Voigt, Gilbert P., "The German and German-Swiss Element in South Carolina, 1732–1752," Bulletin 113, University of South Carolina, September 1922.
27. "Eighteenth Century North Carolina Timeline," North Carolina Museum of History.
28. Churchill, *Great Republic*, 72.
29. Stevens, William B., "Settlement of Georgia," World History International.
30. Churchill, *Great Republic*, 41.
31. Reese, Trevor R., *Frederika: Colonial Fort and Town Its Place in History*, St. Simon's Island, Georgia.
32. Scott, Hamish, and Brendan Simms, eds., *Cultures of Power in Europe During the Long Eighteenth Century*, Cambridge University Press; reprint edition (June 24, 2010), 134.
33. Chronology, "The Germans in America," European Reading Room, The Library of Congress.
34. Barlament, James, "Salzburgers," edited by New Georgia Encyclopedia Staff 10/19/2016, University of Georgia Press, georgiaencyclopedia.org.
35. *Ibid.*
36. Munro, William Bennett, *Government of the United States*, 4–7; Galvin, William Francis, Massachusetts Archive Collection Records, 1629–1799, Historical Sketches Colonial Period, Intercharter Period.
37. New Georgia Encyclopedia, History and Archeology, "Revolutionary War in Georgia," georgiaencyclopedia.org.

Chapter 18

1. Bridenbaugh, Carl, *Myths and Realities: Societies of the Colonial South*, Baton Rouge, Louisiana State University Press, 1952, 30.
2. U.S. Diplomatic Mission to Germany/Public Affairs/Information Resource Centers, Updated: March 2010.

3. Ramsey, Robert, *Carolina Cradle*, 171, 172.
4. Folmsbee, *Annotation*, 749.
5. "Allegheny Mountains," Wikipedia. org.wiki.allegheny-mountains.
6. Summers, *History of Southwest Virginia*, 38–39.
7. *Indian Nations of North America*, Washington, D.C., National Geographic, 76.
8. West Virginia Archives and History, "Native American Clashes with European Settlers."
9. Irving, *Life of George Washington*, chap. 5, 18.
10. Rouse, *Great Wagon Road*, Prologue, 21–36.
11. Merk, *History of the Western Movement*, 49, 54.
12. Ramsey, Robert, *Carolina Cradle*, 18.
13. Paltsits, Victor Hugo, *Scheme for the Conquest of Canada in 1746*, Essay published 1945.
14. "Motivation for Immigration," Davidson County, NC.
15. Hartley and Hartley, "Tar Heel Junior Historian," digitized by Internet Archive in 2013.
16. Ramsey, Robert, *Carolina Cradle*, 150, 17, 21–25, 171.
17. Moravian Archives, Winston-Salem, NC, "Southern Province Moravian Church."
18. Shirley, Michael, *From Congregation to Industrial City*, 6.
19. "Randolph County 1779–1979," Library of the University of North Carolina.
20. "Bethabara Moravian Church," from Moravian Archives, Winston-Salem, North Carolina, 76–79.
21. Mereness, Newton D., "Introduction to the Moravian Diary: Diary of a Journey of Moravians."
22. "The Moravian Story," Historic Bethabara Park, City of Winston-Salem Recreation & Parks Department.
23. Rouse, *Great Wagon Road*, 80, 81.

Chapter 19

1. Boone's letter to Kentucky Gov. Isaac Shelby in 1792 as quoted by Robert Morgan. *Boone*, Intro, 21.
2. Dowd, Gregory Evans, *War Under Heaven*, 275.
3. Creighton, *Eastwind Westwind*; Ramsey, Robert, *Carolina Cradle*, 171–173.

4. Silverman, Sharon H., "A Kentucky Frontiersman's Pennsylvania Roots: The Daniel Boone Homestead," *Pennsylvania Heritage Magazine* Vol. 24, No. 3, Summer 1998.
5. Smout, T.C., *History of the Scottish People, 1560–1830*, 134; Summers, *History Southwest Virginia*, 53.
6. Updated and new information circulated by the Stephen Holston Chapter Tennessee Sons of the American Revolution.
7. Williams, *Dawn of Tennessee Valley*, 124.
8. American Studies at the University of Virginia, "Tour 5."
9. "Journal of Dr. Thomas Walker," in Summers, *History of Southwest Virginia*, 797.
10. Ibid., 798.
11. Thwaites and Kellog, *Documentary History of Dunmore's War*, 58.
12. Hamilton, Emory L., "The Long Hunters," *Historical Sketches of Southwest Virginia*, Publication 5, March 1970.
13. Corlew, *Tennessee*, 41, 42.
14. Bogan, Dallas, "Longhunters Were First to Penetrate Wilds of Tennessee, Kentucky, Then the West," www.tngenweb. org/campbell/hist-bogan/longhunters. html.
15. Kincaid, *Wilderness Road*, 67.
16. Hamilton, "Long Hunters," *Historical Sketches of Southwest Virginia*, Publication 5, March 1970.
17. Bucy, "Chronology of Tennessee History" timeline.
18. Hamilton, "Long Hunters," *Historical Sketches of Southwest Virginia*, Publication 5, March 1970.
19. Bittinger, Lucy Fomey, *Germans in Colonial Times*, 280.
20. Bakeless, John, *Daniel Boone, Master of the Wilderness*, Chapter 4.
21. Fink, Paul M., *Jonesborough: First Century of Tennessee's First Town*, 95–96.
22. Kincaid, *Wilderness Road*, 31 and jacket text.
23. Summers, *History of Southwest Virginia*, 278–83.

Chapter 20

1. Richards, Henry Melchior Muhlenberg, *Historical Sketches by Henry Melchior Muhlenberg Richards Part XV*, 31.

2. Historical Review of Berks County, Summer 1960.
3. Chernow, *Washington*, 332.
4. Chernow, *Alexander Hamilton*, 109.
5. Lockhart, Paul, "The Rich Legacy of a Forgotten Founder." *U.S News*, July 7–14, 2008, 45.
6. Slaughter, Jamie, "Frederick the Great," The National Library for the study of George Washington at Mount Vernon.
7. *Ibid.*
8. Schrader, *Germans in the Making of America*, 139–40.
9. Smith, Randy, history professor, "The Role of the German Hessian in the American Revolution," Lecture presented August 17, 2019, at the Virginia Society of Sons of the American Revolution meeting, General William Campbell Chapter, Abingdon, VA.
10. Head, David, University of Central Florida, The National Library for the Study of George Washington at Mount Vernon, *Home Washington Library Center for Digital History Digital Encyclopedia Hessians*.
11. Chronology, "The Germans in America," European Reading Room, The Library of Congress.

Chapter 21

1. Boone, Nathan, *My Father, Daniel Boone*, 44.
2. English, William Hayden *Conquest of the Country Northwest of the Ohio*, 457–463.
3. McCullough, *The Pioneers*, 7.
4. Excerpted from: National Archives Education Staff. *The Constitution: Evolution of a Government*. Santa Barbara, ABC-CLIO, 2001.
5. *Annual Report of the Society for the Germans in Maryland Volume 11*, January 1, 1899, 124.
6. "German Americans of Cleveland," Cleveland Memory Project, Michael Schultz Library.
7. McCullough, *The Pioneers*, Chapters 1 and 2.
8. *Ibid.*, 20–21.
9. *Ibid.*, 45.
10. Adams, John Kuehm, *German Marietta and Washington County*, Charleston, SC: Arcadia Publishing, 2016, Introduction.
11. McCullough, *The Pioneers*, 255.
12. Fallace, Thomas D., "In the Shadow of Authoritarianism: American Education in the Twentieth Century," Teacher's College Press, Columbia University. 2018, 9.
13. "Neighborhood News" *The Marietta Times*, August 20, 2019.
14. Ohio Historical Marker 2003, Zane's Trace, the Ohio Bicentennial Commission, the Marietta Chapter NSDAR, and the Village of New Concord.
15. U.S. Department of Transportation, Federal Highway Administration.
16. McCullough, *The Pioneers*, 184.
17. "German Heritage Cleveland," Michael Schwartz Library Memory Project, Cleveland State University, Encyclopedia of Cleveland History.

Chapter 22

1. Rath, R. John, "The Failure of an Ideal: The Viennese Revolution of 1848," University of Texas, a paper read at the annual convention of the Southwestern Social Science Association at Dallas, TX, April 3, 1953.
2. Coper, Rudolf, "The German Revolution of 1848," *University of Toronto Quarterly* Vol. 17, No. 2, January 1948, 137–151.
3. Hill, Jonathan Richard, "The Revolutions of 1848 in Germany, Italy, and France" (2005). Senior honors thesis, Eastern Michigan University, 45.
4. "The Europe of Napoleon and Metternich, 1798 to the 1840s," Mount Holyoke College, mtholyoke.edu/courses/rschwart/hist151/metternich.htm.
5. "Germany—German Confederation 1815–66," *Encyclopedia Britannica*, Vol. 10, 1971, 316–323.
6. The Metropolitan Museum of Art, Metmuseum.org.
7. "The Europe of Napoleon and Metternich, 1798 to the 1840s," Mount Holyoke College, mtholyoke.edu.
8. Hill, Jonathan Richard, "The Revolutions of 1848 in Germany, Italy, and France" (2005). Senior honors thesis, Eastern Michigan University, 45.
9. Wittke, Carl, *Refugees of Revolution: The German Forty-Eighters in America*, 18–28.
10. *Ibid.*, 1–5.
11. Hill, Jonathan Richard, "The Revolutions of 1848 in Germany, Italy, and France" (2005). Senior honors thesis, Eastern Michigan University.
12. "Germany—German Confederation

1815-66," *Encyclopedia Britannica*, Vol. 10, USA, 1971, 320.
13. Historical Society of Pennsylvania, hps.org.
14. "Germany—German Confederation 1815-66," 43-57.
15. Schrader, *The Germans in the Making of America*, 242-43.
16. Tolzmann, Don Heinrich, *The German-American Forty-eighters, 1848-1998*, 3.

Chapter 23

1. Zeitlin, *Germans in Wisconsin*, 5.
2. Immigration to the United States, U.S. Census Bureau Statistical Abstract for 2006.
3. Robinson, Gabrielle, *German Settlers of South Bend*, Arcadia, 2003, 19.
4. *Ibid.*, 22.
5. Indiana University, Ruth Lilly Special Collections and Archives, IUPUI University Library.
6. Immigration to the United States, U.S. Census Bureau Statistical Abstract for 2008.
7. "Immigrants Voyage, Germany to Illinois, 1851," Illinois State Museum website accessed November 3, 2018.
8. Bonney, Rachel A., "Was There a Single German-American Experience? The German Americans in Minnesota," Papers written for two conferences sponsored by Concordia College, Moorhead, Minnesota October 1979 and St. Paul, Minnesota, October 1979, https://files.eric.ed.gov/fulltext/ED275571.pdf.
9. Harzig, Christiane, "Germans," *The Electronic Encyclopedia of Chicago 2005*, Chicago Historical Society; *The Encyclopedia of Chicago 2004*, The Newberry Library.
10. Kilar, *Germans in Michigan*, 2, quoting Alan Wolfe's "The Return of the Melting Pot," *The New Republic*, December 1990, 1-7.
11. *Ibid.*, 26.
12. Gross, Stuart D., *Saginaw: A History of the Land and the City*, Woodland Hills: Windsor, 80, 97 as quoted by Kilar, *Germans in Michigan*, 38.
13. Zeitlin, *Germans in Wisconsin*, 10.
14. *Ibid.*, 26.
15. "Germans in Wisconsin," *Ethnic Groups in Wisconsin: Historical Background*, Max Kade Institute for German-American Studies, University of Wisconsin-Madison.
16. Zeitlin, *Germans in Wisconsin*, 40.

17. *Ibid.*, 10.
18. *Ibid.*, 25.
19. Gilman, Rhonda R., "How Minnesota Became the 32nd State," *Minnesota History* Vol. 56, No. 4 (Winter 1998/1999), 157-170.
20. Conzen, Kathleen, *Germans in Minnesota—The People of Minnesota*, Minnesota Historical Society, 2003, 12-18.
21. *Ibid.*, 9.
22. *Ibid.*, 29.
23. Glasrud, Calrence A., ed., *A Heritage Deferred: The German-Americans in Minnesota*, Moorhead, MN: Concordia College, 1981, files.eric.ed.gov/fulltext/ED275571.pdf.
24. Conzen, Kathleen Neils, *Germans in Minnesota*, 46-47.
25. Bonney, Rachel A., "The German Ethnic Experience in Minnesota," *A Heritage Deferred: The German-Americans in Minnesota*, Edited with an Introduction by Clarence A. Glasrud, Moorhead, MN: Concordia College, 1981, files.eric.ed.gov/fulltext/ED275571.pdf.
26. *Ibid.* 28-29.
27. *Ibid.* 29.

Chapter 24

1. Deiler, John Hanno, *The Settlement of the German Coast of Louisiana and the Creoles*, Vol. 8.
2. Moen, Jon, "John Law and the Mississippi Bubble 1718-1720," *Mississippi History*, Mississippi Historical Society.
3. Schrader, *The Germans in the Making of America*, 151-52.
4. *Ibid.*, 236.
5. "John Augustus Sutter," *The West*, PBS, 2001, The West Film Project.
6. Schrader, *The Germans in the Making of America*, 237.
7. "John Augustus Sutter," *The West*.
8. Handbook of Texas Online, Terry G. Jordan, "Germans," June 15, 2010, modified March 7, 2016. Published by the Texas State Historical Association, accessed November 7, 2019, http://www.tshaonline.org/handbook/online/articles/png02.
9. Mellick, Andrew D. "German Emigration to the American Colonies, Its Cause, and the Distribution of the Emigrants." *The Pennsylvania Magazine of History and Biography* Vol. 10, No. 4, 1887, 375-91.

Chapter 25

1. Balfour, Michael Graham, "William II Emperor of Germany," *Encyclopedia Britannica*.
2. *Collier's New Photographic History of the World's War 1918*, New York: P.F. Collier and Sons Publishers, 1918, 10.
3. Morrison, *Oxford History of the American People*, 848–49.
4. *Collier's New Photographic History of the World's War 1918*, 9, 28.
5. Bailey, Thomas A., *American Historical Review* Vol. 41, No. 1, 1935, 54–73.
6. Morison, *Oxford History of the American People*, 852.
7. Lobell, Jarrett A., "What Sank San Diego?," *Archaeology, January/February 2019*, Archeological Institute of America, 40.
8. Herman, Arthur, "His Enemy Across the Ocean," *The Wall Street Journal* "Books," Saturday/Sunday, December 7–8, 2019.
9. Morison, *Oxford History of the American People*, 873.
10. Library of Congress, Teachers, Immigration, German.
11. Wüstenbecker, Katja, University of Jena, "German-Americans During WWI," Thuringia, Germany, 2014.
12. *Ibid*.
13. Siegel, Robert and Art Silverman, "All Things Considered," aired by NPR, April 7, 2017.
14. "House of Saxe-Coburg-Gotha," www.englishmonarchs.co.uk.
15. Huggler, Justin, in Berlin, "Donald Trump, the Once 'Proud German-American,' Has Changed His Tune on the Land of His Forefathers," *Telegraph*, UK, July 11, 2018.

Chapter 26

1. This chapter was written especially for this book by aerospace scientist and university professor, Dr. James Evans Lyne, MD, PhD.

Chapter 27

1. Author's personal Interviews with Max Hermann and Josh Fuller, June 2019 and earlier, through the years.
2. Roosevelt, *New York Times*, 1914 as quoted by Schrader, *The Germans in the Making of America*, 230.

Bibliography

Articles, Newspaper and Magazine
Listed as individual references in endnotes

Books
American Heritage Pictorial Atlas of United States History. New York: American Heritage, 1960.
America's Historylands. Washington, D.C.: National Geographic Society, 1967.
Anderson, Fred. *Crucible of War: The Seven Years' War and the Fate of Empire in British North America, 1754-1766*. New York: Vintage, 2001.
———. *The War that Made America*. New York: Penguin, 2006.
Anderson, George K., and Karl J. Holzknecht. *The Literature of England*, New York: Scott and Foresman, 1953.
The Annals of America: 1755-1783. Chicago: Encyclopedia Britannica, 1976.
Armstrong, Karen. *Islam*. New York: Random House, 2000.
Axelrod, Alan. *A Savage Empire: Trappers, Traders, Tribes and the Wars that Made America*. New York: St. Martin's, 2011.
Azurara, Gomes Eannes de. *The Chronicles of the Discovery and Conquest of Guinea*. Project Gutenberg e-book, released April 1, 2011.
Bakeless, John. *Daniel Boone, Master of the Wilderness*. Bison: University of Nebraska Press, 1989.
Barber, John Warner, and Henry Howe. *Our Whole Country; Vol. I*. New York: George F. Tuttle and Hendy McCauley, 1861.
Bausman, Joseph Henderson. *History of Beaver County, Pennsylvania and its Centennial Celebration*, Volume I. New York: Knickerbocker, 1904.
Baxter, James Phinney. *Sir Ferdinando Gorges and his Province of Maine*, Volume II. Boston: Prince Society, 1890.
Bergreen, Lawrence. *Over the Edge of the World: Magellan's Voyage*. New York: HarperCollins, 2003.
Bittinger, Lucy Forney. *The Germans in Colonial Times*. Philadelphia: J.B. Lippincott, 1901.
Boone, Nathan. *My Father, Daniel Boone*. University of Kentucky Press: Draper Interviews, 1999.
Boorstin, Daniel J. *The Discoverers*. New York: Random House, 1983.
Boucher, John Newton. *Old and New Westmoreland Volume I*. New York: American Historical Society, 1918.
Bource, Edward G., ed. *Original Narratives of the Voyages of the Northmen*. New York: Charles Scribner, 1906.
Bradford, William. *Of Plymouth Plantation*. New York: Knopf, 1952.
Bragdon, Henry W., and Samuel P. McCutchen. *History of a Free People*. New York: Macmillan, 1967.

Branch, Michael P., ed. *Reading the Roots: American Nature before Waldon*. Athens: University of Georgia Press, 2004.
Braun, Wernher von, Frederick Ira Ordway III, and David Dooling. *Space Travel: A History*. New York: Harper and Row, 1985.
Brickell, John. *Natural History of North Carolina*. Dublin: Printed by J. Carson for the author, 1737.
Bucklin, Loraine Pearce. "Life and Times of Isabella of Castile" in Eagle, Mary Kavanaugh Oldham, ed., *The Congress of Women: Held in the Woman's Building, World's Columbian Exposition*,1893. Chicago: Monarch, 1894, pp. 450–457.
Butler, Jon. *Awash in a Sea of Faith*. Cambridge: Harvard University Press, 1992.
Caesar, Gaius Julius. "The Gallic War" in Basil Davenport, ed., *Portable Roman Reader*. Translated by H.J. Edwards. New York: Viking-Penguin, 1951, chaps. 21–28.
Channing, Edward. *A Student's History of the United States*. New York: Macmillan, 1912.
Chesterton, Cecil Edward. *History of the United States*. New York: George H. Doran, 1919.
Churchill, Winston S., ed. *The Great Republic: A History of America*. London: Cassell, 2002.
_____. *The Great Republic: A History of America* (Large Print). New York: Random House, 1999.
Collier's New Photographic History of the World's War. New York: Colliers and Sons, 1918.
Conzen, Kathleen Neils. *Germans in Minnesota: The People of Minnesota*. Minnesota Historical Society, 2003.
Cook, James, with Grenfell Price, eds., *Exploration of Captain James Cook in the Pacific as told by Selections of his own Journals*. Norwalk, CT: Easton, 1998.
Corlew, Robert E. *Tennessee, a Short History*. Knoxville: University of Tennessee Press, 1981.
Cranz, Carl, and K. Becker. *Handbook of Ballistics. Vol. I: Exterior Ballistics, Being a Theoretical Examination of the Motion of the Projectile from the Muzzle to the Target*. London: Majesty's Stationery Office, 1921.
Craven, Wesley Frank. *The Virginia Company of London*. Project Gutenberg e-book, released April 9, 2009.
Creighton, James H. "Eastwind Westwind—The Legacy of John Poore: The Family Poore, Prehistory to the Present," familytreemaker.genealogy.com.
Crosby, Alfred W. *The Columbian Exchange: Biological and Cultural Consequences of 1492*, 30th anniversary edition. Westport, CT: Praeger, 2003.
Clayton, Lawrence A., Knight, Vernon James Jr., and Edward C. Moore, eds. *De Soto Chronicles*, Vol. I. Tuscaloosa: University of Alabama Press, 1993.
Diamond, Jared. *Guns, Germs and Steel*. New York: W.W. Norton, 1997.
Dickens, Charles. "A Child's History of England" in *The Works of Charles Dickens*, Vol. 6. New York: P.F. Collier, n.d.
Doherty, Kieran. *Sea Venture*. New York: St. Martin's, 2007.
Dowd, Gregory Evans. *War Under Heaven*. Baltimore: Johns Hopkins University Press, 2002.
Duncan, David Ewing. *Hernando de Soto*. New York: Crown, 1996.
Durant, Will. *Heroes of History*. New York: Simon and Schuster, 2001.
Durant, Will. *The Story of Civilization: Vol. I, Our Oriental Heritage*. PA: Haddon Craftsmen, 1935, renewed 1963:
_____. *Vol. 3, Caesar and Christ*. New York: Simon & Schuster, 1944.
_____. *Vol. 4, Age of Faith*. New York: MJF, 1950.
_____. *Vol. 5, The Renaissance*. New York: Simon & Schuster, 1953.
_____. *Vol. 6, The Reformation*. New York: Simon & Schuster, 1957.
Durant, Will, and Ariel Durant. *The Story of Civilization: Vol. 7, Age of Reason*. New York: Simon & Schuster, 1961.
_____. *Vol. 8, The Age of Louis XIV*. New York: Simon & Schuster, 1963.
_____. *Vol. 9, The Age of Voltaire*. New York: Simon & Schuster, 1965.
_____. *Vol. 10, Rousseau and Revolution*. New York, Simon & Schuster, 1967.
Dykeman, Wilma. *The French Broad River*. Knoxville: University of Tennessee Press, 1987.
Elson, Henry William. *History of the United States of America*. New York: Macmillan, 1904.
Emison, John Avery. *Lincoln Über Alles*, Gretna, LA: Pelican, 2009.
English, William Hayden. *Conquest of the Country Northwest of the River Ohio, 1778–1783*. Indianapolis: Bowen-Merrill, 1897.

Bibliography 267

English, William Hayden. *Life of Gen. George Rogers Clark.* Indianapolis: Bowen-Merrill, 1897.
"Expedition of Batts and Fallam, 1671, New River Virginia" in Summers, Louis Preston, *Annals of Southwest Virginia 1769–1800,* Vol. I. Abingdon, VA: 1929.
Fink, Paul M. *Jonesborough: The First Century of Tennessee's First Town,* Tennessee State Planning Commission, Publication no. 394. Springfield, VA: National Technical Information Service, 1972.
Fischer, David Hackett. *Albion's Seed: Four British Folkways in America.* New York: Oxford University Press, 1989.
Fogleman, Aaron Spencer. *Hopeful Journey.* Philadelphia: University of Pennsylvania Press, 1996.
Folmsbee, Stanley J. "Annotations Relating Ramsey's Annals of Tennessee to Present Day Knowledge" in Ramsey, *Annals of Tennessee.* Johnson City, TN: Overmountain, 1999.
Franklin, Benjamin. *Autobiography of Benjamin Franklin.* 1923; reprinted Atlanta, Communication and Studies Inc.
_____. "A Narrative of the Late Massacres, in Lancaster County, of a Number of Indians, Friends of this Province, by Persons Unknown With Some Observations on the Same" in *The Writings of Benjamin Franklin, Volume III: London 1757- 1775.*
Fraser, Antonia, ed., *Lives of the Kings and Queens of England.* Los Angeles: University of California Press, 1998.
Friedenberg, Daniel M. *Life, Liberty, and the Pursuit of Land: The Plunder of Early America,* New York: Prometheus, 1992.
Fulbrook, Mary. *A Concise History of Germany.* Cambridge University Press, 1991.
Gaines, John Strother. *American Government in the 20th Century, Teachers Edition.* Eberstein & Mill, 1973.
Garraty, John A., and Peter Gay, eds. *The Columbia History of the World.* New York: Harper & Row, 1972.
Gibbon, Edward. *Gibbon's Decline and Fall of the Roman Empire, Abridged and Illustrated.* Rand McNally, 1979.
Glover, Lorri, and Daniel Black Smith. *The Shipwreck that Saved Jamestown.* New York: Holt, 2009.
Gombrich, E. H. *A Little History of the World, Illustrated edition.* New Haven: Yale University Press, 2011.
Granzotto, Gianni. *Christopher Columbus: the Dream and the Obsession, A Biography.* New York: Doubleday, 1985.
Gray, Mary Preston. *Family Tree.* n.p., 1980.
Grizzard, Frank E., and D. Boyd Smith. *Jamestown Colony: A Political, Social, and Cultural History.* Santa Barbara: ABC-CLIO, 2007.
Hamilton, Emory L. *Historical Sketches of Southwest Virginia, 5: The Long Hunters.* Wise: Southwest Virginia Historical Society, 1976.
Hanna, Charles A. *The Scotch-Irish: or, The Scot in North Britain, North Ireland, and North America.* New York: G.P. Putnam, 1902.
Hatch, Charles E. Jr. *America's Oldest Legislative Assembly and its Jamestown Statehouse.* Washington: National Park Service, 1956.
Hawgood, John A. *America's Western Frontiers.* New York: Knopf, 1967.
Hemstreet, Charles. *The Story of Manhattan.* New York: Charles Scribner, 1901.
Hoig, Stanley W. *Cherokees and their Chiefs in the Wake of Empire.* Fayetteville: University of Arkansas Press, 1998.
Hudson, Charles. *Knights of Spain, Warriors of the Sun.* Athens: University of Georgia, 1998.
Irving, Washington. *Life of George Washington,* Project Gutenberg e-book, released December 1, 2004.
Jacobsen, Annie. *Operation Paperclip: The Secret Intelligence Operation that Brought Nazi Scientists to America.* New York: Little, Brown and Company, 2014.
James, Alfred Proctor. *The Ohio Company: Its Inner History.* New York: University of Pittsburg, 1959.
James, Herman G. *Brazil After a Century of Independence.* New York: Macmillan, 1925, 47, 48.

Jones, David S. *Rationalizing Epidemics*. U.S.A. President and Fellows of Harvard College, 2004.
Jones, Jim. *German Democracy and Justice by Tacitus*. Chester: West Chester University of Pennsylvania, 2012.
Jones, Randell. *In the Footsteps of Daniel Boone*. Winston-Salem, NC: John R. Blair, 2005.
Josephy, Alvin M. Jr. *500 Nations*. New York: Knopf, 1994.
Joyner, Christopher. *Antarctica and the Law of the Sea*. Leiden: Martinus Nijhoff Publishers, 1992.
Kennedy, Paul. *The Rise and Fall of the Great Powers*. New York: Vintage, 1989.
Kilar, Jeremy W. *Germans in Michigan*. East Lansing: Michigan State University, 2002.
Kincaid, Robert L. *Wilderness Road*. Reprinted Middlesboro, KY: Kincaid, 1966.
Kurlansky, Mark. *A Continent of Islands*. New York: Da Capo, 1992.
Lapham, Alice Gertrude. *The Old Planters of Beverly in Massachusetts and the Thousand Acre Grant of 1635*. Cambridge, MA: Riverside, 1930.
Leyburn, James G. *The Scotch- Irish: A Social History*. Chapel Hill: University of North Carolina Press, 1962.
Livy. *The History of Early Rome*, Collector's edition. Norwalk, CT: Easton, 1978. "First published in parts beginning around 24 BC."
Longfellow, Henry Wadsworth. "The Courtship of Miles Standish" in *A Treasury of Great Poems*, selected by Louis Untermeyer. New York: Simon & Schuster, 1955, 810.
Lossing, Benson J. *1776*. New York: Edward Walker, 1847.
MacCulloch, J.A. *The Religion of the Ancient Celts*. New York: Charles Scribner, 1911. Project Gutenberg e-book, released January 12, 2005.
Magaffin, Ralph V.D., and Frederic Duncalf. *Ancient and Medieval History*. New Jersey: Silver Burdett, 1959.
Mann, Charles C., *1491*. New York: Knopf, 2005.
_____. *1493*. New York: Knopf, 2011.
Marshall, Henrietta Elizabeth. *This Country of Ours: The Story of the United States*. New York: George H. Doran, 1917.
McCullough, David. *John Adams*. New York: Simon and Schuster, 2001.
_____. *The Path Between the Seas*. New York: Simon and Schuster, 1977.
_____. *The Pioneers*. New York: Simon and Schuster, 2019.
McGoldrick, Monica, Joe Giordano, and Nydia Garcia-Preto, eds., *Ethnicity and Family Therapy*, 3rd edition. New York: Guilford, 2005.
McMaster, John Bach. *A Brief History of the United States*. California: People of the State of California, 1909.
McSweeney, Edwin F. "Racial Contributions to the United States" in Schrader's *The Germans in the Making of America*. New York: Haskell House, 1972.
Meagher, Jennifer. "The Holy Roman Empire and the Habsburgs, 1400–1600" in *Heilbrunn Timeline of Art History*. New York: Metropolitan Museum of Art, 2000.
_____. http://www.metmuseum.org/toah/hd/habs/hd_habs.htm. October 2002.
Menzies, Gavin. *1421*. Great Britain: Transworld Publishers, 2002.
Merck, Frederick. *History of the Westward Movement*. New York, Knopf, 1978.
Merrell, James H. *Into the American Woods*. New York: W.W. Norton, 1999.
Middleton, Richard. *Colonial America: A History, 1565–1776*. Malden, MA: Blackwell, 2002.
Morgan, Kenneth O., ed., *Oxford Illustrated History of Britain*. New York: Oxford University Press, 1984.
Morgan, Robert. *Boone*. Chapel Hill: Algonquin, 2007.
Morison, Samuel Eliot. "Introduction" in Bradford, *Of Plymouth Plantation*. New York: The Modern Library, 1967.
_____. *Oxford History of the American People*. New York: Oxford University Press, 1965.
_____. ed. and trans., *Journals and Other Documents on the Life and Voyages of Christopher Columbus*. New York: Heritage, 1963.
Munro, William Bennett. *The Government of the United States*. New York: Macmillan, 1919.
Oberth, Hermann. *The Rocket in Planetary Space*. Translated 1923. Berlin: De Gruyter Oldenbourg, 2014.

Ordway, Frederick III, and Mitchell R. Sharpe. *The Rocket Team*. Cambridge: Massachusetts Institute of Technology Press, 1982.
Pagden, A.R. *Hernán Cortás Letters from Mexico*. New York: Grossman, 1971.
Parkman, Francis. *France and England in North America Volume I, Volume II. 1885*. New York: Viking, 1983.
Parry, John Horace. *The Discovery of the Sea*. Berkeley: University of California Press, 1974.
Pastorius, Francis D. "Germantown" in *Annals of America*, 1:310–14.
Patton, James. "Memorial of James Patton to the Governor and Council of Virginia, January 1753" in Williams, *Dawn of Tennessee Valley*, 444–447, Appendix B.
Pennsylvania-German Society. *Pennsylvania-German in the settlement of Maryland*. Lancaster: University of Pennsylvania, 1914.
Perry, Marvin. *Western Civilization, Volume I*. Boston: Houghton Mifflin, 1992.
Philbrick, Nathaniel. *Mayflower: A Story of Community, Courage and War*. New York: Penguin, 2006.
Plumb, A.H. *The Horizon Book of the Renaissance*. New York: American Heritage, 1961.
Powell, T.G.E. *The Celts*. New York: F.A. Praeger, 1958.
Price, Grenfell, ed. *Exploration of Captain James Cook in the Pacific as told by Selections of his own Journals*. Norwalk, CT: Easton, 1998.
Proceedings of the New Jersey Historical Society, Vol III. Paterson, New Jersey, the Press Printing and Publishing, 1906.
Putnam, John J. "The Dutch on the Hudson," *America's Historylands*, National Geographic Society, Washington, D.C., 2D edition, 1962, 1967
Quinn, Hartwell L. *Arthur Campbell: Pioneer and Patriot of the "Old Southwest."* Jefferson, NC: McFarland, 1990.
Ramsey, J.G.M. *The First American Frontier: The Annals of Tennessee to the End of the Eighteenth Century*. C. Hammett. 1853; reprinted Johnson City, TN: Overmountain, 1999.
Ramsey, Robert W. *Carolina Cradle: Settlement of the Northwest Carolina Frontier, 1747–1762*. Chapel Hill: University of North Carolina Press, 1964.
Randall, Willard Sterne. *George Washington*. New York: Henry Holt, 1997.
_____. *Thomas Jefferson: A Life*. New York: Harper Perennial, 1994.
Ranelagh, John O'Beirne. *A Short History of Ireland*, updated edition. Cambridge University Press, 1999.
Rea, Loraine. *Washington County Tennessee Deeds, 1775–1800*. Greenville, SC: Southern Historical, 2001.
Reese, Trevor R.. *Frederica: Colonial Fort and Town, its place in history*. Fort Frederica Association, 1969.
Report and Transactions of the Devonshire Association for the Advancement of Science, Literature and Art. Vol. XIV. Plymouth: W. Brandon & Sons, 1882.
Richards, Henry Melchior Muhlenberg. *Historical Sketches by Henry Melchior Muhlenberg Richard,s Part XV*, Lancaster: Pennsylvania German Society, 1906.
Rolle, Andrew, and John S. Gaines. *The Golden State*, 4th edition, Wheeling: Harlan Davidson, 2000.
Rouse, Parke Jr. *The Great Wagon Road*. Richmond, VA: Dietz, 2004.
Rucinam, Steven. *A History of the Crusades: Volume III, the Kingdom of Acre and the Later Crusades*. New York: Cambridge University Press, 1951.
Sainte-Boeve, C.A. *Portraits of Seventeenth Century History and Literary*. New York: G.P. Putnam & Sons, 1904.
Schama, Simon, *A History of Britain* (London: Bodley Head, 2009) and BBC documentary series.
Schoepperle, Katherine. "A History of German Immigration to New York in 1710," master's thesis, University of Illinois, digitalized by internet archive in 2013.
Schrader, Frederick Franklin. *The Germans in the Making of America*. Boston: Stratford, 1924; reprint New York: Haskell House, 1972.
Schuricht, Herman. *History of the German Element in Virginia*, Volume I. Baltimore: Theo Kroh & Sons, 1898.
Shirley, Michael. *From Congregation to Industrial City*. New York University Press, 1997.

Sipe, F. Henry. "History of Survey and Land Titles" in *Compass Land Surveys*. Parsons, WV: McClain, 1970.
Smith, Bradford. "Jamestown" in *America's Historylands*. Washington, D.C.: National Geographic Society, 1967.
Smith, Robert Lawrence. *A Quaker Book of Wisdom*. New York: Eagle Brook, 1998.
Smout, T.C. *A History of the Scottish People, 1560–1830*. Glasgow: HarperCollins, 1969.
Speidell, Phyllis. "On John Smith's Trail" in *American Spirit Daughters of the American Revolution* 141, no. 5. September–October 2007.
Spoden, Murial Millar Clark. *Historic Sites of Sullivan County*. Kingsport, TN: Sullivan County, 1976.
_____. *Kingsport Heritage, the Early Years 1700 to 1900*. Kingsport, TN: Spoden Associates, 1991.
Stein, Mark. *How the States Got Their Shapes*. New York: HarperCollins, 2008.
Stevens, William Bacon. *A History of Georgia: From its First Discovery by Europeans to the Adoption of the Present Constitution in MDCCXCVIII*. Georgia: D. Appleton, 1847.
Story, Alfred Thomas. *The Building of the British Empire: 1558–1636*, New York: G.P. Putnam and Sons, 1898.
Summers, Lewis Preston. *History of Southwest Virginia, 1746–1786, Washington County, 1777–1780*. Johnson City, TN: Overmountain, 1989.
Taylor, Oliver. *Historic Sullivan*. Bristol, TN: King Printing Co., 1909.
Thwaites, Reuben Gold & Louise Phelps Kellogg, eds., *Documentary History of Dunmore's War 1774*. Compiled from the Draper Manuscripts in the Library of the Wisconsin Historical Society and published at the charge of the Wisconsin Society of the Sons of the American Revolution, 1905. Harrisonburg, VA: C.J. Carrier, 1974.
Tocqueville, Alexis, ed. *Democracy in America and Two Essays on America*. Gerald E. Bevan, trans. London: Penguin, 2003.
Tolles, Frederick B. *Quakers and the Atlantic Culture*. New York: Macmillan, 1960.
Towle, George M. *The Voyages and Adventures of Vasco Da Gama*. Boston: Lothrop, Lee & Shepard, 1878.
Turner, Frederick Jackson. *The Significance of the Frontier in American History*. New York: Henry Holt, 1921.
Tyler, Lyon Gardiner. *England in America 1580–1652*, New York, Harper & Rowe, 1904, Project Gutenberg e-book, released July 14, 2005.
Waddell, J.A. *Annals of Augusta County, Virginia from 1726–1781*, 2nd edition. Staunton, VA: C. Russell Caldwell, 1902.
Walker, Thomas. "Journal of Doctor Thomas Walker" In Summers, *History of Southwest Virginia*, 796–807.
Waller, George M., ed. *Puritanism in Early America*. Boston: Heath, 1950.
Washington, G., D. Maydole Matteson, and J. Clement Fitzpatrick, United States George Washington Bicentennial Commission. *The Writings of George Washington from the Original Manuscript Sources, 1745–1799*. Washington, D.C.: U.S. Government Printing Office, 1931.
Weiser, Clement Zwingie. *The Life of (John) Conrad Weiser: German Pioneer Patriot*. Reading, PA: Daniel Miller Publisher, 1876.
Weiser, Frederick S. "Conrad Weiser, Peacemaker of Colonial Pennsylvania" in *Historical Review of Berks County*, Summer 1960.
Wells, H. G. *The Outline of History*, New York: Doubleday, 1956.
Wheelan, Joseph. *Jefferson's War*. New York: Carroll and Graf, 2003.
Wike, Monte, and Noma Wike. *The Wike Family, Descendants of Jacob M. Weik*. Colorado City, Texas, 1978.
Williams, Samuel Cole. *Dawn of Tennessee Valley and Tennessee History*. Johnson City, TN: Watauga, 1937; reprinted Nashville, Tennessee: Blue & Gray, 1972.
Williams, T. Harry. *History of American Wars*. New York: Knopf, 1981.
Williamson, Hugh. *History of North Carolina*. Philadelphia: Thomas Dobson, 1812.
Wilson, Woodrow, et al., *History of the American People*. New York: Harper and Bros, 1902.
Winawer, Hinda, and Norbert A. Wetzel. "German Families" in McGoldrick, Giordano, and Garcia-Preto, Ethnicity and Family Therapy, 555–572.

Bibliography

Wonders of the Ancient World National Geographic Atlas of Archaeology. Washington, D.C.: National Geographic Society Books, 1994.

Wood, Gordon S. *The Americanization of Benjamin Franklin.* New York: Penguin, 2004.

Wynn, John Huddlestone. *A General History of the British Empire in America, Vol I,* London: Printed for W. Richardson & L. Urquhart under the Royal Exchange, MDCC LXX, 202. Digitized by Google.

Young, Gloria A. and Michael P. Hoffman, eds. *Expedition of Hernando de Soto West of the Mississippi 1541-1543 Proceedings of the de Soto Symposia, 1988 and 1990,* Fayetteville Arkansas, University of Arkansas Press, August 1999.

Zeitlan, Richard H. *Germans in Wisconsin.* Madison: State Historical Society of Wisconsin, 2000.

Zinn, Howard. *A People's History of the United States.* New York: HarperCollins, 1999.

Index

Abenaki 120
Abercromby, Maj. Gen. James 140
Abingdon, VA *170*, 178, 183, 243
ABMA see Army Ballistic Missile Agency
aborigines 73
Acadia 120, 122; *see also* Nova Scotia
Acts of Union of 1800 102
Africa 1, 85, 90, 119, 135
Age of Discovery 1, 15
Age of Enlightenment 201
agent/broker, real estate 71, 149
agriculture 73, 97, 111; *see also* farmer, farming, farmland
Ahlstrom, Sydney E. 88
Alaska 221, 231
Albany 30–32, 110, 120, 212
Albany, Duke of 38
Albany plan 123
Albemarle Sound 159–62
Aldrin, Buzz 242
Algonquin 128, 143
Allegheny County, MD 157
Allegheny Mountains 60, 171
Allegheny River 129
alliance, British-Indian 192; Franco-American 185
Alps 92
Alsace 5–6, 135, 153
Alvarado, Gov. Juan 222
Amana, IA 248
Amelia, SC 164
American Civil War 196, 209, 231
American, English 97
American Expeditionary Force (AEF) 229
American Fur Company 1809 221
American ICBM 240; *see also* ICBM
American Indian 21–2, 33, 60, 70, 132, 147–48, 153, 162, 170, 205
American Revolution 6–7, 9–10, 79, 123, 149–50, 154, 180, 184, 187, 192, 195, 231
American South 207
American Southeast 194
American, Spanish 103
American West 193, 237
Americans, hyphenated 11, 229

Amherst, Jeffery 130, 144–45, 149
Amish 6, 8, 67, 78, 81–2, 172, 178, 207, 229, 247
Amsterdam 31–32, 35, 41
Anabaptist 6, 62–3, 69, 71, 81–2, 162
ancestry, German 11, 178, 196, 220, 224, 229, 231
Anglican, Anglicanism 12, 39, 41, 57–8, 61–2, 64–5, 76, 87, 93–4, 150, 155, 161, 174
Anglican Church 56–7, 61, 63, 76, 93–4
Anglo-Saxon 22
Anne (ship) 166
Anne of Austria 50
Anne, Queen of England 9, 86, 101–2, 106, 108–10, 162–63; *see also* Queen Anne
Anson County, NC 165
Anti-Proprietary Party 138
anti-slavery 72, 82, 196, 204; *see also* slavery
Apalachicola 166
Apollo 52
Appalachian Mountains 6, 59, 60, 124–25, 143, 147–48, 171, 178–79
Arbella (ship) 26
Arbella, Lady 26
Archbishopric of Salzburg 167
Archipelago 30; *see also* East Indies
architecture, German 151
Arctic Ocean 29
Arendt, Hannah 249
Ari de Guinea 40; *see also* Harry from Guinea
aristocrat 203
Arkansas 219
Armstrong, Neil 242
Army Ballistic Missile Agency (ABMA) 240–41
Arnheim, Holland 71
Arnold, Benedict 185
Asia 9, 29–30, 59, 119
Astor, John Jacob 221, 248
Astoria, Oregon 221
atheist 161
Atlantic 247
Atlas ICBM 240–41
Augusta County, VA 171
Augusta, GA 168, 173, 177

273

274 Index

Austin, Ann 27
Austria 5–6, 8, 48–9, 53, 96, 100–1, 103, 116–19, 135, 166, 168, 199–201, 216, 226–28, 235, 247, 250
Austria-Hungary 226, 230
Austrian Empire 102, 130
Austrian Netherlands 116; *see also* Belgium
aviation 237–38
Aviation Medicine, School of 242

Backnang 109
Bacon's Rebellion 59
Baden, Germany 75, 78, 210, 221
Baden-Wurttemberg 72, 75, 78, 106, 151, 189, 210, 243
balance of power 48, 91, 98, 101–2
Baldock 66
Ball, Mary 61
Baltic Sea and States 48, 85, 92, 226, 233
Baltimore, Lord Charles 77, 152, 155, 158–59
Baltimore, MD 155, 169, 208, 223
banjo, African 200
bank barns 151
Bank of England 97
baptism 40, 53, 61–3, 69, 71, 81, 84, 86, 178
Baptist 8, 62–4, 67, 89, 165, 174, 178, 217, 247; *see also* Dunker
Barbados 27, 73, 163
barns, Bank 151
Baron of Bernburg 162
Barter, State Theater of Virginia 243
Bartram, William 194
Battle of Bloody Run 144
Battle of Bushy Run 146
Battle of Great Meadows 128, 154; *see also* Fort Necessity
Battle of King's Mountain 189
Battle of Long Island 188
Battle of Monongahela 129–30
Battle of Oriskany 186–87
Battle of Wiltwyck 34
Batts, Nathaniel 160
Bavaria 8, 48–9, 96, 101–2, 116, 202, 210, 212
Bay Colony 6, 25–7, 189; *see also* Massachusetts Bay Colony
Bay Colony Company 25
beaver 29, 32, 67, 120–21
Beaver Wars 124, 173
Becker, Kurt 233
beer 10, 26, 214, 217
Belgium 30, 32, 101–3, 116–17, 226–27, 229, 234; *see also* Austrian Netherlands
Berkeley, Lord John 39
Berkeley, Sir William 56–62, 64, 161–62
Berkeley's Colony of Virginia 59, 61, 63
Berks County, PA 5, 121
Berlin 13, 48, 53, 118, 202, 233
Berlin Royal Polytechnic School 204
Bermuda 57
Bermuda Hundred 57; *see also* Charles City

Bern, Switzerland 162–63
Bethabara 176
Bethany 168
Bethany Church 189
Bethlehem, PA 85, 89, 122, 247
Beverwijck (Beverwyck) 34
Bible 7–8, 12, 18, 42–3, 47, 69, 82–3, 89, 132, 159, 248
Bienville, Gov. Jean-Baptiste Le Moyne de 220
Big Guts 37–8
Big Lick (Roanoke, VA) 172, 174, 181
Big Meadows 60
Big Stone Gap 180
Bill of Rights 193; English 94–5; U.S. 114
Biloxi 219–20
Bisaner, John Henry 188–89
Bisaner, Simon Pinkney 189
Bismarck, German Chancellor Otto Von 9, 226–27
Black and Decker Corporation 243
Black Forest 4, 243
Black Sea 6, 249
blacksmith 21, 43
Blenheim 102–3
Block, Adriaen 32
Blue Book 185
Blue Ridge Mountains 60, 147, 151–53, 162, 171, 174, 179, 180
Board of Trade 106, 108, 149, 173
Bohemia (Czechoslovakia) 3, 6, 16, 41, 44, 49, 53, 83–5, 89, 101, 116–17, 158, 248; *see also* Czech Republic; Czechia; Prague
Bohemia Manor 158–59
Bohemia River 158
Bonn 46, 235
Books of Suffering 70
Boone, Daniel 177–78, 180–81, 191–92, 243
Boone, Nathan 182, 189
Boone, Squire 177
Boone's Trace 182–83
Boonesborough 181, 191
booster, Juno 240
Boston 26, 70, 77, 194, 223
Boston Globe 231
Boston Harbor 27
bounty 89, 139, 147–48
Bouquet, Col. Henry 132–34, 137, 140–41, 145–46, 149
Bourbon 99–100
Bourbon Dynasty 99–100, 102
Bourbon, Royal House of 49–50, 99–100
bourgeoisie 199, 203
Braddock, Maj. Gen. Edward 128–29, 130, 132–34, 137, 139, 141, 154
Braddock Road 133–34
Braddock's Campaign 128
Bradford, William 74, 113
Brandenburg; Brandenburg Province 24, 48, 53, 96, 202
Brant, Joseph (Mohawk Chief) 115, 186

Index 275

Brant, Molly 115
Brazil 3
Bremen 169, 208
Bremerhaven 169, 208
brewery 87, 176, 214, 249
Bristol, England 17
Bristol, TN 170, 181, 183
Britain 3, 18, 62, 65, 69, 91, 95, 102–4, 116, 119, 123, 130–31, 135–36, 147, 150, 165–66, 170, 180, 187, 200, 205, 227, 231, 248
British America 3–4, 7, 9, 21; see also colonies, British
British Empire 6, 59, 70
British Government 58, 123
British Isles 10, 94, 227
Broad River 164
Brooklyn Bridge 204
Brotherhood of the Euphrates 178; see also Dunkard
Brother's House 176
Brown, John 35–6
Brown, Peter 189
Brown County, WI 212
Bryan, Martha Strode 174
Bryan, Morgan 173–74, 176–78
Bryan, Rebecca 177
Bryan's Settlement 174
Buck, the Rev. Richard 62
Bucks County, PA 83
Budapest 202
Buffalo, NY 212
Bull, Captain (Teedyuscung's son) 143
Bumper, Bumper program 237–38
Bunch of Grapes Tavern, Boston 194
Burke, James 178
Burke County, NC 189
Burke's Garden 178
Buschure, Johann Printz Von 37
Bush People 158; see also Labadists
Bushy Run Creek 145–46
Buzz-bomb 233
Byrd, Col. William 181

Cahokia 149, 192
California 1, 222, 237
California Institute of Technology 240; see also Jet Propulsion Laboratory (JPL)
Calvert, Benedict, 4th Lord Baltimore 155
Calvert, Cecil, 2nd Lord Baltimore 155
Calvert, George, 1st Baron (Lord) Baltimore 155
Calvin, Charles 85
Calvin, John 7, 43
Calvinist 12, 34–5, 41, 43, 45, 52, 54, 135
Cambridge 61
Camden, SC 177
camp(s), internment 229; Milltebau-Dora concentration 234
Canada 31, 119–20, 122–23, 131, 134, 136, 142, 149, 173

canal 197, 210
Cape Briton Island 119, 122
Cape Canaveral 237–38, 240
Cape Cod 31, 228
Cape Henry 21
Cape Horn 19
Cape May 39
Cape Verde Islands 1
captain general 92; see also ruler, stadtholder
Caribbean 85, 90, 163
Carolana ("South Virginia") 159, 161
Carolina 56, 59–60, 107, 145, 159–64, 172–73
Carolina Colony 159–62, 176
Carolina Road 169, *170*, 173–74, 177
carpenter 21, 23, 74, 150, 222
cartel, drug 30
Carter, John 61
Carter, Robert 61–2
Carteret, Sir George 39, 164
Carteret, John 164
cartographer 21
Cassell 72
Catawba 60, 113, 120, 153, 164, 176
Catawba County, NC 189
Catawba River 162, 174
Catawba, Siouan-speaking 172
Catholic Church 7, 41–3, 52, 55–6, 62, 94, 174, 213
Catholicism 3–4, 6–7, 9, 12, 29, 41, 44–5, 48, 52–4, 72, 84–5, 87, 93–4, 100, 105, 107, 135, 150, 155, 161, 165–66, 210, 212–13, 217
Catskills 39
Cavaliers 58–9; see also Royalists
cavalry 186, 188
Cayuga 110, 120
Cecil County, MD 157
Central America 19
C.F. Martin & Co. 200
chalet 216
chamber, privy 57
Charlemagne 41–2, 75
Charles City 57; see also Bermuda Hundred
Charles I, Habsburg King of Spain 15
Charles I, King of England, Scotland & Ireland 25, 57–8, 69, 93, 155, 159
Charles II, King of Great Britain & Ireland 28, 39, 59, 65–7, 69, 93–4, 98, 151, 160
Charles II, Spanish Habsburg King 99–100
Charles VI Holy Roman Emperor 116–17
Charles River 25
Charleston 155, 163, 165–66
Charlestown 167, 173, 177, 188
Charlotte, NC 174, 177
Charlotte of Mecklenburg 167; see also Queen Charlotte
Charter Colony 56, 58
Chattoka (Newbern) 162
Cherokee 60, 113, 125, 130, 153, 176, 178–79, 181–82, 191
Cherokee Nation 172, 179

276　　　　　　　　　　　　　Index

Cherokee War 179
Chesapeake Bay 21–2, 56, 152, 157–58, 160
Chester, PA 68
Chicago 203, 209, 212, 214
Chilhowie, VA 179
chimpanzee Ham 241
China 29–30, 60
Chippewa 124, 143–44, 192, 215
Chota (Cherokee capital) 172, 179
Christ 8, 18, 35, 68–9, 84, 86, 89, 159, 214
Christ Church 61–2, 81, 254
Christian Churches 87
Christianity 8, 15, 17, 25–6, 43, 49, 62–3, 73–4, 83–4, 86, 122, 155
Christiansen, Hendrick 31–2
Christina River 36
Christingle 89–90
church, Gothic 217
Church of England 58, 61, 87, 95, 155, 176
Church of the Brethren 88
Churchill, John Duke of Marlborough 102
Churchill, Winston 15, 19, 22, 135
Cicero 131
Cincinnati 196, 198, 249
City of Brotherly Love 86
Clark, George Rogers 182, 191–92
Clark, William 197
class, middle 1, 9, 26, 49, 61, 87, 97, 201, 203
clavichord 87
Clay, Henry 181
clergy 7, 49, 52, 63, 77, 85; Anglican 61, 70; Catholic 7, 52, 83; Reformed 111
clergymen 53, 106, 111
Cleveland 198
Cleveland Memory Project 194
Clinch River 170, 179
Clinton, Governor of NY 77
Cluerius, Johann Sigismund 24
cobbler 87
Coblenz, Charles 196
Coblenz, Samuel 196
Collins, Mike 242
Cologne 24, 101
colony(ies), Anglican 56, 59, 61; British 6, 8, 16, 57, 67, 76, 91, 123–26, 135, 139, 141, 247; charter 56, 58; Middle 39; royal 58; proprietary 67, 160, 165
Colorado 221, 249
Columbia River 221
Columbus, Christophe 1–2
Comegys (Commegys), Cornelius 157
Command Module 242
Committee of Public Information (CPI) 229
Committee on Aviation (NACA) 240
Communist Manifesto 1848 203
company: joint stock 20, 30, 56; stock 20–1, 30, 56
Concord (ship) 71
Conestoga, PA 75
Conestoga Indians 70

Conestoga Manor 70
Confederation Congress 192
Confederation, German 6, 199–200
conferences, Easton 134, 139–41
confessionalism 84–5
Congregational Church 76, 89, 168
Congress of Vienna, Austria 202
Connecticut 31–2
Connecticut River & Valleys 31–2, 34, 36
Conqueror of the Old Northwest 192
conscription, military 75, 173
Continental Army 185–86, 194, 248
copper 16–7, 22, 118, 211
Corona, spy satellite program 239
Coronado 3
corporation: international stock 30; stock 20–1, 30, 56
Cortés, Hernán 2
Cosby, William (Royal Governor of NY) 114
cotton 30, 61, 216, 223
Cotton, Matthew 27
council, privy 94
Count Zinzendorf 83–4, 87–9, 122, 132, 176
Counter-Reformation, Catholic 41, 43
country, Natchez 178
Covenant Chain 121
CPI *see* Committee of Public Information
Crab Orchard, KY 182
craftsmen 4, 23, 53, 95, 107, 163, 212, 215
Crefelders 158; *see also* Krefelders
Creole 221
Croghan, George 141
crop, cash 157, 161–62, 210, 214
Cromwell, Oliver 58; *see also* Lord Protector of Commonwealth
Crown Point, NY 128; *see also* Fort Crown Point
Cuban-Americans 11
Cuban Missile Crisis 242
Culpeper, Lord Thomas 152
Culpeper County, VA 151
Cumberland Gap *170*, 173, 180–83, 191
Cumberland River 180
Cutler, the Rev. Manasseh 194–95
Cuxhaven 169
Czech Republic, Czechia 16, 41, 44, 83, 89, 96, 116–18; *see also* Bohemia, Prague
Czechoslovakia 5

Dakota (Sioux) Tribe 215, 249
Dalyell, Captain James 144
Damascus, VA 243
Dan River 176
Dane County, WI 212
Danes 34, 68
Dankers, J. (aka Jasper Schilders) 158
Danube 102
Darien, GA 166, 168
Darmstadt 135
Davidson Creek Settlement 174

Index

Daytona Beach 160
Deane, Silas 185
Debus, Kurt 238, 240–41
Declaration of Indulgences 93
Defenestration at Prague 45
Delaware 29–32, 36, 38–9
Delaware Bay 36, 39–40, 68, 76
Delaware Colony 39, 157; *see also* New Sweden
Delaware Indians 125, 128, 137–38, 141, 143, 145–46, 172, 192; Eastern 137–39, 141; Lenape 34, 36–7, 143; Lenni-Lenape 37; Western 137–39, 141
Delaware River 31, 36, 39, 67–8, 73, 150
Delaware Valley 36, 65, 68, 75–7, 81, 138
Delmarva Peninsula 152
Denny, William PA Gov. 138–41
Detroit 134, 143, 145, 192, 210–12
Deutsch 5, 23, 78; *see also* German
Deutschland 4
dialect, German 6, 78, 245; Pennsylvania Dutch 207
dike 92
Dinwiddie, Virginia Gov. 125–26, 153
Discovery (ship) 21, 31
distillery 222
district, Natchez 219
Dixon, Jeremiah 77, 159
Dobbs, Gov. Arthur 174
Doggett, the Rev. Benjamin 61
dogs 10, 230; *see also* German shepherds
Dornberger, Walter 233, 235
doughboys 228
Drachenfels 46
Dragging Canoe 137
Drake, Sir Francis 2, 16–18
Drake, Col. Wilhelm 154
Draper, Lyman 182
Draper's Meadow 181
Dresden 84
Duke of Albemarle 161
Duke of Anjou 99, 101
Duke of d'Orleans 220
Duke of Hanover 86; *see also* George I
Duke of Lorraine and Tuscany 117
Duke of Marlborough 102–3
Duke of Villars 106
Duke of York and Albany 11, 38–9, 67; *see also* King James II of England
Dunkard 178
Dunkers 8, 67, 88, 165, 247; *see also* Baptist; Brotherhood of Euphrates
Dunmore, Lord John Murray (VA governor) 148
Dunmore's War 181
Durlach 135
Dutch 5, 23, 29–40, 56, 62, 67–8, 70–2, 77, 81, 92–4, 103–4, 119, 125, 150, 162; *see also* Low-Dutch
Dutch Colony of New Netherland 11, 29, 32, 36, 247

Dutch colony of Swaanendael (Zwaanendael) 38
Dutch East India (Trading) Company 29–30, 32; *see also* East India Company; VOC
Dutch Empire 92
Dutch Fork 164
Dutch Reformed Church 33, 35–6, 87, 92
Dutch Republic 48, 92; *see also* Netherlands; United Provinces
Dutch War of Independence 30, 32; *see also* War of Independence, Dutch
Dutch West India Company 32, 35–6, 38, 158; *see also* West India Company (WIC)
Dutchman, Dutchmen 23, 30, 34, 96, 152, 157

Earl of Granville 164
East Anglia 25, 27
East-Friesland 208
East India Company 29–30; *see also* Dutch East India (Trading) Company; VOC
East Indies 30; *see also* Archipelago
East Prussia 167
East River 204
Eastern Continental Divide 147
Easton Agreement 1757 139
Easton Treaty 139, 141–42; *see also* Treaty of Easton
Ebenezer, Georgia 167–68, 247
Ebenezer Creek 167–68
ecumenical union of churches 85–7; *see also* worldwide union of churches
Edict of Expulsion 167
Edict of Nantes 52–3
education, educational 8, 51, 66, 80, 87, 119, 187, 193, 195–96, 204, 211–12, 221
Eighteen Forty-eighters 9, 198–99, 202–4, 211–14, 218; *see also* Forty-eighters
Einbeck, Duchy of Hanover 86
Einstein, Albert 12, 247
Eisenberg 134
Eisenhower, Pres. Dwight D. 10, 236, 239–40
El Dorado 1
El Paso 237
Elector of Hanover 116
Elector Palatine 107
Electorate (Duchy) of Wurtemberg 109
Elisha (Elijah) Wallen 180
Elizabeth I, Queen of England 3–4, 20; *see also* Queen Elizabeth I; Virgin Queen
Elizabeth City 57
Elizabethton, TN (Sycamore Shoals, NC) 181
Elk River 158
emigrant 4, 7, 9, 26, 53–4, 57, 74, 77, 79, 105–7, 134, 150, 156, 158, 180, 182, 200, 206, 220, 228
emigration, German 7, 75
endless mountains 60; *see also* Appalachians
Engels, Freidrich 203
engineers, rocket 232, 236
England 1–12, 15–23, 25–6, 28–32, 34, 38–9,

Index

47–8, 53–4, 56–9, 61, 65–6, 68, 70–3, 75–8, 80–1, 85, 89, 91–7, 99–103, 106–12, 116, 119–25, 127–33, 135–37, 141–44, 147, 150–51, 153, 156–57, 159–67, 172–74, 176–77, 179, 181–82, 184–85, 196, 208, 211, 217, 231, 233–354, 243
English Channel 3, 5, 18
English Civil Wars 39, 48, 57–8, 69, 151, 159, 160
English General Marlborough (John Churchill) 102
epidemic 46
Episcopal Church 36, 176
Erie Canal 210, 212
Esopus Creek 35
Esopus Indians, Munsee Nation 34
Esopus Valley 34
Eucharist 53
Eugene, Prince of Savoy (Austrian general) 102
Euphrates 171, 178
Europe 1, 4–7, 9, 15, 19, 21, 29, 30, 41–3, 45–6, 48, 59, 68, 71, 82, 85, 88, 91, 95–103, 116–20, 122, 124, 130–31, 134–35, 160, 163, 165, 173, 185, 196, 199–200, 202–4, 215, 220, 226–27, 229–30, 237, 243
EVA (extravehicular activity) 242
Evangelical (Lutheran) Church 89, 167
Eve of All Saint's Day 42
exodus 25, 75, 99, 106–7, 220, 224, 237
expatriation 46, 106
Explorer 1 satellite 240

Fairfax, Lady Catherine 152
Fairfax, Lord Thomas 151–53
Falkner, Daniel 8
famine 45–6
farmer, farming, farmland 4, 9, 11, 27, 34–5, 53, 58, 74, 76, 78, 81–2, 106–7, 113, 124, 129, 134–35, 137, 141, 163, 169, 172, 188, 204, 206–7, 210–16, 220, 223–23; dairy 214; German 134–35, 214, 249; *see also* agriculture
Father of Space Medicine 242; *see also* Strughold, Hubertus
Father of the Netherlands, William I, the Silent, 1st Prince of Orange 92
feast, love 176
Ferdinand, Archduke Franz 226
feudalism 50, 201–2
fever, yellow 146
fiefdom 204
Fiennes 26; *see also* Lady Arbella
Finnish, Finns 36, 38, 68, 75
fire, Chicago 214
fire engine 77
First English Settlement 17, 22, 25, 160, 163
First Silesian War 116, 118; *see also* Silesian War
Fish, Mary 27
Fisher, Mary 66
Five Nations 172

flag, American 221
fleets: Anglo-Dutch 97, 102; Dutch 67
Flemish 32
fleur de lis 128, 142
Florida 3–4, 15, 20, 56, 159–60, 238; *see also* Spanish Florida
Flushing Remonstrance 35
Fontaine, John 171
Forbes, Gen. John 133, 139–43, 146
Forbes Road 133–34, 140–43, 145
forest, hardwood 171, 195, 214
forestry 211
Forks of the Ohio River (Pittsburg, PA) 127, 129, 133–34, 140–41
Fort Amsterdam 33; *see also* New Amsterdam
Fort Beauséjour 128
Fort Boonesborough *170*, 191
Fort Chiswell 180, 183
Fort Christina 36, 38
Fort Crown Point 128; *see also* Crown Point, NY
Fort Cumberland 126, 129, 154
Fort Detroit 144–45, 170
Fort Douglas in Utah 229
Fort Duquesne 126–29, 133–34, 139–42, 146, 154
Fort Frederika 166; *see also* St. Simon's Island
Fort Frontenac 134, 141–42
Fort Harmar 195
Fort Henry (Wheeling, WV) 197
Fort King George 166
Fort Laramie (New Berlin) 197
Fort Le Boeuf 125–26
Fort Ligonier 141–42, 145
Fort Logan 182
Fort Loudon 179
Fort Louisbourg 119
Fort McPherson, Georgia 229
Fort Michilimackinak 144
Fort Nassau 32
Fort Necessity 127–28, 154; *see also* Battle of Great Meadows
Fort Niagara 128, 145
Fort Oglethorpe, Georgia 229
Fort Orange 32–4
Fort Pitt 134, 137, 142, 144–46
Fort Sackville 170
Fort Snelling 215
Fort Stanwix 186–87
Fort Sutter 222
Fort Vancouver 221
Fort Washington 188
Fort Wayne 207
Forty-eighters (48ers, 1848ers) 9, 198–99, 202–4, 211–14, 218; *see also* Eighteen Forty-eighters
Fox, George 65–6, 77, 80–1
Fox, Margaret Fell 66
France 1–3, 32, 48–50, 52–6, 59, 67, 91–3, 95–7, 99–104, 107, 116, 119–20, 122–24, 130–31,

Index

134–37, 142–43, 166, 185, 197, 200, 202, 208, 219–20, 226–27, 230
Franconia 72
Frankfort Land Company 71, 74
Franklin, Benjamin 70–1, 76–7, 123, 129, 138–39, 185, 194
Frau in Mond 233; *see also* Woman in the Moon
Frederick County, VA 153, 157
Frederick II Hohenzollern, King Frederick the Great 117–19, 130–31, 135, 184, 186
Frederick Parish Vestry 153
Frederick the Great of Prussia 116–17
Frederick Town (Winchester, VA) 153
Fredericksburg 125, 164
Free Society of Traders 76
freedom of press, religion, speech 92–3, 114, 201–1, 247
French 5, 31–3, 46, 51, 53–4, 58, 67–8, 71–3, 75–6, 78, 86, 91–3, 95–102, 106, 116, 119–35, 137–47, 149, 153–54, 166, 172–74, 185, 199, 215, 219–21, 227, 235
French and Indian War 9, 76, 91, 103, 114, 122–25, 128–31, 134–35, 137, 146–48, 153–54, 176–78, 184
French courts of law 54; *see also* parlements
French Huguenot 77, 150, 177; *see also* French Protestant; Huguenot
French Lick (Nashville) 182
French Protestant 46, 52–5, 97; *see also* French Huguenot, Huguenot
French Revolution, Revolutions 199–200
Friedens Lutheran Community 162
Friendly Association 138–39, 141
Friends 8, 65–70, 77, 80–1, 159, 161, 174; *see also* Quakers
Friesland 158
Frisia 62
Fronde 51
Front Street 196
Fuller, Josh 244

Gagarin, Yuri 241
Galveston 223–24
Gans, Joachim 3, 16–8
Gass, Eugen 215
Geneva 53
Georg Ritter Mining Company 162
George I, first Hanoverian king of Great Britain 86, 155, 167
George II, Elector of Hanover; 2nd Hanoverian King of Great Britain and Ireland 116, 118, 125, 130, 164–5, 1687
George III Hanoverian king 167
George V, King 231
Georgia 85–6, 145, 147, 155, 160, 164–68, 173, 177, 229
Georgia Colony 167–68
German-Americans 5, 9–12, 132, 194, 206, 216, 218, 225, 227, 229, 250

German Athens (Milwaukee) 212
German Belt 222–24
German Civil War 43, 47
German Coast 220
German Colony in Charlestown 165
German Confederation 6, 199
German-Jew 17
German Lutheran 4, 8, 40, 84, 86–8, 162, 174, 186, 213, 217
German-Moravian town 110
German Philadelphia Settlement Society 248
German Reformed 39, 75, 83
German Revolution 1848 9, 199
German Valley, New Jersey 39–40, 75
Germanna, Shenandoah Valley of Virginia 172
Germans 2–8, 10, 13, 15–7, 20, 22–5, 27, 29–34, 36–42, 44, 46, 48, 53–4, 67, 69, 72, 75–9, 83, 86, 91, 97, 105–10, 121, 132–33, 137, 140, 144, 150–52, 154–58, 162, 164–65, 167, 171–73, 177, 180, 184, 186, 188, 194–97, 199, 201, 204, 206–7, 209–15, 217, 219–25, 227–28, 230, 235–37, 245; *see also* Deutsch
Germantown 27, 71–6, 81, 107, 158–59
Gibraltar 41, 102–3
Gist (Geist, Guest), Christopher 126–27, 153, 178
Gist, Nathaniel 178
glass 4, 23, 194, 208
glassblower, glassmakers, glassworks 10, 23, 76, 150
Glenn, John 241
Glorious Revolution 1689 91, 94–5, 155
God, god 1, 18–9, 26, 35, 43, 48, 52, 63, 66–9, 71, 80, 82, 86–7, 89, 104, 121, 122, 178, 184, 207–8
Goddard, Robert 238
Godspeed (ship) 21
gold 1–2, 15, 21, 29, 67, 161, 220, 222, 231
Golden Age 3, 15
Golden Hind (ship) 16
Golden Swan 78
goldsmith 43
Gooch, Sir William Lt. Gov. VA 153
Gordon, Patrick, Gov. PA 112
government, Anglican 12; representative 201
governor, proprietary 155
Graffenried, Baron Christoph von 107, 162–63
Grand Alliance (England, the Netherlands & Austria) 95–8, 101, 105
Grand Review 185
grant, land 34, 67, 148, 152, 189, 195; proprietary 152, 160
Granville District 164, 173–74, 176
Gray, Zane 193
Great Appalachian Valley 54, 130, 146, 169, 172, 179
Great Britain 65, 101–3, 119, 124, 134–36, 226–27, 230

Index

Great Elector of Brandenburg 96
Great Indian War-Trading Path 172–74, 179
Great Lakes 124, 137, 192, 210, 215
Great Meadows 126–28, 154
Great Palatine immigration 54
Great Philadelphia Wagon Road 172–73, 169, 171, 176; *see also* Great Valley Road; Great Wagon Road
Great Plains 19
Great Valley of Tennessee 173
Great Valley of Virginia 172–73
Great Valley Road 151; *see also* Great Philadelphia Wagon Road; Great Wagon Road
Great Wagon Road 152, 169, *170*, 171–73, 176, 181; *see also* Great Philadelphia Wagon Road; Great Valley Road
Great War 225, 227, 230, 232; *see also* World War I
Great War for Empire 124; *see also* Seven Year's War
Greater Twin Cities (Minneapolis-Saint Paul) 215
Greek Orthodox 83
Greenbrier River 154
Greene, Nathaniel 81
Greenland 85
grenadier 129, 188
Grenville, Richard 17
grievances 41, 43
Grossaspach in Wurtemberg 109–10
grounds, hunting 137, 145–46, 172, 179, 192
guides, Meherrin Indian 170
Guilford County 162
Guilford Courthouse 188
guitar, German 200
Gulf of Mexico 124, 147, 166, 209, 215, 219
Gulf of St. Lawrence 124
Gutenberg, Johannes 43
Gutenberg Bible 43

Habsburg Dynasty 15, 48, 100
Habsburg Emperor Charles VI 116–17
Habsburg Emperor of Holy Roman Empire 6, 48, 100
Habsburg Empire 103, 202
Habsburg (House of Austria), Royal House of 3, 41, 49–50, 100
Habsburg King of Spain, Charles I 15; *see also* Charles I
Habsburg King of Spain, Charles II 99–100; *see also* Charles II
Habsburg King Philip II 3, 15; *see also* Philip II
Habsburgs 3, 45, 47–8, 50, 96, 117–19, 135
Hacke, Georg Nicolaus 24
Hagen, John 239
Halberstadt 39, 75
Haldimand, Frederick 132
Half King 120–21, 125–28, 139

Half Moon (ship) 29–31, 39
Halle (German town in Saxony) 86
Ham 241; *see also* chimpanzee
Hamburg 4, 23, 60, 151, 169, 229
Hamburger 230
Hamilton, Andrew 114
Hamilton, Lt. Col. Alexander Hanau 185
Hamilton, Lt. Gov. Henry "Hair Buyer" 170
Hanover 86, 135, 167, 212, 233
Hans, German buccaneer 219
Harman, Jacob 179
Harmanson, Thomas 24
Harpers Ferry 60, 154, 171
Harriot, Thomas 17
Harrodsburg, KY 191
Harry from Guinea 40; *see also* Ari de Guinea
Hass, Catherine 189
Hass, Simon 189
Haus Ingeburg 235
Haverford 76
Hawaiian Islands and laborers 221–22
Heath, Sir Robert 159–60
Hebrew 18, 86
Heckewelder, John 194, 196
Heidelberg 46, 105, 221
Heinz, Henry J. 231
Heinz Tomato Ketchup Company 12, 231
Henderson, Judge Richard 181, 191
Hendricks, Garrett 72, 81
Henni, the Rev. John Martin 213
Henrico 57; *see also* Richmond
Henrietta Maria, English Queen 155; *see also* Queen Henrietta
Henry, Gov. Patrick 191–92
Herkimer, Gen. Nicholas 186–87
Herman (Heermans), Augustine 158
Herman (Harman), Heinrich Adam 179
Hermit 159
Herrmann, Max 143–45
Herrnhut 84–5, 87
Hesse-Cassel (Hesse-Kassel) 187, 208
High German 6, 74, 78
Highlanders 133, 145, 165–66, 168
Hindu 36
Hispanic 11, 213
Hite, Baron Joist (Jost) 151–53, 156, 172
Hitler, Führer Adolf 228, 230, 233, 237, 249
Hocking River 197
Hohenzollern, King Frederick II 118
Hohenzollern dynasty 118
Holland 3, 5, 23, 32, 36, 39, 53, 70–1, 75, 77, 92, 96–7, 100, 103, 107, 110, 154, 167, 180
Hollanders 23
Holstein 37, 178, 224
Holstein, Henry 178
Holstein, Matthias (German Dane) 178
Holsteiner, George Michael 181; *see also* Stoner, Michael
Holston (Holstein), Stephen 178
Holston Mountain 178

Holston River 147, 170, 178–79, 181
Holston Valley 130, 172
Holy Roman Emperor 15, 48, 96, 100, 102, 117
Holy Roman Empire 6, 15, 41, 44, *47*, 48–9, 52–3, 96, 100–3, 167, 199
Holy Roman Empress 117
Hondo 224
Hopewell (ship) 29
Hopkins, Steven 62
house, common 159
House of Austria 48–9, 100; *see also* House of Habsburg
House of Bourbon 49–50, 99–100; *see also* Royal House of Bourbon
House of Brandenburg 48, 118
House of Burgesses 58, 61
House of Habsburg 3, 49–50, 100; *see also* Royal House of Habsburg
House of Hanover 167
House of Orange 92
House of Stuart 93; *see also* Royal House of Stuart
House of Windsor 231
Houston 224
Hudson, Henry 29–32, 39
Hudson Bay 31
Hudson River 31, 108, 158, 212, 33–4, 36, 39, 106, 108–10, 119, 152, 158, 212
Hudson Valley 32, 34
Hudson's Bay Company 221
Huguenot 46, 52–5, 77, 88, 96–7, 103, 150, 159, 177; *see also* French Huguenot; French Protestant
humanitarianism 202, 204
Hungarian 49, 117
Hungary 6, 41, 49, 53, 96, 102, 117, 226
hunt, long 179–80, 148, 177–78, 192; *see also* longhunter
Hunter, NY Gov. Robert 108–9
Huntsville, AL 237–42
Hunzel, Dieter 235–36
Huron 130
Hus, Jan 41, 45, 83–4, 88–9
husbandmen 107
hussar 188
Hussite 89
Hutterites 229

ICBM 240; *see also* American ICBM
Idaho 221
immigrant 4–7, 9–11, 30, 39, 58, 70, 79, 91, 106, 108–10, 150, 152, 164, 166, 169, 172–73, 176–77, 179, 183, 206, 210–11, 216, 220, 223, 244; Aryan 228; English 164; French 78; German 4, 7–8, 12–3, 23–4, 40, 46, 54, 60, 67, 71–2, 75, 78–9, 108, 110–11,113–14, 134, 151, 154–56, 162–64, 169, 178–79, 184, 188–89, 196, 198, 204, 207–8, 210–13, 215–16, 221, 227–28, 230, 242, 244–45, 247–50; German-speaking immigrants 7; Irish 208; Polish 22–3; Scots-Irish 7, 150–51, 164, 169; Swiss 78, 84, 163, 213; Welsh 164
immigration, German 8, 10, 26, 72, 75, 108, 134, 196, 210–11, 213, 249–50; Palatine 54, 74
indenture 79, 114
independence 30, 48, 79, 92, 124, 167, 205–6, 222
Independence, MO 198, 221
India 30, 85, 124, 131, 135–36
Indian 12, 17, 21–3, 27, 33–4, 57, 59, 60, 63, 67–8, 70–1, 73–4, 86, 108, 111–13, 119–22, 128–30, 132–34, 137–49, 153, 156, 170, 180, 182, 189, 194–96, 205, 210; *see also* American Indian
Indian Ocean 30, 60
Indian River 178
Indian Trading Path 60, 152, 174
Indiana 80, 122, 125, 144, 192, 205–7, 248
Indianapolis 207
Indians, Conestoga 70
Indigo 161, 165
Indulgences 7, 41–3, 45, 83, 93
industry, mining and mining 16, 211, 220
Institut Pasteur 226
intellectuals, liberal 213
International Geophysical Year 238
interpreter 66, 80, 112, 125, 127, 132, 185, 196
interpreter-negotiator 112–13, 121, 184
Iowa 212, 215, 219, 248
Ipswich, England 61
Ireland 59, 65, 67, 94–5, 102, 106, 114, 129, 173, 227
Irish 7, 11, 106, 156, 177, 208–9, 213
iron 17, 211
ironworks 172
Iroquoia 138
Iroquois 33, 112–14, 121–22, 124–25, 127–28, 139–41, 143, 149, 153, 172–73,186–87
Iroquois Confederacy 34, 110, 119–20, 124, 173
Iroquois League 124
Irving, Washington 38
Isle of Jersey 39, 164
Isle of Skye, Scotland 166
Isle of Wight 5
Italian-American 11
Italy 50, 54, 99–100, 116, 226–27, 230

James I, first Stuart king of England & James VI, King of Scotland 4, 20–2, 56, 58, 67, 102
James II, King of England & Ireland, & James VII, King of Scotland 11, 38–9, 93–5, 97, 101, 155
James Fort 22
James River 22, 171
Jamestowne, Jamestown, Jamestown Colony 4, 6, 16, 20–5, 29, 56–7, 60, 62, 150–1, 189, 247
Jamestowne Massacre 57–8
Jansenism 87
Japan 29, 59, 230, 236

Jersey Isle 39
Jerusalem Evangelical Lutheran Church 167
Jesuit(s) 30, 32, 41, 43, 45); *see also* Society of Jesus
Jesus Christ 18, 68, 84, 86
Jet Propulsion Laboratory (JPL) 240; *see also* California Institute of Technology
Jew 3, 6, 16-8, 35-6, 165-66, 212, 217
Jewish 18, 77, 150, 196
John II, King of Portugul 3
Johnson, Lady Catherine 115
Johnson, Gov. Gabriel 173
Johnson, Sir John 186
Johnson, Col. Sir William 114-15, 128, 138-41, 149
Johnston Atoll 240
Jones, John Gabriel 191
Joseph II 117
jousting 45
Juarez, Mexico 237
Juet, Robert 31
Jumonville, Ens. Joseph Couldon de Villiers 127
Justice of the Peace 72, 121, 152

Kaiser Wilhelm II 201, 225, 230
Kaiser Wilhelm Society 226
Kalmar Nyckel (ship) 36
Kammler, Hans 235
Kanawha River 154
Kansas 205, 215, 221
Kaputnik 240
Kecoughtan 57; *see also* Elizabeth City
Keiser, Herbert J. 207-28
Kelpius, Johannes 8
Kennedy Space Center 241
Kentucky 12, 122, 169, 173, 178-83, 189, 191-92; *see also* Kentucky County of VA
Kentucky County of VA 192; *see also* Kentucky
Kerrville 224
kilns, brick 73, 76
kindergarten 212, 249
King Carter 62
King George's War 1740-1748 116, 119-21, 134, 173
King James II of England 11, 38-9, 67; *see also* Duke of York and Albany
King of Spain 15-6, 99, 102
King Philip's War 27
kingdoms, German 199
King's Highway (Postal Road) 172
King's Royal Rifle Corp 131-35, 137, 144-47; *see also* Royal American Regiment
King's Royal Proclamation 148
Kingston, N.Y 34, 153
Kleve, Germany 32
Knapheide, Rudolph 218-19
knighthood 3, 16, 45, 57, 114, 171
Knights of the Golden Horseshoe 169

Kocherthal, Joshua von 106, 108
Krefeld Colony 71-2
Krefelders 158; *see also* Crefelders
Krisheim 72
Kuhle, Karl 200

Labadie, Jean de 158
Labadists 157-59; *see also* Bush People
laborers 9, 207; agricultural 213; child 211; contract 23, 79; day 73; farm 138; Hawaiian 216; landless 216; skilled 211; slave 234; unskilled 211; *see also* workman
Labrador 20, 90
lacrosse 144
Lady Arbella 26; *see also* Fiennes
Lafayette, Maj. Gen. Marquis de 185
Lake Champlain 128
Lake Erie 120, 125, 134
Lake Michigan 212
Lake Ontario 134
Lancaster County, VA 31-2
Lancaster County and Lancaster, PA 5, 70, 78-9, 121, 124, 172, 174, 248
Lancaster Treaty 124, 172; *see also* Treaty of Lancaster
Lane, Ralph 17
language, German 10, 43, 113, 132, 173, 197-98, 211, 217, 220, 229, 247, 249-50
Lapidists 158; *see also* Bush People
La Salle, René-Robert Cavelier, sieur de 219
Latin America 2-3
Law, John 220
Law Company 220
laws, primogeniture 59; Salic 116
League of Augsburg 96
Lederer, Dr. Johann (John) 60, 162
Lee, Gen. "Light Horse" Harry 186
Lehigh Valley 83
Leicestershire, England 66
Leipzig 87, 220
Leisler, Jacob 11-12
Leopold I of Austria 48-9, 96-7, 100-2
letters 142, 206, 210, 213, 223-24
Lewis, Meriwether 196
Liberalism 9, 200-2
Liberty 65, 68, 186, 204
Licking Creek 181
Lignery, Capt. François-Marie Le Marchand de 141-42
limestone 118, 197; *see also* Maysville, Kentucky
Lincoln, Abraham 204
Lincoln County, NC 188-9
Lindenberg, Hans 235
Lindenberg, Richard 242
Linnaeus, Carolus 194
Linville, Elinor 177
Linville, William 177
Litiz, Pennsylvania 222
Little Tennessee River 179

Index

livestock 4, 26, 32, 46, 143, 188–89, 222
Livingston Manor 110
Livingstone, Robert 109
locksmith 74
Logan, Benjamin 182
London 17, 22–3, 56, 66, 71, 106–7, 109, 125–26, 166, 184, 221, 234
London Company 21, 56–8
Long Island of the Holston 181
longhunter 177–80, 192; *see also* hunt, long
looting 45
Lord Baltimore 77, 155, 158–59; *see also* Calvert
Lord Charles Baltimore 152
Lord Granville's district of North Carolina 164, 173–74, 176
Lord John Berkeley 39
Lord Loudoun 130
Lord Lovelace 106
Lord Proprietor 39, 67, 80, 159, 176
Lord Protector of Commonwealth 58; *see also* Cromwell, Oliver
Lord Thomas Culpeper 152
Lord Thomas Fairfax 151–53
Lost Colony 18, 160
Louis I, duc de Bourbon 100
Louis IV 95
Louis XIII 50
Louis XIV 9, 46, 49–56, 91–97, 99–107, 119, 219–20
Louis XV 220
Louis XVI 119
Louisbourg 119, 122
Louisiana 125, 135, 160, 219–21
Louisiana Colony 219
Louisiana Purchase 1803 215
Louisiana Territory 197, 219
Lovelace, Gov. 106
Low Countries 92, 102, 106, 116
Low-Dutch 74, 158; *see also* Dutch
Lower Peninsula MI 210
Loyalist 8, 186–87
Loyola, Ignatius 43
Lusitania (ship) 227
Luther, Martin 7, 41–3, 45, 84
Lutheranism 4, 6–8, 15, 38, 40–1, 43, 46, 67, 72, 83–9, 106–7, 112, 121, 162, 167, 174, 184, 186, 189, 210, 213, 217, 238, 247–48; *see also* Reformed Church
Luxembourg 6
lynch 230
Lys River 32

Mackinaw City, MI 144
Maine ("North Virginia") 27, 56, 161
Mainz 43
Maliseet 120
Manhattan Island ("the Manhatoes") 29, 32–6, 38
Manheim 105

Mansker, Caspar (Gaspar) 180
Maria Theresa 116–19
Marie Antoinette 119
Marietta 195–97
market, European 213–14, 223
Markham, Gov. William 158
Markneukirchen 200
Marlborough 102–3
Marshall Space Flight Center (MSFC) 241
Martin, Christian Frederick 200
Martinsville, VA 180
martyrdom 41, 45, 62, 83, 89
Marx, Karl 203
Mary and Margaret (ship) 23
Mary II 11–2, 95, 155; *see also* Mary Stuart; Queen Mary
Mary Stuart 93–4, 101; *see also* Mary II; Queen Mary
Maryland 10, 32, 38, 54, 60, 62, 67, 76–8, 113, 121, 124, 131, 133–34, 137–38, 144, 152, 155–59, 169, 171, 173–74, 191, 205, 248
Maryland, General Assembly 10
Maryland House of Delegates 155
mason 21
Mason, Charles 77, 159
Mason, TX 224
Mason-Dixon Line 77–8, 159
Massachusetts 6, 10, 25, 27–8, 31–2, 53, 66, 120, 147, 189
Massachusetts Bay Colony 6, 25–8, 189; *see also* Bay Colony
massacre, Conestoga 70
Maumee 124
Mayflower (ship) 25, 62, 71, 189
Maysville, Kentucky 197; *see also* limestone
Mazarin, Cardinal Jules 50–2, 54
measles 195
mechanics 22, 72, 74, 78
Mecklenburg 167, 210
Mediterranean 3, 102, 124
Mehmen IV (Turkish Emperor) 66
Meidenbauer, John Konrad 212
Mennonite 6, 8, 27, 56, 62–3, 67, 71–5, 82, 135, 217, 229, 247; *see also* Quakers, German; Reformed Church
Mennonite Church 62, 72, 88
mercenaries 30, 45, 75, 132–33, 139, 145, 184, 187–88
merchants, German 1, 196
Mercury Capsule 241
Mercury-Redstone Launch Vehicle (MRLV) 241
Mercury Seven 241
Merrimack River 25
Merrimack River Valley, NH 120
metallurgy 3, 16–7
Methodism 88
Metternich, Age of 202
Mexican-Americans 11
Mexico 3, 15, 19, 222, 237

Miami 121, 124, 130, 145
Michigan 143–44, 192, 205, 209–12
Mid-Atlantic 207
Middle Fork of the Holson River 179
Middle Fork of the Indian River 178
Middle Region of the United States 205
Middle Rhine River 97
Middle Tennessee 181–82, 191
middlemen 124
Midway (aircraft carrier) 237
Midway, GA 168
midwife 82
migration, chain 206, 210, 223
Mi'kmaq 120
Milan 103, 202
militia 11, 76–7, 148, 184–87, 192, 198, 201
militiamen 18, 126–27, 149, 187, 191–92
mill-wrights 4, 23
mills (grist, saw, stamping, textile, wind) 4, 23, 33–4, 54, 73, 82, 168
Milwaukee (German Athens) 10, 212–14, 249
Milwaukee County, WI 212
miner, iron-ore 151
mines, lead 181
Mines Royal 16
Mingo (Western Seneca) Indian 120, 124, 127, 130, 137, 143, 145
ministers, Anglican 63
Minnesota ("Land of 10,000 Lakes") 192, 205, 214–19
Minnesota River 215
Minorca 102–3, 135
Minuit, Peter 29, 33–4, 36–7, 39, 247
missile, Redstone 238, 241
missionaries 27, 83, 85–6, 122, 154, 165–66, 176, 194, 196
Mississippi, ancient culture 149
Mississippi 160, 219
Mississippi Basin 219
Mississippi Bubble 220
Mississippi River 5, 121, 124, 142–43, 146, 148, 164, 173, 178, 197, 207, 209–10, 215, 219–20
Mississippi Valley 134, 147, 220
Missouri 182, 215, 219, 221, 248–49
Mittelwerk 236
Mobile, AL 219–20
Moccasin Gap 182
Mohawk, Indians 32, 34, 38, 109–12, 114–15, 120–21
Mohawk language 109–10, 112, 122, 184
Mohawk River 31, 108, 189
Mohawk Valley 33, 114, 120, 138, 172, 186, 189
monarchies 1, 4, 11, 20–1, 36, 52–3, 56, 58–9, 86, 91, 94–5, 100, 124, 151, 160, 167–68, 199–202
monk 42
Monongahela River 129
Monroe Doctrine 226
Monte Sano 238
Monterey, CA 222

Montgomery's Scottish Highlanders 133
Montreal 119–20, 134
Moon 237, 242
Moravian Brethren 83, 85, 88–9, 176; *see also* Unitas Fractrum; United Brethren
Moravian Church 83–4, 86, 88–9, 174, 176
Moravian Church, Southern Province 89, 176
Moravian Missionary 154
Moravians 8, 67, 83–90, 110, 116, 122, 140, 154, 162, 165–66, 174, 176, 194, 217, 247
Morris County, NJ 40, 75
mosque 36
Mount Spotswood 171
Mount Vernon 125
MRLV 241
MSFC 241–42
Muddy Creek, Forsyth County, NC 164
Mühlenberg, Henrich (Henry) Melchior 83, 86–9, 112, 132
Muncee, Munsee 34, 143
Muscovy Company 29; *see also* Russian Company
musket, musketry 124, 132, 185, 187–88
musketeers 188
Muskingum River 195–96
Muskingum River Valley 146
Muslim 17
mutineer 31
mysticism 8, 158–59

names, Anglicized 72, 178, 211, 230
Nantucket Island 70
Naples 103
Napoleon 199
Napoleonic Wars 199–200
Narragansett Tribe 26
NASA 241–42
Nashville (French Lick) 182
Nassau 135
Natchitoches 219
nation, Huron 144
National Advisory Committee on Aviation, NACA 240
National Aeronautics and Space Act 240
National Science Foundation 239
Native Americans 6, 33–4, 58, 60, 80, 86, 91, 115, 120, 124, 132, 137, 142–43, 145–47, 153, 156, 162, 166, 172, 184, 189; *see also* Indian, American
Naval Research Laboratory 239
navigator 29, 31
Nazareth, PA 85, 200, 247
Nebraska 215, 221, 249
Neckar River 105
neglect, salutary 58
Neolin, Indian religious prophet 144
Netherlands 1–3, 16, 18, 30, 37, 48, 50, 85, 92–3, 95–6, 101, 125, 158, 230; *see also* Dutch Republic; United Provinces
Neuburg (now Newburg) 106

Index

Neuse River 162
New Amsterdam (now New York City) 29, 33–6, 38, 70, 158
New Berlin, OH (now North Canton) 197, 229
New Bern, NC 155, 162–63
New Ebenezer 168
New England 25–9, 34, 56, 62, 114, 122, 132, 143, 161, 173
New England Congregationalists 168
New France 120, 124–25
New Hanover 87
New Helvetia (New Switzerland) 222
New Jersey 12, 32-2, 36–40, 56, 75–6, 132, 141, 237
New Mexico 221, 236, 238
New Netherland (future New York and New Jersey) 11, 29–36, *37*, 38–40, 70, 247
New Northwest Territory 5
New Orleans 169, 197, 207, 209, 220, 223
New Orleans (ship) 197
New Providence 87
New River 147, 179–81
New River Valley 172
New Sweden 36, *37*, 38–40, 75; *see also* Delaware Colony
New Testament 26, 43
New Windsor 109, 164
New World 1–3, 16–7, 26, 38, 56, 71, 89, 119, 151, 223, 226, 228, 248
New York 11–2, 30–3, 35, 38–40, 53, 70–1, 75, 77–8, 85, 106–9, 111–14, 119–20, 128, 132, 138, 150, 155, 158, 162, 169, 172, 186–87, 189, 195, 200, 203, 212, 221, 223
New York City 33, 35, 39, 108, 113, 200, 204, 210, 243
New York Times 231
New York Weekly Journal 114, 247
Newburgh 198
Newburgh on the Hudson 109
Newfoundland 20, 103, 120
Newport, Christopher 21, 23
newspaper, German language 113, 197–98, 206, 211, 229, 247, 249–50
Niagara River 204
Nicolls, Richard 38–9
Nieu Nederlandt (ship) 32
95 Theses 6, 41–3; *see also* grievances
Nolichucky Settlement 164
Nordhausen 235–36
North America 2–4, 7, 10–2, 19–20, 23, 25, 30, 36, 39, 56, 72, 85, 89, 91, 104, 119, 124, 128, 131, 135–37, 142–43, 146, 153, 160, 162, 166, 209, 219, 237
North Canton, OH (formerly New Berlin) 229
North Carolina 3, 16–7, 70, 78, 80, 89, 107, 155, 158, 160–65, 169, 173–74, 176–77, 181, 188–89, 243
North Fork of the Holson River 182

North Pole 29
North Rhine-Westphalia 72, 158
North Sea 4, 30, 226
Northampton County, VA 24
Northeast Passage 29
Northern Neck Proprietary 152
Norway 34, 213
Northwest Ordinance Act 1787 192, 194–95
Northwest Territory (Ohio Country) 5, **140**, 191–94 197–98
Norton, the Rev. John 27
Nova Scotia 103, 122; *see also* Acadia
nuggets, gold 222

oath of allegiance 5
Oberammergau 235
Oberth, Herman 232–33, 238–39, 242
Oglethorpe, Gen. James Edward 85, 165–67
Ohio 81, 122, 125, 146, 180, 190, 192–98, 205–7, 215, 229, 248
Ohio Canal 198
Ohio Company 126, 153, 178, 194–95
Ohio Country (AKA Northwest Territory & the Old Northwest) 5, 119–21, 124, 126–28, 131, 134–35, 137, 140, 146–49, 178, 191–92, 194–95, 197
Ohio Country Indians 120–21, 124, 130, 134, 137–43, 149
Ohio River 5, 120–21, 125–26, 129, 140, 191–92, 194–97, 205, 215
Ohio Valley 120–22, 124–26, 128, 134, 141–43, 153–54
Ojibwa (Chippewa) Tribe 143, 192, 215
Oklahoma Panhandle 221
Old Dominion 59
Old Northwest Territory 5, 9, 190–93, 197–98, 204–5, 219, 222
Old Salem Visitor Center 89
Oldenburg 224
Oley 75
Oley Valley, PA 177
Oneida 110, 112, 120, 128, 139, 186–87
Oneida Creek 187
Onondaga 110, 113, 120, 126
Op den Graeff, Abraham 72, 80
Op den Graeff, Dirk 72, 80
Opechancanough, Chief 57
Operation Paperclip 13, 236, 242; *see also* Project Overcast
Orangeburg 164
Ordnung 82
Oregon 221
Oregon Trail 221
Orient 21, 29, 60, 162
Oriska (Oriskany, NY) 186–87
orphanage 168
orrery 71
Orthodoxy 8, 47, 64, 84
Osenberg, Walter 234
Ottawa 124, 130, 137, 143–45, 177, 192

286 Index

Otto Brothers 196
Ottoman Empire 66, 101, 135
Outer Banks, NC 16–8, 159, 163
Over-the-Rhine 198
Oxford 57–8, 62, 165

Pacific Coast 221
Pacific Ocean 16, 22, 164
pacifism 62, 69, 71, 80–1, 229
Palatinate 8–9, 46, 48, 53–5, 78, 92, 97, 103–7, 109, 114, 121, 167, 186, 189, 220, 247; see also Southwest Germany
Palatine 4, 40, 54, 75–6, 83, 99, 103, 106–11, 132, 135, 156, 162–64, 171, 231
Pamunky Indians 23
Papal Bull of 1493 1
Paris Peace Conference 230
Paris Revolution February 1848 202
Parlements 50, 54; see also French courts of law
Parliament 10, 12, 32, 58, 93–4, 96–7, 100, 131–32, 147, 162, 164, 168, 174
Parma 198
Paspahegh Tribe 22
Passamaquoddy 120
Pastorius, Franz Daniel 8, 71–5, 81, 247
pastry, Bismarck 230
Patriot 9, 71, 79, 186–87, 189, 231
patroon 34
Peace of Paris 134; see also Treaty of Paris 1763
Peace of Ryswick 97
Peace Treaty 192; see also Treaty of Paris 1783
Peace Treaty of Aix-La-Chapelle 119; see also Treaty of Aix-La-Chapelle
Peace Treaty of Westphalia 51, 91; see also Treaty of Westphalia
Peenemunde 233–36, 238
pelts and hides 29, 32–4, 37, 120, 124, 178–79, 221
Penn, British Adm. Sir William 65, 67
Penn, William 8, 39, 65–8, 70–1, 73, 77, 80–1, 91, 138–39, 141, 143, 158–59
Penn's Colony 5, 8, 39, 64, 75, 77–8, 81, 91, 97, 106, 150, 159, 173, 183
Pennsylvania 8, 10, 27, 31–2, 36, 38–9, 53–4, 65, 67–79, 81, 83, 85–7, 89–90, 107–9, 112–13, 120–22, 124–26, 130–34, 137–39, 141, 143–44, 150–53, 155–59, 162, 164–65, 169, 171–74, 176–78, 184, 194, 197, 200, 204–5, 207, 222, 247–48, 250
Pennsylvania Assembly 139
Pennsylvania, Council of 112
Pennsylvania Dutch 5, 78, 207, 248; see also Pennsylvania Germans
Pennsylvania Gazette 123
Pennsylvania Germans 78–9, 83, 121, 135, 157, 197, 215; see also Pennsylvania Dutch
Penobscot 120
Pensacola, FL 146

People of the Dawn 120; see also Wabanaki Confederacy
People of the Longhouse 119; see also Six Nations of the Iroquois Confederacy
Peoria Indian 149
Pershing, Gen. John J. 229
Persian Gulf 226
pestilence 46
Philadelphia 5, 12, 54, 68, 71, 73–7, 80–1, 86–8, 112–14, 134, 138–39, 142, 150, 156, 159, 169, 172, 184, 195, 203, 223, 247–48
Philadelphische Zeitung 113, 247
Philip II of Habsburg King Spain 3, 15, 18
Philip V, King, 1st Bourbon to sit on throne of Spain 99, 101, 103
Philippines 15, 100, 135
Phillips, Henry 161
philosophy 83, 87
Piedmont 6, 165, 169, 173–74, 177, 205
Piedmont Carolina 60
Pietism 6, 8, 46–7, 84, 86–8
Pilgrims 10, 24, 32, 62, 71, 189
pioneers, German-speaking 205
pirate 16, 18, 30, 33
Pisquetomen (Western [Ohio] Delaware chief) 139–42
pitch 22, 108
Pitt, William, the Elder 130–32, 134–36, 142
Pittsburg 124, 126–27, 133, 197, 204
Pittsburgh 142, 248
Pizarro, Francisco 2
Planck, Max 12–3
Planetary Space 232
playwrights 211
Plymouth 5, 18, 56
Plymouth Colony 32, 62, 70, 189
Plymouth Company 21, 56
Plymouth Rock 25
Pocahontas 62
Poland 4–6, 22–3, 38, 92, 101, 116, 118–19, 209, 211, 213
policy, American foreign 226; Indian 59
polka 216–17
Pomaria 164
Pomerania 38, 213
Pontiac (Ottawa chief) 137, 143–45, 147, 149
Pontiac's Rebellion 146, 149
Pontiac's War 137, 143–44, 146–47, 149, 177
Poor Valley 80
Pope 1–2, 41, 43, 45, 49, 248
Port Mahon in Minorca 103
Port of Cowes 5
Port of London 107
Port of Milwaukee 212
Port of New York 212
Port Royal, Monck's Corner 164
Porter, Richard 236
Portland, Oregon 221
Ports of German emigration 4–5, 23, 46, 107–8, 135, 169, 177, 180, 183

Index   287

Ports of immigration into U.S. 5, 54, 75, 169, 223
Portsmouth 5
Portugal, Portuguese 1-2, 15, 33, 92, 134, 136
Post, Christian Friedrich (or Frederick) 154, 194
Postal Road 172; *see also* King's Highway
Potawatomi 143-44, 192, 205
Potomac River 54, 60, 126, 152, 169, 171
Potsdam 48, 225
Powell, Ambrose 179, 182
Powell Valley 170, 179
Powhatan, Chief 22, 57
Powhatan Confederacy 22, 57, 189
Prague 3, 16, 18, 41, 43, 45, 49, 83-4, 89, 158; *see also* Bohemia; Czech Republic; Czechia
Prague Palace Ballroom 44-5
precisionism 87
predestinarian 86
predestine 43
Presbyterian 64, 83, 89, 150, 174, 217
Preston, Col. William 147, 181
Priest 7, 30, 33, 41-2, 45, 53, 62, 83, 167, 248; Catholic 7, 41-2, 45, 62, 83
Prince Albert of Saxe-Coburg-Gotha 231
Prince Carl of Solms-Baunfels 248
prince-electors 49, 96
Prince Eugene of Savoy 102
Prince Frederick 225
Prince Klemens von Metternich 200
Prince of Orange, Orange-Nassau 92
Prince Wilhelm II 225
Prince William III of Orange 92, 95-6
Princess Anne of Denmark 95
Princess Mary 95
Princeton, NJ 12
Princeton University 22
principalities, German 101
Printing Press 43, 113-14
privateers (licensed pirates) 16
Proclamation Line of 1763 70, 147-49; *see also* Royal Proclamation 1763
production, cheese 214
program, Vanguard 239-40
Project Hermes 236
Project Mercury 241
Project Overcast 236; *see also* Operation Paperclip
proletariat 203
propaganda 227-28, 230
Proprietary Party 138
proprietor 34, 59, 67, 71-2, 80, 125, 159, 161-64, 166, 176; *see also* Lord Proprietor
proselytizing 85-6
Protestant England 3, 18-9, 30, 94
Protestant Episcopal Church 176
Protestant Orthodoxy 88
Protestant Parliament 93
Protestant Reformation 7-8, 40-3, 45
Protestant Revolution 43

Protestant 4; *see also* Swiss Zwinglians
Protestantism 6-7, 9, 15, 36, 41, 43-6, 48, 52-5, 58, 65, 75, 81, 83-5, 87-8, 92-7, 100-1, 103, 105-7, 124, 131-32, 150, 155, 160, 162, 165-67, 212, 247-48
Prussia 33, 48, 53, 75, 116-19, 130, 135, 167, 186-87, 196, 199-202, 210, 213, 225
Psalm 66
Puritanism 25-9, 34, 47, 58, 62, 69, 87-8, 155, 161, 189
Purrysburg, SC 164
Putnam, Gen. Rufus 194, 196
Putnam Street 196
Pyrenees 92

Quagnant (Guinant) Chief of the Six Nations 110-11
Quakerism 27, 36, 63, 65-6, 69-70, 72
Quakers 6, 8, 27-9, 35-6, 39, 56, 62-3, 65-72, 74-8, 80-1, 129, 138-9, 150, 156, 159, 161, 171, 174, 177-78, 180, 192, 194, 221; German 62, 68; Pennsylvania 129, 156; *see also* Friends; Mennonites; Society of Friends
Quaker's Friendly Association 138-39, 141; *see also* Friendly Association
Quantum Theory 13
Quebec 119-20, 125, 134-35, 170
Quebec City 133
Queen Anne of England 9, 86, 101-2, 106, 108-10, 162-63; *see also* Anne, Queen of England
Queen Anne's War 9, 99
Queen Charlotte 167; *see also* Charlotte of Mecklenberg
Queen Elizabeth I of England 3, 16, 18, 22; *see also* Elizabeth I, Virgin Queen
Queen Henrietta Maria 155; *see also* Henrietta Maria
Queen Mary 95; *see also* Mary II; Mary Stuart
Queen Victoria 225, 231; *see also* Victoria, Queen
Queens, New York City Borough 35
Quietism 88
quitrent 152, 161, 173

race, Teutonic 12, 157
Radnor 76
Die Rakete du den Planetenraumen 232; *see also* The Rocket into Planetary Space
Raleigh, Sir Walter 3, 16-8, 163
Ralph Lane Company 17
Ramillies, Southern Netherlands (now Belgium) 102
Ramsey, Alexander, Gov. of MN 215
Rappahannock County, VA 60
Rappahannock River 152
Rappahannock River Basin 151
Raritan River 40
Reading, PA 121, 184

288　　　　　　　　　　　　　　Index

Red Prairie, IL 207
Red River Valley 216
redemptioners 8, 78, 114, 247; *see also* servants, indentured
Redstone 238, 240
Redstone Arsenal 237, 241
Reformation 7, 8, 40-3, 45
Reformed Church 7-8, 32, 35-6, 39, 67, 72, 83; *see also* Lutheranism; Mennonites
Reformed Religion 6, 52, 75, 85, 111, 247
refugee 8, 33, 54, 58, 65, 78, 84-5, 106-7, 139, 177, 196, 203, 249-50
regiment 76, 129, 131-33, 140, 144-46; Bavarian 228; Virginian 127; *see also* Royal American Regiment of Corps; 60th Royal American Regiment
region, Siegen 151
Reinickendorf 233
religion, Anglican 21
religious: freedom 4-5, 29, 35, 39, 67, 89, 106, 155, 184, 186, 193, 206, 247; intolerance 8, 95; liberty 65; persecution 7, 25, 68, 198; toleration 36, 46, 64-5, 81, 93, 165-66
republic 11, 50, 182, 202, 204
Republic of Texas 223
Republic of the United Netherlands 29, 32, 35, 100-1
resources, mineral 210
Revolution, American 6-7, 9-10, 79, 123, 149-50, 154, 180, 184, 187, 192, 195, 231; *see also* American Revolutionary War
Revolutions of 1848 9, 198-99
Rhenish districts 220
Rhenish Palatinate (Rheinpfalz) 8, 186
Rhenish Prussia 33, 39, 75
Rhine 4, 92
Rhine Country 7-8, 23, 50, 54, 220
Rhine Province 32, 216
Rhine River 4-5, 11, 97, 105, 107, 221
Rhine Valley 46, 71, 75
Rhineland 33, 54, 65, 74-6, 78, 91, 96-7, 105, 162
Rhineland-Palatinate 43, 109, 113, 231, 249
Rhode Island 53, 70
rice 58, 165, 168
Richards, Henry Melchior Muhlenberg 132
Richelieu, Cardinal 50, 52, 54
Richmond, VA 50, 60, *170*; *see also* Henrico 57, 60
Riedel, Walter 233, 237-38
rifle 54, 79, 179; *see also* long rifle
rifle (long rifle adapted from the German hunting rifle) 79; "Nancy" 180; Pennsylvania or Kentucky 54, 79
riflemen 127
rights 103; corn 178; divine 55, 104, 201; English 161; German 48; inalienable 201-2; Indian 128, 147; land 121; manoral 34; mineral 34; states' 204; trading 38, 121, 56;

women's 66, 117; work 202; writ of habeas corpus 193
Rip Van Winkle 38
Rittenheim 135
Rittenhouse, David 71
Ritter Company 162
ritual 65, 69, 83, 89, 129
road, Kincaid-Calloway 183
Roanoke, VA 171
Roanoke (Big Lick) *170*, 172-74, 181
Roanoke Gap 174
Roanoke Island 16-7, 160
Roanoke River 147, 174, 179
Roanoke Sound (Albemarle) Settlements 18
Roanoke Sound (now Albemarle Sound) 159-60, 163
Robertson, Chief Justice of KY 182
Rock Hill, SC 162
rocket 232, 234, 237-38, 240-42; Redstone 240
The Rocket into Planetary Space 232; *see also Die Rakete du den Planetenraumen*
rocketry 232, 237-38
Rockies 221
Rockingham County, NC 151
Roebling, John August 204
Rolfe, John 62
Roman Catholic Church 9, 41-4, 87, 93-5, 107, 150
Roman Catholic Society of Jesus 30
Rome 83, 238
Roosevelt, Franklin 10
Roosevelt, Theodore 11, 227, 245
Rotterdam 4-5, 71, 107, 157, 159
Roundheads (Puritan parliamentarians) 58
Rowan County, NC 80, 165
Royal Air Force 234
Royal American Regiment of Corps (62nd Foot) 131-35, 137, 144, 149; *see also* regiment; 60th Royal American Regiment
Royal House of Bourbon 49; *see also* House of Bourbon
Royal House of Habsburgs 49; *see also* House of Habsburgs
Royal House of Stuart 92; *see also* House of Habsburgs
Royal Navy 16, 107
Royal New York Regiment 186
Royal Proclamation 1763 147-48; *see also* Proclamation Line of 1763
Royalists 58; *see also* Cavaliers
Rudolf I 49
rule, monarchal 9, 199; primogeniture 49
ruler, stadtholder 8, 15, 48-50, 53, 92, 97, 105, 116-17, 203, 225; *see also* captain general
rum 73-4, 128, 132, 143, 171
Rumbach 113
rush, gold 1, 222, 231
Russell, Capt. William 181

Index 289

Russia 2, 6, 29, 70, 116, 119, 135, 200, 226, 230, 249
Russian Company 29; *see also* Muscovy Company
Russian Germans 210
Ryttinghuysen, Claus 71
Ryttinghuysen, Gerhard 71
Ryttinghuysen, Wilhelm (Mennonite bishop) 71

Sacramento 1, 222
Sacramento River 221-22
Saginaw 210-11
St. Croix River 216
St. Lawrence River 119-20, 124, 134, 142
St. Lawrence Seaway 215
St. Leger, British Col. Barry 186
St. Mary's Whitechapel 61
St. Paul, MN 218-19
St. Petersburg 48
St. Simon's Island 166; *see also* Fort Frederika
Salem, West Jersey 68
Salem Settlement 162; *see also* Wachovia
Salisbury, NC 165, 177
Salisbury, MA 28
salvation 43, 69, 86
Salzburg, Salzburgers 165-68, 247
San Antonio, TX 242
San Francisco, CA 222-23
San Francisco Bay 221
Santa Fe Trail 220
Santee River 164
Sapling Grove (Bristol TN-VA) *170*, 181
Sardinia 103
Saturn 241-42
sauerkraut 10, 230
Sauk 192
Saur, Christopher 12, 248
savages 73-4
Savannah, GA 85, 155, 166-68, 188
Savannah River 165, 167-68
Savoy 96, 101-2
sawmill wrights 151
Saxe-Coburg-Gotha 231
Saxe-Gotha 164
Saxony 49, 84-88, 116, 135, 188, 200
Scandinavia 1, 179, 213
Scarouady, Oneida Chief 128-29
scheme, Law's 220
Schilders, Jasper 158
Schlatter, Michael 83
Schleswig-Holstein 62
Schmitz, Friederich 216
Schoharie 108, 110-12
school 10-1, 41, 46, 66, 78, 80, 87, 107, 109, 111, 176, 185, 188, 195-96, 204, 207, 211, 217-18, 228, 242, 248; high 212; parish 217; parochial 217; Prussian 196; Sunday 168; vocational 212
Schuylkill River 73

Schwenkfelders 8, 67, 88, 247
scientists, rocket 13
SCORE (Air Force satellite) 240
Scotland 7, 20, 34, 59, 67-68, 92, 94-5, 101-2, 133, 150-51, 166
Scots-Irish (Scotch-Irish) 70, 77
Scottish Highlanders 133, 145, 150-1, 165, 168, 172-74, 179, 182, 189, 200
Seneca 110, 120, 143
sentiment, anti-German 10, 227, 229
Serbia 117, 226
serf 49, 117
serfdom 204
servants 8, 10, 57, 59, 79-9, 108, 113-14, 151, 156, 166, 161, 196, 218-19, 247; domestic 79; indentured 204; *see also* redemptioner
settlement, Irish 174
settlers 7, 17, 20, 22-3, 32, 34, 36-9, 67-8, 73-4, 108, 113, 125, 130, 134, 137, 143-4, 147-49, 152-53, 156-57, 160-61, 163-64, 170-74, 177-78, 182, 191, 195, 197, 205, 212-13, 215, 222, 247-48; Anglican 76; British 6, 137; Dutch 33, 37, English 22; English-speaking 76; French 220; German 23, 39, 71, 131-32, 134, 151-52, 156-57, 162, 165, 197, 210, 247; German-speaking 78, 167; Huguenot 77, 150; Jamestown 21-2, 29; Jewish 77, 150; non-English 6; Scots-Irish 165; Swedish 36; Swiss 131-32, 134
Seven Years' War 91, 103, 122, 124, 130, 134-35; *see also* Great War for Empire
sewan 32; *see also* wampum
Shacklewell 66
Shallow Ford 174, 176
Shamokin 112, 122
Shawnee 124, 128, 130, 137, 141, 143, 145-46, 172, 181, 192, 197
Shenandoah County, VA 151
Shenandoah National Park 60
Shenandoah River 60, 171, 179
Shenandoah Valley 60, 86, 130, 151-52, 155, 169, 171-72, 174
Shephard, Alan 241
shepherds, German 10, 230; *see also* dogs
Shepherdstown VA (WV) 154
Shikellamy, Oneida Chief 112-13
Shingas 128
shipwrights 30
shoemakers 66, 72, 74
Sicily 41, 100, 103
Silesia 8, 96, 116-19, 135
Silesian War 116, 118; *see also* First Silesian War
Silverheels 126
Simmons (ship) 85
Simon, Menno 62
Six Iroquois Nations 138, 172; *see also* People of the Longhouse; Six Nations
Six Nations 109-13, 119-22, 124-25, 127, 130, 141, 149, 153, 173, 184; *see also* People of the Longhouse; Six Iroquois Nations

Index

60th Royal American Regiment 133, 137, 146–47; *see also* regiment; Royal American Regiment of Corps
Skippack 75
slavery 34, 62, 68, 72, 78, 81, 148, 157, 161, 167, 193–94, 196, 204, 234; African 6–7, 11, 103, 135, 143–47; galley 53; Negro 161
Sluyter, P. 158
smallpox 101, 145, 164, 195
smith 106
Smith, John 21–3
Smith River 189
Smokies 60
Smollett, Henry 132
Society of Friends 65, 77; *see also* Friends, Quakers
Society of Jesus 30, 43; *see also* Jesuits
society, utopian 199, 203
soldiers Hessian 187–89, 248; *see also* troops, German
Sommerhausen 72
South Africa 90
South America 1–3, 15–6, 19, 100
South Bend, IN 206
South Carolina 27, 53, 78, 127, 133, 155, 160, 162–67, 177, 188
South Carolina Gazette 164
South Sea(s) 22, 29, 60, 160
Southwest Germany 8, 53, 116; *see also* Palatinate
Soviet Union 13, 234–36, 139–42
Spain 1–4, 15–9, 21–2, 30, 43, 48, 50, 92, 96–7, 99–101, 103, 116–17, 134, 136, 166
Spangenberg, Bishop August Gottlieb 85, 88, 176
Spanish Armada 3, 18–9, 22, 94
Spanish Empire 15, 19, 100
Spanish Florida 4, 20, 56, 159–60; *see also* Florida
Spanish Netherlands (Belgium) 101–3, 117
Special Mission V-2 236
specialists, mineral 23
speculators 75, 152–53, 156, 178, 211
speech, Quaker 80
Spencer, NC 162
Spice Islands 15
spices 3, 21, 30, 74, 166
spiritualism 86
Splitdorf, Ensign Carl Gustav 154
Spotswood, Gov. Alexander 151, 169, 171–72
Spotswood Ironworks 172
Spotsylvania County, VA 151, 163
Sputnik 239–40
squatters 152, 222
stadtholder 92–4, 96
Stalnaker, Samuel 178–79
Starnes, Joseph 189
Starnes, Rachel 189
Staten Island 187
states: feudal 6; German 1, 6, 43, 45–6, 48–50,
77–8, 118–19, 200, 202, 207, 212–13, 216; Midwestern 205–7
Stauffer, Johann George 200
Staver, Maj. Robert 236
steamboat 79, 196–97, 203, 207, 209–10, 212, 215
Stephan, Capt. Adam, MD 154
Stephen, Francis (Duke of Lorraine and Tuscany) 117
Steuben, Gen. Friedrich Wilhelm von 248
Stewart, Lt. Charles 235
Stillwater, MN 216
Stoner, Michael 181; *see also* Holsteiner, George Michael
store, dry goods 196
Stowe, Calvin Elvis 196
Stowe, Harriet Beecher 196
Strasbourg, Strasburg 151–53
Strecker Brothers 196
Strughold, Hubertus 242; *see also* Father of Space Medicine
Stuttgart 106, 208, 243
Stuyvesant, Peter 34–6, 38, 70, 158
subaltern 132
submarine, German 228
Sugar Islands 135
sugar, sugarcane 3, 73, 161, 195, 214
Sun King 52
Sunbury, GA 168
Susan Constant (ship) 21
Susquehanna Company 143
Susquehanna River 54, 143, 169
Susquehanna Valley, PA 138
Sutter, John August 221–22
Sutterville, CA 222
Swabia 8, 135
Swallow (ship) 27
Sweden 1–2, 33, 36, 38, 48, 68, 75, 77, 96, 116, 118–19, 135, 150, 177, 209, 231
Swedish Colony 29, 36–7, 247
Switzar, Switzer 23, 135, 164
Switzerland 4–6, 8, 9, 23, 48, 53, 56, 62, 67, 75, 78, 107, 131–35, 137, 140, 144–46, 162–63, 177, 215–16, 220–21; *see also* Zwinglians
Sycamore Shoals, NC (Elizabethton, TN) 137, 180
syrup 73
system, semi-feudal social 206

tailors 21, 74
Tanagharisson 120–21
tanneries 76, 176, 220, 222
tar 23, 107–8, 110
The Tavern Restaurant 243–45
taxes 5, 8, 20, 36, 49, 51, 55, 59, 63, 70, 75, 80, 95, 97, 104–5, 123, 138, 147, 149, 152, 160–1, 173, 187, 206, 213, 220, 222–23
Taylor County, WI 212
Tazewell County, VA 178
Teedyuscung, Lenape Chief 137–39, 141, 143

Index

Tennessee 160, 164, 169, 172–73, 179–83, 188, 191
Tennessee River 179
Tennessee River Valley 179
territory, American Indian 222
Tessmann, Bernard 235
Texas 5, 223–24, 248
Texas German Belt 222; *see also* German Belt
Thames River 162
theology 8, 33, 42, 73, 87
Thirty Years War 7, 40, 43–6, **47**, 48–50, 53, 91–2, 102, 105
Thuringia 234, 236
Tibet 90
Tidewater 22, 57, 59, 150–51, 157, 172, 205
timber 58, 92, 108, 165
Timber Neck, VA 23
tobacco 3, 24, 58, 62, 74, 157, 161–62, 214, 223
Toftoy, Holger 236
Tomepomehala, Shawnee Indian guide 197
Tomochichi, Chief 166
Tories 187
trade 3, 10, 18, 22, 25, 27, 30–5, 37, 46, 56, 58, 60, 73–4, 76, 92, 100, 103, 106, 108, 119–21, 124, 126, 135, 138, 145, 149, 160, 162–63, 166, 172–73, 176, 180, 201, 204, 208, 215, 221, 226, 248; fur 32, 60, 108, 119–20, 124, 160, 180, 215, 221, 248
trailblazer 177, 191
Transylvania 182, 191
Transylvania Land Company 181
Transylvania Purchase 181, 191
treason 12, 58, 186, 204
Treaty 97–8, 113, 119, 139, 196
Treaty of Aix-La-Chapelle 119, 122, 134; *see also* Peace Treaty of Aix-La-Chapelle
Treaty of Albany 172;
Treaty of amity 153
Treaty of Dover 93
Treaty of Easton 141–42; *see also* Easton Treaty
Treaty of Friendship 70
Treaty of Lancaster 121, 124, 172; *see also* Lancaster Treaty
Treaty of Logstown 153, 172
Treaty of Paris 1763 134, 136–37, 143, 154; *see also* Peace of Paris
Treaty of Paris 1783 (Paris Pease Treaty) 192, 215
Treaty of Rastatt 102
Treaty of Tordesillas 2
Treaty of Union 101
Treaty of Utrecht 102–3
Treaty of Versailles 230, 232
Treaty of Westphalia 48, 50, 102
Trent River 162
Trenton, NJ 36, 188
Trinity Lutheran Church 121
Trinity Parish 61
Triple Alliance, Bismarck's 227

troops, German 186–87; *see also* Hessian Soldiers
Trump, Pres. Donald J. 231
Trump, Frederick 231
Tsiolkovsky, Konstantin 238
Tulane 220
Tulpehocken ("Land of Turtles"), PA 106, 112–13, 122
Turkey 66, 230
Turkish Emperor 66
Turks 21, 49, 96, 102
turpentine 108
Tuscarora 110, 120, 163
Tuscarora Indian Wars 163
Two Brothers (ship) 85

Uebele, Anna Magdalena 109
Uncle Tom's Cabin 196
Union County, NC 164
Union Jack 130
Uniontown, PA 126
Unitas Fratrum 84, 86, 88, 176; *see also* Moravian Brethren; United Brethren
United Brethren 83, 87; *see also* Moravian Brethren; Unitas Fractrum
United Congregations 87
United Kingdom 102, 225
United Provinces 35, 48, 92, 96, 101, 116; *see also* Dutch Republic; Netherlands
United States 1–5, 7–13, 17–8, 20–3, 25, 27, 29, 32, 38, 44, 46, 53–4, 56–9, 67, 70, 75, 81–2, 88–9, 91, 95, 99, 103, 106, 109–10, 113, 116, 119, 121–24, 130–32, 134–35, 137, **140**, 146–47, 152–53, 156, 158, 165, 167, 169, 173, 178, 180, 184–90, 192, 194, 196–200, 203–6, 208, 210, 212–16, 221–24, **223**, 226–231, 236, 239, 241–43, 245, 247–50; British 3–4, 7, 9, 16, 21, 57, 125
United States Air Force 243
United States Congress 192, 196
University in Prague 83
University of Oxford 57
University of Wittenberg 42
Upper Peninsula Michigan 211

V-1 and 2 rockets 232–238, 242
Valley Forge 184–85
Van Braam, Jacob 125
Van Meter, Isaac 152–53
Van Meter, John 152–53
Venango, French fort 125
Venice 66
Verein fur Raumschiffahrt (V f R) 233
Verne, Jules 238
Verrazano, Giovanni da 31
Versailles 52, 94
veteran 148, 190, 205, 243–44
Veteran, American Revolutionary War 194–95
Victoria, Queen 225, 231; *see also* Queen Victoria

Index

Vienna 49, 96, 100, 102, 117, 200, 202
Vienna Congress 6, 200, 202
Villars, Gen. Claude-Louis-Hector 106
Villiers, Elizabeth 95
Villiers, Cpt. Francois Louis Coulon de 127
Villiers, Joseph Coulon de 127
vine, vinedressers, vineyard 4, 73, 106-7, 222
Vine Street 198
Virgin Mary 45
Virgin Queen 4, 20; *see also* Elizabeth I; Queen Elizabeth I
Virginia 4, 10, 20-1, 23-4, 53, 57-63, 78, 113, 123-24, 126-27, 130, 133, 138, 144, 150-53, 160-63, 169, 171-73, 178-79, 185, 189, 191-92, 243
Virginia Assembly 182, 191-92
Virginia Beach 21
Virginia Campaign 185
Virginia Cavaliers 58
Virginia Colony 23, 56-9, 61-3, 121, 125, 154, 169
Virginia Company 4, 22-3, 58; of London 21, 56-7, 150; of Plymouth 21
visa 17, 206
VOC 29-30; *see also* Dutch East India (Trading) Company; East India Company
Volga 6, 249
von Braun, Magnus 235
von Braun, Wernher 233, 235, 237, 239-42, 266
von Helmholtz, Hermann 12
von Metternich, Prince Klemens 200, 202
von Steuben, Baron 184-86
Vorstmann, Peter 158; *see also* Sluyter, P.

Wabanaki Confederacy 120; *see also* People of the Dawn
WAC Corporal 236
Wachovia 162, 176
Wade, Robert 68
Wagner, composer 13, 228
Wagner, Lt. Edmund 154
wagon, Conestoga 54, 79, 197, 247
Waldensians 8, 67, 247
Waldorf 220, 248
Wales 68, 81, 101
Walker, Dr. Thomas 149, 178-80
Wall Street 82
Wall Street Journal 29, 82
Wallen, Elisha (Elijah) 180
Wallen's Ridge 180
Walloon 32-3
Waltham 66
Wampanoag Indian Nation 26
wampum 32, 112; *see also* sewan
War of Austrian Succession 116-19, 134
War of Independence, American 136
War of Independence, Dutch 30
War of Spanish Succession 9, 98-9, 101-3, 105-6, 121, 161; *see also* Queen Anne's War

War of the Grand Alliance 95-8, 105
warfare, guerrilla 140
warrants, bounty-land 190
Washington, George 61, 81, 112, 125-29, 133, 148, 153-54, 178, 184-86, 196
Washington County, MD 157
Washington County, VA 80
Washington, D.C. 229
Washington, VA (Rappahannock Co.) 60
Watauga Settlement 164, 182
Watertown, WI 88, 249
Waxhaw Indians 164
Waxhaw Settlement 177
weavers 74-5, 222
Weiser, Anna Eve 112
Weiser, Anna Maria 112
Weiser, Johann Conrad, Jr. 109-10, 112, 121-22, 124, 132, 153, 173, 184, 194
Weiser, John Conrad, Sr. 108, 110-11
Weissenfels, Catherine 114
Welcome (ship) 68, 80
Wesel 33, 158
Wesley, Charles 166
Wesley, John 85, 88, 165-66
West, Capt. Joseph 163
West Coast 221
West Indian Company (WIC) 11, 32, 34, 36; *see also* Dutch West Indian Company
West Indies 2, 37, 85, 106, 124, 163
West Jersey 39, 68, 76
West Virginia 60, 122, 125, 193, 197
Western Hemisphere 226
Western Waters 172
Westphalia 48, 91, 187, 210, 213, 224
wheat 165, 210, 213-14, 216, 222-23, 249
Wheeling, VA (WV) 193, 196-97
Whigs 187
White, John 17, 160
White Oak River 162
White Plains 188
White Sands Proving Ground 236-38
"widow Kriderin" 78
Wienwaert 158
Wiesman, Walter 238
wilderness 7, 17, 46, 73, 113, 133, 156, 159, 176, 178, 180-81, 183-84, 192, 194, 197, 205-6, 215, 221
Wilderness Road 130, 169, *170*, 173, 181-83, 191
Wilhelm II 225-26, 230
William and Mary College 61
William I "the Silent" 92
William II of Orange 92
William III Prince of Orange, King of England 11-2, 93-7, 100-1, 155
William IV 199, 201-2
Williamsburg 125-26, *170*, 171, 191
Wilmington, DE 36, 68
Wilson, Pres. Woodrow 11, 22, 227-30
Wiltwyck 35

Index

Winchester, VA 152–53, 174
windmills 33, 82
wine, Madeira 77
Winston-Salem, NC 89, 174, 176–77
Wirtemberg (Wurttemberg, Württemberg) 78, 135
Wisconsin 12, 88, 192, 203, 205, 212–16, 219, 248–49
Wistar, Carl 156
witchcraft 27
Wittenberg 42, 84, 219
Wittenberg, Susannah 189
Wittenberg's Castle Church 6
Wolf Hills 178, 182, 243
Wolfe, Gen. James 133
Wolfenbuttel 39, 74
Wolfgang, Johann 206
Woman in the Moon 233; *see also Frau in Mond*
Woman in the Wilderness 159
workman 23, 150, 204, 215; metal 211; unskilled 82; *see also* laborer
World War I 9, 11, 45, 80, 99, 135, 211, 217, 225, 227–32
World War II 10–1, 13, 231–32, 250
worldwide union of churches 85–6; *see also* ecumenical union
Wüstenfelde 62
Wyandot 124, 143, 145, 192
Wyatt, Sir Francis 57
Wyoming 221
Wyoming Valley, PA 138–41, 143

Wythe County, VA 80
Wytheville 180–81

Xenophobia 230–31

Yadkin-Catawba Basin 174
Yadkin Ford 162
Yadkin River 174, 176
Yadkin Valley 178
Yalta Conference 236
Yamacraw Bluff (Savannah, GA) 166
Yamacraw Indians 166
yodel 216
York County, VA 24
York River 23
Yugoslavia 6
Yukon, Alaska gold rush 230

Zane (Zahn), Ebenezer 192–94, 197
Zane, John 193
Zane, Silas 193
Zane's Trace *193*, 197
Zeigler, Major Johann 195–96
Zeisberger, David 194
Zenger, Anna 12
Zenger, John Peter 113–14, 247
Zinzendorf, Count Nicholas Ludwig von 83–9, 122, 132, 176
zither 216
Zweibrucken 134
Zwinglians 4; *see also* Swiss

www.ingramcontent.com/pod-product-compliance
Lightning Source LLC
Chambersburg PA
CBHW032032300426
44117CB00009B/1033